Richard A. Henshaw
Colgate Rochester / Bexley Hall / Cruzer
1100 South Goodman St.
Rochester, New York 14620
(716) 271-1320

J. ALBERTO SOGGIN

JOSHUA

old
Test
ament
lib
Rary

J. ALBERTO SOGGIN

JOSHUA

A Commentary

SCM PRESS LTD
BLOOMSBURY STREET LONDON

Translated by R. A. Wilson from the French
Le Livre de Josué
(Commentaire de l'Ancien Testament Va)
first edition 1970
published by Editions Delachaux et Niestlé, Neuchâtel,
with revisions by the author

334 00812 3
FIRST PUBLISHED IN ENGLISH 1972
© SCM PRESS LTD 1972
PRINTED IN GREAT BRITAIN
BY W & J MACKAY LIMITED, CHATHAM

TO THE MEMORY OF
MARTIN NOTH (1902–1968),
WILLIAM FOXWELL ALBRIGHT (1891–1971)
AND
ROLAND GUÉRIN DE VAUX (1903–1971)

עשׂה לך רב
וקנה לך חבר...

Mishnah, Aboth 1 6b

CONTENTS

Part Three: Appendix

PREFACE

THE best preface is useless if a work does not commend itself by its contents. So these lines simply have the object of clarifying several points of detail that I consider useful for the reader; otherwise he may have some trouble in understanding them.

I have found it necessary to maintain the hypothesis of a 'Deuteronomistic' school which would have edited the historical books during the period of the exile, despite some recent objections (which authors of unquestioned standing have refused to accept). This is because the 'Deuteronomic' tradition, about whose presence in Joshua there can be no doubt, seems to me to offer the key for the interpretation of Joshua.

I have had to treat the geographical texts virtually at second hand, using as a basis the works of others, and not my own. I am not in fact a specialist in topography, and I have not had the opportunity of first-hand study of the areas in question, as have for example Alt, Baldi and Noth. At any rate, I hope that I have brought out the problems and the solutions proposed.

Rome, September 1969

PREFACE TO THE ENGLISH EDITION

THE relatively short interval between the publication of the original French edition and the completion of the English translation relieves the author from the task of any major reworking of the commentary. Some of the bibliographies and footnotes have been brought up to date, although the new titles could not be used to update the text. The author was able to correct some slips and errors of fact which had crept into the original, thanks to the very friendly and helpful review by R. North, *Biblica* 52, 1971, pp. 448f.

Rome, November 1971

ABBREVIATIONS

A	Aquila's Greek translation
AASOR	*Annual of the American Schools of Oriental Research*, New Haven
AION	*Annali dell' Istituto Orientale di Napoli*
Aistleitner	J. Aistleitner, *Wörterbuch der ugaritischen Sprache*, Berlin 1963
AJSL	*American Journal of Semitic Languages and Literature*, Chicago
Alt, *KS*	A. Alt, *Kleine Schriften*, Munich I–II 1953, III 1956
ANEP	J. B. Pritchard (ed.), *The Ancient Near East in Pictures relating to the Old Testament*, Princeton 1954, ³1969
ANET	J. B. Pritchard (ed.), *Ancient Near Eastern Texts relating to the Old Testament*, Princeton ²1955, ³1969
AOB	H. Gressmann (ed.), *Altorientalische Bilder zum AT*, Berlin–Leipzig ²1927
AOT	H. Gressmann (ed.), *Altorientalische Texte zum AT*, Berlin–Leipzig ²1926
ArOr	*Archiv Orientální*, Prague
ATANT	Abhandlungen zur Theologie des Alten und Neuen Testaments, Zurich
ATD	Das Alte Testament Deutsch
BA	*The Biblical Archaeologist*, New Haven
BASOR	*Bulletin of the American Schools of Oriental Research*, New Haven
BBB	Bonner Biblische Beiträge
BBLAK	*Beiträge zur biblischen Landes- und Altertumskunde*, Wiesbaden
BH	R. Kittel (ed.), *Biblia Hebraica*, Stuttgart ³1937ff.
BHH	*Biblisch-historisches Handwörterbuch*, Göttingen
BHS	K. Elliger and W. Rudolph (eds.), *Biblia Hebraica Stuttgartensia*, 1968ff.
Bibl	*Biblica*, Rome

BiblRes	*Biblical Research,* Chicago
BJ	*Bible de Jérusalem,* Paris
BK	Biblischer Kommentar, Neukirchen
BL	H. Haag (ed.), *Bibel-Lexicon,* Einsiedeln 1968
B–L	H. Bauer–P. Leander, *Historische Grammatik der hebräischen Sprache des Alten Testaments,* Halle 1922 (repr. Hildesheim 1965)
B–M	(G. Beer)–H. Meyer, *Hebräische Grammatik,* Berlin ³1966ff.
BO	*Bibliotheca Orientalis,* Leiden
BRL	K. Galling, *Biblisches Reallexikon,* Tübingen 1937
BWANT	Beiträge zur Wissenschaft vom Alten und Neuen Testament, Stuttgart
BZ	*Biblische Zeitschrift,* Paderborn
BZAW	Beihefte zur *Zeitschrift für die alttestamentliche Wissenschaft,* Giessen–Berlin
CahRB	Cahiers de la *Revue Biblique*
CahTh	Cahiers Théologiques, Neuchâtel
CBQ	*The Catholic Biblical Quarterly,* Washington
Comm.	*Commentary*
EB	Echter-Bibel, Würzburg
EKL	*Evangelisches Kirchenlexikon,* Göttingen
EncBibl	*Encyclopedia Biblica,* Jerusalem (in Hebrew)
EvTh	*Evangelische Theologie,* Munich
ExpT	*The Expository Times,* Edinburgh
FRLANT	Forschungen zur Religion und Literatur des Alten und Neuen Testaments, Göttingen
FuF	*Forschungen und Fortschritte,* Berlin
GKC	W. Gesenius–E. Kautzsch, *Hebrew Grammar,* translated and revised by A. E. Cowley, Oxford ²1910
Gordon	C. H. Gordon, *Ugaritic Textbook,* Rome 1965
HAT	Handbuch zum Alten Testament, Tübingen
Hex	Origen, Hexapla
HKAT	Handkommentar zum Alten Testament, Göttingen
HS	Die Heilige Schrift des Alten Testaments, Bonn
HSAT	*Die Heilige Schrift des Alten Testaments,* Tübingen
HTR	*The Harvard Theological Review,* Cambridge, Mass.
HUCA	*The Hebrew Union College Annual,* Cincinnati
IB	*The Interpreter's Bible,* New York–Nashville
ICC	The International Critical Commentary, Edinburgh

IDB	*The Interpreter's Dictionary of the Bible*, New York–Nashville
IEJ	*The Israel Exploration Journal*, Jerusalem
Interpr	*Interpretation*, Richmond, Va.
JAOS	*Journal of the American Oriental Society*, New Haven
JBL	*Journal of Biblical Literature*, New Haven
JEOL	*Jaarbericht van het Genootsschap 'Ex Oriente Lux'*, Leiden
JJS	*Journal of Jewish Studies*, London
JNES	*Journal of Near Eastern Studies*, Chicago
Joüon	P. Joüon, *Grammaire de l'Hébreu Biblique*, Rome 1922
JPOS	*Journal of the Palestine Oriental Society*, Jerusalem
JSS	*Journal of Semitic Studies*, Manchester
JTS	*Journal of Theological Studies*, Oxford
K	*K^{e}tib*
KAI	H. Donner–W. Röllig, *Kanaanäische und Aramäische Inschriften*, Wiesbaden 1962ff.
KAT	Kommentar zum Alten Testament, Leipzig–Gütersloh
KHAT	Kurzer Handcommentar zum AT, Tübingen
LTK	*Lexikon für Theologie und Kirche*, Freiburg im Breisgau
LXX	Septuagint: Greek translation
MT	Massoretic text
NRT	*Nouvelle Revue Théologique*, Paris
NS (NF)	New series
OLZ	*Orientalistische Literaturzeitung*, Leipzig–Berlin
OTL	Old Testament Library, London
OTS	*Oudtestamentische Studiën*, Leiden
PEFQS	*Palestine Exploration Fund Quarterly Statement*, London
PEQ	*Palestine Exploration Quarterly*, London
PJB	*Palästinajahrbuch*, Berlin
Q	*Q^{e}rē*
RA	*Revue d'Assyriologie*, Paris
RB	*Revue Biblique*, Jerusalem–Paris
RGG	*Die Religion in Geschichte und Gegenwart*, Tübingen
RHR	*Revue de l'Histoire des Religions*, Paris
RHPR	*Revue d'Histoire et de Philosophie Religieuses*, Strasbourg
RSO	*Rivista degli Studi Orientali*, Rome
RTP	*Revue de Théologie et de Philosophie*, Lausanne
SAT	Die Schriften des AT in Auswahl, Göttingen
SBT	Studies in Biblical Theology, London
SDB	*Supplément au Dictionnaire de la Bible*, Paris

StTh	*Studia Theologica*, Lund
Syr	Syriac translation (Peshitto)
SVT	Supplements to *Vetus Testamentum*, Leiden
T	Targum
ThRev	*Theologische Revue*, Münster
TLZ	*Theologische Literaturzeitung*, Leipzig
TR	*Theologische Rundschau*, Tübingen
TZ	*Theologische Zeitschrift*, Basel
UGS	M. Noth, *Überlieferungsgeschichtliche Studien* I, Halle 1943 (repr. Darmstadt 1957)
V	Vulgate: Latin translation
VD	*Verbum Domini*, Rome
VT	*Vetus Testamentum*, Leiden
WMANT	Wissenschaftliche Monographien zum Alten und Neuen Testament, Neukirchen
WO	*Die Welt des Orients*, Göttingen–Wiesbaden
ZA	*Zeitschrift für Assyriologie*, Berlin
ZAW	*Zeitschrift für die alttestamentliche Wissenschaft*, Giessen–Berlin
ZDMG	*Zeitschrift der Deutschen Morgenländischen Gesellschaft*, Leipzig–Wiesbaden
ZDPV	*Zeitschrift des Deutschen Palästinavereins*, Leipzig–Wiesbaden
ZTK	*Zeitschrift für Theologie und Kirche*, Tübingen
Θ	Greek translation by Theodotion
Σ	Greek translation by Symmachus

BIBLIOGRAPHY

THE recent publication of two important bibliographical studies, E. Jenni, 'Zwei Jahrzehnte Forschung an den Büchern Josua bis Könige', *TR* 27, 1961, pp. 1–32 and 97–146, and R. North, *De Jesu Nave*, Rome (Pontifical Biblical Institute) 1969, means that we need give only a selected bibliography here, referring to these studies for all detailed questions.

A. TEXTS

Septuagint: M. A. Margolis, *The Book of Joshua in Greek*, Paris 1931–38 (a fine critical edition, complete up to 19.38); also S. Holmes, *Joshua: the Hebrew and Greek Texts*, Cambridge 1914; C. D. Benjamin, *The Variations between the Hebrew and Greek Texts of Joshua, Chapters 1–12*, Philadelphia 1921; H. M. Orlinsky, 'The Hebrew Vorlage of the Septuagint of the Book of Joshua', SVT XVII, 1969, pp. 187–95.

B. COMMENTARIES

H. Holzinger, KHAT, Tübingen 1901; H. Holzinger, *HSAT* I, Tübingen, [4]1922; H. Gressmann, SAT I, 2, Göttingen [2]1922 (rightly famous for its introduction to the problems of Joshua on the basis of aetiological legend); C. Steuernagel, HKAT, n.e. Göttingen 1923; A. Schulz, HS, Bonn 1924; J. Garstang, *The Foundations of Biblical History: Joshua–Judges*, Oxford 1931; A. Fernández, *Cursus Scripturae Sacrae* II.5, 1938 (very useful for the study of the text and the geographical data); F. Nötscher, EB I, Würzburg 1950; M. Noth, HAT I.7, Tübingen [2]1953 (a fundamental work for the study of the texts from the point of view of geography and tradition history); D. Baldi, *Bibbia Garofalo*, Turin 1952 (interesting for its solidly conservative attitude in matters of text, tradition history and geography); J. Bright, *IB* II, New York–Nashville 1953 (useful for the study of works published in the USA); É. Dhorme, Bible de la Pleiade I, Paris 1956; H. W. Hertzberg, ATD 9, Göttingen 1957 (excellent from the point of view of geography, tradition history and theology); F. M. Abel, *Bible de Jérusalem*, Paris ²1958; Y. Kaufmann, *Sēfer Yᵉhōsūaʿ*, Jerusalem 1959 (conservative in many matters, but in an original way; his thesis on aetiology and the utopian nature of Josh. 13–21 are unconvincing).

C. MONOGRAPHS

K. Möhlenbrink, 'Die Landnahmesagen des Buches Josua', *ZAW* 56, 1938, pp. 238–68; W. Rudolph, *Der 'Elohist' als Erzähler von Exodus bis Josua*, BZAW 68, Giessen 1938, pp. 165ff.; M. Noth, *Überlieferungsgeschichtliche Studien* I, Halle 1943 (n.e. Darmstadt 1957), pp. 40–47; C. A. Simpson, *The Early Traditions of Israel*, Oxford 1948, pp. 280ff.; F. M. Abel, 'Les stratagèmes du livre de Josué', *RB* 56, 1949, pp. 321–39; Y. Kaufmann, *The Biblical Account of the Conquest of Palestine*, Jerusalem 1953; S. Mowinckel, *Pentateuch, Tetrateuch und Hexateuch*, BZAW 90, Berlin 1964; G. Auzon, *Le don d'une conquête*, Paris 1964; P. W. Lapp, 'The Conquest of Palestine in the Light of Archaeology', *Concordia Theological Monthly* 38, 1967, pp. 283–300; M. Weippert, *The Settlement of the Israelite Tribes in Palestine*, SBT II, 21, London 1971; D. J. McCarthy, 'The Theology of Leadership in Joshua 1–9', *Bibl* 52, 1971, pp. 165–75. We were unable to make use of S. Yeivin, *The Israelite Conquest of Canaan*, Leiden 1971. We shall refer to other works and studies at the appropriate point in the commentary.

D. GEOGRAPHY

M. Noth, 'Studien zu den historisch-geographischen Dokumenten des Josuabuches', *ZDPV* 58, 1935, pp. 185–255; F. M. Abel, *Géographie de la Palestine*, Vol. I, 1933; Vol. II, 1938 (n.e. 1966); D. Baly, *The Geography of the Bible*, London 1957; M. du Buit, *Géographie de la Terre Sainte*, Paris 1958; J. Simons, *The Geographical and Topographical Texts of the Old Testament*, Leiden 1959; Y. Aharoni, *The Land of the Bible*, London 1967.

Maps: Survey of Israel, 1:100,000 (16 sheets); we give the coordinates of these maps in parentheses, following Aharoni, op. cit.

E. ENCYCLOPAEDIA ARTICLES

P. Auvray, 'Josué (livre de)', *SDB* IV, 1949, cols. 1132–41; E. Höhne, 'Josua', *EKL* II, 1958, cols. 383ff.; M. D. (U.) Cassuto, 'Yᵉhōšūa" and 'Sēfer Yᵉhōšūa", *EncBibl* III, cols. 542–65 (Hebrew); R. Bach, 'Josua', *RGG* III, ³1959, cols. 872f.; L. Rost, 'Josuabuch', ibid., cols. 873ff.; J. Scharbert, 'Josue', *LTK* V, 1960, col. 1145; E. M. Good, 'Joshua', *IDB* II, 1962, pp. 988–96; R. Hentschke, 'Josuabuch', *BHH* II, 1964, cols. 895ff.; J. Nelis, 'Josue', *BL*, ²1968, cols. 882–8.

INTRODUCTION

1. THE TITLE AND PLAN OF THE BOOK

IN THE HEBREW Bible, the book of Joshua is the first in the series of 'former prophets'; this title will be explained in §2. The principal theme of the book is the conquest of Palestine west of the Jordan; that part of Palestine east of the Jordan which belonged to Israel had been occupied previously under the leadership of Moses, according to the account which has come down to us in Num. 32 and Deut. 3. 12–20.

The title of the book is taken from that of its protagonist, Joshua the son of Nun, translated in LXX by 'Ιησοῦς υἱὸς Ναυη or Ναυν (probably an internal confusion between the letters H and N; LXX ᴸᵘᶜ: 'Ι. Ναυη) and in Latin by *Iosue filius Nun* or *Nave*. According to the biblical tradition, Israel succeeded under his leadership in obtaining a foothold in extensive regions of the Palestinian plateau. We shall see (§4 below) that for several decades this tradition has been subjected to severe criticism and that the degree to which it can be relied upon is still a matter for debate.

The name *yᵉhōšūaᶜ* in its full form is a typical theophoric name, expressing Yahwist faith in its purest form; it means in fact 'Yahweh saves' or 'May Yahweh save!' It is this longer form which is the most frequent, and the only one to occur in the oldest texts. During the post-exilic period, and in the books of Chronicles, Ezra and Nehemiah,[1] an abbreviated form *yēšūaᶜ* is also found, and the Greek transcription

---

[1] Cf. the concordances to the OT, ad loc.; M. Noth, *Die Israelitischen Personennamen im Rahmen der gemeinsemitischen Namengebung*, BWANT III, 10, Stuttgart 1928 (repr. 1966), s.v. The Greek form of the patronymic, Ναυη, which occurs in LXX and which also appears in Latin (*Nave*), seems to be the original form, before its contraction in front of the Hebrew *n* (from *nāweh* with *n* enclitic). *nūn* in fact means 'fish', while *nāweh* means 'the total of herds and men which makes up a nomad tribe' (as early as Old Babylonian and later especially at Mari), cf. J. L. Kupper, *Les nomades en Mésopotamie au temps des rois de Mari*, Paris 1957, pp. 12ff.;D. O. Edzard, 'Altbabylonisch nawūm', *ZA* 53, 1959, pp.168–73; A. Malamat, 'Mari and

is based on this. The Latin form is probably derived from the contraction of the longer form into *yōšūaʿ*, although this contraction does not occur in our literary records. Finally, another variant of the long form is *hōšēaʿ*, a name borne by, amongst others, the last king of Israel and the prophet Hosea, both of whom lived in the second half of the eighth century BC; it is given to Joshua on two occasions: Num. 13.8–16 and Deut. 32.44.

The book of Joshua is divided into three main parts, each of which can be sub-divided in its turn in the following way:

I. *The actual conquest (chs. 1–12)*

1. Introduction (ch. 1)
2. Exploration of the Jericho region and the Rahab episode (ch. 2)
3. The march towards the west, the crossing of the Jordan and the setting up of memorial stones in the sanctuary at Gilgal (3.1–5.1)
4. Religious ceremonies at Gilgal (5.2ff.)
5. The capture of Jericho (ch. 6)
6. The attack on Ai and related episodes (7.1–8.29)
7. The ceremony at Shechem (8.30–35)
8. The ruse of the inhabitants of Gibeon and their covenant with the invaders (ch. 9)
9. The Gibeon campaign and the expedition to the south (ch. 10)
10. The expedition to the north (11.1–15)
11. General epilogue and list of conquered kings (11.16–12.24)

II. *The Division of the Land (chs. 13–21)*

1. A historical and geographical balance sheet of the operations west of the Jordan (ch. 13)
2. At Gilgal: the apportioning of land to: (*a*) Caleb (14.6–15); (*b*) Judah (ch. 15); (*c*) Ephraim and Manasseh (chs. 16–17)
3. At Shiloh: a new apportioning of land to: (*a*) Benjamin (ch. 18); (*b*) Simeon (19.1–9); (*c*) Zebulun (19.10–16); (*d*) Issachar (19.17–23); (*e*) Asher (19.24–31); (*f*) Naphtali (19.32–39); (*g*) Dan (19.40–48). In 19.49–50, Joshua himself receives an area of land in Ephraim

---

the Bible', *JAOS* 82, 1962, p.146. May it perhaps be a tribal name rather than a patronymic?

4. Cities of refuge (ch. 20), and Levitical cities (ch. 21). Altogether there are twelve tribes listed west of the Jordan and two and a half tribes east of the Jordan; the figure twelve is obtained when one recalls that Caleb and Simeon formed in reality part of Judah

III. *Appendix (chs. 22–24)*

1. The return of the tribes from the east of the Jordan (ch. 22)
2. Joshua's first address (ch. 23)
3. Joshua's second address (24.1–28, and perhaps 8.30–35)
4. Traditions concerning the tombs of Joshua, Joseph and Eleazar (24.29–33)

2. THE WORK OF THE DEUTERONOMIC HISTORY WRITER

The discovery made by Martin Noth during the Second World War[1] supplies the key for the whole interpretation of the 'former prophets' of the Hebrew canon. In their final redaction, these writings are the product of the immense work of collection and compilation which has come to be called, following Noth, the 'Deuteronomic history work' (we shall abbreviate as 'Dtr').

It has long been generally admitted that the books of the Bible from Joshua to Kings are in their present form the product of a Deuteronomic redaction, the importance of which varies according to the history of each literary unit. Thus, for example, it is known that Judges and Kings have virtually been edited from beginning to end by Dtr, apart from a few exceptions; in Joshua and Samuel, we find chapters written in their entirety by Dtr (e.g. Josh. 1.1–18; 8.30–35; 21.43–22.6; 23.1–16). The originality of Noth's discovery lies in his demonstration of the way in which the work of Dtr was one of ordering and preservation, incorporating extremely varied material, sometimes parallel or contradictory (e.g. the account of the crossing of the Jordan, Josh. 3.), which was then placed in order 'according to a well worked-out plan'.[2]

---

[1] M. Noth, *UGS*; A. Jepsen, *Die Quellen des Königsbuches*, Halle [2]1956. Cf. also A. G. Tunyogi, 'The Book of the Conquest', *JBL* 84, 1965, pp. 374–80. Cf. Jenni, 'Zwei Jahrzehnte . . .', pp. 97ff.

[2] Noth, *UGS*, p. 11; *Josua*, p. 9. For the general work of Dt and Dtr in this context, cf. G. von Rad, *Studies in Deuteronomy*, SBT 9, London 1952.

As we know, the work of Dtr begins with Deut. 1.1–4.49, continuing in 31.1–13 and fragments of ch. 34; it is then found throughout the 'historical books' which we have mentioned. In chronological terms, its setting is the situation which followed the reform of Josiah (622–21), king of Judah (640/39–609 BC), and which lasted through the Babylonian exile, probably until the middle of the sixth century. There is no question that the Deuteronomic history formed the most tangible result of the protest of the pre-exilic prophets, between the ninth and the sixth centuries, against the religious syncretism between the traditional Yahwist faith of the ancient nomadic groups, which had settled, and the indigenous religion of Palestine. The prophets saw in this the causes of the decadence of the religion, social ethics and politics of their people. It seems highly probable that this explains the title 'former prophets' given by Israel's tradition to the historical books, which were regarded as an interpretation of the ancient history of the people with the aid of the basic elements of the prophetic preaching.

The aim of the Deuteronomic history as a whole, and therefore of each of its parts, is not to collect and edit facts in the most objective way possible in order to reconstruct a particular situation. It is a work which sets out to show to a community which was ready to listen, the actions which God had carried out through the history of mankind, and in particular of his 'chosen people'. This can be seen clearly in Josh. 23.3, 14; 24.8, 12, 14; these passages form an epilogue which provides a kind of Deuteronomic key to the whole book of Joshua. It is certain that the compilers of the Deuteronomic history recalled the ancient traditions to their audience to prove or illustrate such affirmations as these, and not from a pure and simple spirit of investigation. The present time seemed disastrous, the catastrophe was looming or had already taken place, the future seemed uncertain. But in an age when everything seemed to be unstable, the people were provided with this timely collection and methodical publication of their ancient religious traditions, to draw from them new strength, a renewed faith and a fresh hope in the intervention of God in the immediate future. The ancient promises, the affirmations of the traditional faith on the choosing of Israel, the testimonies of the wonderful works of God in the past, which for a century at least had already been raised to the rank of a liturgical confession of faith in the covenant worship, were all still in force, even though they seemed to be temporarily overshadowed by the judgment which the prophets had elsewhere proclaimed to be imminent. They could even serve as a basis for the future work of restoration, if only the people would at last take seriously, through repentance and a new consecration, the fundamental elements of the prophetic message[1]. Although its premises are different, the work resembles what we find in chs. 40–48 of the prophet Ezekiel.

It is pointless to discuss whether this immense editorial work was carried out by a school or an individual.[2] The question will no doubt never be answered, and is not perhaps as important for the understanding of the Deuteronomic work as some people suppose. It is sufficient to observe that the systematic and unified character of the work suggests a single hand, while the length of the period involved (622/21–550) suggests a collective work.

The work is almost always supposed to have been written in Palestine. For reasons which we give in our commentary on ch. 23, we would suggest that it was written during the Babylonian exile.[3] Assuming this, there are two factors in the way Dtr undertakes the writing of this history, one of which astonishes us and the other of which perplexes us! On the one hand, we cannot but be astonished by the wide range of an attempt at a historical, philosophical and theological synthesis which is without parallel either in classical antiquity or in the ancient Near East, and at the strength of a faith which will not be convinced by the evidence that its cause is already lost, but continues to hope for a restoration at a time when, after the Persian conquest in 539, only a minute fragment of the kingdom of Judah remained. On the other hand, we are perplexed by the inevitable distortions in a historical task of this scope, but which the nature of the

---

[1] The theme of the people of God in Deuteronomy has been particularly emphasized by G. von Rad, *Das Gottesvolk in Deuteronomium*, BWANT III, 11, Stuttgart 1929; H. Wildberger, *Jahwes Eigentumsvolk*, ATANT 37, Zürich 1960. For the whole problem of the theology of Dtr, cf. G. von Rad, *Old Testament Theology* I, London 1962, pp.334ff.; J. M. Myers, 'The Requisites of Response', *Interpr* 16, 1961, pp.14–31; H. W. Wolff, 'Das Kerygma des deuteronomistischen Geschichtswerkes', *ZAW* 73, 1961, pp.171–86 (=*Gesammelte Studien*, Munich 1964, pp.308–24: this last article is particularly valuable).

[2] Noth, *UGS*, pp.97,110, prefers the second alternative; Jepsen and Wolff, op. cit., the first. For a date between 560 and 540 as a *terminus a quo*, according to II Kings 25.27–30, cf. M. Noth, 'Zur Geschichtsauffassung des Deuteronomisten', in *Proceedings of the XXII Congress of Orientalists, Istanbul 1951*, Leiden 1957, vol. II, pp. 558–66 (where he also favours the view that there was one redactor).

[3] Cf. our study 'Deuteronomische Geschichtsauslegung während des babylonischen Exils', in *Oikonomia. Heilsgeschichte als Thema der Theologie* (Hommage à O. Cullmann), Hamburg 1967, pp. 11–77.

history writing which preceded Dtr is not sufficient to justify. With regard to the book of Joshua, for example, the writer gives new dimensions to the conquest of Palestine by the Israelites, and has presented it from an optimistic point of view: 'Many things,' one commentator remarks, 'are taken here in a vertical dimension, where at first sight they give the impression of having happened in a horizontal dimension';[1] which, this commentator continues, is of vital importance for the historical evaluation of the book of Joshua! Without wishing to attribute to the content of the book the character of 'edifying dissimulation' of the facts, 'in a presentation like this the entry into Palestine is more than a historical and secular event; it is a theological fact.' Such a situation naturally requires great prudence of a historian in handling the material! This does not mean, however, that the book is without any historical value. Noth has in fact shown that Dtr displays on the one hand intellectual honesty, and on the other hand a consistent and coherent choice of material.[2] Thus one may have reasonable confidence in the authenticity of the materials, once it is realized that authenticity means that they are in accordance with the tradition which Dtr received and are therefore not the product of the editor's imagination nor of tendentious distortions on his part. Nor is the choice of materials an arbitrary one, as though Dtr had chosen only episodes capable of supporting his own historical and theological theses. On the contrary, Noth demonstrates a remarkable integrity both in the choice of the elements considered as important and in the exclusion of others. This is most clearly seen in the book of Kings, where a constant reference to the sources invites the reader to check the force of the argument, with the aid of material which the compiler did not think it necessary to include. The disappearance of all the sources to which Dtr refers, explicitly or implicitly, faces the modern historian with an insoluble problem, but this is not the fault of Dtr! Thus the whole of the Deuteronomic work is carried out within this dialectic, which for the most part it is impossible to resolve by rational means.

It may be said that this account of the historical books has nowadays almost entirely replaced the documentary hypothesis. That hypothesis regarded Joshua as the sixth book of a Hexateuch, and claimed to trace in it the same sources as in the previous books. It was a conception which seemed to be justified by the obvious fact that the book of Joshua fulfils a promise expressed throughout the Pentateuch, and

[1] Hertzberg, *Comm.*, pp. 9ff.   [2] *UGS*, pp. 95ff.

by the equally evident observation (as Holzinger showed[1]), that it was unthinkable for the Pentateuch to conclude with the conquest of the regions east of the Jordan, without including the conquest of the regions to the west. However, it is to be pointed out that these two themes constantly recur in Deuteronomy, so that it is possible that Joshua may have developed these themes as a continuation of Deuteronomy alone, and not necessarily as a sequel to the whole Pentateuch.[2] Relatively few objections are made to this new way of approaching the problem at the present day, although some are very telling; as has been recently stated, the thesis of the Deuteronomic history work is in the course of becoming 'a commonplace of Old Testament scholarship'.[3]

3. PRE-DEUTERONOMIC ELEMENTS AND THE HISTORICAL PROBLEMS OF THE CONQUEST

Here and there, and particularly in the passages which have come down to us in the best state of preservation, it is possible to go behind the work of the Deuteronomic editor to earlier historical and cultic settings. However, even where this task can be seen to be possible, one must remember that the preservation of this material is not due to the intrinsic quality of its content but rather, as we shall see, to the use to which Dtr believed it could be put – with the exception, it appears, of the second part of the book, chs. 13–31, the content of which is essentially geographical (tribal frontiers, lists of towns and districts, etc.). The latter categories of material have their own history, which it is not too difficult to reconstruct; they were in fact incorporated into the Deuteronomic work at a second stage, when its main out-

---

[1] *Comm.*, 1922, p.328b.

[2] For a good account of studies earlier than that of Noth, cf. Auvray, *SDB*, cols. 1131–38; Cassuto, *EncBibl*, cols.544ff.; D. Baldi, *Comm.*, pp.5ff.; E. M. Good, *IDB*, pp.988–95.

[3] The quotation is from Good, *IDB*, p.992. For the persistence of contrary views, cf. G. von Rad, *Old Testament Theology* I, pp.129ff., who still talks of a 'Hexateuch'; O. Eissfeldt, *The Old Testament: An Introduction*, Oxford 1965, pp.242ff., who disagrees with Noth's theses and supports either the earlier thesis of a Hexateuch or the view which sees the sources of the Pentateuch continued in the 'Former Prophets' (for a detailed criticism of these views, cf. L. Alonso-Schökel, *Bibl* 39, 1958, pp.217–21). Other scholars opposed to Noth are: C.A.Simpson, *The Early Traditions of Israel*, pp.280ff.; G.Hölscher, *Geschichtsschreibung im Alten Israel*, Lund 1952; A.Weiser, *Introduction to the Old Testament*, London 1961, pp.143ff.; G.Föhrer—E. Sellin, *Introduction to the Old Testament*, London 1970, pp.192–5.

lines had been practically completed. The absence of all signs of editorial work in these passages clearly demonstrates, as we said above, the objectivity of Dtr in handling his material.

While the groups of material contained in the second part of the book are very important from the historical and geographical point of view, they are far less important from a theological point of view.[1] These groups of material were added to the Deuteronomic work: cf. the chapter heading, 13.1ff., and the conclusion of 21.43ff. The situation of 24.1–28 (to which 8.30–35 should no doubt be attached) seems similar: it is clear that this passage is based on the recitation, in the course of the cult, of the ancient confession of faith which is attributed to Joshua and localized at Shechem.[2] In its present state, the passage is full of elements which have been edited by Dtr, but it is easy to see that in reality it is a doublet of ch. 23, which is a purely Deuteronomic composition.

We shall also look further on at a valuable attempt to demonstrate the existence in the book of Joshua of the Pentateuchal sources, particularly J and P, and the problems associated with this new presentation of an earlier view. Doubt was cast on the possibility of the presence of E some years before Noth's study and such a hypothesis seems untenable at the present day;[3] but up to twenty years ago the collection of materials contained in the first part, before its redaction by Dtr, was in fact usually attributed to E. Similarly, in the case of P, one can do no more than follow Noth in speaking of a few minor additions formulated in the characteristic style of the Priestly source: 14.1–2; 19.51a; 21.1–2 (often interspersed with other material). In the past, on the other hand, it was usual to attribute to P, as Mowinckel still does, the redaction of the second part. We shall also look at this problem later (cf. (c) below).

Having established these facts, we can now go into details.[4]

---

[1] Consequently no more than a few lines are devoted to them in W. Vischer, *Das Christuszeugnis des Alten Testaments*, II, 1, Zollikon 1942, pp. 26ff.; he simply points to the faith and hope of one who, driven from his own country, remains concerned with its problems. Modern Zionism is no more than a highly secularized version of these feelings (with a strong religious background).

[2] G. von Rad, 'The Form-Critical Problem of the Hexateuch', in *The Problem of the Hexateuch and Other Essays*, Edinburgh 1966, pp. 1–78.

[3] W. Rudolph, *Der 'Elohist'* . . ., and more recently S. Mowinckel, *Tetrateuch-Pentateuch-Hexateuch*, in which, as we shall see, he argues for the retention of J and P.

[4] Noth, *Josua*[2], pp. 11ff.

(a) *In the first part* (*chs. 1–12*), it is easy to see that we are faced with a mosaic of very different materials, almost all of which, however, are associated with the territory of Benjamin and its sanctuary, Gilgal. The exceptions are the Achan episode, a brief sortie into the neighbouring territory of Judah, the assembly at Shechem in 8.30–35, and the two campaigns of 10.16ff.; the list in ch. 12 is neutral from the geographical point of view. We know that the Benjaminite sanctuary of Gilgal was raised to the status of a national sanctuary at the time of Saul the Benjaminite. This is completely in accordance with the episode of the capture of the ark in I Sam. 4, which was probably followed by the destruction of the central sanctuary of Shiloh. But the death of Saul did not bring about the decline of Gilgal, which succeeded in preserving a considerable degree of prestige as long as the kingdom of Israel lasted (cf. I Sam. 11ff.; II Kings 2.1; Amos 4.4; 5.5; Hos. 4.15; 9.15; 12.11; etc.).

Now, according to the traditional account as we find it in the book of Joshua, it was the Gilgal region, if not Gilgal itself, that was the starting place not only of the troops who conquered the territory of Benjamin in the strict sense, but of the expedition to the south (10.8–9) and all the undertakings described in Judges 1 (at least this is a possible explanation of the phrase in Judges 1.1: 'Who shall *go up* first for us . . .', although Gilgal is not explicitly mentioned as a starting point; but the expression assumes that they were in the valley of the Jordan).[1] The first division of the promised land described in Josh. 14–15 probably also took place at Gilgal.

Thus it seems that the traditions of the first part of the book almost all refer to the territory of the tribe of Benjamin, and almost always in relation with its sanctuary Gilgal. However, the other traditions which are recorded show the tendency of the redactor to relate them to this sanctuary, even though by all appearances these traditions have nothing to do with Gilgal, at least in the geographical sense. The only conclusion that can be drawn from these observations is that the sanctuary at Gilgal is the place of origin of the traditions of the first part of the book, for it was there that they were gathered together and from thence that they were handed on. But the unifying influence of the holy place was so strong that it attracted to itself other traditions which in their location and in the ideas they contained were remote from Gilgal and had no links with the tribe of Benjamin. Most present-day commentators draw from this the obvious conclusion that

[1] As Mowinckel, op. cit., pp. 21ff., rightly points out.

the traditions of chs. 1–12 are in great part of Benjaminite origin, with the sanctuary of Gilgal playing a co-ordinating and unifying role. Noth goes so far as to suppose[1] that the sanctuary of Gilgal was not only the unifying factor in the Benjaminite traditions but also the vehicle by which they were handed on; and as a result of this role played by the sanctuary, they provided the pattern for the redaction of the unified account of the conquest. This view is highly probable. Anyone who seeks to refute these statements is faced by the following problem: how is it to be explained that a tradition clearly associated with the tribe of Benjamin could be extended to the whole of Israel and that material which had nothing to do with Benjamin could have come to be linked to the sanctuary of Gilgal? Although the logical construction which we have set out is wholly hypothetical, it enables us to refute in detail the only modern attempt to deny its main assumptions: that of Y. Kaufmann, who denies that the whole of this complex is of Benjaminite origin.[2]

In the main body of the commentary we shall give more detail about the sanctuary of Gilgal. For the moment, it should be noted that the place has not yet been identified with certainty; but the probable locality is a small *tell* without a name, some 4 km north-east of that of Jericho.[3] However, the mosaic map of Madaba, and the testimonies of St Jerome and of Christian pilgrims, record a *dodekalithon* near Jericho on the road to Philadelphia (Amman).

The literary form of the stories collected in the first part of the book is in most cases that which is usually known as 'aetiological' legend.

---

[1] *Josua*[2], p. 12. For the conquest of the territory of Benjamin, now cf. K.D. Schunck, *Benjamin*, BZAW 86, Berlin 1963, pp. 18ff.

[2] Y.Kaufmann, *The Biblical Account of the Conquest of Palestine*, *passim*, and esp. pp. 67ff. This work by Kaufmann is to a large extent a paraphrase of the introduction to his commentary, quoted above. Schunck, op. cit., pp. 25ff., takes a similar view.

[3] J.Muilenberg, 'The Site of Ancient Gilgal', *BASOR* 140, 1955, pp. 11–27, recently supported by K.Elliger, 'Gilgal', *BHH* I, 1962, cols. 572ff. For earlier discussions, cf. Fernández, Baldi and Noth, *Comms*. For Gilgal in the Christian era, cf. F.M.Abel, 'ΓΑΛΓΑΛΑ qui est aussi le Dodécaliton', *Mémorial J. Chaine*, Lyon 1950, pp. 29–34; O.Bächli, 'Zur Lage des alten Gilgal', *ZDPV* 83, 1967, pp. 64–71. The latter suggests that the choice lies between three *tells* and rejects *khirbet mefjir*, which is generally accepted. We cannot deal here with the problem of Jericho at the Roman period; cf. R.de Vaux, review in *RB* 64, 1957, pp. 461f.; C.U.Wolf, 'The Localization of Gilgal', *BiblRes* XI, 1966, pp. 42–51. He identifies the Gilgal of the Roman period with *tell es-sulṭan*, that is, with the *tell* of the Jericho of antiquity; but this is unlikely.

That is, they are legends which set out to explain the names, usages and customs, rites and traditions and other special features of a place or of its inhabitants, etc., by linking them with a hero or with legendary events from pre-history, traditionally associated with the region. At the present day there is considerable controversy about the cultural and cultic milieu of 'aetiological' legends and of their value as sources to the historian; the problem is still far from a satisfactory solution.[1]

Noth holds that in some places one can distinguish the links which joined the episodes before they were edited by Dtr. These, in his view, are: 5.1; 6.27; 9.3–4a; 10.2, 5, 40–42; 11.1–2, 16–20.[2] But the most notable attempt to locate and isolate the pre-Deuteronomic material is certainly that recently carried out by Mowinckel.[3] He regards Josh.2 and 11.13, with certain passages in the second part of the book (cf. (c) below) which are parallel to Judg. 1 (which he naturally includes in his list), as the remnant of what he believes was once the J redaction of the ancient traditions concerning the conquest. The expression 'compiler' (Sammler) which Noth preferred to apply to this early collection seems less risky; in Noth's view, it is wrong to attribute it to J, because of the links with the Pentateuch which this assumes;[4] this 'compiler', however, lived in his view in the tenth century, which would make him the contemporary of J.

(b) The second part (chs. 13–21) contains, incorporated into the geographical passages mentioned above, two documents. The 'system of Israel's tribal frontiers' is a list either of territories actually occupied or territorial aspirations not yet fulfilled. The classical work on this subject is that of A. Alt, written in 1927.[5] The second document consists of a list of localities in Judah divided into twelve districts (cf. Josh. 15.21–62 and 18.25–28, for Judah and Benjamin). Alt[6] sought

---

[1] See B. O. Long, *The Problem of Etiological Narrative in the Old Testament*, BZAW 108, Berlin 1968.

[2] *Josua²*, pp. 12ff.

[3] Op. cit.

[4] *Josua²*, pp. 16ff.

[5] A. Alt, 'Das System der Stammesgrenzen im Buch Josua', 1927, *KS* I, Munich 1953, pp. 193–202; M. Noth, 'Studien zu den historisch-geographischen Dokumenten . . .', pp. 232–48. The use of lists, either of fixed points on a frontier or of towns with their districts, is already found in Ugarit, cf. M. Liverani, *Storia di Ugarit nell'età degli archivi politici*, Rome 1962, pp. 48ff., 73; and R. de Langhe, *Les textes de Ras Schamra et leur rapport avec le milieu biblique de l'Ancien Testament*, Paris 1945, vol. II, pp. 18–68.

[6] 'Judas Gaue unter Josia', 1925, *KS* II, pp. 276–88.

to date it at the period of the reorganization of the kingdom of Judah under Josiah, such a list having become necessary as a consequence of the policy of expansion towards the territories in the north occupied by the declining Assyrian Empire, which would have led to the incorporation of districts I, V and XII, while in the south a district XIII had been conquered. More recent studies[1] prefer to date it a good deal earlier, relating the list to a different historical situation. Here it is assumed to be based on the reorganization of Judah under either David or Solomon, or later, under Rehoboam, on the pattern of that carried out by Solomon for Israel according to I Kings 4. Others have suggested a connection with the measures taken by the kings Abijah (c. 910–908), Asa (c. 908–868), Jehoshaphat (c. 868–847) or at the latest Uzziah/Azariah (c. 787–736).[2] Only Mowinckel still argues for a very late date;[3] in his view, chs.13–19 belong to P or to another even later redaction, likewise from the post-exilic period, even though the presence of older traditional material may be admitted. This view is not convincing. Mowinckel has not produced an adequate reason why these chapters should not be attributed to an earlier period, and does not explain at all why these lists should have played so important

---

[1] F. M. Cross and G. E. Wright, 'The Boundary and Province List of Judah', *JBL* 75, 1956, pp. 209–226; Z. Kallai(-Kleinmann), *The Northern Boundaries of Judah*, Jerusalem 1960 (in Hebrew); id., 'Note on the Town Lists of Judah, Simeon, Benjamin and Dan', *VT* 11, 1961, pp.223–7; a good resumé of the discussion is given in Schunck, op. cit., pp. 156ff. See below, on ch. 15.

[2] For the chronology, cf. the recent study by A. Jepsen and R. Hanhart, *Untersuchungen zur israelitisch-jüdischen Chronologie*, BZAW 88, Berlin 1964, and the chronological tables in Rudolph, *Hosea*, KAT XIII, 1, Gütersloh 1966, pp.271ff. In our *Introduzione all'Antico Testamento*, vol.II, Brescia 1969, pp.235ff., we still followed the chronology of the American school of archaeology, cf. W. F. Albright, 'The Chronology of the Divided Monarchy', *BASOR* 100, 1945, pp.16–22. We would now adopt the chronology of J. Begrich and A. Jepsen, for the reasons given in our articles 'Das Erdbeben von Amos 1.1 und die Chronologie der Könige Ussia und Jotham von Juda', *ZAW* 82, 1970, pp.117–21; 'Amos 6.13–14 und 1.3 auf dem Hintergrund der Beziehungen zwischen Israel und Damaskus im 9. und 8. Jahrhundert', *Near Eastern Studies in Honor of W. F. Albright*, Baltimore 1971, pp.433–41, esp. p.437; 'Ein ausserbiblisches Zeugnis für die Chronologie des Jᵉhô'aš/Jô'āš von Israel', *VT* 20, 1970, pp. 366–8.

[3] Op. cit., pp.61ff. He refers to his previous study, 'Zur Frage nach dokumentarischen Quellen in Josua 13–19', *Afhandl. det Norske Videnskap Akademi i Oslo*, 1946: 1. But he has already been refuted in M. Noth, 'Überlieferungsgeschichtliches zur zweiten Hälfte des Josuabuches', in *Alttestamentliche Studien, F. Nötscher zum 60. Geburtstag* . . ., BBB 1, Bonn 1950, pp.152–62. The study of 1964 to which we refer adds nothing on this subject, cf. our review in *ThZ* 22, 1966, pp.440–2.

a part at a time when a restoration of Israel set out in this form lay beyond even the most daring hope. What had been the faith and hope of Dtr became an absurdity in the decade that followed.

(c) *The second part also contains* a number of very ancient fragments, parallel to Judg. 1, which are in contradiction to the unitary vision of the conquest as the Deuteronomic redactor presents it. These are the descriptions of territories which the tribes did not succeed in occupying; and they show how questionable it is to speak of the conquest of Palestine in the period which preceded the united monarchy: Josh. 15.13–19 ‖ Judg. 1.11–15; Josh. 15.63 ‖ Judg. 1.21; Josh. 16.10 ‖ Judg. 1.29; Josh. 17.11–13 ‖ Judg. 1.27–28; Josh. 19.47 ‖ Judg. 1.34–35.

(d) *The second part also contains* two other lists: that of the 'cities of refuge' (ch. 20) and that of the 'Levitical cities' (ch. 21). Alt and Noth would attribute both to the period of Josiah or a short time later, relating them in both cases to the plan for the restoration of Israel which we have mentioned.[1] Noth, on the basis of the fact that the first list is contained within the second, states that the second is older, although he admits that the first may go back to the ancient holy places which practised the right of sanctuary within their sacred area. Other more recent studies[2] maintain a different chronology: it is argued that the *terminus a quo* of these two institutions is the tenth century, because several of the cities mentioned were first occupied under David and Solomon; but they could not have come into existence much later, because of what Albright calls 'a simple question of chronological incompatibility', for there was no other period when these cities were simultaneously in the hands of the Israelites. A recent study by Mazar[3] has sought to show that each of these cities represented a kind of 'colony' composed of reliable elements to exercise surveillance over recently acquired territory and to organize administration there. He argues from the fact that the cities chosen were either Canaanite or places which lay within Canaanite enclaves. In spite of the lack of definite proof, this seems plausible, in particular as it corresponds in this region to Egyptian practice.

---

[1] Noth, *Josua²*, pp. 123ff.

[2] For the cities of refuge, cf. M. Löhr, *Das Asylwesen im Alten Testament*, Halle 1930; W. F. Albright, *Archaeology and the Religion of Israel*, Baltimore 1953, pp. 123ff. For the Levitical cities, W. F. Albright, 'The List of Levitical Cities' in *Louis Ginzberg Jubilee Volume*, 1, New York 1945, pp. 49–73; *Archaeology* . . ., pp. 121ff.

[3] B. Mazar, 'The Cities of the Priests and Levites', SVT VII, 1960, pp. 193–205.

This does not exclude the possibility, of course, that in the course of the reorganization projected under Josiah, or in the plans of the Deuteronomic school for a restoration, there may have been an attempt to revive ancient institutions which had long fallen into disuse and to give them a new meaning; in this case Noth's theses would be compatible with this latter hypothesis.[1]

(e) *Joshua 24* is certainly a pre-Deuteronomic narrative, both on account of the doublet of the narrative of the assembly at Shechem (vv. 1–33) and also on account of the traditions concerning the tombs (vv. 34ff.).

4. THE PERSON OF JOSHUA IN THE CONTEXT OF THE CONQUEST

After what we have said it will be obvious that there is also doubt about the person of Joshua, at least in the traditional version of the first part of the book. In the first place, if the unifying element of the diverse traditions, including those which have no connection with the Benjamin–Gilgal complex, is the sanctuary at Gilgal, the person of Joshua cannot also provide this unifying function as the whole book intends and as it is now presented to the reader, in accordance with the conviction of Dtr and perhaps even of the 'compiler' before him. The person and work of Joshua presents numerous problems in biblical history. Joshua is already present in the Pentateuch, from the time of the Exodus on, and sometimes takes on exalted and important tasks (e.g. as one of the spies of Num. 13–14); but he never occupies the first rank, because the last four books of the Pentateuch are dominated by the figure of Moses and there is no place for anyone else on a level with him.[2] At the death of Moses, Joshua becomes his successor. An interesting study by A. Alt discusses his role in the book which bears his name; according to Alt, the figure of Joshua, supreme commander of the Israelite forces, has a useful, if not indispensable function, once one admits the view of the Deuteronomic work that there was a single military conquest of the country.[3] But it becomes embarrassing, not

[1] Mowinckel, op. cit., pp. 71ff., naturally disagrees with this view adopted by Noth in *Josua*[2], p. 127, and would also place these elements in the post-exilic period.

[2] Cf. K. Mohlenbrink, 'Josua im Pentateuch', *ZAW* 59, 1942–43, pp. 140–58.

[3] *Josua*, 1936, *KS* I, pp. 176–192. For the general problems cf. the encyclopaedia articles and the histories of Israel. G. C. Aalders, 'Jozua', *Christelijke Encyclopedie* IV, Kampen 1959, pp. 116–119, is an example of a very conservative treatment of the question; D. Baldi, pp. 8ff., is moderately conservative.

to say absurd, once a critical examination of these traditions, and other traditions which have been less subject to editorial revision (e.g. Judg. 1 or Num. 13–14) has shown that the conquest was a process which extended over several centuries of infiltration and progressive occupation of more or less inhabited regions by individual groups with a limited number of battles, except towards the end of the occupation under David, when Israel began to encroach upon the territories of the city states of Palestine. Moreover, it was only in the promised land that the different groups united round a common sanctuary, that of the ark.[1]

Moreover, as we have already asked, how could the Ephraimite Joshua have led an enterprise most of which, in Josh. 1–12, takes part in Benjamin, and the rest of which happens outside Ephraim (apart from the mention of the tomb of Joshua in 24.29 and his own land in 19.49). There is no question that Joshua was an Ephraimite: the two passages which we have just mentioned are a very ancient tradition concerning the location of his lands and his tomb, and there is no reason to doubt it. Moreover, Num. 13.8, 16 and Deut. 32.44 (where he appears under the name of Hoshea), and also the genealogy, unfortunately in disorder, of I Chron. 7.27, state clearly that his tribe was Ephraim.[2] According to Alt, Joshua is 'at home' only in the episode Josh. 10.1–11.25, where he appears as a charismatic hero of the same type as Deborah in Judg. 5, a kind of 'chief judge'.[3] He carries out this role when he resolves problems of territorial controversy, as in Josh. 17.14ff., and this function is in complete agreement with that which he carries out in Josh. 24 during the assembly at Shechem. Thus it has recently been thought that the figure of Joshua is based upon that of the reforming king Josiah, who proclaimed the law and represented the people in the act of stipulation or renewal of the covenant with Yahweh;[4] cf. also Josh. 1, which is clearly of Deuteronomic origin. This view sees Joshua as the pattern of the king of Judah (cf. the generally neglected passage II Chron. 17.7–9) or of the king

---

[1] On this subject, cf., apart from the histories of Israel, A. Alt, 'The Settlement of the Israelites in Palestine', 1925, in: *Essays on Old Testament History and Religion*, Oxford 1966, pp. 135–69; id., 'Erwägungen über die Landnahme der Israeliten in Palästina', 1939, *KS* I, pp. 126–75; also W. F. Albright's call for caution in 'The Israelite Conquest of Canaan in the Light of Archaeology', *BASOR* 74, 1939, pp. 11–22.

[2] Alt, *Josua*, p. 186.

[3] However, Noth, *Josua*[2], p. 61, disagrees.

[4] G. Widengren, 'King and Covenant', *JSS* 2, 1957, pp. 1–32, esp. pp. 12ff.

of Israel. It is only later that the person of Joshua the Ephraimite was introduced, according to Noth by the 'compiler', into other traditions, in so far as this had not already been done at the sanctuary at Gilgal.[1] The result of this is to raise a chronological problem. Because it is not possible to dissociate Joshua from Ephraim, he is brought into relation with the settlement in Palestine of the last group of Israelite invaders, the Rachel group: Ephraim, Manasseh and Benjamin, which took place no earlier than the first years of the thirteenth century BC.

With regard to the conquest, the following geographical and literary units can easily be distinguished:

(a) In Gen. 34 we possess the traces of an attempt on the part of the tribes of Levi and Simeon to settle in the Shechem region, an attempt which apparently failed; this failure seems to have caused the group in question to disperse. At the present moment the narrative, full of legendary elements, is to be found amongst the traditions of the patriarchs; it refers to a very ancient stage in the conquest.[2]

(b) In Num. 13–14 (cf. Josh. 14–15 and Judg. 1.9ff.) we possess the three stages in the literary evolution of one and the same text, the theme of which is the conquest of the southern plateau by Judah and the groups associated with that tribe. This was an operation which was originally carried out independently of the narrative of the unitary conquest, but which as we have it is presented, outside Judg. 1, as a preliminary exploration (Num. 13–14) or as the taking into possession of a territory assigned to the tribe (Josh. 14–15). This is confirmed by the fact that up to the time of David Judah had only marginal contact with the twelve tribes, having only very infrequent relations with them (certain of which appear only in the later synchronization of the text).[3] The connections with the narrative of Josh. 10.28–43 are not clear; the course of events seems to have been reversed in order to adapt the episode to a conquest which set out from

[1] Josua², pp. 12ff.

[2] M. Noth, Überlieferungsgeschichte der Pentateuch, Stuttgart 1948, pp. 93–95 (= UGP); G. von Rad, Genesis, OTL, London ²1963, pp. 287ff.; A. De Pury, 'Genèse XXXIV et l'histoire', RB 76, 1969, pp. 5–49.

[3] M. Noth, UGP, pp. 143–50; id., Numbers, OTL, London 1968: id., The History of Israel, London ²1960, pp. 55ff. For the links between Judah and the 'twelve tribes' before the monarchy, see R. Smend, 'Gehörte Juda zum vorstaatlichen Israel?', in the papers of the Fourth World Congress of Jewish Studies, vol. I, Jerusalem 1969, pp. 57–62.

Gilgal. Perhaps this is a mutilated variant of the tradition mentioned above, which simply records anecdotes from it.

(c) Josh. 1.1–10.15 describes, as we have noted, the conquest of the territory of Benjamin.

(d) Josh. 11.1–14 refers to two episodes in the conquest of the north, the battle of Merom and the destruction of Hazor. The 'waters of Merom' lie near the present-day *ṣafed*; the city of Hazor a little to the south of Lake Huleh. This passage seems to be independent of the narrative of the unitary conquest, and Joshua the Ephraimite does not seem to have played any part in its origin.

(e) Josh. 19.47ff. and Judg. 17–18 describe, the first in a schematic and laconic form, and the second in a more extended narrative, the conquest by Dan of its territory in the extreme north, after the abandonment, probably under Philistine pressure, of the territory which it originally possessed west of Benjamin. The *terminus a quo* of this story, therefore, is not earlier than the second half of the twelfth century.

(f) Regions not occupied but remaining in the possession of the Palestine city states by virtue of their military superiority (cf. above §3c).

(g) The unopposed occupation of the territory of Shechem by the Joseph group after the episode discussed above in (a) is one of the most typical examples of peaceful penetration by agreement with the indigenous population. The non-belligerent nature of this occupation is fully confirmed by the fact that excavations show no destruction until the very end of the twelfth century, no doubt in connection with the episode of Abimelech, Judg. 9.[1]

(h) The territories east of the Jordan seem to have been occupied under Moses, although we do not possess any historical or geographical details on this (cf. Num. 32; Deut. 3.12–20; Josh. 1.12–18; 13.8–32).

These elements taken together furnish a fresh proof that the unitary conquest of the country under the sole command of Joshua is a fictional construction, which was perhaps already to be found, even before the Deuteronomic preaching, in the pre-exilic cult. The very complicated history of the conquest is reduced to a handful of typical elements largely drawn from Benjaminite tradition and placed under

---

[1] L. E. Toombs and G. E. Wright, 'The Fourth Campaign at Balata (Shechem)', *BASOR* 169, 1963, esp. pp. 25f. On this text see our article, 'Il regno di 'Abimelek in Sichem (Giudici, 9) e le istituzioni della città-stato siro-palestinese nei secoli XV–XI avanti Cristo', *Studi in onore di Edoardo Volterra*, to be published shortly.

the aegis of Joshua, because he was a well-known person who had
been active either militarily or in resolving controversies between the
regions. In a sense, just as the king was later to be the acknowledged
representative of the people, who were able to speak in their own persons through him as mouthpiece, so Joshua became the man in whom
the people realized themselves, made decisions, prayed, suffered and
acted. It is consequently quite likely that in the cult and in preaching
the role of Joshua was taken by the representative of the community,
either priest, king or prophet.

As we have tried to show elsewhere, whereas the picture of the conquest would be incomplete if one left out Josh. 1–12, so one cannot
adopt the Deuteronomic version of the conquest, which perhaps even
goes back to the 'compiler', without taking into account passages providing a different historical framework to which more consideration
is due.[1] Thus one episode must always be distinguished from another,
and one region from another. In this way, the country can be divided
into three zones, each presenting its own historical and literary problems: the southern zone, the central zone, which can be sub-divided
into a south-central and north-central zone, and the northern zone.
The story we possess of the conquest corresponds in a greater or lesser
degree in each case to the factual reality, as we shall see in detail,
though of course within the limits of the book of Joshua.

5. THE TEXT AND ITS TRANSLATIONS

The Hebrew text of Joshua is generally good, although it has preserved, as Baldi has observed,[2] a number of traditional errors: thus in
7.17 it has *lagge^{b}bārīm* for *labbattīm*, and in 15–28 *ūbizyōt^{e}yā* for *ūb^{e}nōtēm*.
After 21.42 the Massoretic text lacks a passage of one or two verses
which are usually restored on the basis of LXX. Some authors believe that there are frequent later additions in the text, which we shall
examine in detail below.

The ancient translations of the Vulgate (V) and the Syriac (or
Peshitto) do not present any special problems, and any variants they
contain will be examined in their place. LXX displays its usual complexity, which is due to the existence of several different recensions;[3]

[1] 'La conquista israelitica della Palestina nei secoli XIII e XII e le scoperte archeologiche', *Protestantismo* 17, 1962, pp. 193–208.

[2] *Giosuè*, pp. 3ff.

[3] For a comparison between MT and the various recensions of LXX, cf. S. Holmes, *Joshua: the Hebrew and Greek Texts*, Cambridge 1914; Baldi, pp. 3f.

here the work of Margolis, unfortunately interrupted at 19.38, is worthy of note. The most authoritative recension is that known as the 'Egyptian', or Hesychian, from which derive Codex B (Vaticanus, LXX^B) and Pap. Oxyr. 1168 (fourth century; 4.23–5.1 only); its readings are often shorter than those of MT and better for the spelling of proper names. Other recensions are: the 'Constantinopolitan' from which is derived Codex A (Alexandrinus, LXX^A), the 'Syrian' or Lucianic, from which derives the Vetus Latina, and which is distinguished by a number of important variants (LXX^Luc), and finally the 'Palestinian', from which are derived the Hexapla and the Tetrapla of Origen, as well as the Syriac translation. Sometimes the Constantinopolitan recension agrees so closely with MT that one suspects that it has been edited to follow it more closely. The text of LXX^B can be found in Hebrew in two manuscripts from Qumran which have not yet been either published or studied in detail.[1]

6. THE BOOK OF JOSHUA IN THE CONTEXT OF THE BIBLICAL MESSAGE

After what has been said above about this history writing of the Deuteronomic school, it is now possible to distinguish the particular message of the book of Joshua. The Deuteronomic school presented itself to the people at a moment of terrible crisis, at one and the same time to make known to them that the judgment pronounced by the prophets had been carried out, to call them to repentance and to lay once again the foundations of the people of God, drawing for this purpose on the ancient traditions. In this context, the role of the book of Joshua is to show how the ancient promises were carried out. From the time of the patriarchs until the Exodus from Egypt, and then in particular in the book of Deuteronomy, the promise of a land is one of the most characteristic elements in the relationship between the leading figures in the tradition and their God. There is no doubt about the antiquity and authenticity of this element; to possess land is one of the most basic desires determining the actions of semi-nomads occupied in stock-rearing and sometimes, when circumstances permit, in agriculture. We know that this was true of the Israelites, or more exactly of the ancestors of the groups who ultimately came to form Israel, be-

---

[1] Hitherto this fact has been mentioned only by P. Benoit, etc., 'Editing the Manuscript Fragments from Qumrân', *BA* 19, 1956, pp. 75–96, esp. p. 84 (= *RB* 59, 1956, pp. 49ff.), and by Jenni, 'Zwei Jahrzehnte', p. 23.

fore they occupied their lands in Palestine. The presentation of the facts by Dtr, in spite of their simplification, therefore, remains in outline historically reliable from this point of view.[1] It is based on numerous earlier traditions about the conquest. All of them are local or tribal; many of them had already been gathered together by the 'compiler'; several of them, epic and savage, glorified in battles prolonged to the last drop of blood that could be shed and even to the extermination of whole populations (ignoring for the moment the veracity of these events, or at least taking them as they stand in the form of seminomadic epic). Others, profoundly religious in nature, were the testimony of men overcome by the terrible experience of a personal encounter with the deity. Others again, gathered together in methodical collections, were the relics of ancient lists of tribes, frontiers and territories, and describe the division of the land which Israel had received as a gift when the promise had been fulfilled. With regard to the narrative elements, the choice fell largely on the traditions of Benjamin. Historically they were not very reliable, but they had the advantage of already forming an organic whole, and perhaps of being an integral part of the liturgy of the sanctuary at Gilgal, and the further advantage of possessing their own theological content. They brought to the audience of Dtr the message which he wished to hand down: intransigence towards the indigenous population and the elimination of all syncretism even to the point of extermination. Now we know today, and Dtr probably also knew, that the conquest before the time of Saul was largely the peaceful fusion of two populations. The military element scarcely began before the arrival of the Philistines, from the middle of the twelfth century, while in addition the resistance of the local population to the invaders was in more than one case rewarded by flattering success, as is clearly shown by the list of territories which were not conquered.[2]

Naturally, the redactor is presenting a thesis rather than established facts, because the same Deuteronomic history records the difficulties which the prophets and the reforming kings encountered in carrying out their functions, an evident sign that the indigenous

[1] For the problem of 'sacred history' (=Heilsgeschichte) and 'profane history', and for our view of this matter, cf. 'Alttestamentliche Glaubenszeugnisse und geschichtliche Wirklichkeit', *ThZ* 17, 1961, pp. 385–98, and also 'Geschichte, Historie und Heilgeschichte im Alten Testament', *TLZ* 89, 1964, cols. 721–36.

[2] This has been made clear by V. Maag, 'Malkut Jhwh', SVT VII, 1960, pp. 129–53, esp. pp. 134ff.

populations, far from having been exterminated, were still alive, powerful and even capable of absorbing the invaders! Dtr could not or would not do anything to prevent the presentation by other traditions remaining on the margin of his own work, or altogether outside it, of a picture quite different from his own.

It was in this way that a people which was in exile, or which had only just set out for home, was given a message of hope. According to the preaching of the Deuteronomic school, the ancient traditions were true; the promise of the land was a promise which remained in force, although at the present time it had been veiled by the judgment. It is in this paradoxical and apparently unreasonable proclamation that we can look for the roots of the epic of Judah's reconstruction in a fragment of its original territory, the progressive elimination of syncretism in Israel, or the absorption of its less scandalous elements, and the ultimate setting up of the theocratic state. The latter was able to operate thanks to the absence of political independence and of all nostalgia for the monarchy. Only the person of David, and to some extent that of Solomon, were henceforth raised to the dignity of semi-legendary figures in pre-history, while the monarchy itself was presented as an unnecessary element (in Joshua and Judges everything functioned without it), an element, moreover, which was responsible for the decadence of Israel.

Such a historical and theological situation was obviously unfamiliar to the church of the early centuries, and even to the primitive church, which is the reason for sometimes exaggerated typological interpretations such as that of St Jerome. On the other hand, the theme of the divine promise fulfilled in the conquest could easily be applied as a figure of the promise received by the church and fulfilled in the person of him whose name was identical with that of the ancient tribal chief. As a result, the New Testament exhorts the 'Hebrews' of Hebrews 11.30–31 to turn, with the same faith as had inspired Rahab and Joshua, to Jesus Christ, described in 12.2 as the 'pioneer of our faith'. Moreover, when the New Testament draws comparisons from agriculture, it does so not only in order to use examples taken from the daily life of its audience, but also to maintain a continual relationship with the land, the object of the ancient promise, which was 'conquered' under Joshua. This land was always considered by Deuteronomic theology not so much as a right of Israel but as a free gift made by Israel's God, which could be withdrawn and entrusted to others (cf. Deut. 12.9). The first example of this, of course, was the

tragic episode, which resounds throughout the whole of the Deuteronomic literature, of the double exile of the years 597 and 587, preceded
by that of the northern kingdom in 722–21, though the exile was
followed, it is true, by a restoration. The primitive church in its turn
witnessed the events of AD 67–70, which were not followed by a restoration, as a result of which it identified itself henceforth with Israel,
an Israel which was no longer 'according to the flesh'. But the church
knew that it, too, could not claim any right, that the gift received
could be entrusted to others, and that it shared with ancient Israel
sin and unfaithfulness, unworthiness of grace, and inability to be
God's faithful steward. This could have led to a magnificent dialogue
between the church and Israel if the initial breach had not been
sealed and perpetuated by the persecution begun by the church after
the fourth century.

All this springs immediately to the mind the moment one looks
from a Christian point of view at the book of Joshua and its dominant
theme: the 'conquest' as the fulfilment of ancient promises. This point
of view goes beyond the level of pure exegesis, but it has its place in a
commentary such as ours, for we are certain that it is only in this
word, into which is incorporated the witness of Joshua, foreshadowing
him who is the Word himself, that the church and the synagogue can
find the one way to salvation.

PART ONE

THE NARRATIVE OF THE CONQUEST

The Introduction

1 ¹After the death of Moses the servant of the LORD, the LORD said to Joshua the son of Nun, Moses' minister, ²'Moses my servant is dead; now therefore arise, go over this Jordan, you and all this people, into the land which I propose to give to them, to the people of Israel. ³Every place that the sole of your foot will tread upon I have given to you, as I promised to Moses. ⁴From the wilderness and from the Lebanon, and from the great river, the river Euphrates [all the land of the Hittites] to the Great Sea toward the going down of the sun shall be your territory. ⁵No man shall be able to stand before you all the days of your life; as I was with Moses, so I will be with you; I will not fail you or forsake you. ⁶Be strong and of good courage; for you shall cause this people to inherit the land which I swore to their fathers to give them. ⁷Only be strong and very courageous, being careful to do according to all [the law] that Moses my servant commanded you; that you may have good success wherever you go. ⁸This book of the law shall not depart out of your mouth, but you shall meditate on it day and night, that you may be careful to do according to all that is written in it; for then you shall make your way prosperous, and then you shall have good success. ⁹Have I not commanded you? Be strong and of good courage; be not frightened, neither be dismayed; for the LORD your God is with you wherever you go.'

10 Then Joshua commanded the 'scribes' of the people, ¹¹'Pass through the camp, and command the people, "Prepare your provisions; for within three days you are to pass over this Jordan, to go in to take possession of the land which the LORD your God gives you to possess." '

12 And to the Reubenites, the Gadites, and the half-tribe of Manasseh Joshua said, ¹³'Remember what Moses the servant of the LORD commanded you, saying, "The LORD your God has set tled you, giving you this land." ¹⁴Your wives, your little ones, and your cattle shall remain in the land which Moses gave you beyond the Jordan; but all the men among you who can bear arms shall pass over armed before your brethren and shall help them, ¹⁵until the LORD settles your brethren as well as you, and they also take possession of the land which the LORD your God is giving them; then you shall return to the land of your possession [and shall possess it], the land which Moses the servant of the LORD gave you beyond

the Jordan toward the sunrise.' [16]And they answered Joshua, 'All that you have commanded us we will do, and wherever you send us we will go. [17]Just as we obeyed Moses in all things, so we will obey you; only may the LORD your God be with you, as he was with Moses! [18]Whoever rebels against your commandment and disobeys your words, whatever you command him, shall be put to death. Only be strong and of good courage.'

Bibliography: W. Rudolph, *Der 'Elohist'* . . ., pp. 164ff.; M. Noth, *UGS*, pp. 40ff.; Auzou, pp. 59ff.

[1.1] *'ebed yhwh* is lacking in LXX[BA] and the recensions which derive from it, but is present in V, T and Syr. An interesting variation is found in the Arabic version, which read *n^{e}bī' yhwh*. For the name *nūn*, cf. the introduction, p. 1 n. 1. [2] *hazzeh*: lacking in almost all recensions of LXX, but is found in V and T. Syr has it, but lacks *lāhem*. The Arabic translation paraphrases: 'To the land which I promised to Abraham, Isaac and Jacob'. *lib^{e}nē yiśrā'ēl* seems to be superfluous to the construction of the sentence and is probably a gloss defining *lāhem* more accurately. [4] The list as we have it is in disorder: 'From the wilderness and this Lebanon as far as the great river, the river Euphrates' would in fact include the whole desert region east of Jordan, between Jericho and the river in question! LXX read the names as the object of 'I shall give' in the previous verse: '(I shall give you . . .) the desert and the Antilebanon . . . as far as . . .' (note that LXX always says 'the Antilebanon'), and omits *hazzeh*, which cannot refer to the Lebanon (which cannot be seen from east of the Jordan opposite Jericho), but at best to the 'wilderness'. The Arabic version attempts a solution by attaching 'from the wilderness' to the previous verse; but this solves nothing, particularly as V, T and Syr confirm the 'from the wilderness' of MT. Similarly, 'all the land of the Hittites' is lacking in LXX, but is found in the other versions; the expression reflects the Assyrian terminology of the first half of the first millennium BC for what is now Syria, and seems exaggerated; it is probably (cf. its absence from LXX) a defining gloss, introduced because of the lack of clarity in what precedes. The passage is probably a corrupt reading of the parallel text in Deut. 11.24–25: 'from the wilderness and the Lebanon and from the river, the river Euphrates . . . to the western sea . . .', on the basis of which we can no doubt restore: . . . *mēham-midbār w^{e}hall^{e}bānōn* . . . *min hannāhār haggādōl n^{e}har p^{e}rat* . . .: 'From the wilderness and from the Lebanon, and from the great river, the river Euphrates' (cf. Deut. 1.7, which has 'the Lebanon as far as the great river, the river Euphrates'). It is impossible to tell how this textual corruption came about. [5] *l^{e}pānēkā*: LXX, V and Syr read the second person plural.

[6] la'abōtām: LXX has the plural. [7] me'ōd is lacking in LXX. la'asōt: LXX puts the conjunction before the verb, making two separate actions, 'being careful and doing . . .' kekol etc.: LXX has only ka'aser and suppresses the mention of the tōrāh, which, however, is found in the other versions. Cf. also mimmenū with the masculine suffix, a possible but rare construction. [8] wehāgītā, root hgh, 'coo', of birds, 'mutter'; it is also a technical term for meditation in a low voice, cf. Ps. 1.2. bekol: the ancient translations did not read the b (except for T) and render: 'to do all that . . .' derākekā: LXX has the plural. [9] yhwh 'elōhēkā: T precedes it by mēmrā = 'the word of Yahweh our God', an interesting example of the interpretative translation of late Judaism, which sought to emphasize the mediating word. tēhat, qal perfect or infinitive of tht. [10] šōterē: šōtēr is the scribe; not, of course, in the NT sense, but an official, usually a civilian official, sometimes military, who seems to have been specially in charge of keeping lists and catalogues, but whose other functions are obscure. In Exod. 5, the term is used for an Egyptian official. In Israel, the term is mainly used in D, Dtr, P and Chron., and presupposes an organized state. LXX reads γραμματεύς, and V princeps. T, more accurately, has sārekā = high official. [11] hammahaneh: LXX adds τοῦ λάου, but this seems to be a repetition of the object of the verb that follows. 'elōhēkem: LXX has ὁ κύριος ὁ θεὸς τῶν πατέρων ὑμῶν, that is, yhwh 'elōhē 'abōtēkem; it is the only such variant, but as in the case of the Arabic translation of v.2, the mention of the 'God of the fathers' in the context of promise and fulfilment seems very apt. [12] The singular adjective referring to a people is common. [13] zākōr: note the archaic use of the infinitive absolute with the value of a finite mood, here the imperative, cf. Exod. 20.8, etc. (cf. GKC § 113 and B-M § 103.5). mēniah: the verb nwh literally means 'give rest'. [14] mōšeh be'ēber hayyardēn: the words are missing in LXX. [15] wīrištem 'ōtāh: missing in LXX; probably a dittography with the preceding word, even though it is found in the other versions. The expression makes no sense, since v.14 assumes that the territory east of the Jordan has already been taken into possession. This is why it is not possible to keep it by placing it at the end, as Hertzberg does. [17] 'elōhēkā: LXX has ἡμῶν = 'elōhēnū. [18] lekōl: LXX has καθότι, i.e. kekōl.

Chapter 1, an introduction displaying typically Deuteronomic features, can be sub-divided as follows: (a) vv. 1–9, Yahweh's address to Joshua; (b) vv. 10–18, Joshua's orders to the people. The text does not present any particular difficulty, except in v.4, where a traditional list is quoted.

(a) God's address to Joshua (1.1–9)

[1.1] The book of Joshua sets out not to be a new beginning, but a continuation, as can be seen from the expression *wayᵉhī*, which need not be translated. In fact the book takes up Deut. 34, which tells of the death of Moses, who was not allowed to take part in the conquest of Canaan because of the events recorded in Num. 20.12; 27.14; Deut. 3.26; 31.1–8. The hero of our book is presented as the successor of Moses with the command to complete his work; not only Deut. but also P agree with our text in seeing Joshua as the person responsible for this task: Num. 27.15ff.; Deut. 3.23ff.; 31.1ff. From one point of view, then, the death of Moses forms a break in the course of sacred history; from another point of view, it is only one episode amongst others. God has already thought of everything, the sacred history continues, and, now that the great leader of the people is dead, God appoints a successor (Calvin) to him who, in Hertzberg's words, inherits the task from him, receiving it as it were at second hand. Note the difference between the title of Moses and that of Joshua: the former is the 'servant of Yahweh' (Deut. 34.5; Josh. 1.1 (omitted in the LXX), 2,7,13,15; etc.) throughout the whole book (and only at his death is this title accorded to Joshua himself, Josh. 24.29). Joshua is called *mᵉšārēt mōšeh*, a title very similar to that of *ᶜebed*, but distinguished from it by its strictly 'secular' sense, whereas *ᶜebed* possesses not only a secular meaning but also a specifically theological meaning, illustrated in Deutero-Isaiah. Joshua's title is equally well known (cf. Exod. 24.13; 33.11; Num. 11.28 [P]), but instead of relating him to God, like Moses' title, it relates him to a man. Thus in the Deuteronomic sacred history something similar happens to what can be observed in the handing on of the message of the apostles: Moses, like the apostles, is a first-hand witness; his successor, like the disciples of the apostles, from henceforth belongs to a different economy and receives the message from a human predecessor. This is, in fact, one of the numerous aspects of the New Testament christology of the *ᶜebed yhwh.*

[2–3] The scene takes place in the region east of Jordan, also called *ᶜarᵉbōt mō'āb*, 'the plains of Moab' (Num. 22.1; 33.48). This, then, is the first in a series of local aetiologies which are characteristic of the first part of the book, that is, of the conquest of the greater part of the south-central zone corresponding to the territory of the tribe of Benjamin. The tradition of entry into Palestine from the east, across the Jordan, is in fact typical of the Rachel groups (Joseph, i.e. Ephraim and Manasseh, and Benjamin); from them it came to be adopted by the whole of Israel, in circumstances which we have tried to describe (cf. §3a in the introduction). According to this description, the scene is close to the Jordan ('this Jordan') opposite Jericho, in the region defined at the present day by two bridges, that in the north carrying the road for heavy lorries and that in the south carrying the motor road from Jerusalem to Amman. Not only is it a peculiarity of the Jordan that almost its entire course flows below sea level (350m below sea level near Jericho), but in addition, far from forming a means of communication like so many rivers in antiquity, it is a divisive factor, in spite of being so narrow. It has cut a deep channel between banks which easily crumble away, and is useless to agriculture because it is too low-lying to be useful for irrigation; thus it forms the very type of a 'natural frontier' between two countries. Although the region is potentially very fertile, its climate is no encouragement to people to settle there. Consequently, its crossing was legitimately compared in the cult to the crossing of the Red Sea (cf. ch. 3 below), with the difference that here the enemy is in front and not behind. As in Exod. 14–15 the people of God are faced with a superhuman task (Hertzberg). This problem is indicated directly by the two verbs employed: the first, *nōtēn*, a participle, indicates intention: I propose to give; the second, *netattīw*, in the perfect, means 'I have given to you'. The first bears witness to the divine plan, while the second expresses a divine decree in which all things have already been accomplished. The people see themselves faced with a future which, although it is not yet realized, is already irrevocably decided. The theological contrast in these few lines appears throughout the Deuteronomic history. According to the view expressed in this history, it is enough in the present case for the people to touch the lands in question with the sole of their foot for the divine plan to take immediate effect. In its paradoxical character, the phrase recalls certain affirmations in the New Testament about faith, e.g. Matt. 17.20 ‖ Luke 17.6. All this takes on a startling significance when one considers it against the background of the actual situation of the people at the period when the Deuteronomic message was being proclaimed: they were exiled and dispersed and their country, partly abandoned and partly occupied by others, was under foreign domination.

[4] The bounds of the land of Israel are defined here by three fixed landmarks: the desert ('from the wilderness') of the south and southeast, that is, the Negev of ancient and modern times and the land east of the Jordan; the Euphrates in the north-east and the Mediterranean

in the west ('the Great Sea towards the going down of the sun').
The Lebanon, rather than being a fixed landmark, is a point of
great importance, included in the territory of Israel. Two things must
be noted: (1) This territory, of surprising extent, includes virtually
the whole of present and ancient Syria; by comparison, the country
divided in Josh. 13–21 (with the exception of the Deuteronomic passage 13.1–6), cf. Judg. 20.1, is much smaller, since it is limited to
Palestine proper. (2) We know of only a single period when the
frontiers were actually as extensive as this: the period of David and
Solomon, from about 1000 to 926 BC (cf. II Sam. 8.3–10 || I Chron.
18.3–10; I Kings 4.24f. || I Chron. 9.26f.). These facts entail the
following conclusion: the natural frontiers in question do not occur
exclusively in Deuteronomy and Dtr, but are also to be found in the
geography of JEP, deriving probably from the reign of David (cf.
Gen. 15.18; Exod. 23.31; Num. 13.21; 34.2–12). They are taken up
in this form by Deuteronomy and Dtr (Deut. 1.7; 11.24–25; Josh.
13.1–6; Judg. 3.3) and also by the other writer of the restoration:
Ezek. 47.15–20.[1] As far as the north-eastern frontier is concerned,
there are two variants: according to the first, this frontier ran along
the Euphrates in the north; according to the second, it lay in Syria at
the 'entrance of Hamath' (cf. 13.5), the narrow channel through
which the Orontes runs towards the north. Thus it does not seem
right to follow Noth (p. 28) in affirming that this description assumes
'a probably somewhat vague conception of the great empire of David',
or to follow Kaufmann (ad loc.), who believes that it is a description
of the 'ideal frontiers' of Israel. On the contrary this description,
reliably attested in various strata of the tradition (in this case that of
the frontier on the Euphrates), corresponds to historical facts which
can be checked. It is not necessary to go into the problem of the
mutual relationship between the two traditions. The expression 'all
the land of the Hittites', which is lacking in LXX, may have been a
later gloss, but it is not essential to assume this. In fact, the expression
is quite plausible in the first half of the first millennium BC, and is
found in the contemporary terminology of the Assyrian annals,[2] and

___

[1] Y. Kaufmann, *The Biblical Account* . . ., pp. 48ff.; *Comm.*, p. 90; cf. A. Alt,
'Das Grossreich Davids', 1950, *KS* II, 1953, pp. 66–72; H. J. Kraus, *Psalmen* I, BK
XV, 1, Neukirchen ²1961, pp. 14f.

[2] Cf. the annals of the ninth to the seventh centuries in *ANET*, pp. 275ff., which
also show that at this period the Euphrates was in fact the frontier between Assyria
and the West.

during the final period of the neo-Babylonian kingdom,[1] whereas half a millennium later it may have seemed unsuitable to the LXX translators and for that reason was suppressed in the text. In the programme of restoration under Josiah, who as we know tried to reconquer the north at the fall of the Assyrian Empire and to re-establish the great Davidic kingdom, as well as in the reconstruction programme of Dtr, Ezekiel and others both during and after the exile, these frontiers of the empire of David and Solomon seem to have formed the ultimate aim; in this sense, one can talk in Kaufmann's words of 'ideal frontiers'. Once again, then, as in the previous verses, we have this paradoxical affirmation which nothing, neither the failure of the work of Josiah nor the total collapse of the nation, was able to shake. For the Deuteronomic theologian of history, the divine promise cannot be retracted.

[5–6] The promise is followed by a further statement; it is not just a question of calling for faith; certain guarantees must be given as well. The continuity of history is stressed once again: God was with Moses. He will be with Joshua and with those whom he leads. Assuming the validity of the promise down the centuries, this historical continuity extends not only to the people in the time of Joshua, but also to those who at the time of Dtr were mourning the destruction and enslavement of the nation. Here (as throughout the Bible) cowardice and weakness would amount to a lack of faith, above all on the part of the leader designated by God, to whom much was given, and of whom, therefore, much would be asked. Hence the exhortation: 'Be strong and of good courage' rings out more than once in this chapter (vv. 6, 7, 9, 18). The basis of this command, and that which follows, [7] is that Yahweh has called on the people to take possession of the territories which have been accorded to them, and has promised to remain at the side of Joshua, as he had been at the side of Moses; this statement can now be followed by the command 'be not frightened' and 'be careful' to obey (the two verbs 'be strong and of good courage' already appear in Deut. 31.6–8, 23). In its original form the text probably spoke only of 'doing according to all that Moses my servant commanded you', but the later gloss naturally understood by this statement the *tōrāh*, that is, the teaching, the ordinance, the law. The theme of success, seen as a consequence of carrying out the law, is one

---

[1] Cf. K. Galling, *Studien zur Geschichte Israels im persischen Zeitalter*, Tübingen 1964, p. 15.

of the most typical in Deuteronomy (cf. Deut. 5.32ff.; 29.8; cf. 17.11, 20). This is not, however, as it has been suggested, a cheap legalism, but the requirement which Deuteronomy has, in common with all the prophets, of making life correspond with the confession of faith in a coherent fashion; otherwise this confession becomes hypocritical and brings a greater condemnation than any other fault. These themes recur in Matt. 7.24ff. ‖ Luke 6.47ff.

[8] This later adaptation, transforming Moses' command into the *tōrāh*, is continued. Whereas in the previous verse the *tōrāh* was explicitly mentioned, here the idea of a book on which one has to meditate is firmly embedded, and is still accompanied by the idea of success in life. The spiritual atmosphere to which this statement corresponds is well described in Ps. 1, where the same verb is employed. It is clear that in this passage we are rapidly tracing the course taken by post-exilic Judaism, leading from the word of God to the identification of this word with the book, and then with the very letter of the book. But we must take care not to think at once, as is too often done, of a substitution of the book for the living word of God. Certainly this danger is always present in passages such as this; but we are faced here with something which rather resembles the *sola scriptura* of the Reformation, in the sense of a concrete basis, really and wholly incarnate, but inspired by faith, and opposed to all romantic and mystical enthusiasm and to all human traditionalism. Thus it is above all the sacred history which is being preached to the people, with the purpose of calling them to faith and trust in their God, who has chosen them from the first; and they are then called to obey the written witness of this sacred history, which is both human and inspired. This theme is continued in [9]: in obedience to the gospel promise, the believer can set out in confidence.

(b) Joshua's orders to the people (1.10–18)

These verses form an almost symmetrical parallel to those which precede them: just as Joshua has received the command from Yahweh he now hands it on to the officers of the people. The organization of Israel set out here is essentially that which existed in the organized monarchical state of the first half of the first millennium BC. [10–11] It is interesting to note that the 'conquest' is described as something very peaceful, like a cultic procession, for which it is necessary to carry provisions, but where one has nothing else to worry about, as the liturgy has laid down everything. The possession of Canaan had already been decreed by God and the people had only to act accordingly. **[12–15]** With regard to the tribes who had already obtained territory east of the Jordan (for this information cf. Num. 32; Deut. 3.18–20), it is confirmed that they will have to take part in the common enterprise (v. 13 takes up Num. 32.28; Deut. 3.10ff.), but it is the latter passage only which is followed by the text here. This common enterprise must already have been represented as a present reality in the Israelite cult (cf. chs. 3ff.), and was then re-historicized by Dtr. For the return of these groups, cf. ch. 22.

[14] Whereas in vv. 10ff. the conquest was presented as a peaceful process to be carried out as it were on a liturgical pattern, it now clearly appears as a military enterprise, and the whole people, both those of the land east of Jordan and the future inhabitants of Palestine west of the Jordan, have to appear in the line of battle. It is also possible, in the opinion of Hertzberg, that there are in Dtr two strata, an older one which still mentioned the military expedition, and the other, already set in a fixed cultic form, where everything is carried out in a peaceful fashion. For the first stratum, cf. Deut. 3.18–20.

[15] This verse contains another technical Deuteronomic term, 'to give rest', which in the context we can translate as 'settle' (cf. Deut. 12.9; 25.19; Josh. 21.4ff.; I Kings 8.56). Hertzberg has rightly observed that the concept of 'rest', which is equivalent of the idea of returning home after a long day's work, is an allusion to the return to the holy land after the exile. Deutero-Isaiah, the prophet *par excellence* of the return from the exile, also includes amongst his principal themes that of rest, and follows the patterns of the Exodus and the conquest. The theme is also taken up in Pss. 95.11 and 132.8, as well as by Chronicles, assuming its final form in Heb. 3.11 and 4.1ff. (these passages refer negatively to Num. 14.21–23 [P], where, however, the terminology is different: 'the land which I swore to give to their fathers'). To dwell in the Promised Land is the tangible sign of the divine act of salvation through which a great part of this school's very reduced eschatology is realized.[1] Von Rad has shown that this concept of rest was the link between the work of God in the creation (according to Gen. 2.1ff.) and the fulfilment of the ancient promises, and that on this double basis Heb. 3–4 constructs its own theory of the ultimate 'rest'.[2] With regard to the related problems of the tribes

[1] Cf. G. von Rad, *Das Gottesvolk im Deuteronomium*, Stuttgart 1929, pp. 6off., 71ff.; M. Noth, *UGS*, pp. 102ff., 107ff.

[2] G. von Rad, 'There Remains Still a Rest for the People of God: an Investiga-

and the connections between the tribes on the west and the east of the Jordan, we are obliged because of their complexity to refer readers to the commentary on the passages quoted in Numbers and Deuteronomy.

Finally [16–18], we have an interesting account of the Deuteronomic conception of human authority: the necessary condition for obedience to be accorded to it is that Yahweh should be with the person who exercises authority. David is described in this way (I Sam. 16.18; cf. 17.37; 18.28); and the result is that everyone follows him, even against their own interest (e.g. Jonathan), and abandons Saul.[1] Deuteronomy is much concerned with this problem of authority, both royal and prophetic (cf. Deut. 17.14ff.; 18.9ff.). The reason is no doubt the discredit into which the monarchy had fallen after the death of Josiah and the number of false prophets who opposed the true prophets. This is the reason for the people's insistence, found here, too, upon the 'letters of credit' required of those who were to guide them.

CHAPTER 2

The Spies at Jericho

2 [1]And Joshua the son of Nun sent two men secretly from Shittim as spies, saying, 'Go, view the land, especially Jericho.' And they went, and came to Jericho, and came into the house of a harlot whose name was Rahab, and lodged there. [2]And it was told the king of Jericho, 'Behold, certain men of Israel have come here tonight to search out the land.' [3]Then the king of Jericho sent to Rahab, saying, 'Bring forth the men that have come to you, who entered your house; for they have come to search out all the land.' [4]But the woman had taken the two men and hidden them; and she said, 'True, men came to me, but I did not know where they came from; [5]and when the gate [of the city] was to be closed, at dark,

---

tion of a Biblical Conception', *The Problem of the Hexateuch and Other Essays*, Edinburgh 1966, pp. 94–102.

[1] Cf. J. Pedersen, *Israel, Its Life and Culture*, I–II, Copenhagen 1926, pp. 182ff.

the men went out; where the men went I do not know; pursue them quickly, for you will overtake them.' ⁶But she had brought them up to the roof, and hid them with the stalks of flax which she had laid in order on the roof. ⁷So the men [of the king] pursued after them on the way to the Jordan as far as the fords; and as soon as the pursuers had gone out, the gate was shut. ⁸Before they lay down, she came up to them on the roof, ⁹and said to the men, 'I know that the LORD has given you the land, and that the fear of you has fallen upon us, and that all the inhabitants of the land melt away before you. ¹⁰For we have heard how the LORD dried up the water of the Red Sea before you when you came out of Egypt, and what you did to the two kings of the Amorites that were beyond the Jordan, to Sihon and Og, whom you utterly destroyed. ¹¹And as soon as we heard it, our hearts melted, and there was no courage left in any man, because of you; for the LORD your God is he who is God in heaven above and on earth beneath. ¹²Now then, swear to me by the LORD that as I have dealt kindly with you, you also will deal with my father's house with kindness and [give me a sign of] truth, ¹³and save alive my father and mother, my brothers and sisters, and all who belong to them, and deliver our lives from death.' ¹⁴And the men said to her, 'Our life for yours! If you do not tell this business of ours, then we will deal kindly and faithfully with you when the LORD gives us the land.'

15 Then she let them down by a rope through the window, for her house was built into the city wall, so that she dwelt on the wall. ¹⁶And she said to them, 'Go into the hills, lest the pursuers meet you; and hide yourselves there three days, until the pursuers have returned; then afterward you may go your way.' ¹⁷The men said to her, 'We will be guiltless with respect to this oath of yours which you have made us swear. ¹⁸Behold, when we come into the land, you shall bind this scarlet cord in the window through which you let us down; and you shall gather into your house your father and mother, your brothers, and all your father's household. ¹⁹If any one goes out of the doors of your house into the street, his blood shall be upon his head, and we shall be guiltless; but if a hand is laid upon any one who is with you in the house, his blood shall be on our head. ²⁰But if you tell this business of ours, then we shall be guiltless with respect to your oath which you have made us swear.' ²¹And she said, 'According to your words, so be it.' Then she sent them away, and they departed; and she bound the scarlet cord in the window. ²²They departed, and went into the hills, and remained there three days, until the pursuers returned; for the pursuers had made search all along the way and found nothing. ²³Then the two men came down again from the hills, and passed over and came to Joshua the son of Nun; and they told him all that had befallen them. ²⁴And they said to Joshua, 'Truly the LORD has given all the land into our hands; and moreover all the inhabitants of the land are fainthearted because of us.'

Bibliography: A. Windisch, 'Zur Rahabgeschichte, zwei Parallelen aus
der klassischen Literatur', *ZAW* 37, 1917–18, pp. 238–68; G. Hölscher,
'Zum Ursprung der Rahabsage', *ZAW* 38, 1919–20, pp. 54–7; K. Möhlenbrink, 'Die Landnahmesagen des Buches Josua', pp. 250ff.; W. Rudolph,
Der 'Elohist' als Erzähler . . . pp. 165–69; F. M. Abel, 'Les stratagèmes
du Livre de Josué', pp. 321–39; id., 'L'anathème de Jéricho et la maison
de Rahab', *RB* 57, 1950, pp. 321–30, esp. pp. 327ff.; M. Astour, 'Benê-
Iamina et Jéricho', *Semitica* 9, 1959, pp. 5–20; A. Vincent, 'Jéricho, une
hypothèse', *Mél. de l'Université St-Joseph* 37, 1960–61, pp. 81–90; J. Heller,
'Die Priesterin Rahab', *Communio Viatorum* 8, 1965, pp. 113–7; Auzou,
pp. 64ff.; W. L. Moran, 'The Repose of Rahab's Israelite guests', *Studi
sull'Oriente e la Bibbia* . . . G. Rinaldi, Genoa 1967, pp. 273–84; also
D. J. McCarthy, 'Some Holy War Vocabulary in Joshua 2', *CBQ* 33, 1971,
pp. 228–30; F. Langlamet, 'Josué II et les traditions de l'Exateuque', *RB*
78, 1971, pp. 5–17, 161–83, 321–54 (which appeared too late to be used.)

[2.1] *'ªnāšīm*: LXX has *νεανίσκοι* = *nᵉ'ārīm*, a term which is also used to
mean men of arms, cf. II Sam. 2.14ff. *ḥereš*, which emphasizes the secret, a
secret from his entourage as well, is lacking in LXX and Syr; the latter
has instead: 'who knew the region'; we shall return to this point.
wᵉ'et-yᵉrīḥō: the ancient translations either agree with MT (LXX,T) or
else read 'the region of Jericho' (Syr), or 'the region and the city of Jericho'
(V), the latter version being the most logical. *wayyēlᵉkū*, etc.: LXX has a
longer text: *πορευθέντες εἰσῆλθοσαν οἱ δύο νεανίσκοι εἰς 'Ιερειχώ* (LXXᴬ:
εἰσῆλθον); the expression *wayyābō'ū yᵉrīḥō wayyābō'ū*, which we have restored in the translation, was probably omitted by homoioteleuton; the
other translations confirm MT. *zōnāh* is the technical term for a prostitute
in the OT, but one cannot tell here whether it refers to a 'sacred' prostitute or an ordinary one. Josephus, *Antt.* V, 1, 2 (Thackeray, vol. 5, pp. 4ff.)
and T tried to water down the impropriety by reading 'inn'. *wayyiškᵉbū*:
the root has the same ambiguity as the expression 'sleep with', and the
writer uses it on purpose in order to let us know the opinion of the inhabitants of Jericho. [3] *habbā'īm*: LXX once again has a longer text: *τοὺς
εἰσπορευομένους εἰς τὴν οἰκίαν σου τὴν νύκτα*; so too Syr; which instead
of 'into your house' has 'to you'. MT has both readings, but omits 'this
night'. [4] *šᵉnê* is lacking in LXX and V. *wattišpᵉnō*: for this unusual form
(= *wattišpᵉnēm*) cf. *GKC* § 60 d. The suffix is lacking in V, and some
scholars (*BH³*) would omit it. [5] For the passive sense in the infinitive
construct cf. *B-M* II § 102 1 c. [6] *bᵉpištē hā'ēṣ*: our translation follows the
versions, assuming it is possible to regard the expression as a 'reverse'
construct; but cf. Baldi and Noth, *ad loc.* [7] *'al* can have the meaning 'as

far as', attested in Ugaritic (Aistleitner, no. 2030, 4), and the correction (*BH³*) does not therefore seem necessary; cf. V: *ad vadum*. *'aḥᵃrē*: the form is clumsy, but not impossible, cf. Noth *ad loc*. LXX replaced it by καὶ ἐγένετο = *wayᵉhî*. [12] The last part of the verse, confirmed by the translations, is lacking only in LXX; but it is superfluous, because there is no question of this sign later. It must no doubt be omitted, as Noth does, giving full weight to the association of the two words *ḥesed weᵉmet*, cf. v. 14. [13] *wᵉet -'aḥōtay*: K has the singular and Q the plural, which seems more correct. Instead of this phrase, LXXᴮ has καὶ πάντα τὸν οἶκον μου, a repetition, but one which harmonizes with v. 18. [14] LXX puts the phrase *wᵉhāyāh . . .* into the mouth of the woman; but this would give a repetition which would be meaningless. Similarly the second person masculine plural is not very meaningful, and is usually corrected into the second person fem. sing. Of course this could well refer to the house of Rahab, who in some way or other would have had to be made aware of what was happening. [15] Verses 17–21 would certainly be better placed before v. 15, to avoid the continual repetition of the conversation in the most uncomfortable circumstances (Abel). LXX (cf. *BH³*) has a much shorter text, and the concluding words are lacking in V. [17] This verse presents certain illogicalities in the persons, genders and numbers. [18] *bā'āreṣ*: LXX has εἰς μέρος τῆς πόλεως, more logical in the context. [20] Cf. v. 17. [21] The second part of the verse is lacking in LXXᴮᴬ (*BH³*).

1. The nucleus of our text appears to be very old (it almost certainly belongs to Noth's 'compiler' or to Mowinckel's J, and was taken up by Dtr without great modification). In the past, several authors divided it into sources, because of certain internal tensions which are fairly evident: the spies are hidden twice (vv. 4a, 6), the house is built either on or against the wall (v. 15), the spies are twice in the process of leaving and twice declare themselves absolved from the oath they have given (vv. 15, 21; 17, 20, etc.) Gressmann and Eissfeldt have both tried to separate and then to reconstruct two parallel narratives. But an examination of the text as it stands, or of the two texts resulting from the separation into sources, shows that certain irregularities, if in fact they exist (we shall look at them in a moment), do not affect the fundamental unity of the story. Only the statement of Rahab (vv. 9ff.) presents some difficulties. It appears in fact to be inspired by themes drawn from the ancient confessions of faith of Israel (Deut. 26.5b–9; Josh. 24.2b–13) and sounds very improbable coming from this woman, even allowing for her sudden conversion. It is probable that the Deuteronomic redaction made numerous changes here, in an attempt to give a 'theological' justification for the conduct of

Rahab, which in fact can be explained in a much more probable way.

2. The attentive reader will immediately notice another problem: that of the relationship between ch. 2 and the narrative of chs. 1 and 3–6. In fact, ch. 2 is substantially independent of ch. 1 (we shall look at the problems of chronology further on), because an exploration of this nature is normally a preparation for an act of force carried out by a ruse. We find an echo of this in the variant which LXX gives in v. 18: 'and if we succeed in penetrating into a part of the town . . .', which assumes an attack in force and a house-to-house combat; while the 'confession of faith' of 24.11 records explicitly that the inhabitants of Jericho fought against the invaders. On the other hand, these preparations would have been completely useless if the town was to fall by a miracle, and would only have detracted from the marvellous nature of the event. The gratitude of Israel towards Rahab and her house likewise seems exaggerated if all this woman had done was to hide the two spies and to help them to flee. The fact that she is told to keep silent implies that she has been informed of the intentions of the attackers, and even that they entrusted a part to her in their plan of attack. Not all these elements are equally clear, but they form an impressive list of indications in favour of the view that this chapter originally recounted the capture of the city by a military attack, on the basis of information gathered by the spies, and perhaps also through the help of Rahab. In other words, ch. 2 presents a version of the conquest parallel to but different in substance from the narrative actually given in ch. 6. Of course the question of a conquest by military attack must be distinguished from that of the part played by Rahab in this affair, which is more uncertain and which some authors, such as Baldi and Hertzberg, regard as improbable. In any case, the version of events given in ch. 2 seems older, and more historically probable, than that attested by ch. 6, which is simply a liturgical and cultic transfiguration of the events, retold as history at a later period. No doubt 6.25 preserves part of the primitive epilogue, later separated from its context and amalgamated with the second version. To regard such a reconstruction as 'a false interpretation' (Baldi) requires the objector to propose an acceptable explanation, which Baldi does not do. Moreover, if we look closely, the chronology of this chapter is incompatible with that of chs. 1 and 3ff. On the one hand, we have a chronology of 1–2 days to get to Jericho, 3+1–2 days for the return of the spies, while on the other hand, there are only 3

days of waiting before the crossing of the Jordan (cf. 1.11 and 3.2–5) and the older chronology was even shorter (cf. 3.1ff.)! We would have a supplementary proof of this if we could accept, following Vogt, the existence in ch. 3 of a 'historical' recension.

3. This chapter contains no important aetiological elements, by contrast with other passages in the first part of the book, and contrary to the idea which is currently held. The aetiology reappears only if one restores the missing part of the epilogue which is preserved in 6.25. But this element is not primitive and is important only because of the disappearance of the rest of the epilogue. There is no question elsewhere in the Old Testament of 'descendants of Rahab' living in Jericho and friendly towards Israel, and it would be hazardous to assume their existence, because the city had barely been restored in I Kings 16.34, that is, towards the end of the first half of the ninth century, even though, according to II Sam. 10.6 (beginning of the tenth century), the place seems to have been more or less inhabited. For the presence of other aetiological elements, cf. Noth, ad loc.

4. The profession of Rahab has often been related to 'Canaanite' fertility cults, of which this woman is supposed to have been the priestess and sacred prostitute. This thesis, put forward for the first time, as far as I know, by Gressmann in 1914 and supported by Hölscher, has recently been taken up again by Mowinckel (pp. 13ff.) and by Heller. According to these writers, the sanctuary where she exercised her ministry would have been that of Astarte, or that of the moon (cf. the name of the town). But Noth rightly points out that there is no trace in the whole story of any kind of priesthood exercised by Rahab or her family, while the term $z\bar{o}n\bar{a}h$, in contrast to the term $q^e d\bar{e}\check{s}\bar{a}$, which is semantically similar but is used exclusively to refer to sacred prostitution in the fertility cults, does not make it possible to say whether Rahab's profession was sacred or secular. Even if it could be explained, the point seems completely secondary in this narrative, apart from the *a posteriori* theological conclusions that have been based on it, because the role which this woman plays has nothing to do with her profession.

5. The assurance with which the spies go to Rahab's house is striking. They certainly know who she is, where she lives, what her profession is, and consequently, that in the continual coming and going in her house there is little risk of their being noticed. But one should also note the attitude of this woman: she receives the spies knowing who they are, she hides them and collaborates closely with

them, helps them to escape, and compromises herself hopelessly with regard to her fellow-citizens; these services go far beyond what is ordinarily to be expected of a prostitute! We had tried to resolve some of these problems on the basis of the Mari text no. 16, vol. III (1950),[1] but W. L. Moran has shown that this solution is impossible.[2]

6. M. Astour has tried to identify the Benjaminites of Israel, who were presumably the invaders here (cf. Introduction, §3), with those in Mari who bore the same name. Unfortunately, this attractive thesis labours under a major difficulty: the impossibility in the present state of our knowledge of bridging half a millennium of history which is virtually unknown to us, particularly as the two names (semantically equivalent, even if one should read *mārū-yāmīnā*) refer to the geographical position of these groups in the south rather than to their name as a people in the ordinary sense. Although the similarities exist, the absence of sources makes this thesis a pure guess. The most ancient Benjaminite traditions which we possess[3] show this tribe in the region of Bethel (Judg. 1.22–26) and not (any longer?) at Jericho, which would agree with the theories discussed in the introduction. For other chronological questions, cf. the end of this chapter.

7. Shittim (*šiṭṭīm*) (cf. Num. 25.1; 33.49), means 'acacias' and is nowadays identified with *tell el-khammān*, or else with *tell el-kefrēn* (212–139), both of which are approximately 11–12 km east of the Jordan and 1–2 km apart. The remains of the Jericho of the conclusion of the Bronze Age are to be found on the present *tell es-sulṭān* about 2 km from present-day Jericho (*er-riḥa*, 192–142), on the route for heavy lorries which leads towards the north. The mountain of vv. 16ff. is probably the 'Mountain of the Forty' (*jebel qarantāl*, 191–143), which is full of natural caves and outcrops; but it is not impossible that it refers to the eastern ramparts of the south-central hill country, which are more or less at the same latitude as Jericho and Jerusalem.

[2.1] The name of the woman is a good example of a West Semitic

---

[1] On the basis of the official transcription and translation, used by M. du Buit, 'Quelques contacts bibliques dans les Archives royales de Mari', *RB* 66, 1959, pp. 576–81, esp. pp. 577ff.; cf. M. Noth, *Die Ursprünge des alten Israel im Lichte neuer Quellen*, Köln-Opladen 1961, p. 17; J. A. Soggin, 'Giosué, 2 alla luce di un testo di Mari', *RSO* 39, 1964, pp. 7–14.

[2] On the basis of the new transcription and translation proposed by A. Finet, *L'accadien des lettres de Mari*, Brussels 1956, § 84 k.

[3] Cf. the excellent study by H. J. Zobel, *Stammesspruch und Geschichte*, BZAW 95, Berlin 1965, pp. 107ff.

name, no doubt linked with a divine name or title, e.g. *rāḥāb-'el*.[1]
Whether independently or not of the explanation given above, the
choice of the house is significant. The Old Testament often insists on
the despicable or apparently inappropriate character of the persons
whom God calls to carry out key functions in the realization of his
plans, cf. the choosing of David (I Sam. 16.11ff.) or of Jeremiah
(Jer. 1.6). In this case there is also the unsuitable nature of the
woman's profession; Josephus and the Targum make her out to have
been only an innkeeper. All this assumes a considerable labour of
re-interpretation on the text down the centuries, in the course of
which the theme of the military conquest of the town has been lost.

[2–7] The presence of aggressive nomads a short distance east of
the city had naturally put the inhabitants on the alert and increased
their vigilance. We shall consider the situation of Jericho in the
thirteenth century in ch. 6. The two men were only able to get away
thanks to the assistance of Rahab. The events took the following
course: (*a*) Rahab, realizing the atmosphere prevailing in the town,
hid the two men as soon as they arrived at her house; (*b*) she replied
to those who were looking for them by putting them on a false track;
(*c*) she had her guests sent up on to the roof and hid them under the
stalks of flax. A flat roof is the typical covering of an ordinary house in
Palestine, and the Hebrew word used simply means 'roof' (*gāg*). During the dry season it could be used as a storage place, and as a resting
place on the very hot days which, at Jericho, form the greater part of
the year. Flax is already attested at Ugarit,[2] appears frequently in the
OT, and is also found in the 'agricultural calendar' of Gezer (second
half of the tenth century, cf. *KAI*, no. 182). It was no longer cultivated
in the region by the Arabs, but has recently been reintroduced into
Israel.

[8–14] This first speech is full of elements borrowed from the
ancient confession of faith which an Israelite might put into the
mouth of a stranger whom he was trying to describe as sympathetic to
his compatriots. It is composed of Deuteronomic fragments and comments by the ancient 'compiler' (Noth), the purpose of which is to
explain why this woman accepted the point of view of the invader; as
we have seen, the original explanation had disappeared. The reply of

---

[1] M. Noth, *Die Israelitischen Personennamen im Rahmen der gemeinsemitischen Namengebung*, BWANT III, 10, Stuttgart 1928, repr. 1966, p. 193. Other names with this
root are *reḥabyāh*, *reḥob'ām* and *reḥōb*.

[2] Cf. J. Aistleitner, *Wörterbuch der ugaritischen Sprache*, Berlin 1963, no. 2296: *ptt*.

the two men reads literally: 'Let our life be delivered to death in your place!', a self-cursing formula which guarantees the promise that they give.

[15–21] These verses give the woman's second speech and describe the flight of the spies. If vv. 17–21 are placed before v. 15, the problem of the logical succession of events is avoided (Abel and, in part, Baldi). In this way one avoids a curious dialogue between the two men who have been lowered from the wall and the woman who remains up above, a dialogue which is unimaginable when one considers that the town was in a state of alert—while the handing over of the scarlet thread is equally impossible. But the more reasonable explanation is that of Moran, that we have here a case of prolepsis, in which the text anticipates an important element by placing it earlier than its logical position in the context.[1] Verse 17 is strange: it is either an interpolation from v. 20, or else it immediately implies certain conditions to be fulfilled for the oath to be valid. In the second case, however, the expression is too weighty, and the first case is the more probable. If that is so, it must be admitted that this textual error is fairly ancient, because it is reproduced in all the translations. The conditions for the promise of the two men to save Rahab and her family are the following: that the sign should be placed outside the house and that all concerned should be gathered inside it. Perhaps the scarlet thread at the window may also have been the agreed signal for the attack on the city, as some commentators have supposed. It is not possible to be certain about this, seeing that the greater part of the epilogue has disappeared; the fact that Rahab tied the thread immediately is against this hypothesis. With regard to the colour of the thread, it reminds one curiously of the blood with which the Israelites in Egypt had to sprinkle the lintels of their doors during the last plague (cf. Exod. 12.13).

[22–24] After these adventures the spies return to the camp and make their report to Joshua: the situation is favourable for an attack. The final statement assumes the speech of Rahab and therefore shows that it was written at a late period; it now forms a link between ch. 2, of which the logical conclusion has no doubt disappeared, and ch. 6.

[1] Cf. also the recent study by W. J. Martin, '"Dischronologized" Narrative in the Old Testament', SVT XVII, 1969, pp. 179–86, which gives us examples in the OT where the order of the sentence is not chronological but according to the importance of the arguments.

The NT included Rahab in the genealogy of David as the mother of Boaz, the husband of Ruth, and therefore in the genealogy of Jesus (Matt. 1.5, expanding on I Chron. 2.10f.). All commentators agree in identifying the two Rahabs. According to this genealogy, the capture of Jericho would have taken place four generations before David, that is something like 120–160 years previously, which takes us back into the twelfth century. But this is a statement which is difficult to verify, and it tells us only about the chronological speculations indulged in at certain periods. It is probable, although it cannot be proved, that legends in Judaism underlie such speculations (Holzinger). Hebrews 11.31 makes Rahab an example of faith, and James 2.25 an example of meritorious works. In Judaism, Rahab became the prototype of the proselyte who abandoned a life of sin to accept the faith of Israel; and so she is often presented as a living example of the effectiveness of Israel's proselytization when Israel is faithful to its calling. Judaism also possessed various genealogies which made Rahab the ancestor of certain prophets of the priestly line (including amongst others Jeremiah and Ezekiel). This was done by means of exegetical procedures which in most cases seem illegitimate to us; but it did not possess any genealogy making Rahab the ancestor of David, and therefore of the Messiah, although other well-attested genealogical speculations suggest that the existence of a genealogy such as this is at least probable.[1]

CHAPTER 3.1–5.1

The Crossing of the Jordan

3 [1]Joshua aroused the camp early in the morning and they set out from Shittim, and they came to the Jordan, he and all the people of Israel, and they lodged there before they passed over. [2]*At the end of three days the* '*scribes*' *went through the camp* [3]*and commanded the people,* '*When you see the ark of the covenant of the* LORD *your God being lifted up by the priests* [*the*] *Levites, then*

---

[1] For this problem cf. H. L. Strack—P. Billerbeck, *Kommentar zum Neuen Testament aus Talmud und Midrasch*, I, Munich 1924, pp. 20–33.

you shall set out from your place and follow it, ⁴*that you may know the way you shall go, for you have never passed this way before. Yet there shall be a space between you and it, a distance of about two thousand cubits; do not come near it.*' ⁵And Joshua said to the people, 'Sanctify yourselves; for tomorrow the Lord will do wonders among you.' ⁶*And Joshua said to the priests, 'Take up the ark of the covenant, and cross [the river] before the people.' And they took up the ark of the covenant, and went before the people.* ⁷*And the* Lord *said to Joshua, 'This day I will begin to exalt you in the sight of all Israel, that they may know that, as I was with Moses, so I will be with you.* ⁸*And you shall command the priests who bear the ark of the covenant, "When you come to the brink of the waters of the Jordan, you shall stand still in the Jordan." '* ⁹*And Joshua said to the people of Israel, 'Come hither, and hear the words of the* Lord *your God.'* ¹⁰*And Joshua said, 'Hereby you shall know that the living God is among you, and that he will without fail drive out from before you the Canaanites, the Hittites, the Hivites, the Perizzites, the Girgashites, the Amorites, and the Jebusites.* ¹¹Behold, the ark of the covenant [of the Lord] [Lord of all the earth] is to pass over before you into the Jordan. ¹²Now therefore take twelve men from the tribes of Israel, from each tribe a man. ¹³And when the soles of the feet of the priests, the bearers of the ark of the Lord, the Lord of all the earth, shall rest in the waters of the Jordan, the waters of the Jordan shall divide, the waters of the Jordan from upstream, and the waters shall be stopped in one heap.'

14 So, when the people set out from their tents, to pass over the Jordan with *the priests,* the bearers of the ark [of the covenant] before the people, ¹⁵and when the bearers of the ark had come to the Jordan, and the feet of *the priests,* the bearers of the ark were dipped in the brink of the water (the Jordan overflows all its banks throughout the time of harvest), ¹⁶the waters coming down from above stood and rose up in a heap far off, by Adam, the city that is beside Zarethan, and those flowing down toward the sea of the Arabah, the Salt Sea, were wholly cut off.

And while the people passed over opposite Jericho, ¹⁷the *priests,* bearers of the ark [of the covenant of the Lord] stood on dry ground, in the midst of the Jordan, while all Israel passed over on dry ground *until all the nation finished passing over the Jordan.*

4 *When all the nation had finished passing over the Jordan,* the Lord said to Joshua, ²"Take yourselves twelve men from the people, from each tribe a man, ³and command them, "Take from here out of the midst

4 Then Joshua called the twelve men from the people of Israel, whom he had appointed, a man from each tribe; ⁵and Joshua said to them, 'Pass on before

of the Jordan, *from the very place where the priests' feet stood,* twelve stones, and carry them over with you, and lay them down in the place where you lodge tonight." '
(8aβ) And they took up twelve stones out of the midst of the Jordan, as the LORD had told Joshua, according to the number of the tribes of the people of Israel, and they carried them over with them to the place where they lodged, and laid them down there.

{the ark of the LORD your God
{me, before the Lord (LXX)
into the midst of the Jordan, and take up each of you a stone upon his shoulder, according to the number of the tribes of the people of Israel, *6that this may be a sign among you, when your children ask in time to come, "What do those stones mean to you?" 7Then you shall tell them that the waters of the Jordan were divided before the ark of the covenant of the LORD; when it passed over the Jordan, the waters of the Jordan were cut off. So these stones shall be to the people of Israel a memorial for ever.'*
8aα And the men of Israel did as Joshua commanded. 9And Joshua set up twelve stones in the midst of the Jordan, in the place where the feet of *the priests,* the bearers of the ark *of the covenant,* had stood; and they are there to this day.

10For the *priests,* the bearers of the ark, stood in the midst of the Jordan, until everything was finished that the LORD commanded Joshua to tell the people, *according to all that Moses had commanded Joshua.* The people passed over in haste; 11and when all the people had finished passing over, the ark of the LORD passed over *and the priests were before the people.* 12The sons of Reuben and the sons of Gad and the half-tribe of Manasseh passed over armed before the people of Israel, as Moses had bidden them; 13about forty thousand ready armed for war passed over before the LORD for battle, to the plains of Jericho. 14*On that day the LORD exalted Joshua in the sight of all Israel; and they stood in awe of him, as they had stood in awe of Moses, all the days of his life.*

15*And the LORD said to Joshua,* 16*'Command the priests, the bearers of the ark, to come up out of the Jordan.'* 17*Joshua therefore commanded the priests, 'Come up out of the Jordan.'* 18*And when the priests, the bearers of the ark of the LORD, came up from the midst of the Jordan, and the soles of the* *priests' feet were lifted up on dry ground*, the waters of the Jordan returned to their place and overflowed all its banks, as before.

¹⁹The people came up out of the Jordan *on the tenth day of the first month*, and they encamped in Gilgal on the east border of Jericho.

²⁰And those twelve stones, which they took out of the Jordan, Joshua set up in Gilgal. ²¹And he said to the people of Israel, '*When your children ask their fathers in time to come, "What do these stones mean?*," ²²*then you shall let your children know, "Israel passed over this Jordan on dry ground.*" ²³The LORD your God dried up the waters of the Jordan for you until you passed over, as the LORD your God did to the Red Sea which he dried up for us until we passed over, ²⁴*so that all the peoples of the earth may know that the hand of the LORD is mighty; that you may fear the LORD your God for ever.*'

5 ¹When all the kings of the Amorites that were beyond the Jordan to the west, and all the kings of the Canaanites that were by the sea, heard that the LORD had dried up the waters of the Jordan for the people of Israel until they had crossed over, their heart melted, and there was no longer any breath in them, because of the people of Israel.

Bibliography: J. Wellhausen, *Die Composition des Hexateuch*, Berlin ⁴1963, pp.118ff.; W. Rudolph, *Der 'Elohist' als Erzähler* . . . pp.169–78; K. Möhlenbrink, 'Die Landnahmesagen . . .', pp. 254–8; P. P. Saydon, 'The Crossing of the Jordan, Josue 3 and 4', *CBQ* 12, 1950, pp.194–207; A. George, 'Les récits de Gilgal en Josué', *Mémorial J. Chaine*, Lyon 1950, pp.169–86; H. J. Kraus, 'Gilgal, ein Beitrag zur Kultusgeschichte Israels',

VT i, 1951, pp. 181–99; C. A. Keller, 'Über einige alttestamentliche Heiligtumslegenden II', *ZAW* 68, 1956, pp. 85–97; H. J. Kraus, 'Zur Geschichte des Passa-Massot-Festes', *EvTh* 18, 1958, pp. 47–67, esp. pp. 54ff.; O. Kaiser, *Die mythische Bedeutung des Meeres in Ägypten, Ugarit und Israel*, BZAW 78, Berlin 1959, pp. 135–40; J. Dus, 'Die Analyse zweier Ladeerzählungen de Josuabuches (Jos. 3–4 und 6)', *ZAW* 72, 1960, pp. 107–34, esp. pp. 120–34; H. J. Kraus, *Worship in Israel*, Oxford 1966, pp. 125–9; E. Vogt, 'Die Erzählung vom Jordanübergang Josue 3–4', *Bibl* 46, 1965, pp. 125–48; J. Maier, *Das altisraelitische Ladeheiligtum*, BZAW 93, Berlin 1965, pp. 18–32 (cf. my review in *RSO* 41, 1966, pp. 85–9); Auzou, pp. 70ff., 76ff.; J. A. Soggin, 'Gilgal, Passa und Landnahme', SVT XV, 1966, pp. 263–77. It was not possible to make use of F. Langlamet, *Gilgal et les récits de la traversée du Jourdain (Jos. III–IV)*, CahRB 11, Paris 1969 (but see my review in *ThRev* 67, 1971, cols. 174f.); J. N. M. Wijngaards, 'The dramatization of salvific history in the Deuteronomic Schools', *OTS* XVI, 1969, pp. 3ff.

For the arrangement of the text, see below. Dtr passages are printed in italics.

[3.1] is part of the ancient liturgy. *wayyis'ū*: LXX[BL] and the recensions deriving from them read the singular. For the place, cf. 2.1. Verse 1aβ is lacking in LXX[BA], while Syr lacks *hū' we* . . . *terem*, on its own and as an adverb, = 'before' (time). With [2] the Deuteronomic passage begins; it can be recognized from the *šōṭerīm*, who have already occurred in 1.10, and who pass 'through' the camp (against Fernández, Saydon and Baldi). Note the construction of the verse, which is not simple, and which we have to modify in translating it. V translates the beginning by *et morati sunt ibi tres dies*, which it adds to the end of v. 1. [3] For MT, priests and Levites belong to the same category (cf. V, which reinforces this identification: *et sacerdotes stirpis leviticae*), while LXX, T and Syr on the contrary stress the distinction between them, as happens in Chronicles. For Deut. (cf. 18.1) and Dtr, there is only one priesthood, and it is of Levitical origin. *hālak 'aḥēr* is a technical term, found in Accadian (*alāku arki* . . ., cf. also Jer. 2.2) for taking part in a procession behind a sacred image or religious symbol. [4] V slightly changes the order of the verse, putting at the end *et cavete, ne appropinquetis ad Arcam*, adding *lema'an*: *ut procul videre possitis*. We adopt the order proposed by Abel, placing the second half of the verse, which goes better with what precedes, at the beginning of the verse. *ūbēnāw*: cf. K and Q; it exists either in the plural vocalization of the noun (rare: 3 times) or in the singular form (*GKC* § 103; *B-M* § 87, 3c). *bammiddā*: LXX has στήσεσθε, perhaps having read *'imedū* (Noth in *BH*[3]). The expression 'neither yesterday nor the day before yesterday' is equivalent to 'never'. [5] This does not seem to be at home in the present Deuterono-

mic context; perhaps it, too, belongs to the ancient liturgy. After *hitqaddāšū*,
LXX adds εἰς αὔριον. [6] Takes up the Deuteronomic narrative again: the
order given previously is carried out. [7] After *kol* LXX inserted υἱῶν =
benē (perhaps by haplography with *beʿēnē*?). For this theme cf. 1.5b. Note
the use of *ʾašer* to introduce a final clause (rare, B-M 88, 2b). [8] *weʾattā*:
LXX has καὶ νῦν = *weʿattā*, 'and now'. [9] *gōšū* from the root *ngš*, cf.
GKC § 66 c. *dibʿrē*: LXX and V have the singular = 'the Word' (capital
W!); there may be a dittography: the *yod*, an early abbreviation for *yhwh*,
was later confused with the suffix, at a time when the divine name was
once again written out in full. [10] LXX omits the first two words and
continues Joshua's address in direct speech. [11] is not Deuteronomic but
also belongs to the earlier text. The expression 'ark of the covenant, Lord
(?) of all the earth' seems strange, although it is confirmed by all the
ancient translations (which, however, read 'of the Lord . . .') except Syr,
which has 'the ark of the covenant of the LORD, Lord . . .' This reading
seems much more probable, and has a parallel in v. 13. LXX, V and T
regarded the first phrase as in a *status constructus* to 'Lord'. This assumes the
existence of a *nomen regens* governing several words, a form which, although
rare, is not impossible;[1] but the reading of Syr seems better. [12] LXX
omits *weʿattā* and reads, instead of *miššibtē*, τῶν υἱῶν, i.e. *mibbenē*. [13] The
root *nwḥ* can give as infinitive construct either *nūaḥ* or *nōaḥ*, *GKC* § 72q.
[14] The construction of this sentence seems extraordinarily heavy for an
oriental, Semitic text. In Noth's view, the mention of the priests, here and
in the verses that follow, is of Deuteronomic origin. For *habberīt* here and
below, cf. v. 11. [15] *ūkebō*': LXX adds οἱ δὲ ἱερεῖς here, adapting the text
to the context. *hammāyim*: LXX has εἰς μέρος τοῦ ὕδατος τοῦ Ἰορδάνου =
mē hayyardēn, perhaps a dittography with the following verse. *ml'* may be
either the third person masc. sing. of the perfect *qal*, or the active *qal*
participle; the second possibility is preferable here. It is not a question of
an abnormal flood but of a recurrent seasonal phenomenon (against Noth,
who would take it as a perfect). *kōl*: LXX has ὡσεί, i.e. *kemō* or *kaʾašer*. By
adding πυρῶν (from πυρός, —οῦ, 'winter corn'), LXX may have wished
to stress the connection between the phenomenon and the season of
spring. [16] *bēʾādām*: K read *beʾādām*, while Q read *mēʾādām*, with T and
Syr; but we must read K: the waters were held back 'by Adam . . .' and
not 'from Adam . . . to the Sea'. The text, however, is not very clear, and
there are notable variants in the ancient versions: LXX[BA] has ἔστη πῆγμα ἕν
ἀφέστηκας μακρὰν σφόδρα σφοδρῶς ἕως μέρους κιθαιρειν, i.e. (LXX[A] καριαθιαριμ)
'forming a single heap over a very wide area, as far as the frontier of K'
(probably reading *bimʾōd* instead of *beʾādām*—Baldi), a reading which Abel
would accept in place of MT, and which assumes a phenomenon on a far

---

[1] Cf. our observation in *Bibl* 44, 1963, p. 521 n. 2, for some examples and a bibliography.

vaster scale. On the other hand, V has *et ad instar montis intumescentes apparebat procul ab urbe quae vocatur Adom, usque ad locum Sarthan* (note that instead of *nēd 'eḥad*, V probably read *nir'eh har*, and instead of *meʿ'ōd* read *meʿ'ad*). Syr presents yet another reading, while T is like MT. W. Albright proposes a correction, reading *mibbad lō mēʿ'ᵃdāmā ʿad miṣṣad ṣ* . . . N. Glueck perfects this conjecture by reading *mēṣad* for the last part.¹ This gives us 'far from Adam(ah)' and 'beside Zarethan' in the first case and 'as far as the fortress of Zarethan' in the second case. But these suggestions do not give a better sense than MT, which it is preferable to retain, in spite of all. **[17]** For *hā'ārōn* cf. on v. 11. *wᵉkol*: cf. v. 12. *hākēn* in itself would be an infinitive absolute *hiphil* of *qwn*, but this form would be meaningless in the context. Noth rightly points out that it is no doubt a composite of *kēn* = 'here' (cf. 2.17), and the article is used in a demonstrative sense, as in *hayyōm*, 'today'. **[4.1]** The first part of the verse, which can be recognized as deriving from the Deuteronomic redaction, is omitted in LXX and the Arabic version. The Massora itself leaves a space after this first part. **[2]** *qᵉhū*: LXX, V and the Eastern Syriac translation read the verb in the singular, and the dative pronoun is lacking in LXX and V. It will be noted that this order finds an exact parallel in 3.12, even though the choice of words is slightly different and the purpose different also. The exact figure is omitted in LXXᴮ. **[3]** The verb continues to be in the singular in the translations mentioned in connection with the previous verse; *lākem* is omitted only in LXXᴮ. *mimmaṣṣab* is lacking in LXXᴮᴬ, but reappears in later translations. Abel would omit the phrase, which he regards as an anticipation of v. 9, but in spite of the readings in LXX, such an emendation does not seem to be justified from the textual point of view. *hākīn* is a curious form: as the *hiphil* infinitive of *qwn*, it makes no sense, and it is doubtful that it is a rare form of infinitive absolute (*GKC* § 72z) used in a finite sense, because it lacks the appropriate conjunction. Noth and Kaufmann are no doubt right in supposing that it is an analogous form to *hākēn* in 3.17, or perhaps a dittography (cf. Holzinger, and Noth in *BH*³). **[5]** The name is omitted in LXXᴮᴸ and V. The mention of the ark is lacking in LXX, which has ἐμπροσθέν μου (*lᵉpānay*), πρὸ προσώπου κυρίου. Thus here again LXX seems to be trying to harmonize two recensions, by implying that the men took the stones from the bed of the river after those carrying the ark had passed by (as can be seen from v. 8, which, however, belongs largely to the first recension), putting other stones in their place. Some conservative Catholic scholars still attempt the same harmonization. For MT, on the other hand, the idea is that the twelve men carry the stones from the bank they set out from into the river, to serve as stepping stones, however precarious, for

---

¹ W. F. Albright, 'The Administrative Division of Israel and Judah,' *JPOS* 5, 1925, p.33 n.37; N. Glueck, 'Three Israelite Towns in the Jordan Valley', *BASOR* 90, 1943, p.6.

those carrying the ark; these stones henceforth remained visible through the water, which at this point would have formed a small rapids, and would have excited the curiosity of later generations precisely because they were the double of the pillars at Gilgal (Noth and Abel). [6] *tihyeh*: LXX and T add *lāhem*; LXX lacks *beqirbekem* but has διὰ παντός = *'ad 'ōlām*, followed by a second ἵνα, 'in order that, when . . .'. Syr does the same. [7] LXX begins καὶ σὺ δηλώσεις τῷ υἱῷ σου. Some scholars cannot accept *nikretū mē*, as being a useless repetition and lacking in LXX (although it occurs in T, Syr and V). But such repetitions are common in West and South Semitic; they may be omitted in Indo-European languages for reasons of style, but they are retained by Semitic translations. This is a matter of form and not of substance. [8] This verse consists largely of the recension concerning the stones taken from the river bed and set up on the west bank. After *ṣiwwā* LXX adds κύριος τῷ 'Ιησοῖ. *lemispar*: LXX read ἐν τῇ συντελείᾳ τῆς διαβάσεως τῶν υἱῶν etc. [9] LXX precedes the mention of the twelve stones by καὶ ἄλλους, as does V: *alias quoque XII lapides*, continuing in this way the attempt to harmonize the two recensions (cf. on v. 5). After *habberīt*, LXX and Syr add 'of Yahweh'. [10] LXX has ἕως συνετέλεσεν 'Ιησοῦς πάντα ἃ ἐνετείλατο κύριος instead of *'ad tōm*, and omits the two mentions of Joshua and that of Moses. [11] Instead of *hakkōhanīm* LXX read *hā'abānīm* (οἱ λίθοι), with the intention (Baldi) of correcting and harmonizing the difficulties arising from the combination of the two recensions. At the end, LXX has ἔμπροσθεν αὐτῶν as well. [13] LXX, V, Syr give the exact figure without adding 'about'. [18] *nitqū* etc.: LXX has καὶ ἔθηκαν τοὺς πόδας ἐπὶ τῆς γῆς. [20] *lāqeḥū*: LXX^BA and the recensions deriving from them read the singular. [21] *wayy'ōmer* . . . *yiśrā'ēl* is lacking in LXX^BA and the recensions depending on them. For the use of *'ašer* cf. 3.17. *māḥār* is lacking in LXX^A and recensions. [23] *'ašer*: for its use here, cf. *GKC* § 159a and *B-M* §88.2b. *mippenēkēm*: LXX and Syr read the third person pl. masc. [24] *yerā'tem*: almost all commentators and Kraus, p. 157, propose reading *yir'ātām* with the same consonants (= *yir'āh* with a third person pl. suffix), but the remedy is no better than the malady, which is not very great in any case! The text is quite comprehensible, and is supported by the ancient versions. [5.1] *kol* and *yommā* are lacking in LXX^BA and the recensions which derive from them. *'obrānw*: Q, LXX and V (ἐν τῷ διαβαίνειν, *donec transirent*), T and Syr read *'obrām*, while K has the first person plural , 'until we had crossed over'. *'ōd* is lacking in all the ancient versions. LXX translated 'the Canaanites' by τῆς Φοινίκης.

Reading chs. 3–5 of Joshua, one has an immediate impression of a series of episodes which all refer to the crossing of the Jordan and derive from it their literary unity, but which on the other hand seem to lack any original internal unity of any kind (in spite of the various attempts at harmonization which were still being made a few years ago, especially amongst conservative Catholic commentators). Several incoherences concerning dates and places, which resist all attempts at harmonization, will be immediately obvious to the reader in particular in ch. 4. Notwithstanding this, the section we are dealing with ultimately presents a unity which is imposed upon these differences, to which we shall return.

The first thing one notices is a striking analogy with the account of the Passover and the crossing of the Red Sea, Exod. 12–15, to the extent that it seems safe to affirm a substantial unity of content between these two passages (in our study listed above, we give a synoptic table). This observation is important in determining the literary category and *Sitz im Leben* of Josh. 3–5, which is obviously linked with the sanctuary at Gilgal. But a second unifying factor in chs. 3–4 and 6 is the procession with the ark, so that the total section 3–6 seems eventually to have formed a whole, transcending differences of detail.

Kraus has concluded that in chs. 3–5 we possess a celebration of the event of the Exodus and the crossing of the Red Sea, made a present reality in the new historical and geographical context which was from now on that of Israel. This would mean that we have an interesting example of the liturgical actualization of ancient traditions, with the one exception that the course of events has been reversed, the celebration of the Passover closing the solemnity instead of opening it. This liturgical tradition has been historicized, either already by the 'compiler', or, more probably, by the Deuteronomic redaction, the result of which is to produce an independent episode of the conquest, which is the first in chronological order. This historicization has lead to a version of events incompatible with the facts recorded in ch. 2, which, as we have seen, made necessary the suppression of the end of that episode. The only difference by comparison with the text of the Exodus concerns the presence of the ark, as we shall see.

The first part can be divided as follows: (*a*) The preparations for the crossing of the Jordan (3.1–13); (*b*) The miracle of the waters (3.14–16a); (*c*) The crossing (3.16b–17; 4.10–11, 14–18); (*d*) The twelve stones (4.1–9); (*e*) The crossing of groups from the east of the Jordan (4.12–13); (*f*) The arrival at Gilgal (4.19–5.1).

The text clearly shows the diversity of its origins before the liturgical ritual was composed. Noth attributes Deuteronomic origin to the whole of ch. 1 and then (Rudolph differing slightly from him here) to

3.2–3, 6–10; 4.4–7, 11b–12, 14–18a, 21b–24, together with the phrases mentioning the Levitical priesthood, and the chronology; the other material, he holds, forms part of the ancient liturgy, and was either handed on by the 'compiler' or came down independently. The division into sources on the lines laid down by Wellhausen was brought to its ultimate expression in the study by Möhlenbrink, but was rejected by Noth. However, it has been attempted once again by Dus, Maier and Vogt, although they do not mention any 'sources' in the proper sense. In the view of both Maier and Dus, six recensions each introduced additions before the present text was finally formed: I. The aetiology of the stones in the Jordan; II. The aetiology of the stones set up at Gilgal (both of these being Benjaminite: 3.14a, 16 [with additions]; 4.1–2 [additions], 3, 8 [additions], 9 [additions], 20 [additions]); III. An Ephraimite recension which introduced Joshua (3.1, 5 [additions], 11, 3–5; 4.4–5 [additions], 14, 19 and 21 [additions]); IV. The extension to 'all Israel' by means of additions here and there; V. The recension which introduced the ark (3.13 [additions], 14b, 17 [additions]; 4.11, 18 and fragments in 3.11 and 4.5); VI. Deuteronomic re-elaborations (3.2–4, 6–10; 4.6–7, 12–13, 24; some glosses in 4.10, 16–17).

This breakdown, which is complicated enough, is continued to ch. 6, but with certain variations which we shall examine in their place.

Much more simple, and revolutionary because it eliminates the passages attributed to the Deuteronomic reaction, is the solution proposed by Vogt. This distinguishes two narratives, one historical and the other liturgical and ritual, giving the following result:

I.   A narrative from the same tradition as in ch. 2, introducing a
      holy war: 3.1, 7, 14a, 16; 4.10b, 12, 13a, 14, 13b.
II.   The liturgy, in which two parts can be distinguished:
      A.   Up to the miracle at the Jordan, 1.10; 3.2, 3, 4, 5, 6, 8, 9,
           10, 11, 13, 14b, 15.
      B.   The crossing and the stones: 3.12, 17; 4.4, 5, 6, 7, 9, 10a.
      B¹. The crossing and the stones: 4.1a, 2, 3, 8, 11, 20, 21, 22, 23,
           24.
Finally, 3.15b and 4.15–19 are later additions.

The summary of these three recent hypotheses is sufficient to give an idea of the extreme complexity of the problem of the primitive sources of this passage, before the insertion of the different passages in the liturgy, as well as that of the Deuteronomic passages, which were hitherto regarded as well established.

In any case, in ch. 4, two parallel recensions referring to the crossing of the river can be distinguished: that of the foundation of the sanctuary at Gilgal by the setting up of twelve standing stones, and that of the twelve stones in the middle of the river, at the place of the traditional ford, each with its own aetiological reference. This can be regarded as having been established ever since Wellhausen, in spite of certain disagreements about details, and has not been contested except by conservative Christian writers and by Y. Kaufmann.

If the section we are discussing is the product of the historicization of an ancient liturgy, which has gone so far as to replace in part the narrative tradition (the conclusion of ch. 2), it is pointless to raise the question of the historicity of the events. What is certainly historical is the celebration of the cult at Gilgal near Jericho; and the content of this celebration, the Passover, the Exodus and the conquest (in ch. 6) is also historical. For a possible dating of this feast, we must turn to the period of Saul, when the importance of the sanctuary at Gilgal was at its greatest, and when it was out of reach of the Philistine attacks which probably destroyed Shiloh (last quarter of the eleventh century). No doubt the cult existed before this period, and it is not too daring to suppose that it was in this setting that the events of the sacred history to which the cult was linked passed from the tribe of Benjamin and became associated (Joseph) with all Israel. What for the moment cannot be established is the nature of the sanctuary of Gilgal: did it exist in the pre-Israelite period, or was it founded by Israel? The presence of a circle of standing stones, with their close resemblance to the layout of Phoenician open-air sanctuaries, makes the first alternative by far the most likely.[1] In Judg. 3.19 we have an allusion to these same stones, but without any mention of their being set up by Israel.

If the dating is fixed at the period of Saul, or a little earlier, this raises a new problem which is not easy to solve: from 1050 on the ark was in the hands of the Philistines. Maier has maintained independently and on quite different premises (pp. 27ff.) that the introduction of the ark into this context is later and was carried out on the pattern of

---

[1] Cf. K. Galling, *BRL*, cols. 268ff.; L. Woolley, *Medio Oriente*, Milan 1961, p. 96; T. A. Busink, 'Les origines du Temple de Salomon', *JEOL* VI, 17, 1963, pp. 165–92, esp. pp. 177ff.; J. Gray, *The Canaanites*, London 1964, fig. 25; L. Delekat, *BHH* II, 1964, col. 1169; see also the later Punic sanctuaries.

the insertion of its story into I Sam. 4–6, with the purpose of giving
the possession a specifically Yahwist nature. This, he holds, did not
take place before the period of the kings. It is one of the problems, and
not the least complicated, which we shall encounter and which will
no doubt never be solved.

Thus we are faced with what we can call a sacred drama, a kind of
mediaeval 'mystery': the people who take part know that everything
has already been decided in their favour; each of the various liturgical acts celebrates a miraculous intervention on the part of Yahweh,
and the ancient aetiological traditions have been completely incorporated into them. Furthermore, as often happens in West Semitic
style, when the intention is to stress the importance of an action, an
attempt is made to repeat a key word as often as possible. In chs. 3–4,
Hertzberg has noted that the root ʿbr (to pass over) and the verb ʿmd
(to stop, stand) occur five times. These two terms summarize the main
theme of these stories, in particular because the Jordan is not any
river but the traditional frontier of the promised land towards the
east, which is now crossed in order to take possession of this land. Thus
the crossing of the river is synonymous with the conquest and the beginning of the fulfilment of the ancient promises. Dtr has taken up
again the ancient liturgy, which had perhaps fallen into disuse at that
period, to provide the skeleton of a programmatic narrative: at that
time too, Dtr asserts, it was absurd to hope for the success of Israel; at
that time too, both nature and men were aligned against Israel, but
God fulfilled the ancient promises. Declarations such as 3.10 take on
a particular meaning if we consider that they were made at a period
when nothing seemed further from the people than the presence of
God (who had abandoned his people, cf. Ezek. 11.22ff.!), the power
of God (who had not been able, he had said, to protect his people, Jer.
31.29; Ezek. 18.2), and the promises of God, which the prophets had
proclaimed for centuries to have been suspended. To all this the Deuteronomic preacher replies that God is the same as at the first, that
the promises still hold, and that now, as in past centuries, God would
bring about all he had said to his people.

(a) The preparations for the crossing (3.1–13)

[3.1] This verse is linked to ch. 2 by the usual literary construction:
the two waw consecutives make the raising of the camp and the setting
out to be the direct consequence of the good news brought by the
spies, that at Jericho and round about the situation is favourable to

the invaders: Rahab has promised her collaboration and it is now certain that Yahweh has delivered the place into their hands (2.21–24). But in fact the narrative takes up 1.18: having received an assurance on the part of the people that they will accompany him wherever God sends him (1.16ff.), Joshua raises camp and sets out. Towards the end of ch. 2, we in fact have an independent tradition (cf. also Introduction §3), which probably assumes the crossing of the Jordan by force (cf. 24.11a) and almost certainly also assumes the conquest of Jericho thanks to the treason of Rahab (we find a similar case in Bethel, Judg. 1.22–26). In chs. 3–5 and 6, on the contrary, the crossing and conquest are represented as a cultic act, in which the ark is carried in procession, an act which has later been historicized. The present verse also gives a clear impression that Israel spent only a single night on the bank of the river, ready to cross. [2–4] These verses seem very loosely connected to v. 1 (in spite of the arguments by Fernández and Baldi) and in fact belong, as we have seen, to the Deuteronomic redaction. Israel camps for three days on the eastern bank of the Jordan (cf. 1.11), which gives the following chronology for chs. 3–5: the people come up from the river on 10 Nisan (March–April), the first month of the lunar year on the spring reckoning (note the use of the neo-Babylonian calendar, contrary to other texts which have followed tradition and maintained the ancient Canaanite terminology: Exod. 13.4; 23.15; 34.18; Deut. 16.1; I Kings 6.38; 8.2; 6.1, 37). Thus they left Shittim to camp alongside the bank of the Jordan on the 8th of that month. The date, then, is exactly a week before the celebration of the Passover (the night of 14–15 Nisan, 5.10–12). This halt, useless in itself, may have played a liturgical role of preparation for the Passover. The chronology is irreconcilable with that of 2.22, where there is a wait of a further three days (against Kaufmann). Thus it is obvious that Dtr completely restructured the original chronology of the feast, which did not include the preparatory phrase; for him, on the contrary, one could not begin the Passover without a week of preparation. In the original account, the departure must have been on 9 Nisan and the arrival at Gilgal on the 10th. The distance which had to remain between the ark and the people seems to be an element deriving from the ancient ritual. This explanation would naturally have been offensive to Calvin, who was equally aware of the chronological difficulties of this passage and tried to harmonize them.

The presence of the ark here, as we have noted, is a difficulty. We would simply recall that :(a) the ark never appears elsewhere in the narratives of the conquest; (b) it never appears elsewhere at Gilgal; and during the years when the sanctuary enjoyed its greatest importance, under Saul, it could not have been there, because according to I Sam. 7.1 (cf. II Sam. 6) it was at Kiriath-jearim, on the boundaries of Judah and Benjamin, west of Jerusalem. In any case it is clear that even in the oldest version, it was the task of the priest to carry it (against Noth, who would attribute the mention of the priest to Dtr), because the people could not come nearer than a certain distance to the ark.[1] Nor could a non-consecrated person touch it. This comment agrees with the account of the carrying of the ark in I Sam. 6 and II Sam. 6, where the risk of not handling the ark with the necessary ritual precautions is clearly emphasized. All these indications, as well as the fact that no attempt is made to give an aetiological explanation of the presence of the ark, which is assumed, argue, as Noth states, in favour of the presence of the ark in the primitive ritual, even though we are unable to determine the circumstances of this in the context of the amphictyony. In these verses, the ark still carries out the functions of a guide, as a sign of the presence of Yahweh (cf. the very ancient passage, removed from its context, of Num. 10.35, where the ark and Yahweh are wholly identified). The people did not know the way, because they had never followed it, while the spies belong to a different tradition incompatible with this (against Baldi); the priests, too, would have been in the same situation if God, by means of the ark, had not guided them according to his will. We find a similar case in I Sam. 6.7ff. In the ritual, this element has a slightly different significance. Those who took part in the cult, the pilgrims, mostly did not know the route which led through the desert valley of the Jordan, whereas the priests, who were acquainted with this cult, knew it; and since the ceremony took place almost entirely on the banks of the river and partly in the water, at a place where the bank is quite steep and loose, it was wise to be prudent.

[5] This verse also derives from the ancient tradition. The call, 'sanctify yourselves', is common to several liturgical and ritual traditions in the OT, and is found on the occasion of every extraordinary event brought about by Yahweh; this 'sanctification' consists of a series of rites of purification and an abstinence from all sexual activity

---

[1] 2,000 cubits is about 900 metres. The length of the cubit can be calculated only indirectly: the aqueduct of Hezekiah, which is 533 m long, contains in its inscription the statement that it is 1,200 cubits long, so that a cubit is approx. 444.25 mm. Cf. G. Barrois, *IB* I, pp. 153ff.

and from certain foods (Exod. 19.10–15; Num. 11.18; Josh. 7.13, etc.). Here the expected event described by the term *niplā' ōt* (the root *pl'* exists solely in the *niphal, piel, hithpael* and the *hiphil*) which means 'extraordinary actions', 'miraculous works' (and in a derivative sense, 'unheard-of words'), with the emphasis on the supranormal nature of the event. The word LXX uses is θαυμαστά, which is often used for miracles when they provoke the reactions of astonishment and marvelling. A terrifying prodigy is usually described by *nōrā'* (root: *yr'*); there are also more neutral terms.[1] A divine intervention of this kind obviously requires an adequate human preparation (which appears here independently of the preparatory week for the Passover which Dtr records).

[6] In the present state of the text, this verse tells us what happened the next day, the 'tomorrow' mentioned in v. 5. In fact, with the readjusted chronology of Dtr, we are 'at the end of three days'. There is no question about the attribution of these verses, because they take up themes already noted in 1.5, 17. The verb *ns'* means both 'take up' and 'carry'. The idea, as Hertzberg quite rightly points out, is that when the ark is taken up and carried, God begins to act. Here, that is, he begins to lead the procession. That this in no way means that it is possible to make Yahweh do what is required of him by ritual means, is something Israel was to learn at its cost, cf. I Sam. 4. This view is to some extent confirmed by [7]. Joshua is gradually introduced to the office of Moses, the servant of Yahweh, until he himself becomes a 'servant' (Josh. 24.29). Hertzberg makes an acute observation that Yahweh is raising up a charismatic leader, through whose person he proposes to guide the people (cf. 4.1, 4 below). This theme is not necessarily linked to the Gilgal cult, as we saw in the introduction, but [8] presents Joshua in this role from this point on, and to it is added the role of intermediary between God and the people. It is probable, as Hertzberg suggests, that in the earliest narrative Joshua had the specific function of parting the waters, or at least of stopping them (cf. Moses in Exod. 14.21), although there is no direct indication of this. The simple contact of the priests' feet with the water seems neither sufficient nor adequate to the phenomenon which results; this element is replaced more effectively in [9] by preaching (cf. the emphasis placed on what LXX and V call 'the word', a typical emphasis in the theology of Deuteronomy and Dtr). While this is taking place, the

---

[1] For this problem cf. W. Eichrodt, *Theology of the Old Testament*, II, London 1967, pp. 162ff.

people, whom one must assume were fairly small in numbers, assembled along the river bank. The address proper follows in **[10]**. The
beginning of it is particularly important. It is as it were the proof
offered to the people 'that a living God' is amongst them. The expression occurs elsewhere in the OT; Pss. 42.2; 84.2; Hos. 1.10 (there
is also a similar expression: *ḥay yhwh*, as truly as Yahweh lives) and in
general serves to distinguish God positively from the gods of Canaan
who died and rose again periodically, in connection with the seasonal
cycle of nature to which they were subject. This made them all the
more incapable of intervening in the course of history, whereas on the
contrary the living God actually guides the course of history, con-
trols nature himself and does not tolerate either a 'natural' order of
things or the intervention of anyone else in what is his own domain.
As the Lord of nature and of history, he can drive out or submit to
others the inhabitants of any region. In this way, in the present case,
he fulfils his promise to Israel. The verb *yrš* here has two senses, the
connection between which is striking: in the *qal*, 'to trample grapes',
whence it takes the meaning 'trample down', 'submit', 'take possession'; and in the *hiphil*, 'drive out', 'occupy' (whence the noun *yᵉrūšā*
'possession, property'). Here it has the negative sense with regard to
the indigenous inhabitants; they are listed in a standard form which
contains seven names (cf. Gen. 15.19; Exod. 3.8, 17; Deut. 7.1; 20.17;
etc.). The full list is not always given, but it constitutes a simple resumé of the very complex ethnic situation of the region. The 'Canaanites', which LXX transcribes here by το χαναναῖον, but which it often
translates by φοίνικες, generally refers to the populations of the coastal
cities who survived the numerous invasions from the interior during
the early centuries of the second millennium. In the OT, similarly, this
name is used by preference to designate the people of the coast and the
plains. The Hittites appear in small colonies, here and there, throughout the whole territory of Syria and Palestine, far from their country,
which is of course in northern Syria and Asia Minor. The OT tells of
one of these colonies at Hebron (Gen. 23). We also find Hittites defined as such individually, apart from the inhabitants of Hebron, in
Gen. 26.34; 36.2; I Sam. 26.6; II Sam. 11–12; 23.39; while the people of Jerusalem are said to be partly descended from Hittites in Ezek.
16.3. According to LXX the Hivites are a Hurrite clan and are to be
found above all at Shechem (Gen. 34.2 [LXX]) and in the four Gibeonite cities (Josh. 9.7 [LXX]). The Amorites are always described as
the population of the hill country as opposed to that of the coast (cf.

Deut. 1.7, 19, 20, 44; Gen. 48.22; Josh. 10.5; etc.), and are probably
the remnants of the previous wave of West Semitic invaders. The
Jebusites are the inhabitants of Jerusalem (18.16, 28; Judg. 19.10),
though Ezek. 16.3 regards it as composed of Amorites and Hittites.
This description is so rare that other commentators have preferred to
regard it as late and artificial. We know nothing about the two other
peoples mentioned.

Hertzberg comments that as far as we know, this list does not seem
to refer to anything south of Jerusalem. However, since one tradition,
possibly late (P), connects Hebron with a Hittite colony (Gen. 23),
this is not so certain: we know too little about the indigenous populations of Palestine to hazard opinions which are barely probable.

The formula 'hereby you shall know . . .' seems to be a typical
one, especially in Ezekiel, but it is also employed elsewhere to connect the knowledge of God with his marvellous acts, so removing it
from the purely conceptual sphere and relating it to the history where
God judges and forgives.[1]

[11] Together with v. 13, this verse contains another attribute of
Yahweh which is only found in this setting. We have restored the formula used here on the pattern of v. 13. The expression seems normal,
as Noth points out, in fairly late passages such as Micah 4.13; Zech.
4.14; 6.5. But here, as also in Ps. 97.5, it is in the pre-Deuteronomic
passages that we find a confession of God's sovereignty over the universe, and therefore of God's right to dispose of the world. In [12] we
have a description of the choice of twelve men, one from each tribe,
without saying what for; the verse is 'left hanging' (Noth), which
gives the impression either that it has been displaced from its original
context or that it has been separated from it by a fairly lengthy interpolation. According to Noth, the original context is 4.4aβ, 4b, 5 (4aα
having been introduced to harmonize this passage with its new context), whereas Hertzberg holds the view that the verse should be
placed before 9.1–9, or the latter passage transferred here. For some
conservative Catholic commentators, these reasons are sufficient to
exclude the verse, whereas for other more modern commentators
(such as Baldi), the verse has been left here in this form to create a certain 'suspense'; this latter suggestion obviously cannot be taken very
seriously. It is clear that the twelve men have been picked in con-

[1] For this problem, which we cannot examine in detail here, cf. the study by W.
Zimmerli, *Das Erkenntnis Gottes nach dem Buch Ezechiel*, Zurich 1954 (*Gesammelte Auf-
sätze*, Munich 1963, pp. 41–119), esp. pp. 34, 74ff.

nection with the twelve stones in the following chapter, where, however, we find two themes in uneasy combination: that of the twelve
stones in the river bed, which is fragmentary, and that of the twelve
columns of the sanctuary. [13] This verse announces what is going to
happen: 'the waters of the Jordan shall be divided' (*krt*, 'to cut', in the
niphal here) and 'will stop in a single heap' ('*md*, 'stop' – v.t. and v.i.,
but originally, 'stand still'). Logically, there is some confusion between
waters which divide and those which stop, but we find the same in
Exod. 14.21b (where, however, the root employed is *bqʻ*), where the
waters 'part' or 'divide', and in Exod. 14.22b, where they stay 'like a
wall' (*ḥōmāh*), while the same term as in Joshua is employed in Exod.
15.8c: *nēd*, 'heap'. Thus the terminology is not absolutely alike, but
the fundamental conception is the same, apart from certain adapta-
tions to the new geographical setting, where the miracle of the Red
Sea is realized once again in the present in the cult. Thus, since the
pattern is exactly the same as that of the crossing of the Red Sea, it is
preferable to refer to the commentary on Exod. 14–15 for the literary
problems which may arise with regard to certain incoherences or contradictions.

(*b*) *The miracle of the waters* (*3.14–16a*)

[14–16] This miracle, equivalent in its external features to that of
the Red Sea (Exod. 14–15), is adapted here to the situation of the
sanctuary of Gilgal, which is not that of a gulf in the sea or a lake, but
that of a river. The translation seeks to emphasize both the miraculous
nature of the event and its parallelism with that of the Exodus. With
regard to the miracle itself, if it had taken place at a period when the
river was at its lowest, the ford would have been passable without any
special device, because the stream is reduced at such a time to a narrow trickle of water; the same phenomenon can also be observed after
a 'dry' winter, that is, when there has been no snow on the mountains,
and the river is reduced to a very low level. But the tradition goes out
of its way to point out that we are at the beginning of the second week
of Nisan (March–April), in the framework of the Passover calendar,
and that this spring was normal from the point of view of the level of
the waters. Thus the river was overflowing because of the melting of
the snow, principally upon Hermon (v.15). If LXX is not always
clear here, it, too, evidently intends to stress the fact that it was the
time of the first harvest, as MT confirms.

The geographical aspect of the miracle is most interesting. The waters stopped near a locality called *'ādām* (elsewhere *'ᵃdāmāh*, cf. a biblical concordance), the present day *tell ed-dāmiye*, which has preserved the ancient name (201–167), at the junction of the Yabbok (nowadays *nahr ez-zerqā*) and the Jordan, near the bridge on the road for heavy lorries from *nāblus* to *es-salṭ*.[1]

Thus the miracle proper took place several kilometres north of Jericho and Gilgal, where only its effects were seen.[2] We owe to Garstang a complete explanation of the natural factors which might lie behind the description of the miracle.[3] On the night of 7–8 December 1267, according to a contemporary Arab chronicler, the high banks of the Jordan, which in this region runs deep down between two walls of very soft limestone rock, gave way, forming a natural dam which succeeded in holding back the water for about 16 hours, while the waters downstream disappeared into the Dead Sea. The phenomenon was repeated in 1906, and during the serious earthquake of 11 July 1927 (cf. Table *XXV*, 1 and *III*), when the waters were held back for 21 hours and 30 minutes. Earthquakes are relatively frequent in the region of Syria and Palestine, and occur at least once a generation. Naturally the phenomenon is of short duration, because the waters very quickly succeed in cutting out a bed.

Thus it is perfectly logical that in the representation of the miracle of the Red Sea as a present event, in the cult of the sanctuary of Jericho, this phenomenon should have been chosen as an illustration, and should have permitted the historicization of the miracle. The latter process takes nothing away from the miracle itself, which is reduced neither to a normal phenomenon nor to a 'routine', but on the contrary is effectively given a setting in history, outside the whole mythical sphere.

We do not know the exact site of the other locality mentioned. According to I Kings 4.12; 7.46, *ṣārᵉtān* must be somewhere in the region of Succoth, and in any case north of Adam, and near the river, without it being possible to say exactly where. That is why the location given in the *Westminster Atlas* or in Grollenberg's atlas (which place Zarethan respectively rather less than 20 km north of Adam or about

[1] Cf. G. E. Wright and F. V. Filson, *The Westminster Historical Atlas to the Bible*, Philadelphia and London ²1946, map IX; L. H. Grollenberg, *Atlas of the Bible*, London 1956, maps 11, 14.

[2] Cf. for the geographical problems the commentaries of Baldi, p. 34, and Noth, pp. 36ff.

[3] J. Garstang, *Comm.*, p. 136; cf. also F. M. Abel, *Géographie de la Palestine*, I, Paris 1933, p. 481; Baldi, p. 35; Noth, p. 37.

10 km wsw of Adam) are somewhat questionable; moreover, they assume the phenomenon was on an absurd scale. For these reasons, Zarethan has been identified until recently with the present-day *qarn ṣarṭabe* (194–167), which is exactly opposite *ed-dāmiye*. This is the Hellenistic Alexandrium[1] and the Sartaba of the Talmud,[2] but here the main difficulty is that in these places there have been no archaeological discoveries earlier than the Hellenistic period. Glueck has also proposed a point further north, east of the Jordan (204–186), which is given in the *Westminster Atlas*: *tell es-saʿīdīye*;[3] Baldi and Noth agree with Glueck but reject any correction of the text. The reading Zarethan has also been disputed; cf. the two variants in LXX. The two names that occur there are so far outside the geographical setting of our text (we know of two places called Kiriathaim, one in northern Galilee and the other in Moab) that they are impossible. The same remark is true of the conjectures of Albright and Glueck of which we spoke.

In the cultic representation of the event, which we can reconstitute only with the aid of a number of indications in the text, it seems that the crossing of the Jordan was no longer carried out physically: the sporadic nature of the natural phenomenon, which in any case depended upon the time of the flood, made this impossible. The procession probably started from Gilgal; the priests, followed by the people at a respectful distance, touched the water with their feet and then came back up to the point which they had left.[4] This is why the Jordan narrative has remained within its original limits, without undergoing the re-elaborations or the amplifications from one source to another that are found in the case of the Red Sea narrative. By comparison with the miracle in Exodus, that celebrated on the Jordan has maintained several of the more ancient elements, such as the connection with natural causes (in Exod. 14.21b J we have only a brief mention of the east wind, whereas the later recasting, Exod. 14.21a–22b P, makes the waters part, allow Israel to cross and rush back over their pursuers).

The Deuteronomic redactor has preserved with hardly any alteration the original components in so far as they were in full accord with his own message. Just as Deutero-Isaiah (cf. Isa. 40.3; 41.17; 43.2, 16;

---

[1] *Westminster Atlas*, map IX, c-4.

[2] A view also defended by E. Dhorme, *Comm.*

[3] *Westminster Atlas*, loc. cit. Cf. recently J. B. Pritchard, *RB* 72, 1965, pp. 257–62; his excavations seem to confirm this identification.

[4] A view accepted by E. Vogt, loc. cit., p. 142; F. Langlamet, op. cit., p. 18.

51.10; etc.) likes to refer often to the miracles of the Exodus to picture the glorious return of the exiles into their homeland, the Deuteronomic preacher of the liberation recalls the celebration of this event at Gilgal near the Jordan and makes use of the liturgy for his own message.

(c) *The crossing of the river* (*3.16b–17; 4.10–11, 14–18*)

As in the case of the celebration of the crossing of the Red Sea, the crossing of the Jordan constitutes one of the principal elements of the cultic act, closely related to the miracle of the waters. The participants felt themselves completely identified with their ancestors and in communion with them by virtue of the dramatic side of this liturgy. We are no longer in a position to determine exactly what took place in the cult celebrating the crossing, but it seems that at a certain moment those who carried the ark stopped and that the people, who had hitherto kept a respectful distance from the ark (cf. 3.4), could then walk in front of the ark. Ritually, the scene took place 'in the midst of the Jordan', held back upstream by the miracle. For the ancient liturgy, the presence of the ark in the bed of the river was the effective cause of the miracle. Thus the people were so to speak 'reviewed' by the ancient palladium; in it dwelt God himself, who had chosen this sign of his presence in the midst of the people. God had chosen to accompany his community every year in this celebration, thus establishing an uninterrupted link with past generations. In the same way Dtr, by means of a reference in 3.7 and 4.14, seeks to emphasize the historical continuity between the primitive period and the present time within the sacred history.

Our text presents a number of confusions: in 4.11 all seem to have crossed the river; in 4.15ff. the priests still have to come up out of the bed of the river. We have seen that LXX tries to harmonize the two recensions (by a deliberate correction of the text it substitutes the 'stones' for the 'priests'), but this is a facile solution which cannot be accepted. Equally improbable is the solution proposed by Fernández and followed by Baldi, according to which the priests preceded the people all the way from Gilgal but not during the crossing of the river. In fact, as Hertzberg has rightly noted, the situation is somewhat reminiscent of a harmony of the gospels, where material which is completely parallel has been re-united but where the joins are often quite obvious.

Once again, the accent is placed on the astonishment of the believer at the sight of the mighty acts of God: God acted with power in the past, and also was always present when his people recounted in the cult his ancient and marvellous works. On this basis, Dtr, like other prophetic writers, could set about his work of the spiritual re-edification of his people, whose situation was after all so similar to that of their nomad ancestors on the point of undertaking an enterprise which was to succeed completely. In this way he gives a concrete historical basis for the fulfilment of the ancient promises.

(d) The twelve stones (4.1–9)

From the beginning of ch. 4 it is possible to distinguish with reasonable certainty the elements of two parallel recensions, which share the theme of twelve stones, and give an aetiological explanation of them to the descendants of the heroes of the past. In the first case, we have twelve pillars set up at Gilgal, on the western bank of the river, after the crossing (4.1–3, 6–8a, b, 20; cf. 3.16c–17). In the second case, we have stones taken from the eastern bank of the Jordan and put into the stream at the point where the priests passed with the ark (4.4–5, 8a, 9, 15–19, 21–24; cf. 3.12). Verses 10–12 seem to be common to the two recensions, but follow the second rather than the first. Attempts at harmonization (usually made by conservative Catholic writers and by Kaufmann) do not provide a more satisfactory solution than the division of the fragments proposed above, but, on the contrary, make an already complex situation more complicated still.

[4.1–9] The confusion of the text here, which results from the failure of an attempt to harmonize two traditions which are very different, although they share the common theme of the twelve stones, makes any more thorough study impossible. The best-preserved tradition seems to be that of the twelve stones set up in the sanctuary. This is not surprising, because these stones could not be overlooked, whereas the stones set down in the river could easily remain unnoticed, depending upon the level of the water and how clear it was. This second tradition now appears in an incomplete form, to the point that the redactor and unifier of the history no longer had any clear idea of what really happened. Hertzberg would regard this tradition as one of the supplementary and secondary devotions which are always found around places of pilgrimage. What is certain is that these two elements are typical local elements, and that the narrative here departs from the Exodus and the Passover, for these aetiologies are closely linked with the river and the sanctuary and must go back behind the combining of the narrative with Israel's confession of faith. The insistence on the number twelve makes it probable that there is a primitive connection between the sanctuary and the amphictyony which is independent of the ancient confession of faith. No doubt the 'twelve tribes' celebrated there, as soon as they were organized in an amphictyony, a commemoration of the crossing of the river which was still independent of the sacred history. This would obviously take us back to a very early period, probably before the monarchy.

Later, as the ritual developed, the number twelve very quickly became a means for those who took part in the amphictyonic cult to make the past a present reality. This cult recalled what God had done for each of the groups who saw themselves represented first of all by the pillars in the sanctuary, and in the second place by the stones in the river. Finally, in the Deuteronomic preaching, the presence of the pillars and stones became the signs of a promise which was capable of defying the passage of time, a promise already fulfilled in the distant past and which was going to be carried out once again, after having been suspended for a time by the judgment. Thus this promise was still a present reality for the exiles, and was an incentive to them to prepare for the return. Historical and liturgical interest now take a second place, and the emphasis is placed on the equivalence between the present Israel, scattered and defeated, and the Israel of the past, both now united both by their weakness and by the strength which comes from the eternal promises of God, the signs of which are evident.

[6-7] See after vv. 20ff.

(e) The crossing of the groups from the east of the Jordan (4.12-13)

[12] The crossing of the groups from the east of the Jordan constitutes a brief interlude which takes up 1.12-15, where the order carried out here is given. Thus we seem to have an addition to the work of Dtr, to which ch. 1 belongs, with the aim of emphasizing that the whole of Israel took part in the conquest. But one cannot exclude the possibility of participation by representatives of tribes east of the Jordan in the Gilgal cult, with a special ritual function (cf. ch. 22). In any case, it is probable that [13] already belonged to the ritual, perhaps in fact in connection with the participation in it of the tribes of the east of the Jordan. Noth points out that the sudden mention of their military intentions (13b: '. . . for battle') is in contrast to the context and gives the impression of representing an older and independent element in the tradition. This passage is echoed in the

affirmation of 24.11, which explicitly states: 'The men of Jericho fought against you'. Thus originally the passage was separate from its present context, into which it was incorporated in circumstances about which we know nothing, and belongs rather to the tradition of ch. 2, which records the preparation for the siege of Jericho. Consequently, it is also separate from the context of Josh. 6 (against Noth, who would separate the present chapters from both 2 and 6, but without giving reasons). Thus one may grant, at least as a working hypothesis, to explain the apparent incoherence of this military expedition, that we have here a fragment of a very ancient tradition. The preparations in Josh. 2 and the allusion to 24.11 bear witness to this, as both talk of a military siege of Jericho, no doubt as a reprisal for an attack by the inhabitants of that region against the invaders (24.11 clearly alludes to this). Verse 13 survived and reappears in a liturgical context from which every trace of the battle has disappeared, even though something of the ancient spirit of the holy war may remain. Finally, for the Deuteronomic editor, the passage has been totally dedramatized and reduced to a statistical fact referring to tribes east of the Jordan who crossed the river, and to their intentions. It is probable that before the rehistoricization of the episode by Dtr, there was a time when the tribes from the east of the Jordan took an effective part in the ritual, but we know too little about this to be able to propose anything except a pure hypothesis. Fundamentally, all that interests Dtr is to make a present reality of the ancient ritual, in which there was no place for the bravery and cunning of men, but only for the mighty acts of God.

(*f*) *The arrival at Gilgal (4.19–5.1)*

In [19] we have the second chronological indication (for the first, cf. 1.11 and 3.2a), which is more precise than the former: 10 Nisan. This is an important stage in the spring feast at Gilgal, when celebration of the Exodus as a present reality came to be held. Does it belong to the ancient ritual or to the Deuteronomic redaction? It is difficult to say. Noth prefers the second alternative and seems to be right, for what is recorded here forms part of the week of preparation for the Passover, which, as we have seen, is a specifically Deuteronomic preoccupation. This apart, there is nothing against the attribution of this element to the ancient ritual.

[20–23] As in vv. 6–7, which we have not considered until now because their content is identical with the present verses, we have an explicit reference to a question posed by the sons of those who in the past had undergone the original experience – in reality, that is, a question which those taking part in the Gilgal cult would put to the celebrants at a particular moment: 'What do these stones mean?' For a very long time, the sight of the stones in the river, in the middle of the ford, and of the twelve pillars in the sanctuary, was the occasion of a liturgical dialogue between the community taking part in the celebration and the priests, who not only carried out the ritual but were also the guardians of the ancient tradition. The version in vv. 20–23 (the first recension) is also the one which introduces an explicit reference to the miracle of the Red Sea (v. 23), relating it to the ἱερὸς λόγος of the Gilgal sanctuary. In the present state of the text, this reference is amplified by [24], which extends the scope of the event to the whole known universe, setting it free from its local limitations. What was valid 'then' is proclaimed to be still valid 'today', at a time when the people are groaning in exile and believe that the promises and miracles of God belong to the past, with no connection to the present miserable reality. This cosmic dimension is also found in the Servant Songs of Deutero–Isaiah, but there the subject is dealt with in relation to the salvation of the nations (42.6; 49.6). The recognition of God by the heathen nations has an automatic effect on the people of God (and this is why MT should be retained in spite of the change of person), still astounded as they are by the terrifying acts of Yahweh. The Deuteronomic redactor, to whom this verse is due, is here developing a concept similar to that of Paul in Rom. 11.11–15, where the favourable reaction of the heathen to the preaching of the gospel is destined to bring about, if only by jealousy, the conversion of Israel.

[5.1] The ancient liturgy to which this verse belongs could conceive of only one immediate reaction: that of the nations who have heard of the miracle and who tremble. This aspect must have found expression in the liturgy itself; it is also highly appropriate to the Deuteronomic preaching, addressed to a people who had been conquered by nations who were in part the same as those mentioned here, and who no longer dared to hope for salvation.

CHAPTER 5.2–9

The Circumcision at Gilgal

5 [2]At that time the LORD said to Joshua, 'Make yourself (or 'get yourself') stone knives and *begin again to* (LXX 'sit down to') circumcise the people of Israel *the second time.*' [3]So Joshua made stone knives, and circumcised the people of Israel on the 'Hill of the Foreskins'.

MT, V, Syr, T	LXX
[4]*And this is the reason why Joshua circumcised them: all the people who came out of Egypt (the males, all the men of war) had died in the wilderness on the way after they had come out of Egypt.*	[4]Joshua purified the Israelites in this way: all who were born on the way, all those who were uncircumcised amongst those who came out of Egypt,
[5]*Though of course all the people who came out had been circumcised, yet all the people that were born in the wilderness on the way after they had come out of Egypt had not been circumcised.*	[5]all those Joshua circumcised. For Israel had wandered 42 years through the Madbaritide (sic!) desert.
[6]*For the people of Israel walked forty years in the wilderness, till all the nation, the men of war that came forth out of Egypt, perished, because they did not hearken to the voice of the LORD.*	[6]That is why most of them were uncircumcised, of the warriors, those who came out of Egypt, who had disobeyed the commandments of God.

To them the LORD swore that he would not let them see the land which the LORD had sworn to their fathers to give us, a land flowing with milk and honey. [7]*So he raised their children in their stead, and them Joshua circumcised; for they were uncircumcised, because they had not been circumcised on the way.* [8]When the circumcising of all the nation was done, they remained in their places in the camp till they were healed. [9]And the LORD said to Joshua, 'This day I have rolled away the reproach of Egypt from you.' And so the name of that place is called Gilgal to this day.

Bibliography: W. Rudolph, *Der 'Elohist'* . . ., pp. 178–82; F. Sierksma, 'Quelques remarques sur la circoncision en Israël', *OTS* IX, 1962, pp.

136–39, esp. pp. 141ff. (a study containing irrelevant psychoanalytical observations); G. Posener, *Dictionnaire de la civilisation égyptienne*, Paris 1959, p. 56b–c; F. R. Lehmann and K. Galling, 'Beschneidung', *RGG*[3] I, 1957, cols. 1090f.; W. Bunte, id., *BHH* I, 1962, cols. 223–35; Auzou, pp. 79ff.

[5.2] Note the stereotyped character of the formula which links this passage to the preceding one: 'At that time . . .'. *šūb* . . . *šēnīt* does not seem to have much meaning here: 'Begin again . . . the second time'; this double expression is lacking in V but is found in T and Syr, while LXX has καθίσας (cf. VL, *sedens*), that is, *šēb*, 'sit down'. Hertzberg prefers this latter reading because the Egyptian ritual of circumcision required the operator to be seated (cf. an example in *ANEP*, no. 629). This was a very ancient ritual provision which soon was no longer understood and therefore altered (in a text without *scriptio plena* both words are written *šb*). Abel, on the other hand, would omit the verb and keep 'the second time'. Noth considers that both terms are redactional, which would explain the incoherence. After *ṣurīm* LXX adds ἐκ πέτρας ἀκροτόμου, a detail which conveys nothing. *mōl*: an imperative formed as for double *ʿayin* verbs, whereas it ought to follow the pattern of *ʿayin yod* and *ʿayin waw* verbs; but exchanges between these two classes of verbs are frequent. [3] *lō* is lacking in all the translations but causes no difficulty. It could be a *lamed* of emphasis, in which case the translation would be: 'Joshua did make stone knives . . .' *ʾel gibʿat*: LXX has ἐπὶ τοῦ καλουμένου τόπου, while in T we read *bgbʿt wqrʾ lyh . . . gbʿt*; this longer phrase is evidently meant as a preparation for the aetiological reference in v. 9. [4–6] The text of LXX is substantially different, so that in the translation we give it separately, in another column. For MT the situation is as follows: those who had fled out of Egypt were circumcised, the generation born in the desert was not, and Joshua wished to remedy this. For LXX, on the contrary, there were also uncircumcised persons amongst those who came out of Egypt, and this was their sin, but the way in which Joshua remedies this wrong is not clear. [5] Note *kī* in the sense 'though of course'. [6] Note *ʾašer* in the sense 'because'. Instead of 40, LXX has 42, for no apparent reason; chronological differences are common in any case between the different translations and recensions.

[2–3] The aetiology of the place name, 'Hill of the Foreskins', is intimately connected with this narrative and with the celebration of the circumcision and the Passover at Gilgal. It seems unlikely to suppose that the people could have believed the hill to have been formed by the piling up of discarded foreskins in the course of the centuries! The name refers rather to the rite, localized on a particular hill in the neighbourhood, and it is of little importance whether the localization is artificial or not. In any case, could there not have been near the sanctuary of Gilgal a place where the circumcisions were carried out? For a possible site, cf. Baldi. If the place actually existed, it may have been marked by the presence on the ground of a large number of dressed flints, as Dhorme points out. At the present moment, the narrative is included in the ceremonial of the feast at Gilgal and almost certainly refers to the practice of circumcising those who had not yet been circumcised before admitting them to the celebration of the Passover.

We cannot go into the inextricable problem of circumcision here. All that need be said is that during the first half of the first millennium BC, circumcision was practised amongst all West Semitic people (cf. Jer. 9.24ff.), whereas during the second half of the second millennium the situation was not so uniform: the Megiddo ivories (*ANEP*, no. 332) in fact show us two circumcised prisoners, whereas nothing of this kind is found at Ugarit. In Egypt, circumcision was a regular practice, particularly in the upper classes, but was not an obligatory custom and formed an initiation rite at puberty. On the other hand, it was not practised in Mesopotamia nor amongst the Philistines, who were probably Indo-European in origin, and the OT has preserved the memory of this (cf. Judg. 14.3 || 15.18; I Sam. 17.26; 18.25ff.; 31.4 || 1 Chron. 10.4; II Sam. 1.20, etc.). Thus the reference to the reproach of Egypt presents certain difficulties to which we shall return (v.9). In Israel, circumcision was soon brought forward to early infancy (Exod. 4.24–26), which removed all connections with the rites of puberty; but our passage is one of the numerous traces of a circumcision at the age of adulthood, where there is a clear connection with Egyptian practice, if we read with the LXX that the person who carried out the rite sat.

The word 'covenant' does not once occur in this passage, and yet we are at the very heart of the subject, because circumcision was the visible sign of the covenant. MT tries to harmonize this rite with that described in Gen. 17, which LXX does not attempt to do, probably not without some motive. By its incorporation into the ideology of the covenant, this rite, which amongst other nations was no more than an initiation rite, became in Israel an act of decision for Yahweh, and was repeated from one generation to another, always bearing this significance. For Dtr, who was preaching to the exiles, the act, together with other rites and practices such as the strict observance of the sabbath and the dietary laws, was one of the fundamental elements of the confession of faith appropriate to Israel in a foreign

milieu, either indifferent or hostile. At the end of the exile this decision of faith was to replace a purely ethnic attachment to the community of Yahweh (cf. Isa. 56.1–8).

In the present case, the explanation given of the circumcision of
the whole people seems to be incidental. Verses 5ff. imply that the
rite was not possible throughout the journey (that is, it is an attempt
to justify the fact that the rite was not carried out on infants). But the
primitive ritual certainly supposed that amongst those who came to
Gilgal there would be families living far from the great cultic centres
(one would think particularly of those who lived in the region east of
the Jordan), amongst whom the circumcision of children would not
always have taken place at the prescribed time. Thus there was an
opportunity of carrying the rite out before the family participated in
the public celebration of the Passover. In this way, the ancient ritual
offered Dtr a number of very useful themes for his preaching, such as
that of the awareness of Israel's special vocation, or that of the fulfilment of the divine promises of the covenant even in a foreign country.

The instrument used in the rite is also very ancient: this flint knife
in fact carries us back to the Stone Age. As Hertzberg observes, the
existence of such a practice in the Bronze Age, like the custom of setting up altars of undressed stone or of earth (Exod. 20.24), can be explained by a preference for materials in the raw state; one might say
as they left the hands of the Creator.

[4–7] These verses consist of a historical and apologetic digression
about the reasons why the people had not previously been circumcised
and why they had to be at the moment when they entered the holy
land. But it will be noted that amongst the reasons given, that of
taking part in the Passover is not mentioned, so that our text, in its
most ancient form, and even before it came to be incorporated in the
ritual of Gilgal, was either written in ignorance of the condition required by Exod. 12, or had no link with the Passover. The chosen
explanation is long, complicated and artificial, and its chronology assumes that the various themes which form the ancient confession of
faith have already been drawn together. None of this, however, provides a satisfactory answer to the question why the generation who
travelled through the wilderness could not have been circumcised.
The explanation given by LXX is even more improbable. Perhaps at
an ancient date, before the narrative was incorporated into the Gilgal liturgy, there existed another explanation which was more mythical and less closely attached to the history of salvation, the present

explanation being intended to replace it. This is probable, because the place name is a proof of the antiquity of the practice of this ritual act in this region. The 'land flowing with milk and honey' is the almost proverbial definition of Palestine as seen by a nomad, or a semi-nomad aspiring toward a settled life. Moreover, Caanan, before millennia of exploitation took their effect, was a really rich country, although not as rich as Egypt or Mesopotamia.

[8–9] give us a second aetiology, that of the name of Gilgal. This name is derived from the root *gll*, to roll, turn over. Thus in this place Yahweh is supposed to have 'rolled away' the reproach of Egypt, which is why the place is called 'rolling'. Now we saw that the fact that the Israelites were not circumcised cannot be explained by Egyptian practice, as mediaeval Jewish exegesis usually asserted (e.g. Qimḥi). Hertzberg, therefore, explains the reproach of Egypt as the insult which Israel received from the Egyptians because of their own uncircumcision. But the problem remains unresolved. Certainly etymological aetiology is one of the kinds of aetiology which is of the least historical value, and it would not be surprising if this comment recalls the assumption of a later commentator that in Egypt circumcision was not practised (from whence it passed to mediaeval Jewish exegesis). K. Galling[1] has proposed another solution: 'to roll away the reproach of Egypt', in his view, refers in fact to a rite similar to that described in Josh. 24.23–24 (cf. the commentary on this passage) and Gen. 35.1ff.: the putting away of foreign gods, applied here to whole groups and sealed by the circumcision. Although we do not think that the solution can be accepted, it has at least the merit of explaining a text which would otherwise remain obscure.

[1] K. Galling, 'Das Gemeindegesetz in Deuteronomium 23', *Festschrift für Alfred Bertholet*, Tübingen 1950, pp. 176–91, esp. p. 190.

CHAPTER 5.10–12

The Celebration of the Passover at Gilgal

5 ¹⁰The people of Israel were encamped in Gilgal and they kept the passover *on the fourteenth day of the* [first] *month* at evening in the plains of Jericho. ¹¹And [on the morrow after the passover] *on that very day*, they ate of the produce of the land, unleavened cakes and parched grain. ¹²And the manna ceased on the morrow (or: that day), when they ate of the produce of the land; and the people of Israel had manna no more, but ate of the fruit of the land of Canaan that year.

Bibliography: J. Jeremias, *Die Passahfeier der Samaritaner*, BZAW 59, Berlin 1932; L. Rost, 'Weidewechsel und altisraelitischer Festkalender', *ZDPV* 66, 1943, pp. 205–26 (*Das Kleine Credo*, Heidelberg 1965, pp. 101–11); E. Kutsch, 'Erwägungen zur Geschichte der Passafeier und des Massotfestes', *ZTK* 55, 1958, pp. 1–35, esp. pp. 20f.; H. J. Kraus, 'Zur Geschichte des Passah-Massot-Festes im Alten Testament', *EvTh* 18, 1958, pp. 47–67, esp. pp. 50–8; H. Haag, 'Pâque', *SDB* VI, 1960, cols. 1120–49, esp. 1132; R. de Vaux, *Studies in Old Testament Sacrifice*, Cardiff 1964, pp. 10f.; G. Fohrer, *Überlieferung und Geschichte des Exodus*, BZAW 91, Berlin 1964, pp. 93f.

[10] The name of Gilgal is lacking in LXX, but is found in the other versions. It will be noted that the giving of two place-names is superfluous: either 'Gilgal' or 'the plains of Jericho'. The latter is the *lectio difficilior*. After *pesaḥ*, Syr and some Hebrew MSS add *bārīšōn* = 'in the first month'. [11] *mimmāḥᵃrat happesaḥ* is lacking in LXX; MT and the other versions had in mind two ritual meals: on the day of the Passover nothing but the unleavened cakes and the parched grain, and the produce of the land after the Passover. LXX understood it as follows: 'And they ate of the produce of the land: unleavened cakes and parched grain, on that day.' It would therefore be hazardous to refer to this rite to date a text which has under-gone too much alteration to allow such deductions. [12] LXX replaces *mimmāḥᵃrat* by ἐν ταυτῇ τῇ ἡμέρᾳ . . . μετὰ τὸ βεβρωκέναι αὐτούς.

In the liturgical context supposed here, the carrying out of the rite of circumcision on all the uncircumcised before the celebration of the

Passover is quite logical. In Exod. 12, it is assumed that all the participants are circumcised (v. 44). Circumcision is the outward bodily sign
which bears witness before all of one's membership of the covenant,
and this is an indispensable condition for taking part in the Israelite
solemnity of the Passover, rather as in the Christian church baptism
is a condition for taking part in the eucharist. Moreover, both rites
recall the liberation that has come about through God's mighty acts
in the past.

[10] The fourteenth day of the first month (that is, the month
March–April in the spring reckoning) is the first full moon of the
year. The Passover has always been celebrated at this date, even
though this was not explicity specified before Deuteronomy (Deut.
16) and the requirement is not found in the oldest sources, JE. The
present passage is found in a Deuteronomic context, and we have
seen above (cf. the commentary on 4.19) that the chronological indications of chs. 3–5 probably belong to this source and are not primitive: that is, it is the Deuteronomic redaction which has the celebration of the Passover preceded by a preparatory week (3.2–4). The
mention of the date and the combination of the Passover and the
unleavened bread, problematic because of the state of the text, do
not allow us to place a late dating on this text, even if it is admitted
to be part of the Deuteronomic redaction (cf. Kraus and De Vaux,
against Kutsch and Fohrer). This is the only place other than in the
centralization of the cult carried out by Josiah, that we are present at
a *public* celebration of the festival, and the account of the reform of
Josiah does not omit to comment on this (II Kings 23.21ff.; cf.
Deut. 16.1ff.). There is, in fact, no doubt, according to Kraus, that
the reference of II Kings 23 to the period of the Judges owes its
existence to a public festival celebrated at Gilgal until the period of
the Judges and then abandoned for reasons of which we are ignorant,
or else rejected by orthodox theology because of the contaminating
elements which had been introduced into it. Thus we continue to
regard this ceremony as an ancient one, although we recognize that
the passage is due to a late redaction. Morevoer, it is not necessary to
follow Noth in regarding the date itself as Deuteronomic, because
there is nothing elsewhere to suggest that the Passover was ever celebrated at a different date.

The mention of the 'plains of Jericho' seems to recall the practice
of celebrating the festival outside the sanctuary, which is in line with
what was stated above. There is clear evidence of this usage as early

as Exod. 5, where we find Moses asking Pharaoh to let the people go and hold a feast 'in the wilderness'. But apart from the difficult problem of knowing which of the two traditions is the older (everything suggests that the Joshua tradition is the older), the original festival here was probably the celebration of a move to a new pasture in the spring, of 'transhumance' (Rost), and was a memory of the nomad period amongst a settled population, later completely swallowed up by the feast of the Passover. In the setting of the Gilgal sanctuary, this archaic aspect of the feast was no doubt preserved for a long period, and even today the Samaritans maintain the custom of celebrating the Passover camping on Gerizim on the edges of the holy place, outside their dwellings in Nablus.

[11] The pastoral festival has been amalgamated with the agricultural celebration of the first fruits of the harvest by the eating of unleavened bread and roasted barley, the mention of the *qālūy* here being unique. However, the text does not make the course of events very clear: in MT the unleavened loaves, etc., are for the Passover and the products of the land for the days that follow; for LXX, on the contrary, the unleavened bread, etc., are the products of the land. MT probably preserves an ancient usage which was found only in the locality, and differed from the current practice reflected in LXX. The link between the Passover and the unleavened bread, however, is a very ancient one, even if it did not always exist. It is found as early as the J passages of Exod. 12, but is secondary in the festivals themselves. Here there is still an awareness of the ancient distinction, whereas in Exod. 12 (J), the two rites are already linked with the sacred history of the Exodus. For we are told that the unleavened bread and the grain belonged to the 'products of the earth', that is, that they are the first fruits of the holy land, the first element of the carrying out of the divine promise. The parched grain is no doubt an element peculiar to Gilgal. Hertzberg remarks: 'the semi-nomad becomes a peasant, but the God who has brought this about remains the same'.

[12] The gift of manna ceases automatically with the possibility of living by the products of the country itself. This tangible sign of divine providence (Exod. 16) no longer has any purpose, and so we pass from one period of the sacred history to the next. The miraculous help given in the wilderness is replaced by the equally great miracle which is constantly experienced anew by the devout Israelite (cf. Hos. 2), the spring harvest. Free of the fears to which the Canaanite

was subject because of the weakness and unreliability of his gods, the Israelite, as long as he does not allow himself to drift into syncretism but remains determined to rely upon his own tradition, can look forward with assurance, without making a divinity of nature and without fearing it.

Similarly, in the Deuteronomic preaching the celebration of the first Passover in the holy land was a source of confident hope: everything at Gilgal bore witness to God's faithfulness to the ancient promises, and Dtr, too, could call on this faithfulness in his preaching.

CHAPTER 5.13–15

The Appearance of the Commander of the Army of Yahweh

5 [13]When Joshua was $\left\{ \begin{array}{l} \text{in} \\ \text{in the region of} \\ \text{on the outskirts of} \end{array} \right\}$ Jericho, he lifted up his eyes and looked, and behold, a man stood before him with his drawn sword in his hand; and Joshua went to him and said to him, 'Are you for us, or for our adversaries?' [14]And he said, $\left\{ \begin{array}{l} \text{'No;} \\ \text{'Indeed;} \end{array} \right\}$ but because I am commander of the army of the LORD, I have now come . . .' And Joshua fell on his face to the earth and gave him worship, and said to him, 'What does my lord bid his servant?' [15]And the commander of the LORD's army said to Joshua, 'Put off your shoes from your feet; for the place where you stand is holy.' And Joshua did so.

Bibliography: H. M. Winer, 'The Conquest Narratives', *JPOS* 9, 1929, pp. 1–26, esp. pp. 3f.; W. Baumgartner, 'Zum Problem des "Jahwe-Engels" ', 1944, in *Zum Alten Testament und seiner Umwelt*, Leiden 1959, pp. 240–46; F. M. Abel, 'Les stratagèmes du livre de Josué', *RB* 56, 1949, pp. 321–31; id., 'L' apparition du Chef de l'armée de Yahveh à Josué', *Miscell. Bibl. et Orient. A. Miller oblata (Stud. Anselmiana* 27–28), Rome 1951, pp. 109–13; L. Rost, 'Engel', *BHH* I, 1962, cols. 410f.; J. A. Soggin, 'La "negazione" in Gios. 5.14', *Bibbia et Oriente* 7, 1965, pp. 75–6.

---

[13] *bīriḥō* is confirmed by LXX and T, while V has *in agro urbis Jericho*, Syr 'in the plain of Jericho' and the Arabic version 'in the environs

of Jericho'. The three latter versions obviously present a more plausible version in the present historical and geographical setting, and the two former a reading which is at once a *lectio brevior et difficilior*. Noth, Abel and most commentators translate 'in the environment of Jericho', and Noth points out that this is how the text is understood in its present context, but that originally it must have referred to an event which took place *within* the city and not near it (Gressmann accepts this reading, taking it literally and seeing in it originally a pilgrimage by Joshua to the local sanctuary of Baal or Astarte; but there is nothing to prove this). [14] The *lō'* (which LXX and Syr read wrongly as *lō*, because they did not expect a negative reply, but a clear affirmative) cannot refer to the first part of the question, which calls for an affirmative reply; thus either it refers to the second half (in which case the style is clumsy, cf. the solution of LXX and Syr) or else it refers equally to the first half and is probably not a negation but an emphatic *lāmed* = 'indeed'. *wayyištāhū*, root *ḥwh*, a causative in *šin* (*šap* ʿ*ēl*) with an intrusive *taw*, one of the rare forms present with certainty in the OT, which (as is well known) only has the causative in *h-*. For this problem cf. *B-M* § 72d. Note the interruption of the sentence in the middle of the verse. [15] The phrase is identical with that in Exod. 3.5. The second part of the verse is lacking in LXX.

[13] The apparition of the commander of the army of Yahweh takes place literally 'in Jericho' and, according to three translations, in the outskirts of the city. But the purpose of these translations was to eliminate or at least to reduce the confusion arising from the mention of a place situated inside a city which the Israelite troops still have to conquer. In all probability, this passage originally belonged to the tradition which includes ch. 2, 6.22ff. and 24.11, which spoke of a campaign carried out against the city of Jericho, which was finally conquered by a ruse. In this case Joshua could in fact have been inside the city, after its conquest and destruction, in order to take stock of what had been conquered (which is why he 'lifted up his eyes'), perhaps on the ruins of the sanctuary (cf. the *māqōm* of v. 15: this word often has the meaning 'holy place', a meaning which persists in the corresponding Arabic term *maqām*). In the ritual, once the story of the military conquest of Jericho had been eliminated, and replaced by the liturgical narrative of ch. 6, where the only personage worthy of attention is God himself, this passage is retained but altered at the end of v. 14 (although it is not easy to determine at what stage in the tradition the alteration was made) and changed into a favourable prediction for the remainder of the operations. Thus V, Syr and

the Arabic version give the sense required by the present liturgical context, while MT, LXX and T retain the sense of the ancient tradition which had not yet been adapted to the new context of the Gilgal cult.

The angel with the drawn sword appears in the autonomous tradition preserved in II Sam. 24, according to which, in the parallel passage in I Chron. 21.16, the destroying angel appears with a drawn sword in his hand (cf. also II Kings 19.35 and parallels, where, however, the sword is not mentioned). Joshua, moreover, is well aware of the angel's role as a destroyer, and he is concerned to know why the angel has been sent.

[14] The angel's reply is affirmative with regard to the first half of the question, and consequently implicitly negative with regard to the second half. The commander of the army of Yahweh can only declare himself to be favourable to the people of the promise. We cannot deal here with the question of the 'army of Yahweh'. We need only recall that twice, in the ancient traditions, the heavenly bodies submit to the divine will and fight on behalf of the people of God: Josh. 10.12–13a and Judg. 5.20. The theme of the angels and the army of Yahweh reappears in Judaism, and we have examples in Dan. 9–10, but in a completely different ideological context. The conclusion of the text is lacking: the angel seems to have come to announce something to Joshua, but the message does not follow. We might perhaps translate: 'It is because I am the commander of the army of the LORD that I have come', but this is not very convincing.

Joshua's reaction is what one normally finds in such a case and we shall not dwell on it. Note, however, that here, as in other passages which deal with the prehistory of Israel, the angel is not a being distinct from Yahweh, but in a sense is one of his hypostases, to the extent that the worship paid to him is directed to Yahweh himself (cf. Gen. 16.7ff.; Judg. 6.12, 24; 13.22; etc.). For LXX an angel is already a creature distinct from its creator, and consequently to accord it worship is a sin (cf. in the NT, Rev. 19.10; 22.9); here, too, the mention of Joshua's worship is suppressed.

[15] The reply of the angel to Joshua's question is modelled exactly on that given by Yahweh to Moses in Exod. 3.5. Was its function in the liturgy to introduce Yahweh's revelation to Joshua, like the revelation to Moses in Exodus? If something of this sort existed, only a trace remains of the liturgical celebration in which the ancient tradition must have had a part.

CHAPTER 6

The Conquest of Jericho

6 ¹Now Jericho was shut up and barricaded before the people of Israel; none went out, and none came in. ²And the LORD said to Joshua, 'See, I have given into your hand Jericho, with its king and mighty men of valour. ³You shall march around the city, all the men of war going around the city once. Thus shall you do for six days. ⁴And seven priests shall bear seven trumpets of rams' horns before the ark; and on the seventh day you shall march around the city seven times, the priests blowing the trumpets. ⁵And when they make a long blast with the ram's horn, as soon as you hear the sound of the trumpet, then all the people shall shout with a great shout; and the wall of the city will fall down flat, and the people shall go up every man straight before him.' ⁶So Joshua the son of Nun called the priests and said to them, 'Take up the ark of the covenant, and let seven priests bear seven trumpets of rams' horns before the ark of the LORD.' ⁷And he said to the people, 'Go forward; march around the city, and let the armed men pass on before the ark of the LORD.' ⁸And as Joshua was addressing the people, the seven priests bearing the seven trumpets of rams' horns before the LORD went forward, blowing the trumpets, with the ark of the covenant of the LORD following them. ⁹And the armed men went before the priests who blew the trumpets, and the rearguard came after the ark, and as they went the trumpets blew. ¹⁰But Joshua commanded the people, 'You shall not shout or let your voice be heard, neither shall any word go out of your mouth, until the day I bid you shout; then you shall shout.' ¹¹So he caused the ark of the LORD to compass the city, going about it once; and they came into the camp, and spent the night in the camp. ¹²Then Joshua rose early in the morning, and the priests took up the ark of the LORD. ¹³And the seven priests bearing the seven trumpets of rams' horns before the ark of the LORD passed on, blowing the trumpets continually; and the armed men went before them, and the rearguard came after the ark of the LORD, while the trumpets blew continually.¹⁴And the second day they marched around the city once, and returned into the camp. So they did for six days. ¹⁵On the seventh day they rose early at the dawn of day, and marched around the city in the same manner seven times: it was only on that day that they marched around the city seven times.¹⁶And at the seventh time,

when the priests had blown the trumpets, Joshua said to the people, 'Shout; for the LORD has given you the city. [17]And the city and all that is within it shall be devoted to the LORD for destruction; only Rahab the harlot and all who are with her in her house shall live, because she hid the messengers that we sent. [18]But you, keep yourselves from the things devoted to destruction, lest when you have devoted them you take any of the devoted things and make the camp of Israel a thing for destruction, and make it untouchable. [19]But all silver and gold, and vessels of bronze and iron, are sacred to the LORD; they shall go into the treasury of the LORD.' [20]So the people shouted, and the trumpets were blown. As soon as the people heard the sound of the trumpet, the people raised a great shout, and the wall fell down flat, so that the people went up into the city, every man straight before him, and they took the city. [21]Then they utterly destroyed all in the city, both men and women, young and old, oxen, sheep, and asses, with the edge of the sword. [22]And Joshua said to the two men who had spied out the land, 'Go into the harlot's house, and bring out from it the woman, and all who belong to her, as you swore to her.' [23]So the young men who had been spies went in, and brought out Rahab, and her father and mother and brothers and all who belonged to her; and they brought all her kindred, and set them outside the camp of Israel. [24]And they burned the city with fire, and all within it; only the silver and gold, and the vessels of bronze and of iron, they put into the treasury of the house of the LORD. [25]But Rahab the harlot, and her father's household, and all who belonged to her, Joshua saved alive; and she dwelt in Israel to this day, because she hid the messengers whom Joshua sent to spy out Jericho. [26]Joshua laid an oath upon them at that time, saying, 'Cursed before the LORD be the man that rises up and rebuilds this city, Jericho. At the cost of his first-born shall he lay its foundation, and at the cost of his youngest son shall he set up its gates.' [27]So the LORD was with Joshua; and his fame was in all the land.

Bibliography: cf. the works of W. Rudolph (pp. 182–8), J. Dus, J. Maier and J. A. Soggin referred to in the bibliography to ch. 3. For the archaeological problem of Jericho, cf. J. Garstang, 'The Walls of Jericho', *PEFQS*, 1939, pp. 186–96; id., *SDB* III, 1938, cols. 410–14; H. H. Rowley, *From Joseph to Joshua* (index, s.v. 'Jericho'), London 1950; K. M. Kenyon, 'Excavations at Jericho, 1954', *PEQ* 86, 1954, pp. 45–63; W. F. Albright, *Recent Discoveries in Bible Lands*, New York [2]1955, pp. 46ff., 87f.; M. Noth, 'Hat die Bibel doch Recht?', *Festschrift G. Dehn*, Neukirchen 1957, pp. 7–22, esp. pp. 13f.; K. M. Kenyon, *Digging up Jericho*, London 1957, ch. XI; A. Kuschke, 'Jericho', *RGG*[3] III, 1959, col. 591; H. Haag, 'Jericho', *LTK* V, 1960, cols. 896–98; M. Noth, 'Der Beitrag der Archäologie zur Geschichte Israels', SVT VII, 1960, pp. 262–82, esp. pp. 273ff.; J. L.

Kelso, 'Jericho', *IDB* II, 1962, pp. 835–39; J. Gray, *Archaeology and the Old Testament World*, London 1962, pp. 93ff.; G. E. Wright, *Biblical Archaeology*, Philadelphia-London, ²1962, pp. 78–80; J. Bright, 'Jericho', *BHH* II, 1964, cols. 816–19; Auzou, pp. 91ff.; H. J. Franken, 'Tell es-Sultan and Old Testament Jericho', *OTS* XIV, 1965, pp. 189–200; J. Robinson, 'Who cares about Jericho?', *ExpT* 78, 1966–67, pp. 83–6; H. Muszyń-ski, 'Sacrificum fundationis in Jos. 6.26 and I Reg. 16.34?', *VD* 46, 1968, pp. 259–74.

[6.1] *sōgeret ūmᵉsuggeret*, as Baldi and Noth have rightly pointed out, is an idiomatic expression, literally 'closing and reclosed'. 'Before the people of Israel' is lacking in LXX. The latter has a text which is often shorter than that of MT, and to which we shall refer only when it is of exegetical interest; apart from this, see the apparatus in *BH³*. T, on the contrary, has a longer text: *bdšyn dᵽrzl' wmtqᵽ' bᶜbryn* = 'it was closed with iron gates and strengthened with bolts of bronze'. This is no doubt a narrative ampli-fication. [2] 'Mighty men of valour' is not preceded by the particle *'et* which appears in the rest of the context; it seems to be a useless appendage here. Most commentators regard the phrase as a gloss; Abel connects it with the beginning of v. 3: 'And you, mighty men of valour, you shall go round . . . etc.' [3–4] LXX omits a good part of these two verses, so that the Israelites no longer march round the town, but simply surround it; is this a reminiscence of the preparations for an armed conquest (cf. 2.18a, LXX)? [6–7] LXX^BA once again have a shorter text: the statement by Joshua, in v. 6, is omitted, while that in v. 7 is addressed to the priests so that it is they who give the signal to the people (cf. *BH³*). This distinction is also preserved, it seems, in K, which read *wayyᵉʾōmᵉrū*, corrected by the Q and the other translations into *wayyōmer*. The ark is also lacking in LXX, which simply has 'before Yahweh'. [9] LXX has a different version of the second part of the verse: 'The priests, as a rearguard behind the ark of the covenant of the Lord, sounded', which once again seems to explain K, which has *tāqᵉᶜū*. T is to some extent a paraphrase, but contains a true variant: after 'the priests who sounded the trumpet' it inserts *wšbṭ' dbyt dn 'zl btr 'rwn'*, i.e. 'and the tribe of the house of Dan went behind the ark', a statement the point of which is unknown, unless it is simply a narrative elaboration. [11] *wayyassēb* in the hiphil has Joshua as its subject in MT; LXX, V and Syr read the *qal* (*BH³*), 'and the ark went round'; V, like T and Syr, read *semel per diem* after *hāᶜîr*: [12] LXX has τῇ ἡμέρᾳ τῇ δευτήρᾳ, an element which MT introduces further on. [13] T once again has the tribe of Dan following the ark. [14] For the LXX text, cf. v. 12. [17] The last part of the verse is lacking in LXX^BA (*BH³*). For *heḥᵉbᵉʾatāh*, attested in two of the earliest codices, cf. *GKC* § 75 and *B–L*, p. 375. It is one of the cases where the *lāmed* '*āleph* verbs have the vocalization of *lāmed hē* verbs.

The normal form occurs in v. 25. [18] *šāmar* with *min* in the sense of 'keep yourself from' (confirmed here by the ancient versions) is not found in the OT in the *qal*, which is why the reading of the *niphal* imperative is usually proposed here (cf. *BH³*). *taḥᵃrīmū* is corrected by many to *taḥᵉmīdū*, 'desire', following LXX εὐθυμήντες, cf. Syr, and also 7.21 and Deut. 7.25. The correction is useful but not essential. '*ākar* is a technical term of the cult and indicates a passage from the profane sphere to the sacred, the latter being understood in its most negative sense (Köhler); the root is also that of '*ākōr* in 7.24ff. and seems to form a prelude to the Achan ('*ākān*) episode. [19] 'Go': LXX and V have the passive 'are carried'. [21] LXX^B has 'Joshua utterly destroyed . . .' [24] *bēt*: an evident allusion to a temple (that of Gilgal, or already that of Jerusalem?); it is omitted by LXX, V and Syr, but nevertheless is the *lectio difficilior*.

1. The division into sources (e.g. J and E) attempted by Gressmann and Eissfeldt has been virtually abandoned today. Only Baldi mentions the possibility that 'the final redactor . . . may have combined two parallel redactions or *traduzioni* (translations!—he must have meant 'traditions') which had a different psychological background . . .'. This is so in spite of the evident irregularities presented by the text as we find it. In the opinion of Holzinger, adopted, although for different reasons, by Kaufmann, the text as we possess it presents a real unity, even though at certain points it is still possible to identify elements which have been added to the original. Thus for example between 2–3aα and 3aβ–4 there is a clear parallelism, strengthened by verbs which are semantically equivalent in this context, *sbb* and *nqp*; there are also tensions within 5a, 6–7, 8a, 9a, 10a and 11a. The same situation is found within vv. 14–15, notably in 15b. Nor can one say with certainty that the shorter text of LXX often succeeds in removing one of the apparently contradictory elements! A further example: it is not at all clear who is to sound the trumpet; in vv. 4, 6, 8, 13, 16 it is the priests, but in 9b and 13b the rearguard, the composition of which is not certain, is also to sound the trumpet. Similarly, the relationship between the sounding of the trumpet and the people's war cry is not clear; in v. 5 the second is meant to follow the first without special orders and is to come before the assault; but in v. 20 the sequence is: shouts, the sounding of the trumpet, a great shout. In vv. 8ff. the trumpets sound, but the people have to remain silent until the order is given to shout, and this order is given in vv. 16ff., whereas elsewhere the order to shout is given by a longer blast on the trumpet; and in v. 16 Joshua in fact gives the order to shout, and

then goes on talking when the people should have shouted. Thus Noth is right when he remarks that this chapter was not produced as a single unit (p.40), but is quite a complicated construction. One final difficulty is that of the topography of Rahab's house. In 2.15 this house is on top of the wall or adjoins it; but in this case, how could it avoid being destroyed, or at least seriously damaged, when the walls fell? This is a further proof that chs. 2 and 6 are independent.

2. The present text mentions the ark, vv. 4, 6, 8b, 11, 12, 13. This reference is identical to that found in chs. 3–4 (where, however, the trumpets are absent, and where the priests are 'Levites', which is an addition; moreover, in ch. 6 the priests carry trumpets and not the ark). It shows that at one of the stages in its re-elaboration this chapter was considered as logically following chs. 3–4. Thus just as the latter chapters recorded the celebration of the Passover and the Exodus, here the conquest is celebrated in an essentially similar ceremony, which includes amongst other things a symbolic action representing the event which is being celebrated. Consequently, our text is originally a liturgical text, as was clearly perceived by Hertzberg and others, in which only a minimal part of the original narrative has been preserved, outside its original context. (This remnant probably consists only of vv. 1–3a and 24ff.; Vogt, in the opinion already quoted, thinks it also includes part of ch. 3.)

3. Maier (cf. J. Dus), pp. 323ff., has attempted to divide the chapter into different strata of tradition. In his view we have:

I. The Benjaminite saga of Rahab (of which all we can now trace is the narrative content, cf. the concluding verses, and ch. 2);

II. The Ephraimite recension introducing Joshua (vv. 2, 5, 12a, 20aβ, all with various insertions);

III. The national recension by the compiler (of which virtually nothing remains);

IV. A first recension introducing the ark (vv. 1, 7b, 8, 12b, 16a, all with additions);

V. A second recension concerning the ark (vv. 5a, 7, 8aβ, ba, 11, 15–14a, all with additions);

VI. The Deuteronomic re-elaboration (v. 6 and elements in 8, 10, 16b–20aa), together with various Deuteronomic glosses (vv. 4, 13, 15b).

As in the previous case, such a division into sources is extremely complicated, and is impossible to check in depth. According to

Maier's study it is probable in any case that, as in chs. 3–4, the ark was introduced at a second stage. Thus we shall not adopt Maier's division.

4. Consequently, the historicity of the fall of Jericho in the ritual circumstances described in this chapter seems extremely unlikely; on the other hand, the existence of a liturgy including a procession is unquestionably historical, even though, as was the case for chs. 3–4, it is no longer possible to give a date to it. It was probably established in the last decades of the second millennium, and it is possible that the rite continued to be celebrated for a certain period beyond that date. The acceptance of this dating would exclude the presence of the ark, which would only be a later insertion, in a more orthodox sense, as an attempt to conceal the true nature of the object carried in procession.

Thus for the historian the true problems only begin with the artificial rehistoricization carried out either by the 'compiler' or later by Dtr. It is this which has led to our passsage becoming, without any objective reason, an episode (the first) in the conquest, which, moreover, has replaced a narrative of the capture of Jericho by armed attack and with the aid of a ruse (cf. the commentary on ch. 2).

5. The literary facts and the tradition history of the chapter being as they are, it is no longer surprising that the results of archaeological excavations give a picture of a Jericho of the end of the Bronze Age and the beginning of the Iron Age which is totally incompatible with the narrative recorded here. Those who maintain to the bitter end the historicity of ch. 6 can only regard these findings as discouraging.

The excavations carried out on the *tell* of Jericho (for its site, cf. the commentary on ch. 2) on various occasions from the beginning of the century until the middle of the 1930s (1908–1910 by E. Sellin for the *Deutsche Orientgesellschaft*, and 1930–1936 by J. Garstang for the Palestine Exploration Fund) exposed the foundations of a strong rampart, formed by a double row of walls, the inside walls being about 3 m thick and the outside walls about 2 m thick. This rampart had fallen in such a way that an earthquake was suggested. But the quantity of ashes and food residues bore impressive witness to the fact that there had been either a fire or a recent harvest (cf. 3.15; 5.10–12). For the details, compare the excellent accounts in *SDB* III by Baldi, Noth and Bright. This defensive system was dated approximately between 1450 and 1250 BC, but in any case in the second half of the second millennium, and the dating was regarded as fundamental in

determining the beginning of the Israelite occupation. These findings
seemed definitely established, when they were completely overturned
by the excavations carried out on behalf of the British School of
Archaeology by Miss K. M. Kenyon from 1952 to 1958. So far we
have only provisional accounts, but they suffice to establish two un-
questionable facts:

(a) The wall that was believed to be that connected with Joshua
cannot be dated later than the early Bronze Age (third millennium
BC, cf. ch. 7), in view of the fact that during the first half of the second
millennium (the Middle Bronze Age) other defence systems were
constructed on its ruins, equipped with the particular type of sloping
plane known generally as a glacis, the purpose of which was to prevent siege engines, and particularly the battering ram, being brought
up to the fortifications. Now this system of defence was introduced
during the period of Hyksos domination and is certainly earlier than
the middle of the second millennium.[1]

b. From the late Bronze Age (approximately 1550–1300 BC, cf.
pp. 26off.) there is no trace either of ramparts or of other constructions, because extensive erosion rapidly brought about the disappearance of the upper part of the city, which was abandoned at that time
(other finds, especially in the cemetery of that period, show that the
locality was more or less inhabited). This process was all the more
rapid in that construction was largely of unbaked brick (the adobe of
the Iberian peninsula and Latin America, still used today in Arab
countries). Miss Kenyon's conclusion is that the excavations cast no
light upon the presumed period of the Israelite conquest.

Whereas the first assertion is beyond question, and the wall which
was for so long considered to be that of the conquest is shown to be
hundreds of years earlier, the second, as is often the case with negative
assertions, leaves several possibilities open. For the American school
the destruction of all traces by erosion prevents any assessment of the
facts whatsoever.[2] But the members of this school are ready to admit
that the town could not have been a very large one and that if it
possessed walls, these were simply a re-used fortress of the sixteenth
century BC, even if proofs are lacking. Noth, and European scholars
in general, believe that so impressive a wall could not have disappeared without leaving any trace, and that since there have been

---

[1] Kenyon, *Digging Up* . . ., pp. 214ff.
[2] W. F. Albright, *The Archaeology of Palestine*, Harmondsworth ⁴1960, pp. 108ff.;
id., *Recent Discoveries* . . ., pp. 46ff., 87f. Cf. Wright, p. 80; Bright, col. 818.

so many intensive excavations carried out on the *tell*, it is improbable that traces of this wall still remain to be found somewhere. They point out that there is no example in the history of archaeology of a stratum which has *completely* disappeared. Consequently, for Noth the absence of any evidence of the wall is an unequivocal proof that the wall itself did not exist.[1]

This situation, which is what we would expect to find after our analysis of the literary condition and tradition history of ch. 6, forms a striking analogy with the situation of Ai (which we are going on to consider), even if the circumstances are different. In any case, since there are traces of habitation on the *tell*, the taking of Jericho must have been simply an incident in the task of infiltrating sparsely inhabited regions which, according to the theses of Alt, formed the early stages of the 'conquest'.

6. The purpose of the liturgy which celebrates the conquest is to make known to the community which takes part in it that Yahweh carried out the final element in his ancient promises, and that this took place through no human merit. The ritual proceeds, adopting certain elements of the holy war which had already taken on a stereotyped form, and as they are found above all in Chronicles (cf. II Chron. 13.13–16; 20.1ff.). They have nothing warlike about them except the name; it is enough for Israel to go out in procession and finally to sound the trumpet. In other respects, this literary form is perfectly adapted to a liturgical celebration where Yahweh is the principal actor. The people are limited to carrying out the liturgical acts which God orders through the instrument of those who are ordained to this purpose, and the divine plan is carried out in Israel.

[1–3a] To a group of nomads, a fortified town must seem impregnable. But here the attempt succeeded, thanks to divine intervention, and this is what is being celebrated. These verses contain one of the typical formulas of the holy war, by which God proclaims victory to Israel.[2] As we have seen, the holy war is reduced here to a special vocabulary and stereotyped actions. There is no trace of a battle in the proper sense of the word (we have seen in our commentary on ch. 2 how the tradition recorded such a battle). But the command to 'encircle' the city shows that there is a recollection of a siege.

[3a–5] The liturgical aspect is now superimposed upon the military

---

[1] M. Noth, 'Hat die Bibel . . .,' pp. 13f.

[2] G. von Rad, *Der Heilige Krieg im Alten Testament*, ATANT 20, Zurich 1951, pp. 6ff.

aspect by means of a series of clever devices: 'encircle' (root *sbb*) now becomes 'going round' (*nqp* II) the city in procession, with priests and trumpets, a theme which also appears in II Chron. 13.13ff. Hertzberg has pointed out in this respect that the 'men of war' appear here not for the purpose of a battle but for a ceremony. The confusions and internal contradictions clearly bear witness to successive additions and possibly to the inclusion of liturgical elements intended to explain the course of the ceremonial.

The relation of cause and effect between the liturgical act and the collapse of the walls is explicitly affirmed here, and this miracle, celebrated in the ritual, sums up the whole religious experience of Israel, for whom God carried out his ancient promises by way of his mighty acts in history. Thus Jericho appears as something of a pattern and model for the conquest, in which everything, including the terminology, has become a matter of ritual: cf. in vv. 5 and 20, the use of the word *'lh*, 'to go up', typical of the processional ascent to the sanctuary.

[6–10] The course of the liturgy as our text describes it seems fairly simple. The procession is opened by a detachment of armed men, followed by priests carrying trumpets, then comes an object later identified with the ark, which for this reason must have been some equivalent (was it a golden bull, in view of the markedly northern nature of the tribes? There are no grounds for certainty). It could have been the ark only from 1050 on, although we encounter it earlier in various places, from Shiloh to Jerusalem, but never at Gilgal. A rearguard concludes the procession. The participation of the people in the ceremony is expressed by means of a 'war cry' uttered either on a given signal by the trumpets or following the explicit order of the person conducting the ceremony; it formed the climax of the celebration.[1] The feast was to last seven days, and this recalls the fact that the feast in chs. 3–5, culminating in the Passover, lasted for this period. Thus the first week was concluded with the Passover on the sabbath, and the second with the representation of the present reality of the conquest, by means of the ritual of the destruction of the first city to be conquered.

The 'trumpet' (*šōpar hayyōbēl* or *qeren hayyōbēl*) is formed of a ram's horn (*yōbēl* means 'he who leads the flock') used in the cult, above all for the jubilee (the name of which is probably derived from this).

---

[1] P. Humbert, *La 'Terou'a'. Analyse d'un rite biblique*, Neuchâtel 1946.

Thus it was not a metal trumpet such as is seen in most representations of the story.

[11–19] These verses record another element in the ritual: a circuit of the town every day for six days, followed by a return to the camp. The rite is repeated seven times on the seventh day in order to draw together what has already been carried out, the epilogue then being added: the people's war cry and the fall of the walls. Instructions about Rahab and her family have been added to the speech of Joshua, which is actually finished in v. 16. In this way the redactors hoped to harmonize this chapter with ch. 2. In v. 18 we have a brief exhortation on the subject of devotion to destruction which is a preparation for the Achan episode in chs. 7–8.

[20–24] The mention of the temple treasury in v. 24 is not without importance. It may be an anachronistic mention of the Jerusalem temple, or merely an allusion to the temple at Gilgal. The reading should not be omitted, not only because it is the *lectio difficilior*, but also because it supplies a liturgical indication about what had to be done with the sacred objects which were brought out of the sanctuary before the procession.

[25–26] As we have seen in discussing ch. 2, v. 25 is no doubt a fragment of the ancient narrative of the military capture of Jericho, while v. 26 presupposes the account of I Kings 16.34. But Josh. 18.21 and II Sam. 10.5 show clearly that in some fashion the locality remained inhabited, so that the history of Rahab could have been retold in a neighbourhood of the city in which there remained people who could boast of being the descendants of Rahab. For this problem see ch. 2, § 3.

CHAPTER 7.1–8.29

The Episode of Achan and the Conquest of Ai

7 ¹But the people of Israel broke faith in regard to the ban; for Achan the son of Carmi, son of Zabdi, son of Zerah, of the tribe of Judah, took some of the devoted things; and the anger of the LORD burned against the people of Israel.

2 Joshua sent men from Jericho to Ai, which is near Beth-aven, east of Bethel, and said to them, 'Go up and spy out the land.' And the men went up and spied out [the region of] Ai. ³And they returned to Joshua, and said to him, 'Let not all the people go up on the expedition, but let about two or three thousand men go up and attack Ai; do not weary the whole people, for they are but few.' ⁴So about three thousand went up there from the people; and they fled before the men of Ai, ⁵and the men of Ai killed about thirty-six men of them, and chased them from before the gate as far as the 'Ravines', and slew them at the 'Descent'. And the hearts of the people melted, and became as water.

6 Then Joshua rent his clothes, and fell to the earth upon his face before the ark of the LORD until the evening, he and the elders of Israel; and they put dust upon their heads. ⁷And Joshua said, 'Alas, O Lord GOD, why hast thou brought this people over the Jordan at all, to give us into the hands of the Amorites, to destroy us? Would that we had been content to dwell beyond the Jordan! ⁸And I, O Lord, what can I say, when Israel has turned their backs before their enemies! ⁹For the Canaanites and all the inhabitants of the land will hear of it, and will rebel against us, and cut off our name from the earth; and what wilt thou do for thy great name?'

10 But the LORD said to Joshua, 'Arise, why have you thus fallen upon your face? ¹¹Israel has sinned; they have transgressed my covenant which I commanded them; they have taken some of the devoted things; they have stolen, and lied, and put them among their own stuff. ¹²Therefore the people of Israel cannot stand before their enemies; they turn their backs before their enemies, because they themselves have become a thing devoted to destruction. I will be with you no more, unless you destroy the devoted things from among you. ¹³Up, sanctify the people, and say, "Sanctify yourselves for tomorrow; for thus says the LORD, God of Israel, 'There are devoted things in the midst of you, O Israel; you cannot stand before your enemies, until you take away the devoted things from among you.' " ¹⁴In the morning therefore you shall be brought near by your tribes; and the tribe which the LORD takes shall come near by clans; and the clan which the LORD takes shall come near by households; and the household which the LORD takes shall come near man by man. ¹⁵And he who is taken with the devoted things shall be burned with fire, he and all that he has, because he has transgressed the covenant of the LORD, and because he has done a shameful thing in Israel.'

16 So Joshua rose early in the morning and brought Israel near tribe by tribe, and the tribe of Judah was taken; ¹⁷and the clans of Judah drew near, and the clan of the Zerahites was taken; and the clan of the Zera- hites drew near by households, and Zabdi was taken; ¹⁸and he brought his household near man by man, and Achan the son of Carmi, son of Zabdi, son of Zerah, of the tribe of Judah, was taken. ¹⁹Then Joshua said to

Achan, 'My son, give glory to the LORD God of Israel, and render praise to him; and tell me now what you have done; do not hide it from me.' 20And Achan answered Joshua, 'Of a truth I have sinned against the LORD God of Israel, and this is what I did: 21when I saw among the spoil a beautiful mantle from Shinar, and two hundred shekels of silver, and a bar of gold weighing fifty shekels, then I coveted them, and took them and behold, (the shekels of silver) are buried in the earth inside my tent, with the bar underneath the mantle.'

22 So Joshua sent messengers, and they ran to the tent; and behold, (the mantle) was buried in his tent with the silver underneath it. 23And they took them out of the tent and brought them to Joshua and all the people of Israel; and they laid them down before the LORD. 24And Joshua and all Israel with him took Achan the son of Zerah, and the silver and the mantle and the bar of gold, and his sons and daughters, and his oxen and asses and sheep, and his tent, and all that he had; and they brought them up to the Valley of Achor. 25And Joshua said, 'Why did you bring trouble on us? The LORD brings trouble on you today.' And all Israel [stoned him with stones; they] burned them with fire, and stoned them with stones. 26And they raised over him a great heap of stones that remains to this day; then the LORD turned from his burning anger. Therefore to this day the name of that place is called, the Valley of Achor.

8 1And the LORD said to Joshua, 'Do not fear or be dismayed; take all the fighting men with you, and arise, go up to Ai; see, I have given into your hand the king of Ai, and his people, his city, and his land; 2and you shall do to Ai and its king as you did to Jericho and its king; only its spoil and its cattle you shall take as booty for yourselves; lay an ambush against the city, behind it.'

3 So Joshua arose, and all the fighting men, to go up to Ai; and Joshua chose thirty thousand mighty men of valour, and sent them forth by night. 4And he commanded them, 'Behold, you shall lie in ambush against the city, behind it; do not go very far from the city, but hold yourselves all in readiness; 5and I, and all the people who are with me, will approach the city. And when they come out against us, as before, we shall flee before them; 6and they will come out after us, till we have drawn them away from the city; for they will say, "They are fleeing from us, as before." So we will flee from them. 7Then you shall rise up from the ambush, and seize the city; for the LORD your God will give it into your hand. 8And when you have taken the city, you shall set the city on fire, doing as the LORD has bidden; see, I have commanded you.'

9 So Joshua sent them forth; and they went to the place of ambush, and lay between Bethel and Ai, to the west of Ai; but Joshua spent that night among the people (or 'in the middle of the Plain'). 10And Joshua arose early in the morning and mustered the people, and went up, with the

elders of Israel, before the people to Ai. [11]And all the people who were with him went up, and drew near before the city, and encamped on the north side of Ai, between the 'Ravine' and Ai. [12]And he took about five thousand men, and set them in ambush between Bethel and Ai, to the west of the city. [13]So the people set up the camp, which was north of the city, and its 'heel' west of the city. But Joshua went away that night into the middle of the Plain. [14]And when the king of Ai saw this he made haste and went out early, he and all his people, to the Place of Assembly on the Arabah side to meet Israel in battle; but he did not know that there was an ambush against him behind the city. [15]And Joshua and all Israel let themselves be beaten by them, and fled in the direction of the wilderness. [16]So all the people who were in the city were called together to pursue them, and as they pursued Joshua they were drawn away from the city. [17]There was not a man left in Ai or Bethel, who did not go out after Israel; they left the city open, and pursued Israel. [18]Then the LORD said to Joshua, 'Stretch out the javelin that is in your hand toward Ai; for I will give it into your hand.' And Joshua stretched out the javelin that was in his hand towards the city. [19]And the ambush rose quickly out of their place, and as soon as he had stretched out his hand, they ran and entered the city and took it; and they made haste to set the city on fire. [20]So when the men of Ai looked back, behold, the smoke of the city went up to heaven; and they had no power to flee this way or that, for the people that fled to the wilderness turned back upon the pursuers. [21]And when Joshua and all Israel saw that the ambush had taken the city, and that the smoke of the city went up, then they turned back and smote the men of Ai. [22]They had come forth from the city to meet them; and there they were in the midst of Israel, some on this side, and some on that side; and Israel smote them, until there was left none that survived or escaped. [23]But the king of Ai they took alive, and brought him to Joshua. [24]When Israel had finished slaughtering all the inhabitants of Ai in the 'Field' where they pursued them (and all of them to the very last fell by the edge of the sword), all Israel returned to Ai, and smote it with the edge of the sword. [25]And all who fell that day, both men and women, were twelve thousand, all the people of Ai. [26]For Joshua did not draw back his hand, with which he stretched out the javelin, until he had utterly destroyed all the inhabitants of Ai. [27]Only the cattle and the spoil of that city Israel took as their booty, according to the word of the LORD which he commanded Joshua. [28]So Joshua burned Ai, and made it for ever a heap of ruins, as it is to this day.

29 And he hanged the king of Ai on a tree until evening; and at the going down of the sun Joshua commanded, and they took his body down from the tree, and cast it at the entrance of the gate of the city, and raised over it a great heap of stones, which stands there to this day.

Bibliography: A. *On the whole passage*: K. Möhlenbrink, 'Die Landnah-mesagen . . .', pp.259ff.; W. Rudolph, *Der 'Elohist' als Erzähler* . . ., pp. 189ff.; Y. Kaufmann, *The Biblical Account* . . ., pp. 71ff., 74ff. B. *On Achan and Achor*: B. J. Alfrink, 'Die Achan Erzählung', *Miscell. Bibl* . . . A. *Miller oblata*, Rome 1951, pp. 114–29; H. W. Wolff, 'Die Ebene Achor', *ZDPV* 70, 1954, pp. 76–81; M. Noth, 'Das Deutsche Evangelische Institut für Altertumswissenschaft des Heiligen Landes', Lehrkurs 1954, *ZDPV* 71, 1955, pp. 42–55; F. M. Cross and J. T. Milik, 'Explorations in the Judaean Desert', *BASOR* 142, 1956, pp. 5–17, esp. p. 17; F. M. Cross, 'A Footnote to Biblical History', *BA* 19, 1956, pp. 12–17, esp. p. 17. C. *On the conquest of Ai*: R. Dussaud, 'Note additionelle', *Syria* 16, 1935, pp. 346–52; A. Lods, 'Les fouilles d'Aï et l'époque de l'entrée des Israe-lites en Palestine', *Mélanges F. Cumont*, Brussels 1936, pp. 847–57; L. H. Vincent, 'Les fouilles d'et-Tell-Aï', *RB* 46, 1937, pp. 231–66; W. F. Albright, 'The Israelite Conquest of Canaan in the Light of Archaeology', *BASOR* 74, 1939, pp. 11–22, esp. pp. 16ff.; J. Simons, 'Een opmerking over het "Aj-probleem"', *JEOL* III, 9, 1944, pp. 157–62; F. M. Abel, 'Les stratagèmes . . .', pp.329ff.; J. Marquet-Krause, *Les fouilles d'Aï (et-Tell)*, Paris 1949; J. M. Grintz, ' "Ai, which is beside Beth-Aven". A re-examination of the identity of Ai', *Bibl.* 42, 1961, pp.201–16; J. A. Callaway, 'The 1964 'Ai (et-Tell) excavations', *BASOR* 178, 1965, pp. 13–40, cf. *BA* 28, 1965, pp.26–30; H. W. Hertzberg, 'Ai', *BHH* I, 1962, cols. 52f.; Auzou, pp. 101ff.; J. A. Callaway and M. B. Nicol, 'A Sounding at Khirbet Haiyan', *BASOR* 183, 1966, pp. 12–19; J. A. Callaway, 'New evidence on the Conquest of Ai', *JBL* 87, 1968, pp.312–20; id., 'The 1966 'Ai (et-Tell) excavations', *BASOR* 196, 1969, pp.2–16. We were unable to make use of the last article.

[7.1] After 'to the ban' LXX adds ἐνοσφίσαντο 'and they took of it', an explanatory gloss on the previous phrase. LXX usually has a shorter text, and sometimes minor variants. We will mention them only when they are of importance for the meaning of the text. As between MT and LXX we often have a variation in wording: Ai is replaced by 'the city', 'the inhabi-tants', and once by 'the district' (v.2); Israel by 'the people', 'Joshua', which does not change the fundamental meaning of the text. Note, finally, in LXX, a tendency to suppress topographical indications. There are two possible reasons for this: either LXX suppressed unfamiliar ideas, or else MT added them. The former is more likely. 'Achan': I Chron. 2.7 (except a handful of MSS), LXX[B] at this point in the present text and Josephus, *Antt.* V, I, 10 read *ākār* (Ἄχαρ), the same root as the name of the city and of the verb used in vv. 25f. I Chron. 2.7 refers explicitly to this episode: 'Achar . . . who transgressed (*'ōkēr*) in the matter of the devoted thing'. It is a typical case of confusion between *reš* and *nun* at the end of a word, even more understandable in that Achor is perhaps pejorative, as Holzinger maintains. 'Zabdi': I Chron. 2.6 and LXX[B] at this point in the present text read *zimrī* (*Ζάμβρι*); LXX[A] has *Ζάβρι*. The latter case is one of confusion between *rēš* and *dālet*. [2] 'From Jericho' is lacking in LXX[B A], which may not have used a text which made this connection between this episode and the previous one. The best solution is to consider, like Benjamin, that MT has been expanded. 'Beth-aven, east of . . .' occurs in V, but is lacking in LXX, which has: LXX[B], *ἥ ἐστι κατὰ Βαιτήλ*; LXX[A], *Βηθαῦν* in place of the whole expression. T has the whole expression, but in a different order. The phrase could be a gloss, and so would be parallel to 'near Bethel', but there is also a possibility, which Albright takes into consideration (p. 15), as does Grintz (p. 212 n. 3), that this name is not a contemptuous form of Bethel, as it was generally understood by the prophets from the eight century on, but derives from *bēt 'ōn* (*'ōn*: 'generative power', 'richness'). Albright and Grintz base their interpretation of the whole passage on this possibility. The latter understands *'im* literally, 'with Beth-Aven', and identifies this locality with Ai. The region of Ai is implied in the end of the verse. [3] 'Expedition': this sense of *'lh* is already attested in Ugaritic;[1] 'weary': MT read the *piel* of *yg'*, LXX (*ἀναγάγῃς*) the *hiphil* of *ng'*. [5] 'From before the gate', *lip'nē haššā'ar*. Either a *mem* has been lost (*millip'nē*), by haplography with the preceding plural, or else we have *l'* with the meaning, already found in Ugaritic, of 'from'. LXX and V have correctly translated in the latter sense. 'As far as the "Ravines"' is not omitted in LXX, as *BH*[3] erroneously states: LXX, followed by Syr and T, read, with the same consonants, 'to the point of destroying them', *καὶ συνέτριψαν αὐτούς*, i.e. *'ad šibrām* (root *šbr*, Aramaic = Syriac *tbr*, break); no doubt they did not understand the name of the place, which V transcribes correctly, while the others rendered the text by 'as far as the quarries (of stone)'. [6] 'The ark' is missing in LXX[B], which simply read 'before *yhwh*'. [7] 'Why hast thou brought this people over . . .': LXX has 'Why did thy servant bring this people over the Jordan . . .'. This is either a misreading, or, more likely (but one explanation does not exclude the other) a theological correction which avoids placing the responsibility for what has taken place on Yahweh, even an indirect responsibility. *hē'*abartā; cf. *GKC* § 63p for this form. *ha'*abīr: *GKC* § 113x, unless we should read *ha'*abēr (*BH*[3] and commentators), a rare form for the infinitive absolute, *GKC* § 53k. 'Beyond': LXX has 'near (*παρά*) the Jordan'. [17–18] LXX has all the verbs in the impersonal passive: 'and the approach was made by clans . . . was taken . . .' We have accepted this reading in

---

[1] Cf. M. Liverani, *Storia di Ugarit nell'età degli archivi politici*, Rome 1962, p. 42.

v. 17, where MT makes Joshua the subject of 'took'. 'The clans of Judah';
we read the plural, following LXX (κατὰ δήμους); MT has the singular,
which is meaningless. 'The clan of Zerah . . .': MT adds 'man by man',
which comes in v. 18, but is out of context here; we have replaced it,
following V and Syr, by *bātīm*, according to the order indicated in vv. 14ff.
Some of the proper names are lacking in LXX. For the use of *lᵉ*, cf. on
v. 5. [19] 'My son' is lacking in LXX, which has σήμερον. [21] At the beginning of the verse K has the *waw* copulative, while Q has the *waw* consecutive. The latter is required here. 'Mantle from Shinar'; LXX has φιλὴν
ποικίλην, that is, 'many coloured mantle', cf. Gen. 37.3 for the same. V has
coccineum, 'scarlet' (but not in Gen. 37). The nature of this garment was
not clear to the ancient translators. 'Bar': in Hebrew literally 'tongue'; it
was in fact a very flat strip, cf. *BRL* c. 380. *hā'ohᵒlī*: for the problem of the
double determinative (unless in fact there is a textual error) cf. our article
in *Bibl* 44, 1963, p. 521 n. 2. [23] LXX has 'the elders of Israel'. 'Laid
them down': LXX has ἔθηκαν, that is *wylgm* (confusion between *gimel* and
qoph?). [24] LXX omits the mention of the objects and restricts itself to
persons and animals. It inserts the reference after 'Achan' in the second
half and omits the end of the verse. Note the play on words, already mentioned in v. 1, between the verb '*kr*, 'bring misfortune, trouble', the place
'*ākōr* and the name as it is preserved in LXX and I Chron. 'Plain'; Hebr.
'*ēmeq*, usually = 'valley'; for this meaning cf. Noth, ad loc. [25] 'And
burned them . . .' is missing at the end in LXX. Syr and V omit the
second mention of the stoning; although the verb *sql* is older, in this sense,
than *rgm*. Since a double stoning is improbable, and in accordance with
v. 15, which puts the burning first, we have the following sequence of
events: burning, covering of the remains by stoning, the erection of a heap
of stones. In this way, we preserve the root *sql*. [8.2] '*ōrēb*, literally 'ambush'. The term is used here either in a participial sense, to indicate those
who are 'waylaying' or, less properly, as a substantive, to indicate the
thing in itself and the place. [3] '30,000 men' seems too many, but the
figure is confirmed by the ancient versions. Some propose a reduction to
3,000, cf. the parallel passage, v. 12, which has 5,000; but there too the
figure is unreasonably large. One must regard these figures as reflecting
the tendency, attested from the Exodus to the early period of the kings, to
exaggerate figures; it is better not corrected. [6] 'Till we have drawn them
away' is lacking in Syr (cf. *BH*³, n. *a-a*; the note is not quite accurate as
far as LXX is concerned). The final phrase is missing in the ancient translations and is no doubt a repetition of the end of v. 5. [7] The correction
in *BH*³, n. a, does not seem necessary, cf. v. 1. 'You shall seize the city'.
LXX read: 'you shall approach the city' (πορεύεσθε); V has *vastabitis
civitatem*; T, 'you will sack the city' (root *rkn*). The reference in *BH*³ to the
course followed in v. 11 is false, because it is the general body which is in-

volved there, and not the group placed in ambush. LXX omits the end of
the verse and the beginning of the next. **[8]** 'As Yahweh has bidden';
LXX has only: 'Do according to this order . . .' and omits the end. The
whole phrase is lacking in V. **[9]** With v. 3b it is parallel to vv. 12–13; at the
end of the latter verse we also find *beṭōk hāʿēmeq*, which Noth (*BH*³ and
Commentary) would also read here, assuming the loss of the final *q*; this
suggestion is not supported by the versions but provides a more logical
text, because we are never told that Joshua was in the habit of sleeping
anywhere other than in the midst of the people. 'The Plain' (for the meaning, cf. on 7.24) would then be the proper name of a locality on the opposite
side of the city to the ambush. **[11]** 'The people': the Hebrew expression is
either a scribal error (a gloss *hāʿām* which has found its way into the text
and which is lacking in T) or else a new example of a double determinative
(cf. above on 7.21 and the way LXX has rendered the text). The whole
expression is lacking in V. **[12]** LXX has a shorter text: 'While the ambush
against the town was on the west', a reading which is not confirmed by the
other versions. **[13]** This verse, forming a parallel to v. 9, is totally lacking
in LXX. Instead of 'he went away', confirmed by T and V, Noth (*BH*³
and *Commentary*) proposes *wayyālen*, 'and he spent the night', cf. v. 9. 'In
the middle of the Plain', cf. v. 9; Syr has 'in the middle of the people';
these variants are typical of the same text transmitted by different agents.
[14] We have translated the text following LXX and V, which omit 'the
men of the city' at the beginning, and keep the verb in the singular. This is
more logical, since throughout the sentence the subject remains: the king.
The first mention of the 'men' is tautological and anticipates, out of context, the second mention. LXX, and in part V, also omits the topographical references, which, however, we keep. 'In battle': LXX has ἐπ' εὐθείας,
i.e. 'in a straight line', in Hebrew *beyešārā*, originally no doubt an abbreviation, later misunderstood, of 'against Israel' (*beyiśrāʾēl*). **[15]** The end
of this verse and the beginning of the next are lacking in LXX. **[17]** The
mention of Bethel is strange in this context, apart from the fact that it is
not appropriate and is lacking in LXX. It may have been introduced
following vv. 9 and 12, and should consequently be omitted (Noth); on
the other hand it may be a case of a *lectio difficilior* (though not *brevior*), and
one must carefully consider retaining it; it clearly favours the theses of
Albright (see below). **[18]** LXX has a longer text, somewhat confused, in
which, however, it is clear that it is the hand of Joshua and not the
javelin which is raised; the gesture is thus similar to that in Exod. 17.11f.
kīdōn is generally understood as being a javelin; at Qumran it has the
meaning 'sword'. **[20]** LXX omits the last part of the verse. **[22]** LXX read,
instead of 'in the midst of Israel', 'in the midst of the camp (παρεμβολή)'.
'There was left none . . .': LXX and V read the passive; no doubt we
should follow Noth in reading the infinitive and not the third person sing.

of MT. **[24]** 'In the wilderness' is tagged on to 'Field', to which it is obviously parallel. LXX read instead 'on the mountain, near the descent', which recalls the *mōrād* of 7.5. For the explanation, cf. Noth, ad loc. The text of LXX is much shorter in two places (cf. *BH*³) and makes Joshua the subject of the final phrase. **[29]** 'Tree' (gallows): LXX has 'on a double post (ἐπὶ ξύλου διδύμου) and on the post he remained until the evening', an allusion to the crucifixion. 'Entrance of the gate of the city': LXX has εἰς τὸν βόθρον, i.e., 'in the ditch', in Hebrew *happaḥat (BH*³). 'Gate of the city' would be a (correct) gloss to explain the use of the unusual expression 'entrance'.

This fourth section of the first part, consisting of the whole of ch. 7 and the first 29 verses of ch. 8, presents a number of problems which have not yet been resolved. Scholars before the war (Gressmann, Holzinger and, even later, Simpson, pp. 293ff.) have tried to resolve them by postulating the existence of at least two sources, but this method has not proved very useful, in view of the extremely fragmentary nature of the various narratives obtained in this way. We give here a list of the principal problems.

1. It is obvious that the narrative, which at first sight is a unity, is composed in reality of at least two narratives which have been combined only later. This has long been noted. We have first of all the episode of Achan, aetiologically associated with the valley of Achor, into which is inserted the narrative of the conquest of Ai, which is linked with the cycle of Gilgal and Jericho.

2. The geographical and topographical condition of the second narrative, which abounds in place names and other indications, is extremely complex. This makes the whole narrative even more difficult.

3. The two narratives must each be considered in themselves, with regard to problems of historicity, of their localization and of their literary category, and also with regard to their inclusion in the larger context of the conquest.

4. Whereas in the Gilgal cycle the cultic element was dominant, here it is virtually absent. Consequently these two narratives are clearly distinguishable, even in literary respects, from the story which here provides their starting point. We shall discuss some of these problems.

1. The Achan narrative, 7.1, 5b–26, located in the valley of Achor, is a question of an interdiction or ban, applied to an individual

Israelite and his family. We cannot give here a detailed discussion of the problems of this institution, except in outline.[1]

This practice assumes the total destruction of the enemy and his goods by means of devotion or extermination (in Hebrew *ḥerem*) at the conclusion of a campaign (cf. e.g. Josh. 6.24; I Sam. 15). There are also examples outside Israel, e.g. on the stele of Mesha, King of Moab (lines 10ff., cf. *ANET*, p. 320; *KAI*, no. 181) from the second half of the ninth century. Precious metals could be excluded from the ban and were then deposited in the sanctuary (as in Josh. 6), but looting, as in this episode, was never allowed in any circumstances. Thus 8.2b and 27 form an exception where looting is a fact admitted, and this variant is to be noted by contrast with current practice. In I Sam. 15, Saul is reproached precisely because he allowed his men to loot, instead of seeing that everything was destroyed.

In the Achan episode, the fault of an individual is extended to the whole community, and contaminates it in a particular way, beginning with the people who are most closely linked with the guilty person, cf. similar cases in Judg. 19–21 (the Benjaminites); I Sam. 13–14 (the Israelite troops, as a result of the act committed by Jonathan); II Sam. 21.1–10 (the surviving sons of Saul, as the result of an act committed by Saul). There is nothing here which suggests that a collective fault has priority over individual guilt, as Alfrink proposes on the basis of the demand made that the whole people should sanctify itself; 7.13 tells us of an individual fault (here the appropriation of devoted things) which produces effects on the whole people. The sole remedy is the identification and punishment of the guilty person. The theme of collective guilt, and the means used to discover the responsible person (drawing lots) are already mentioned in I Sam. 14.40ff., which is unquestionably a very early passage, and in which the identification of the guilty person by lot is carried out, according to a variant in the LXX, with the aid of the urim and thummim. It is not stated here that a similar procedure was used.

The recent studies of Noth, which have since been verified by Cross and Milik, have shown beyond all doubt that the valley (or plain) of Achor must be located in the northern part of the present-day *el-buqēʿa*, on a horizontal line between the Ircania of the Hellenis-

---

[1] G. von Rad, *Der Heilige Krieg im Alten Testament*, ATANT 20, Zurich 1951, pp. 15ff.; W. Eichrodt, *The Theology of the Old Testament*, I, 1961, pp. 139–41; W. Richter, *Traditionsgeschichtliche Untersuchungen zum Richterbuch*, BBB 18, Bonn 1963, pp. 177ff.

tic period (now *khirbet mird*, 185–125) and Qumran. It is a region
which Josh. 15.7 places within the frontiers of Judah, which include
the plain of Achor in the north. This is in agreement with the tradition which makes Achan a man of Judah. Originally the narrative probably represented a Benjaminite polemic directed against Judah, the
southern neighbour of Benjamin, though we have no way of being
sure of this.

In the context of Josh. 1.1–10.15, which is based upon Gilgal, with
excursions in the direction of the Benjaminite hill-country, this localization distinguishes the narrative as the only one taking us outside
Benjamin, except of course 8.30–35, which no doubt belongs to the
Shechem cycle (chs.23–24). The episode of the capture of Ai, to which
this passage serves as an introduction, also takes place in the central
hill country, at least according to the identification of Ai and Bethel
which has long been traditional and is widely maintained. We shall
return to this problem later. As the crow flies, this region is about 30
km from the plain of Achor, a considerable distance when one considers that the very rough terrain does not allow a direct route between the two regions, that is, across the hill country itself. In other
words, the details of the itinerary, Gilgal-Ai, Gilgal-Achor and then
Gilgal-Ai again, with at least two journeys back to the sanctuary, is
geographically correct, even if it only confirms the original independence of the two narratives.

Apart from its purpose as a Benjaminite polemic against Judah,
which we have already considered, the purpose of the story of Achan
seems to have been mainly to give an aetiological explanation for the
existence of a human tomb under a heap of stones, which seems to
have attracted attention in this desert region. The practice of stoning
may have provided the starting point for the explanation, which was
then completed by the attachment to this place of a tradition referring to a man stoned for having committed an act of sacrilege. Kaufmann's argument in *The Biblical Account*, pp. 70ff., that a heap of
stones in a place where there are so many cannot be regarded as sufficient to give rise to an aetiological legend, should be read with
caution: on p. 74, Kaufmann himself recognizes the presence of aetiological elements in this story, especially in vv. 24–26.

2. The geographical aspect of the narrative of the conquest of Ai
is extremely complex, in spite of (or perhaps really because of) its extremely detailed nature and the abundance of different references, all
of which present problems.

(a) 7.2 tells us that Ai is 'near Beth-Aven, east of Bethel'. LXX[B] gives only the first name, while LXX[A] gives only the second, but V and T confirm MT. Recently, J. M. Grintz has put forward weighty arguments for the view that Beth-Aven was in fact a third locality, still near Bethel, but distinct from it (pp. 211ff.). He believes that its name, afterwards understood in its derogatory form ('*āwen*, 'pain, sin', for '*ōn*) was preserved as an example after the destruction of the place, and was often quoted in this sense by the prophets of the eighth century in the attacks made at Bethel (cf. Hos. 4.15; 5.8; 10.5; Amos 5.5b). Because of the links between the two places, Bethel and Beth-Aven later came to be regarded as identical (during the rabbinic period the word *miqqedem* in v. 2 was generally translated 'in the past' rather than 'east of', a meaning which the expression can equally well have). The *tell* of Beth-Aven, now without a name, was renamed *hattel*, a name which is still found in the Arabic *et-tell*. Grintz notes in fact that Ai means not so much 'heap of ruins' (i.e. *tell*) but 'heap of stones', and there are quite a number of places (both in the OT and at the present day) which have a name consisting of, or derived from, the same element. Naturally, the identification of Beth-Aven with Ai, and the transfer of the name of the first place to Bethel, are pure conjecture, because we have no proof of this. In any case, Ai must be sought in the immediate neighbourhood of Bethel (cf. also 12.9).[1]

(b) 7.5 mentions 'ravines', which others translate by 'quarries' (of stone); these 'ravines' are linked with the gate of the city, but no other details are given by which they might be located. If we translate 'ravines', the expression may refer to the beginning of the sheer drop from the hill country towards the Jordan depression.

(c) 7.5a, cf. 8.24 (LXX), mentions the 'descent', which once again we would locate at the eastern edge of the hill country just where the descent towards the Jordan depression begins. Today, again following the traditional localization in this region, two tracks lead from Jericho to Beitin: one by '*ain ed-dūd*, and the other rather further to the south (cf. map 4 in Baldi), both covering a distance of about 20 km. If there was also a track at that period, one can see why this 'descent' is distinguished from the 'ravines' mentioned above.

(d) 8.4ff., 12–13: The ambush was laid 'behind' the city, and in vv. 9ff., 12 between Bethel and Ai, that is, east of the former and west of the latter.

[1] Z. Kallai (-Kleinmann), 'Notes on the Topography of Benjamin', *IEJ* 6, 1956, pp. 180–5, had located *bet awen* on *tell maryan* (141–75).

(e) In 8.11 the camp was set north of Ai, opposite the site of the 'ravine'. Did the original narrative describe Israel as coming from the north (i.e. from Shechem), rather than from Gilgal?

(f) 8.13 and perhaps v.9 talk of a 'valley' (or 'plain') which is different from the above.

(g) 8.13 speaks of a 'heel' in relation to the camp.

(h) 8.14 mentions a *mōʿēd*, literally 'the place for the assembly'. Other translations are also possible, but this one seems to be the best. It faced the Arabah, an expression which Deuteronomy often uses to indicate the Jordan depression, rather than the valley leading from the Dead Sea to the Red Sea to which this name usually refers. Thus this place was in a similar position to that of (b) and (c).

(i) 8.15, 20, 24 (?) mention the 'wilderness' towards which Joshua and his party fled. In v.24 LXX identifies the locality with that mentioned in (c). This region, too, it seems, must be sought at the extreme eastern edge of the hill country. According to this explanation, Joshua and his party fled in the direction of the depression from which they had come, which would have put them in a very difficult strategic situation.

(j) Finally, 8.24 mentions a 'field'.

The possibility of understanding the topography of this region as it is described in Josh. 7–8 is entirely dependent upon the possibility of setting the indications given in a real topographical context. M. Noth (pp. 48f.), however, rightly points out the difficulty of an operation of this kind: only someone who knew the topography of the region at that time could attempt to localize the particular places mentioned, and it is not possible for us to check them today. In fact writers are almost unanimous in their identification: Bethel is identified with the present-day *bētīn* (172–148), a few km ENE of the present-day *rām-ʾallah*; Ai is identified by almost all writers with *et-tell* (174–158) (an identification which Noth regards as beyond all question), except for Kallai (-Kleinmann) and Grintz; it is situated about 2km SE of *bētīn*. An identification with *khirbet ḥayar*, another *tell* in this region (175–145), which seems at least to have retained some connection with the name of Ai, cannot be maintained because recent test excavations have shown no trace of any occupation earlier than the Roman period.

Even if these two identifications are admitted, we encounter a series of difficulties. First of all, the position of *et-tell* is only close to *bētīn* in theory, for there are considerable difficulties of communication between these two places, which are separated by a small range of mountains (as J. Simons pointed out in 1944.) Moreover, the excavations carried out at *et-tell* before the war and recently continued show the existence of a large town at the end of the third millennium followed only by a brief Israelite reoccupation lasting from the beginning of the Iron Age (eleventh century) to the second half of the tenth century. Thus at the period of the Israelite conquest the place was certainly uninhabited, and the most one can suppose (Vincent, Abel) is that in its ruins the inhabitants of Bethel set up a forward post (which would also explain why at the beginning of the story the scouts believed that a small number of men would be enough; in any case the figures given in the course of the narrative are completely exaggerated). The results of the excavations recently taken up again under the direction of J. A. Callaway only confirm the results of the excavations carried out before the war, and the perplexities of Kaufmann, *The Biblical Account*, pp. 76ff., who believes that the excavations before and immediately after the war were hasty and inadequate, are no longer justified.

The disagreement between the archaeological and the literary data, which recalls the situation with regard to Jericho, but cannot be resolved by similar explanations, has now been smoothed over by an ingenious hypothesis put forward by Albright and maintained by his disciples (G. E. Wright and J. Bright). This is that in reality the Israelites conquered Bethel (i.e., the present passage would be parallel to Judg. 1.22ff.) and repopulated it. Later, the theme of destruction, which was difficult to reconcile with a flourishing city, was transferred to the neighbouring *tell*, to which the name 'heap of stones' was applied. But even with this explanation there is a difficulty, largely literary in nature: Josh. 7–8 and Judg. 1.22ff. would then be two substantially different narratives concerning the same event; and there are other difficulties, archaeological in nature.

The excavations at the present-day *bētīn*, restricted to the neighbourhood of the locality which partly covers the site of the ancient town, were carried out in 1934 by Albright himself, and then by G. L. Kelso in 1954, 1957 and 1960. These excavations prove beyond doubt that the place was destroyed towards the end of the thirteenth century, at the same time as a series of sites in the central and southern hill country,[1] followed by an occupation by a people at a lower technical

1 Cf. W. F. Albright, 'The First Month of Excavation at Bethel', *BASOR* 55 1934, pp. 24–25; id., 'The Kyle Memorial Excavation at Bethel', *BASOR* 56, 1934, pp. 2–25; J. L. Kelso, 'The Second Campaign at Bethel', *BASOR* 137, 1955, pp.

level, which the excavators identified with the Israelites. There are two points to note in this thesis:

(*a*) It is possible, and even probable, that the destruction of *bētīn* and the other sites in the hill country were carried out by the Israelite invaders. But it is not certain, since other peoples were moving about in the region and civil wars between the various city states were numerous.

(*b*) In order to explain the connection between Bethel and Ai, the hypothesis assumes a transfer of names and identities. It was proposed for the first time by Alt, but he later withdrew it. It was extended by Albright, who based it on a study by Dussaud. Apart from the fact that it is only a hypothesis, it raises the question of the connection between the present narrative and that of Judg. 1.22ff., and can also easily be refuted for a number of detailed reasons which cannot be gone into here.[1]

(*c*) There is another quite different point to consider. While it is true that Bethel is nowadays unanimously identified with *bētīn*, so that Ai (closely linked in the OT to Bethel, cf. Gen 12.8 and 13.3) would have to be located in the immediate neighbourhood, this identification is based solely on the mention of Bethel as the frontier point between Benjamin and Ephraim (cf. 16.2; 18.13), and on the etymology *bēt'ēl→bētīn*, with the transformation of the Hebrew *lāmed* into the Arabic *nūn*. Only the first argument is valid. The second was maintained for the first time by Edward Robinson in the last century, and taken up again by Albright in the 1920's.[2] Now, apart from the

5–10; 'The Third Campaign at Bethel', *BASOR* 151, 1958, pp. 3–9; 'The Fourth Campaign at Bethel', *BASOR* 164, 1961, pp. 5–9; W. F. Albright, *Recent Discoveries* . . ., pp. 47ff.; J. L. Kelso, 'Excavations at Bethel', *BA* 19, 1956, pp. 36–48; O. Eissfeldt, 'Bethel', *RGG³*, I, 1957, cols. 1095f.; K. Elliger, 'Bethel', *BHH*, I, 1962, cols. 231–3; J. L. Kelso, 'Bethel (Sanctuary)', *IDB* I, 1962, pp. 391–3; J. L. Kelso et al., 'The Excavation of Bethel (1934–1960)', *AASOR* XXXIX, 1968. The thesis of Albright and his disciples is also found in M. Bič, 'Bet'el—le sanctuaire du Roi', *ArOr* 17, 1, 1949, pp. 46–63.

[1] Cf. already L. H. Vincent, 'Les fouilles d'et-Tell-Aï', *RB* 46, 1937, pp. 231–66, where *et-tell* is considered to be a precarious forward post in front of Bethel; M. Noth, 'Hat die Bibel doch recht?', *Festschrift Günther Dehn*, Neukirchen 1957, pp. 7–22, esp. pp. 13ff. and nn. 6, 7, 8. We have discussed some aspects of this problem in 'Zwei umstrittene Stellen aus dem Überlieferungskreis um Schechem', *ZAW* 73, 1961, pp. 78–87, esp. pp. 85ff.

[2] Edward Robinson, *Biblical Researches in Palestine and the Adjacent Regions*, I, London 1856, pp. 448–50; W. F. Albright, 'Ai and Bet Awen', *AASOR* IV, 1924, pp. 140–9. Simons, in 1944, was already expressing his doubts on this matter.

inherent weakness of any purely etymological solution of problems of this kind, the etymology in itself is doubtful. Even if we admit that in some cases the Hebrew *lāmed* can become an Arabic *nūn*, this does not always necessarily happen. Terminations in '*ēl* and derivatives are also to be found in Arabic. Moreover, any proposed solution must take into account the Samaritan traditions which locate Bethel on Mt Gerizim, identifying it with the Samaritan sanctuary on that mountain,[1] and these traditions should be subjected to a critical examination before any categorical affirmation is made about the site of Bethel. In fact, if the traditions have preserved reliable information, we would have an explanation of the reason why the redactor placed Josh. 8.30–35, which belongs to the Shechem traditions, after this episode, and it would also be clear how the latter could have fallen into Israelite hands without a struggle. Moreover, the famous pilgrimage from Shechem to Bethel[2] would at once be set in a completely different geographical perspective. The same is true for the connection found in I Kings 12 between the new capital of Israel, Shechem, and the national sanctuary at Bethel. We will return to these important factors in our commentary on Judg. 1.2ff.

As for the text itself, its composite character clearly appears from the doublets of 8.4, 9; 8.12, and in the insertion of the Achan episode. The underlying basis may be reasonably supposed to be an ancient story, perhaps of Benjaminite origin, which spoke of a reverse suffered by Israel in the hill country that was remedied by aid of a ruse. Since it concerned a period in which the Canaanites were usually the victors (cf. Judg. 1 and the parallels in Joshua), it is not surprising that the episode was well known and for a long time was the basis of various versions which include the narrative which we now possess. This has now become the model and pattern of such incidents: the obedience of faith is the only thing which can give victory to Israel, while disobedience leads to disaster. To develop his thesis, the Deuteronomic redactor, probably drawing on elements already present in the work of the much earlier 'compiler' (M. Noth), uses the ancient aetiological legend linked with the plain at Achor, and grafts on to it the theme of disobedience to the order to carry out the ban, with the extension of the ban to the guilty person. We know that the reform of Josiah tried to bring back into force the ancient ideology of the holy

[1] J. Macdonald, *The Theology of the Samaritans*, London 1963, cf. index s.v. Bethel.
[2] A. Alt, 'Die Wallfahrt von Sichem nach Bethel', 1938, *KS* I, Munich 1953, pp. 79–88; and our article quoted above (n. 37).

war which had lapsed for centuries (Deut. 20f.), This narrative, linked in such a way with the conquest of Jericho and that of Ai, presented numerous opportunities for an attempt of this kind. The application of the story takes on a very special sense if we can perceive in it
the echo of a message addressed to the exiles of the sixth century, ex-
horted not to return to the errors of their fathers, which first the prophets and then the Deuteronomic school saw as leading directly to
the disaster of the exile. Unfortunately, one can no longer, as in Joshua 2, go back here to the primitive stage of the tradition; nor can we
be certain that Ai was the original name of the place. The description
of the topography of the region could be a vestige of the primitive version of the story, because if it was the work of the 'compiler' or of Dtr,
it would be a good deal clearer. On the other hand, the emphasis
placed in the story as we have it on the theological and ethical necessity of customs which reflect the faith professed make it quite clear
why strictly historical and geographical elements were pushed into the
background.

After these observations, our comments on individual verses may
be reduced to the minimum.

[7.5] The death of thirty-six people out of a total of two to three
thousand does not seem to be a sufficiently important factor to justify
the reactions described. In reality, it is the figures given in our text
which are questionable.

[6] The rites described are part of the usual ceremonies of mourning
(cf. Exod. 32.11; Num. 14.13ff.; Deut. 9.26; etc.). The mention, here
and in 8.10, of the 'elders of Israel' presents a problem: from ch. 1 on,
Dtr has always used the word 'scribes' (*šōṭᵉrîm*). The reason for this
change of terminology is not clear. Perhaps the expression is that of
the 'compiler', and was adopted by Dtr. Similarly, the presence of the
ark of Yahweh, apart from the fact that it is uncertain from the textual point of view, raises the same problems as in ch. 3.

[7–9] The dialogue emphasizes that the people have no guarantee.
The fact that they are conducting, or believe that they are conducting,
a holy war in the name of Yahweh does not imply any obligation on
the part of God, as his reply in vv. 10–15 makes clear.

[19] The confession of praise seems to have been necessary in order
that no one should believe that the method employed was arbitrary.

[21–22] 'A mantle from Shinar' is a garment of Mesopotamian
origin (for the name, cf. Gen. 11.2ff.), a region celebrated for works of
art of great value. The presence of riches at Jericho, a point to which

all traffic from the east to the west of the Jordan had to pass, is not improbable. The 'shekel' weighs rather less than 11.5g, so that the sum is one of some value. The connection between the various objects in not always clear in the narrative: in v. 21, the silver is buried, while the bar of gold is wrapped in the mantle; in v. 22 even the mantle is buried (which is improbable, considering it was made of perishable material), while the bar of gold, as above, was rolled in the mantle.

[24ff.] According to the text the stoning, that is the collective execution of the guilty person by the community, who thereby declared that they shared responsibility for the sentence pronounced, took place in the presence of the family and the goods of the guilty person. This latter detail suggests that the whole clan of the condemned man, even if it was not considered directly responsible for what had happened and therefore subject to the same penalty, had to be expelled from the community, being as it were contaminated. Perhaps a narrative also existed which described the extermination of the whole group, a severe sentence which had come to be mitigated by the Deuteronomic period, when the emphasis began to be placed on the individual responsibility of the guilty person.

[8.1] 'Do not fear or be dismayed' is a typical phrase of the oracle of salvation, customarily pronounced by a prophet or a priest[1], and sometimes by Yahweh himself. It also belongs to the ritual of the holy war, where it appears in a similar context, but naturally refers to the results of the battle. Thus the death of the guilty person has removed the curse.

[2] We are told nothing in the previous chapters of the death of the king of Jericho; the end of ch. 6 mentions only the extermination of the whole city. The extermination of the inhabitants of a city is explicitly enjoined in Deut. 20.16–18. [29] Deut. 21.22–23 explicitly orders that the body of an executed person should be taken down from the gallows before sunset. The theme of the heap of stones is found here in similar circumstances to 10.26–27 (cf. the commentary on that passage, and cf. also 7.26). In I Sam. 31.10 a similar treatment is inflicted on a body. Here we have a double aetiology (Möhlenbrink): that of the *tell* and that of the heap of stones in the ruins of the gate.[2]

---

[1] For an analysis of this literary form which has become classical, cf. J. Begrich, 'Das priesterliche Heilsorakel', *ZAW* 52, 1934, pp. 81–92 (*Gesammelte Studien*, Munich 1964, pp. 217–31). A comment: to make this literary form a *priestly* form is to restrict its setting in life to a particular class and excludes its use by the prophets.

[2] For Josh. 8.30–35, see the commentary on Josh. 24. LXX inserts it after 9.2.

CHAPTER 9

The Covenant with the Gibeonites

9 ¹When all the kings who were beyond the Jordan in the hill country and in the foothills and all along the coast of the Great Sea toward Lebanon, the Hittites, the Amorites and Canaanites, the Perizzites, the Hivites, and the Jebusites, heard of this, ²they gathered together with one accord to fight Joshua and Israel.

3 But when the inhabitants of Gibeon heard what Joshua had done to Jericho and Ai, ⁴they on their part acted with cunning, and went and made ready provisions, and took worn-out sacks upon their asses, and wineskins, worn-out and torn and mended, ⁵with worn-out, patched sandals on their feet, and worn-out clothes; and all their provisions were dry and crumbly. ⁶And they went to Joshua in the camp at Gilgal, and said to him and to the men of Israel, 'We have come from a far country; so now make a covenant with us.' ⁷But the men of Israel said to the Hivites, 'Perhaps you live among us; then how can I make a covenant with you?' ⁸They said to Joshua, 'We are your servants.' And Joshua said to them, 'Who are you? And where do you come from?' ⁹They said to him, 'From a very far country your servants have come, because of the name of the LORD your God; for we have heard a report of him, and all that he did in Egypt, ¹⁰and all that he did to the two kings of the Amorites who were beyond the Jordan, Sihon the king of Heshbon, and Og king of Bashan, who dwelt in Ashtaroth.

11 And our elders and all the inhabitants of our country told us to take provisions in our hand for the journey, and to meet you, and say to you, "We are your servants; come now, make a covenant with us." ¹²Here is our bread; it was still warm when we took it from our houses as our food for the journey, on the day we set forth to come to you, but now, behold, it is dry and crumbly; ¹³these wineskins were new when we filled them, and behold, they are burst; and these garments and shoes of ours are worn out from the very long journey.'

14 So the men partook of their provisions, and did not ask the oracle of the LORD. ¹⁵And Joshua made peace with them, and made a covenant with them, to guarantee their lives; and the leaders of the congregation confirmed by oath.

16 At the end of three days after they had made a covenant with them, they heard that they were their neighbours, and that they dwelt among them. [17]And the people of Israel set out and reached their cities on the third day. Now their cities were Gibeon, Chepirah, Beeroth, and Kiriath-jearim. [18]But the people of Israel did not kill them, because the leaders of the congregation had sworn to them by the LORD, the God of Israel. Then all the congregation murmured against the leaders.

19 But all the leaders said to the congregation, 'We have sworn to them by the LORD, the God of Israel, and now we may not touch them. [20]This we will do to them, and let them live, lest wrath be upon us, because of the oath which we swore to them.'

21 And the leaders said to them, 'Let them live, but let them become hewers of wood and drawers of water for all the congregation.' When the leaders had spoken to them, [22]Joshua summoned them, and he said to them, 'Why did you deceive us, saying, "We are very far from you," when you dwell among us? [23]Now therefore you are cursed, and some of you shall always be slaves, hewers of wood and drawers of water for the temple of my God.' [24]They answered Joshua, 'Because it was told to your servants for a certainty what the LORD your God had decided with his servant Moses, to give you all the land, and to destroy all the inhabitants of the land before you; so we feared greatly for our lives because of you, and did this thing. [25]And now, behold, we are in your hand: do as it seems good and right in your sight to do to us.' [26]So he did to them, and delivered them out of the hand of the people of Israel: and they did not kill them. [27]But Joshua made them that day hewers of wood and drawers of water for the congregation and for the altar of the LORD, to continue to this day, in the place which he should choose.

Bibliography: A. *Archaeology and geography*: Z. Kallai -Kleinmann), 'B^e'ērōt', '*Ereṣ Iśrā'el* 3, 1959, pp. 111–15 (in Hebrew); J. B. Pritchard, 'Gibeon's History in the Light of Archaeology', SVT VII, 1959, pp. 1–12, esp. pp. 3f.; id., 'A Bronze Age Necropolis at Gibeon', *BA* 24, 1961, pp. 19–24; id., *Gibeon–Where the Sun Stood Still*, Princeton 1962; K. Galling, 'Kritische Bemerkungen zur Ausgrabung von eğ-ğib', *BO* 22, 1965, pp. 242–5; also J. A. Callaway–R. E. Cooley, 'A salvage excavation at Raddana, in Bireh', *BASOR* 201, 1971, pp. 9–19; A. Ibáñez Arana, 'El pacto con los gabaonitas (Jos. 9) como narración etiológica', *Estudios Bíblicos* 30, 1971, pp. 161–75, which appeared too late to be consulted.
B. *History and Literature*: K. Möhlenbrink, 'Die Landnahmesagen . . .', pp. 241–5; W. Rudolph, *Der 'Elohist' als Erzähler* . . ., pp. 200–4; J. Liver, 'The Literary History of Joshua IX', *JSS* 8, 1963, pp. 227–43; F. C. Fensham, 'The Treaty between Israel and the Gibeonites', *RA* 27, 1964, pp. 96–100; Auzou, pp. 111ff.; J. Blenkinsopp, 'Are there Traces of the

Gibeonite Covenant in Deuteronomy?', *CBQ* 28, 1966, pp. 207–19.
C. *Hivites and Hurrites*: E. A. Speiser, 'Ethnic Movements in the Near East in the Second Millenium B.C.', *AASOR* XIII, 1933, pp. 13–54; R. T. O'Callaghan, *Aram Naharaim*, Rome 1948, pp. 54f. n.8; E. A. Speiser, 'Hivite', *IDB* II, 1962, p. 615.

[9.1] LXX has 'Antilebanon' instead of 'Lebanon' as in ch. 1, and in the list of peoples, in the last place but one, 'Girgashites', which has no doubt been lost in the Hebrew and the other translations. Note the expression 'beyond the Jordan' to indicate the land west of the Jordan; thus the point of view here seems to be of someone east of the Jordan. LXX has in each case 'the kings of . . .' [2] LXX inserts 8.30–35 after this verse. [3] Instead of 'Joshua', LXXᴮ has 'the Lord'. Some scholars (Baldi) regard this as a mistaken reading, but it could also be a theological correction as in 7.7, with the purpose of giving all glory to Yahweh. [4] *wayyiṣeṭayyārū*: following some MSS this is usually read *wayyiṣeṭayyādū* (confusion between *dālet* and *rēš*). *ṣyd* means 'go hunting', and in the *hithpael* 'get ready for hunting', whence the derivative sense 'carry provisions'. The verb also appears in vv. 5b and 12 and in the ancient translations. *ṣyr*, which MT reads, is found only here as a verb, and its primary meaning is 'messenger', so that the *hithpael* would have to be understood to mean 'disguise oneself as a messenger', or simply 'disguise oneself' (Abel). Both verbs are found in LXX. The terminology of vv. 4–5, cf. vv. 12–13, is that in use in the desert (cf. Deut. 8.4; 29.5). [5] 'All their provisions': LXX read εὑρωτιῶν, i.e. *wbl(h)* 'mouldy, spoilt' instead of *kl* (probably a confusion between *kap* and *bēt*). [6] 'And to the men of Israel' is lacking in LXX. This is a doublet which anticipates the following verse. [7] 'They replied': Q and Tᴶ read the singular ('and the Israelite replied'), while K, Tᴹˢˢ, LXX, V and Syr read the plural. *haḥiwwī* tells us about the inhabitants of Gibeon and the tetrapolis (v. 17). LXX (as in Gen. 34.2; 36.20) has χορραῖον = *ḥōrī*, 'Hurrite', perhaps a confusion between *rēš* and *waw*. In II Sam. 21.2 they are called Amorites. 'How can I make a covenant with you?': LXX and V have the plural, Q and K the singular; for the form cf. *B–L* § 50v. The problem of this verse and the few verses that follow is probably that originally the subject was 'the Israelites' (cf. LXX and V), now replaced in the redaction by 'Joshua the Israelite' ('*īš yiśrā'ēlī* perhaps understood as a collective, which is what is usually done, but also as a singular). [9] The mention of Egypt is lacking in LXX. 'We have heard a report', in Hebrew *šōmeʿō* from *šōmaʿ*, 'a rumour'; some scholars (Noth) propose *šimʿō*, 'the news', while others (Hertzberg) propose *šāmōaʿ* 'we have indeed heard': LXX rendered it by τὸ ὄνομα, reading *šemō*, 'its name', 'the renown of it', a repetition caused by assonance, which seems to suggest a reading like *šimʿō*. [10] 'Who dwelt in' is in LXX and Syr but is lacking in MT and V. After Astaroth LXX adds Edreï, as in 12.4 and

Deut. 1.4. Instead of Heshbon, LXX^B has 'Amorites', owing to an error. [11] 'Your servants': LXX^B has 'thy servants', cf. v. 7. We have put the second statement, by the elders, into indirect speech; in Hebrew, all three are in direct speech. [12] 'From our houses' is lacking in LXX. [14] 'The men': LXX has οἱ ἄρχοντες, i.e. *hann^eśî'îm* (cf. *BH*³), as in v. 15b. But this is not a better reading, because the Gibeonites appear before Joshua and the Israelites, not before a meeting of chiefs; in v. 15 the situation is different. 'The oracle': literally, 'the mouth of Yahweh'. LXX omits 'the mouth', no doubt in order to eliminate an anthropomorphism (Benjamin). [15] 'To guarantee their lives'; literally, 'to let them live'. [17] 'The third day' is lacking in LXX; it serves no purpose in MT, but is confirmed by the other versions. [18] 'Murmur': root *lwn*, a technical term in Exod. 15–17; Num. 14–17 for the 'murmuring in the wilderness' against Yahweh and Moses. [20] 'And let them live', in Hebrew *haḥ^ayeh*, inf. absolute *hiphil* with a finite value. LXX has 'having left them alive' (ζωγρῆσαι = *w^ehaḥayyeh*). [21] LXX and V omit the beginning, which effectively interrupts the context. 'But let them become': Hebrew has 'and they became', *waw* copulative instead of *waw* consecutive, but LXX with the future and V with the final clause, cf. T^{MSS}, read a *waw* consecutive, which we introduce. After the statement by the leaders, LXX ^{MSS} and Syr added: LXX: 'And the whole assembly did as the leaders . . .'; Syr: 'And the leaders said to them: "Let them live and let them be hewers of wood and drawers of water for the congregation of Yahweh to this day" ' (cf. *BH*³). The latter phrase anticipates v. 27 out of context. [22] LXX read the pronouns in the singular. [23] LXX omits 'the temple of' and has 'for me and for my God', perhaps in order to avoid the anachronism of the mention of the Jerusalem temple, cf. v. 27. [27] In LXX the pronouns and verbs are in the plural. [26–27] Slight variants in LXX. The second part of the verse is clearly a Deuteronomic addition and is anachronistic.

The history of the alliance between Gibeon and Israel presents a situation somewhat different from that of the stories of Jericho and Ai.

1. In the first place, the topography (as in the case of Jericho) is now clear. The excavations carried out at *ej-jib* (approximately 12 km NE of Jerusalem, 167–139) in 1956, 1957, 1959, 1960 and 1962 by the expedition organized by the University of Pennsylvania Museum and led by J. B. Pritchard revealed the remains of a town fully equipped for the production of wine, and a store of earthenware jars for the bottling and transport of this wine. The handles of these jars carried the inscription *gb'n*, the name of Gibeon in defective spelling, as could be expected at that period. With this discovery, the arguments still adopted by Alt and Noth (p. 112) against this identification can be

regarded as refuted. At the present day, only K. Galling continues to
doubt the identification of Gibeon with *ej-jib*, on the grounds that the
etymological relationship between the two names is not clear, and that
the amphorae for the wine could have been brought into the town,
from Gibeon itself. The latter statement seems unlikely, since there is
good evidence of the production of wine in large quantities, so that it
would seem absurd for the place to have had to import it—unless, of
course, the wine was for blending with wines produced locally, But in
this case it would not seem logical to have bottled and transported it in
amphorae, because these were reserved for more costly products. Until recently an important difficulty lay in the lack of findings from the
late Bronze Age, a phenomenon similar to that observed at Jericho.
But this difficulty has been overcome by the discovery of a cemetery
belonging to precisely this period. Thus one can conclude that the
town was inhabited at the period of the conquest. Perhaps the remains of the town lie under the present-day settlement. Gibeon is also
mentioned in Josh. 10.1–15; II Sam. 2.12–17; 20.4–13; 21.1–11; I
Kings 3.3ff. From then on we hear nothing more of Gibeon until the
time of Jeremiah.

2. The literary history of Joshua 9 is not simple. Möhlenbrink, and
more recently Kaufmann in his commentary, in discussing vv. 7ff.,
where Joshua alternates with the Israelites, have attempted to distinguish two different strata of tradition. Möhlenbrink thinks there
was a 'Joshua' recension and an 'Israelite' recension, while Kaufmann
believes there was a 'priestly' (*kōhenît*, with Joshua or the Israelite as
the subject) recension, containing the ruse, the covenant, the discovery of the deceit, the conquest of the city and the reduction of the
Gibeonites to hewers of wood and drawers of water for the altar, and a
second recension, with the congregation and the leaders as the subject, with the reduction of the Gibeonites to servants of the congregation. But apart from the fact that by this system neither of the two succeeds in reconstructing two coherent narratives, the making of a covenant by Joshua and the Israelites, a covenant which they both keep,
even after the discovery of the deceit of the Gibeonites, rather suggests a later and tendentious re-elaboration of an ancient tradition,
the theme of which was simply the making of a covenant between the
invaders and the inhabitants of Gibeon. Rudolph already thought
there was a primitive J stratum, cf. the recent studies of Mowinckel.
He considered that the work of Noth's 'compiler' and then the Deuteronomic redaction were imposed upon this. In the course of the re-

elaboration and redaction of the text, he believed, Joshua was introduced alongside the Israelites, the name of whom thereafter being
regarded as in apposition in the singular to the name of Joshua, virtually disappeared. It is significant that it was the elders who 'confirmed by oath' what Joshua had done and that the enmity of Israel
was directed against them. This implies that it was the elders who
promoted this covenant, and who were no doubt originally the ones
to make the agreement in v. 14 (cf. v. 19). It is also the people (in
LXX it is the chiefs) who eat the Gibeonites' provisions (v. 14). In all
this Joshua clearly has a secondary role, in spite of the re-elaboration
of the text. Except in v. 15, quoted already, he does no more than ask
questions and make statements (vv. 8b and 22).

As Liver has rightly pointed out, the story of the ruse itself contains evident confusions. If the Gibeonites claimed to come from a
long way off (vv. 6b, 9, 22), why did they ask for a covenant? What
use would it have been to them? And how could the Israelites have
allowed themselves to be deceived? Verse 7 states explicitly that at
first the Israelites had some doubts! Liver concludes that in reality
both Joshua and the chiefs had good reason to allow themselves to be
deceived, which explains the animosity of the people towards them a
little later (v. 18). But in addition, the language of the request made
by the Gibeonites is typical of the inferior party who demands from
the more powerful an alliance for his own safety:[1] 'Come now' (vv.
6b and 11b); 'We are your servants' (that is, 'vassals', v. 11). The redactors were later able to interpret this demand and this offer in the
pejorative sense which 'ebed can also have: 'slave'. Again, it is clear
that vv. 1–2, the speeches in vv. 9–10 and 24–25, cf. the appendix v.
27b, are Deuteronomic, and in v. 24 the Gibeonites seem to be aware
of the commands given in Deut. 20.10–18.[2] The speeches have the
same theme as the exchanges between Rahab and the spies in Josh.
2.9–11, and their literary category is that of the Deuteronomic confession of faith put into the mouth of a stranger who is willing to submit himself to it. The appendix, v. 27b, is an anachronistic reference
to the temple of Jerusalem, because for Dtr, to carry out a cultic act
in any other place is regarded as impious; but originally the allusion
could only have referred to an altar at Gibeon (see below).

[1] Cf. J. Begrich, 'Berit', ZAW 60, 1944, pp. 1–11 (Gesammelte Studien, Munich
1964, pp. 55–66); G. E. Mendenhall, 'Govenant Forms in Israelite Tradition', BA
17, 1954, pp. 50–76, esp. pp. 56ff.

[2] Noth, p. 9, considers vv. 9b–10, 24, 27b to be Deuteronomic.

The final question which must be raised is that of the historical basis of the mention of the enslavement of the Gibeonites, the circumstances which led to their having this servile role in Israel. There is no reference elsewhere in the OT to such a situation on the part of the Gibeonites, but it is often related (cf. Bright and Liver) to that of the $n^e\bar{t}\bar{\imath}n\bar{\imath}m$ (v. 27 contains the root ntn). But these persons do not appear until the post-exilic period: Ezra 2.58; 8.20; Neh. 7.46–60. The second of these texts reads the '$n^e\bar{t}\bar{\imath}n\bar{\imath}m$ (the 'given': RSV: 'temple servants') whom David and his officials had set apart to attend the Levites'; there is no connection, even hypothetical, with the Gibeonites. This means that the aetiological motive which Gressmann, Alt and Noth strongly maintain is present in the final verse amounts to very little. Nor do we know anything of the altar: in spite of the final injunction, it is clear that it was an altar at Gibeon, where Solomon later repaired (I Kings 3), cf. the traditions recorded by I Chron. 21.29; II Chron. 1.3, which place the tent of meeting beside the altar, while II Chron. 1.5 seeks to identify it with the altar made in the desert; but these are only speculations, because we possess no historical information which we can work on. Another possibility would be that the Gibeonites served an altar at Gilgal, where according to I Sam. 11.15 and 13.9 sacrifices were offered; but these two texts tell us nothing about the nature of the altar or of the personnel associated with it. Finally, Dtr may have had the altar of Shechem in mind (Josh. 8.30–35), but the pre-Deuteronomic stratum could not have reflected this view.

The situation described in 10.1ff. suggests rather that there was a treaty of mutual assistance, in which the Gibeonites may perhaps have been the inferior party, but which must have been made by means of a normal agreement between the parties and not through the deceit of the inferior party. The logic of 10.1ff., as we shall see, is that the kings of the region formed a coalition when they learned that Israel had succeeded in obtaining a foothold in the hill country following an agreement with Gibeon: it would be absurd to mount an expedition to attack a population who had been reduced to a condition of helotry! In fact, as Blenkinsopp has pointed out, the Deuteronomic passages in ch. 9 reflect a terminology which is also found in Deuteronomy; amongst others, the terms 'hewers of wood' and 'drawers of water' appear in Deut. 29.11 to indicate an inferior form of membership of the community.

The conclusion which follows is that the narrative of a making of an alliance between Israel and the Gibeonites was re-elaborated at a later period to justify the existence of a situation which was a flagrant violation of the norms laid down by Deut. 20.10–18. This theme may already have been present in the work of the 'compiler', but it is no longer possible to be sure of this in the present state of the text. Thus we must give serious consideration to the possibility that this passage, of whose primitive form traces are still present here and there, takes us back to a very early period, when Israel, in spite of the covenant, had taken steps against the allied Gibeonite cities. In this case, the origin of the story would be the ideological preparation for the steps taken, which would be justified by the claim that the Gibeonites had exercised deceit. See below for details.

3. All our conclusions so far show that underlying the present account is a very early narrative relating to a covenant concluded between the invaders and the Hivite tetrapolis, which is mentioned only in v. 17. The important study by Fensham is devoted to this subject. II Samuel 21.1–14 supplies us with an excellent proof of the basic historicity of this story. Saul had broken the covenant with the Gibeonites in circumstances about which we are not told but which we may connect, hypothetically, with an attempt to eliminate an enclave which for some reason was regarded as dangerous (as we have seen in the preceding section, this may be the context which gave rise to the polemic re-elaboration of the story). The violation of the covenant, a crime which throughout the ancient Near East was punished by the deity by means of a whole series of curses explicitly called down by the contracting parties in their original stipulation, resulted in a severe drought over the whole country; only the punishment of those who were guilty could bring matters back into order.[1] This attack of Saul on the Gibeonites, an attack which apparently succeeded, also casts light on the hostility of the exiles from Beeroth in II Sam. 4.2ff., which otherwise would be incomprehensible. This allows us to put forward a probable suggestion about the action undertaken by Saul against the tetrapolis: that it was for the purpose of expelling the inhabitants and incorporating their territory into that of the tribe of

[1] A. Malamat, 'Doctrine of Causality in Hittite and Biblical Historiography', *VT* 5, 1955, pp. 1–22; H. Cazelles, 'Davidic Monarchy and the Gibeonite Claims', *PEQ* 87, 1955, pp. 165–75; cf. our *Das Königtum in Israel: Ursprung, Anfang und Entwicklung*, BZAW 104, Berlin 1967, pp. 48ff., 69; also the articles cited above by Liver, pp. 239ff., and Fensham.

Benjamin, i.e., his own tribe. We know from elsewhere that Benjamin was always short of land.[1]

These two passages show, the first directly and the second indirectly, that the mention of a treaty between Israel and Gibeon is historical; this treaty, even if it had been made only by Benjaminite invaders, must have in one way or another come to be binding on the whole amphictyony.

There are features drawn from the covenant formula which are clearly visible in our text. These are: (a) The request of the Gibeonites (v. 6; cf. 8, 11), formulated in the language of the inferior party who seeks to become a vassal; (b) The exchange of food (perhaps for a common meal) (v. 14); (c) The granting of 'peace' on the part of the superior party (v. 15a); (d) The final oath which in every circumstance effects the inviolability of what has been concluded, on the part of the superior party (v. 15b, cf. 18); (e) Amongst the clauses it seems that there was always one concerning mutual defence (cf. 10.1ff); (f) Curses on the transgressor, indirectly attested by their fulfilment in II Sam. 21ff; the primitive and irrational character of these curses appears from the fact that the plagues which resulted could strike either the guilty person or the victim, and that the fault must be expiated in all circumstances, if necessary in the person of the relations of the guilty person, if he himself was no longer available. The exposure of the bodies to the elements and the wild beasts, attested in II Sam. 21.1ff., also forms part of the curses in question. The attitude of Rizpah, the unique exception in the biblical text, succeeded in saving the bodies of the victims, whose burial was ultimately ordered by David.

We can now go on to comment on individual verses:

[1–2] There is no connection between the beginning and what has taken place in the previous chapters; the situation assumed seems to be rather that of Josh. 10.1ff. The 'hill country', the 'foothills' and the 'coast of the Great Sea' are the three zones into which Palestine is divided towards the west.

[3–4] These verses, on the other hand, refer to the conquest of Jericho and Ai, but in the context of a development on the part of the redactor around the central theme: the ruse. [6] Gilgal also appears in the same context, whereas it is not mentioned in the rest of the chapter. 'Make a covenant . . .': kārat berīt, with le, in general indica-

---

[1] Cf. Liver, p. 241, and our articles 'Il regno di 'Esba'al, figlio di Saul', RSO 40, 1965, pp. 89–106, pp. 103ff.; Das Königtum . . ., loc. cit.

tes the inferiority of the party referred to by that preposition; between equal parties one usually finds ʿ*im*, or, ʾ*et*: 'with'.

[7] The Hivites (LXX: Hurrites) are mentioned in the list of peoples in Gen. 10.17 ‖ I Chron. 1.15 and in the stereotyped lists of inhabitants of Palestine conquered by Israel (cf. v. 1). They appear in a number of independent texts: Gen. 34.2 (LXX: Hurrites): in the present passage (LXX: Hurrites); Josh. 11.3a (LXX only), 3b (LXX: Hittites), 19 (LXX omits); Judg. 3.3 (the same phrase as in Josh. 11.3b); Isa. 17.9 (LXX: Hivites and Hurrites; MT is corrupt). The frequent confusion between Hivites and Hurrites may be, as we have seen, the consequence of the confusion between *wāw* and *rēš*, or else an indication that the Hivites were originally a Hurrite group, as Speiser holds.

[17] Here we have the only mention in the OT of the names of the tetrapolis. *hakkᵉpîrā*, which in Hebrew means 'lioness', can probably be identified with the present-day *tell kefîre* (160–137), which in Arabic means 'citizeness', approximately 7 km ESE of Gibeon. The site of *bᵉʾērōt*, in Hebrew 'wells', is uncertain, but its name is preserved in the present-day *el bire*, approximately 7 km north-east of Gibeon; an identification with *khirbet raddāna*, some 300 m from *el bire*, was recently proposed by J. A. Callaway. *qiryat yᵉʿārîm*, meaning in Hebrew 'town of the woods' (159–135), is beside the present day *abū ghūš*, a little more than 10 km east of Jerusalem on the present-day route for heavy lorries from Jerusalem to Tel-Aviv. Some of these places are mentioned again in Josh. 18.25, 26 (Gibeon and Chephirah) and in 15.9, 60; 18.14ff., 28 (Kiriath-Jearim), but as then forming part of the territory of Benjamin.

[18] An oath, even if it is violated by a deceit, cannot be annulled by the person who has given it, cf. a similar case in Gen. 27.35ff.

CHAPTER 10

The Battle of Gibeon and the Expeditions to the South

10 ¹When Adoni-zedek king of Jerusalem heard how Joshua had taken Ai, and had utterly destroyed it, doing to Ai and its king as he had done to Jericho and its king, and how the inhabitants of Gibeon had made peace with Israel and had been integrated with them, ²he feared greatly, because Gibeon was a great city, like one of the royal cities, and because it was greater than Ai, and all its men were mighty. ³So Adoni-zedek king of Jerusalem sent to Hoham king of Hebron, to Piram king of Jarmuth, to Japhia king of Lachish, and to Debir king of Eglon, saying, ⁴'Come up to me, and help me, and let us smite Gibeon; for it has made peace with Joshua and with the people of Israel.' ⁵Then the five kings of the Amorites, the king of Jerusalem, the king of Hebron, the king of Jarmuth, the king of Lachish, and the king of Eglon, gathered and set out on an expedition with all their armies and encamped against Gibeon, and made war against it.

6 And the men of Gibeon sent to Joshua at the camp in Gilgal, saying, 'Do not abandon your servants; come up to us quickly, and save us, and help us; for all the kings of the Amorites that dwell in the hill country are gathered against us.' ⁷So Joshua went up from Gilgal, he and all the people of war with him, and all the mighty men of valour. ⁸And the LORD said to Joshua, 'Do not fear them, for I have given them into your hands; there shall not a man of them stand before you.' ⁹So Joshua came upon them suddenly, having marched up all night from Gilgal. ¹⁰And the LORD threw them into a panic before Israel, who slew them with a great slaughter at Gibeon, and chased them by the way of the ascent of Beth-horon, and smote them as far as Azekah and Makkedah. ¹¹And as they fled before Israel, while they were going down the ascent of Beth-horon, the LORD threw down great stones from heaven upon them as far as Azekah, and they died; there were more who died because of the hailstones than the men of Israel killed with the sword.

12 Then, in the day when the LORD gave over the Amorites, Joshua spoke to the men of Israel; and he said in the sight of Israel,
'Sun, stand thou still at Gibeon,
and thou Moon in the valley of Aijalon.'
13 And the sun stood still, and the moon stayed,
until the nation took vengeance on their enemies.

Surely this is written in the 'Book of the Just'. The sun stayed in the midst of heaven, and did not hasten to go down for about a whole day. ¹⁴There has been no day like it before or since, when the LORD hearkened to the voice of a man; for the LORD fought for Israel. ¹⁵Then Joshua returned, and all Israel with him, to the camp at Gilgal.

16 These five kings fled, and hid themselves in the cave at Makkedah. ¹⁷And it was told Joshua, 'The five kings have been found, hidden in the cave at Makkedah.' ¹⁸And Joshua said, 'Roll great stones against the mouth of the cave, and set men by it to guard them; ¹⁹but do not stay there yourselves, pursue your enemies, cut off their retreat, do not let them enter their cities; for the LORD your God has given them into your hand.' ²⁰When Joshua and the men of Israel had finished slaying them with a very great slaughter, until they were wiped out, and when the remnant which remained of them had entered into the fortified cities, ²¹all the people returned safe to Joshua (in the camp) at Makkedah; not a man moved his tongue against any of the people of Israel. ²²Then Joshua said, 'Open the mouth of the cave, and bring those five kings out to me from the cave.' ²³And they did so, and brought those five kings out to him from the cave, the king of Jerusalem, the king of Hebron, the king of Jarmuth, the king of Lachish, and the king of Eglon. ²⁴And when they brought those kings out to Joshua, Joshua summoned all the men of Israel, and said to the chiefs of the men of war who had gone with him, 'Come near, put your feet upon the necks of these kings.' Then they came near, and put their feet on their necks. ²⁵And Joshua said to them, 'Do not be afraid or dismayed; be strong and of good courage; for thus the LORD will do to all your enemies against whom you fight.' ²⁶And afterward Joshua smote them and put them to death, and he hung them on five trees. And they hung upon the trees until evening; ²⁷but at the time of the going down of the sun, Joshua commanded, and they took them down from the trees, and threw them into the cave where they had hidden themselves, and they set great stones against the mouth of the cave, which remain to this very day.

28 And Joshua took Makkedah on that day, and smote it and its king with the edge of the sword; he utterly destroyed them and every person in it, he left none remaining. So he did to the king of Makkedah as he had done to the king of Jericho. ²⁹Then Joshua passed on from Makkedah, and all Israel with him, to Libnah, and fought against Libnah; ³⁰and the LORD gave it also and its king into the hand of Israel; and he smote it with the edge of the sword, and every person in it; he left none remaining in it; and he did to its king as he had done to the king of Jericho. ³¹And Joshua passed on from Libnah, and all Israel with him, to Lachish, and laid siege to it, and assaulted it; ³²and the LORD gave Lachish into the hand of Israel, and he took it on the second day, and smote it with the edge of the

sword, and every person in it, as he had done to Libnah. ³³Then Horam king of Gezer set out on an expedition to help Lachish; and Joshua smote him and his people, until he left none remaining. ³⁴And Joshua passed on with all Israel from Lachish to Eglon; and they laid siege to it, and assaulted it; ³⁵and they took it on that day, and smote it with the edge of the sword; and every person in it he utterly destroyed that day, as he had done to Lachish. ³⁶Then Joshua went up with all Israel from Eglon to Hebron; and they assaulted it, ³⁷and took it, and smote it with the edge of the sword, and its king and its towns, and every person in it; he left none remaining, as he had done to Eglon, and utterly destroyed it with every person in it. ³⁸Then Joshua, with all Israel, turned back to Debir and assaulted it, ³⁹and he took it with its king and all its towns; and they smote them with the edge of the sword, and utterly destroyed every person in it; he left none remaining; as he had done to Hebron and to Libnah and its king, so he did to Debir and to its king.

40 So Joshua defeated the whole land, the hill country and the Negeb and the foothills and the slopes, and all their kings; he left none remaining, but utterly destroyed all that breathed, as the LORD God of Israel commanded. ⁴¹And Joshua defeated them from Kadesh-barnea to Gaza, and all the country of Goshen, as far as Gibeon. ⁴²And Joshua took all these kings and their land at one time, because the LORD God of Israel fought for Israel. ⁴³Then Joshua returned, and all Israel with him, to the camp at Gilgal.

Bibliography: (a) *On the battle of Gibeon*: K. Möhlenbrink, 'Die Landnahmesagen . . .', pp.264ff.; W. Rudolph, *Der 'Elohist'* . . ., pp.207–9; G. E. Wright, 'The Literary and Historical Problem of Joshua 10 and Judges 1', *JNES* 5, 1946, pp.105–14; W. J. Phythian-Adams, 'A Meteorite of the Fourteenth Century', *PEQ* 78, 1946, pp.116–24; F. M. Abel, 'Les stratagèmes . . .,' pp.332ff.; J. de Fraine, 'De miraculo solari Josue', *VD* 28, 1950, pp.277–86; R. B. Y. Scott, 'Metereological Phenomena and Terminology in the Old Testament', *ZAW* 64, 1952, pp.11–25, esp. pp.19f.; G. Lambert, 'Josué à la bataille de Gabaon', *NRT* 76, 1954, pp.375–91; J. Heller, 'Der Name Eva', *ArOr* 26, 1958, pp.636–56, esp. pp.653ff.; J. B. Pritchard, 'Gibeon's History in the Light of Excavation', *SVT* VII, 1960, pp.4f.; J. Dus, 'Gibeon', *VT* 10, 1960, pp.353–74; K. D. Schunck, *Benjamin*, BZAW 86, Berlin 1963, pp.29ff.; Auzou, pp.115ff.; J. R. Halliday Jr, 'The Day(s) the Moon Stood Still', *JBL* 87, 1968, pp.166–78; M. Balában, 'Kosmische Dimensionen des Wunders von Gibeon', *Communio Viatorum* 12, 1969, pp.51–60; G. E. Wright, 'A Problem of Ancient Topography: Lachish and Eglon', *HTR* 64, 1971, pp.437–50 (to which we were unable to refer.). (b) *The five kings in the cave of Makkedah*: K. Elliger, 'Josua in Judäa', *PJB* 30, 1934, pp.47–71; M. Noth, 'Die fünf Könige in der Höhle von Makkeda', *PJB* 33, 1937, pp. 22–36; K. Möhlenbrink, 'Die Landnahmesagen . . .', pp. 264ff.; W. Rudolph, *Der 'Elohist'* . . ., pp. 209ff.; Y. Kaufmann, *The Biblical Account* . . ., pp. 72ff. (*c*) *The campaign in the southern hill country*: M. du Buit, *Géographie* . . ., p. 98.

---

[1] *'adōnī-ṣedeq*: LXX^B, here and in the verses that follow, has *'adōnī-bezeq*, as in Judg. 1.5ff.; Noth[1] regards this latter reading as the original one, and thinks that the former is a later attempt to adapt this tradition to that of Jerusalem. This view must be taken seriously, although there is no definite proof. 'Had made peace': LXX, here and in v. 4, has αὐτομόλησαν, cf. V: *quod transfugissent*. It is difficult to say whether this is a variant, or a particular view of the meaning of *šlm*. [2] The comparison with the treatment of Ai is lacking in LXX. 'Royal cities': LXX has the more general expression, 'one of the capitals', μητροπόλεων, perhaps because the meaning of the original institution was no longer understood. [3] The names, here and in v. 5, present notable variants in LXX:

> *hōhām Αιλαμ*
> *pir'ām Φιδων* (confusion of *rēš* and *dālet*?)
> *yāpīa' Ιεφθα*
> *'eglōn Οδολλαμ*

Cf. also the note on v. 10. The other versions confirm MT, apart from a few variants in the vocalization. *d^ebīr* was never the name of a person, but always a well-known locality in the southern hill country. [4] For *'ālāh*, 'set out on an expedition', cf. the commentary on 7.3, p. 93. 'Make peace' is equivalent to 'make an alliance'. [5] 'Gathered' is lacking in LXX, which has the unlikely 'Jebusites' instead of 'Amorites'. 'All their armies', literally, 'their camps'. LXX and V render this by 'their people' and 'their armies' respectively. [6] 'Do not abandon', literally, 'Do not withdraw your hand from . . .'. [10] 'Threw them into a panic': LXX and V read 'troubled them'. For 'Beth-horon', LXX^B has Ὡρωνειν, i.e. *hōrōnaim*, an improbable reading, since it introduces a town which is found only in Moab in the OT and on the Mesha stele, lines 31–32. Perhaps the Hebrew text of LXX had a *mem* enclitic which was no longer understood as such. [12] 'The men of Israel': LXX read: 'When God delivered the Amorites into the hands of the Israelites, when he destroyed them at Gibeon; and they were destroyed before the Israelites . . .'; there are certainly redundant features in this text, but it shows all the characteristics of an omission by homoioteleuton in MT. [13] 'Surely': instead of translating *h^alō'* by the rhetorical question, 'Is it not written?', it seemed better to translate it as a *lāmed* affirmative. In vv. 16–27, the text of LXX has a

---

[1] M. Noth, 'Jerusalem und die israelitische Tradition', 1950, *Gesammelte Studien*, Munich ²1960, p. 172.

number of omissions: we will mention them only when they modify the meaning. [19] 'Cut off their retreat': Hebrew root *znb*, literally 'tail', that is, 'attack from behind'; in other words, deprive them of the possibility of continuing their journey to their own cities (Baldi, Noth). The expression is also found in Deut. 25.18. [21] LXX and V lack 'in the camp'; followed by 'Makkedah', this word is meaningless, unless one supposes that Joshua had established a camp near the cave, which we are not told. 'Not a man': in Hebrew: *lō . . . leʾīš*: the prefix on *ʾīš* need not necessarily be removed as a dittography (*BH*³, Baldi, Noth, etc.). It is probably a *lāmed* emphatic with an affirmative sense: 'Absolutely no one . . .' At the end of the verse we have a proverbial expression, which in Exod. 11.7 is found with a different subject (perhaps the original one): 'Not a dog . . .'. [24] 'Who had gone with him . . .': the Hebrew has a strange form, *hehālekū*', the final consonant of which is usually considered a dittography, cf. *GKC* § 23i; for the article introducing a relative clause cf. *GKC* § 138i. [25] 'Against whom': in Hebrew *ʾōtām*, confirmed by LXX, which also has an accusative. Some scholars propose the reading *ʾittām*, but this is not necessary, because the *niphal* with *ʾet* (the accusative particle) is well attested, *GKC* § 117i.[1] [28] 'And its king' is lacking in LXX, and from the stylistic point of view is an addition in Hebrew. Here and in the verses that follow, LXX has the verbs in different persons, and a complete formulation where this is not so in MT. The mention of the king of Makkedah is unique in this passage. 'He utterly destroyed them': this phrase, apart from being clumsy here, is clearly a repetition from the stylistic and syntactic point of view, and is only found in part in LXX: 'And they destroyed (ἐξωλέθρευσαν) every living being . . .' At the end LXX read οὐδεὶς διασεσωσμένος καὶ διαπεφευγώς. Cf. 8.22; 10.30,33, where a complete formulation is attempted. [30] After 'into the hands of Israel', LXX adds καὶ ἔλαβον αὐτήν, i.e. *wayyilkedāh*, 'and conquered it'; and so in the other cases. [32] After 'and smote it with the edge of the sword'‹ LXX adds καὶ ἐξωλέθρευσαν αὐτήν, i.e. *heherīm ʾōtāh*, 'he utterly destroyed it', once again the full formulation. [33] 'To help': the form *lāʿezōr*, although grammatically irregular, is well attested. *hišʾīr* is a perfect, and this form is always found with *ʿad biltī*, although an infinitive would seem preferable (*BH*³, Noth). For a discussion of the perfect in this context, cf. *GKC* § 53.1 and the dictionaries of Gesenius-Buhl[17], under *šʾr* I, and Köhler-Baumgartner, under *biltī*. The formula appears at least six times, so it is preferable not to correct the verb. LXX once again has a complete formulation: after 'smote' it adds ἐν στόματι ξίφους, i.e. *lepī hereb*. There are once again differences between LXX and MT in the name. [35] LXX once again has the full formulation. [37] The final sentence is missing from

---

[1] For the use of *ʾet* with the *niphal*, cf. recently J. Hoftijzer, 'Remarks concerning the Particle *ʾt* in Classical Hebrew', *OTS* XIV, pp. 1–99.

LXX, which no doubt, and rightly, considered it a repetition of the first. [39] LXX lacks Libnah. [40] LXX does not seem to have understood 'Negeb', which in B read Ναβαί, later corrected in A to Ναγεβ, following MT. The Greek text of Rahlfs misleads the reader. 'The slopes': LXX (and probably V) mistakenly read τὴν 'Ασηδωθ here, i.e., in the locality of Ashdod. In reality the term comes from the root 'šd, attested in the Elephantine papyri and in the Aramaic of Judaea in the sense 'pour' (liquids), 'flow down', 'turn aside' (of a watercourse, as in Num. 21.15), so that here we have 'falls' of water (Noth), or else, and perhaps more probably, 'partings of water'. The expression recurs in 12.8; 13.20. In the latter case it may also form part of a proper name.

Chapter 10 is composed of three units, now gathered into a single narrative: (a) The anti-Gibeonite coalition, conquered by Joshua in the battle of Gibeon, (vv. 1-15); (b) The execution of the five kings in the cave of Makkedah (vv. 16-27); (c) The campaign in the southern hill country (vv. 28-42). We shall deal with them separately.

(a) *The Battle of Gibeon (10.1-15)*

Chapter 10, in its present form, has a link with the events in ch. 9. The coalition of Canaanite ('Amorite') kings of the southern hill country against the invader seems to have been the direct consequence of the ruse of Gibeon, or of their going over to the enemy, according to LXX and V. For as a result of this, Israel (probably Benjamin, as we have seen) established an important bridgehead in this region (cf. vv. 1b and 4). Several general observations can be made on the text of ch. 10.

1. First of all, there is a notable difference between the importance placed upon the city in the two chapters, Josh. 9 and 10. Chapter 9 shows us the Gibeonites wishing to obtain at any cost a treaty which made them vassals. This suggests a situation of military weakness that did not permit them to resist the invader effectively, which (as Baldi points out) does not mean that one should assume them to be cowards, as is often done. Chapter 10, on the contrary, explicitly states (v. 2) that Gibeon was an important place, the defection of which might weaken the whole defensive system of the hill country, and that its inhabitants were 'mighty'. To a very limited extent this is due to the Deuteronomic redaction (of which there are few signs here, as Noth observes, p. 56, rather than p. 9: vv. 1a, b and 25). Thus everything suggests that this theme was present before the redaction was carried

out. In any case, is Joshua really 'at home' in this episode and in
11.1ff., as A. Alt holds?[1] Noth denies this as well (p. 61), and believes
that the connection of this episode and the next with the person of the
leader is secondary; but he does not explain why this should be so.
This statement is regarded with scepticism by Wright and by Bright,
but had already been criticized previously by Möhlenbrink (pp. 264ff.)
who also maintains the independence of 10.1ff. with regard to ch. 9.

2. The quotation from the 'Book of Yashar' or 'of the Just'[2] contradicts the description of the battle. For the sun not to have set is
directly related to the continuance of the battle until victory was
achieved, but then the mention of the moon makes no sense, unless
one accepts with Halladay (p. 169) a parallelism in which the two
major heavenly bodies are involved. No doubt the quotation originally goes back to another event, and was later attached to the present
narrative, the geographical situation of which it shared. The theme
in itself is also found in the *Iliad*, II, 412ff., in almost identical circumstances: Agamemnon prays Zeus not to let the sun go down before
the Achaeans have been victorious, and this is what happens. Abel
has made a list of other examples of this nature in classical antiquity.

The position of the quotation in the present context and the occurrence of the same phenomenon elsewhere in a similar context cannot
be ignored by those who wish to study the phenomenon in an attempt
to evalute its historical value. The principal meaning of the verb *dmm*
is 'to be silent', whence the explanation of Heller and Dus: the sun
and the moon no longer gave any oracles.[3] For Scott the verb here

---

[1] A. Alt, *Josua*, pp. 187ff., cf. the introduction to this book, § 4.

[2] Another explanation of this name has recently been given by I. L. Seeligmann,
'Menschliches Heldentum und göttliche Hilfe', *ThZ* 19, 1963, pp. 385–411, esp.
p. 396 n. 23. He believes it is the result of an abbreviation which has later not been
understood: *spr h'yšr'* i.e. *sēper h^adar yiśrā'ēl* – 'Book of the worth, the glory of Israel'.
There are no grounds for this view. We have other mentions of the book: in II Sam.
1.18 and probably, according to LXX, in I Kings 8.13, 53: ἐν βιβλίῳ τῆς ᾠδῆς
=*b^esēper haššīr*, that is, there has been a metathesis of the first two consonants. The
question which reading should be chosen remains open: 'The Just' is a common
epithet for Yahweh, in which case we would have a kind of *res gestae* of God; 'The
Song' would imply a collection of ancient epic songs. In fact, the presence in the
work of the elegy of David on the death of Saul and Jonathan suggests rather that
the second is correct, in particular as it makes no mention of the deeds of Yahweh.
We have another work of the same kind in the 'Book of the Wars of Yahweh', Num.
21.14. Apart from a few fragments, none of these books has come down to us.

[3] Of course these explanations are unconvincing; there is no miracle in the absence of oracles.

means 'no longer shine', hence 'hide in the clouds' before a storm. The derivative sense is traditionally translated 'stand still'. Amongst the rationalizing explanations of the event (for a good summary of these and others, cf. Baldi, pp. 85ff.), and ignoring metaphorical or allegorical explanations, that which seems the most plausible was proposed by J. Phythian-Adams[1], who linked it with the fall of a meteorite in Asia Minor, accompanied by a rain of smaller meteorites, and the persistence for some time of a diffused light. This event took place in the fourteenth century. The difficulties here are considerable. First of all, there is the chronological difficulty, for the event is a century before the beginning of the conquest, according to the usual dating. If this chronology is accepted, the present episode would have to be backdated by a century and related to the activities of the first wave of invaders to which the episode described in Gen. 34 makes allusion. But there is nothing to suggest that we can assume this. Secondly, even if we admit that this explanation is substantially based on the truth, one would have to be sure that it was materially possible for the light of the meteorite to be visible in Palestine, a distance of several hundred miles, and whether the small meteorites could have fallen on the area. The examples quoted by Ceuppens (Poland, 1868 and Siberia, 1908) describe events which had no effect beyond a region of some 40 km in extent. Thus it seems more prudent to regard the phenomenon as one of the numerous miracles of which the Bible tells us (such as are found elsewhere in the ancient world), remembering that in the biblical message a miracle is always a 'sign' of an extraordinary divine intervention which imparts a grace unmerited by man and inconceivable in any other way. Ultimately this explanation is more satisfactory than others, which, without any adequate basis, seek to prove the possibility of the phenomenon from a purely scientific and geographical point of view.

3. We must also make some comment about the traditions which the present chapter contains. As it stands, we have three episodes drawn into a single narrative by a common chronological order. In the first episode we have the five kings setting out against Gibeon (v. 3; the last, as we have seen, is not the name of a person but of a locality), who are mentioned as signifying their respective city states. They reappear, without their names, in v. 5 (which repeats what we

---

[1] On the basis, amongst others, of the study by F. Ceuppens, *Le miracle de Josué*, Études Religieuses 548, Liège 1944.

already know from v. 3) and in v. 23; but in vv. 29ff., a text which is
clearly connected with vv. 1–15, as Schunck has rightly observed,
the list of cities is rather different: Gezer is suddenly introduced, as a
place whose king comes to the help of Lachish, but which is not to be
destroyed itself, while Jerusalem and Jarmuth are missing. And this
time Debir occurs normally as a city and not as the name of a person.
The link made in the chapter between vv. 16ff. and vv. 29ff. is that it
was the death of the kings which enabled the invaders to attack and
destroy their respective cities, profiting from the dismay caused by
the news and by the destruction of their armies. Noth proposes the
following solution to these problems. A more general designation must
have been given in the first place, e.g., as in v. 6: 'all the kings . . .
that dwell in the hill country' or something of this sort; the names of
persons and cities were a secondary introduction. On the other hand,
as we shall see below, the *tells* of this region were all destroyed at the
end of the thirteenth century, so that the flight of the enemy described in vv. 10ff. becomes perfectly logical and coherent from a
historical and geographical point of view, if we accept that vv. 29ff.
in their present form provide the conclusion to them (Schunck). Thus
in order to accept Noth's solution, one would have to admit that the
list of kings and cities in the present narrative referred to traditions
which are reliable, but originally independent of the present narrative. It is perhaps less complicated to grant that behind ch. 10 lies a
tradition of conquest which mentions the destruction of the cities
listed and the execution of their kings, a tradition now linked to ch. 9
on the one hand and to the aetiology of 10.16ff. on the other. In
spite of the questions which remain unanswered, this is a good working
hypothesis.

4. In spite of these affirmations, we must recognize that the theme
of a coalition against the invaders and the group of cities which had
gone over to the enemy is completely in accord with the logical
requirements of the chapter as we have it. In other words, as long as
the invaders were content to infiltrate into uninhabited or thinly
populated regions of the wilderness or the hill country,[1] their immi-
gration did not disturb the indigenous population, and might even in
certain circumstances appear desirable (cf. the arguments put forward

[1] This is the thesis of A. Alt, 'The Settlement of the Israelites in Palestine', 1925,
Essays, pp. 135–69, and 'Erwägungen zur Landnahme der Israeliten in Palestina',
1939, *KS* I, pp. 126–75. As we have seen, the episodes of the conquest of Jericho and
Ai present almost insuperable historical difficulties.

in Gen. 34.21, which certainly reflect the advantages which an urban population could derive from the settlement of semi-nomads with numerous flocks and herds). But once the invaders succeeded in reducing any sections of the local population to subjection (and we have seen that there is no reason to doubt the substantial historicity of the pact between Israel and the Gibeonites), thereby becoming the masters of certain regions, they ceased to be more or less desirable guests and turned into powerful enemies, involved from henceforth in the struggles of the city states and the whole region, which was trying to maintain an already precarious balance (cf. Hertzberg). Here, the league of Canaanite kings seemed to have realized the course of events only too late; the negative outcome of the battle of Gibeon did the rest. Thus whereas behind the story of the battle of Ai there may lie the memory of a very early victory won by the invaders by means of a ruse, there is all the more reason for assuming a similar situation here, with the one difference that in this case there was a pitched battle, won by Israel in an astonishing fashion, exactly as in Judg. 4–5.

5. The geographical setting of the district in question (cf. Schunck for the details and for a very detailed bibliography) gives us in the first section the following localities: Jerusalem (which is no longer mentioned in vv. 29ff.); Hebron; Jarmuth (no longer mentioned in vv. 29ff.), probably the present-day *khirbet yarmūa* (147–124), approximately 25 km SE of Jerusalem; Lachish, the present-day *tell ed-duwēr*, in Hebrew *tell lākiš* (153–108).[1] Japhia, which appears in 19.12 as a place name, is not mentioned in this chapter. Up to a few decades ago Eglon was identified with *tell ʿajlān* (Dhorme maintains this identity up to the present day), which has preserved the name and which is ESE of Lachish, but this identification should be rejected, because excavations there have not shown any remains earlier than the Byzantine period. Elliger and Noth (cf. n.[2] below) suggest that it may be identified with *tell bēt mirsim* (141–096), generally identified with Debir, see below. Others think it may be *tell el-ḥesi* (124–106), approximately 11 km ESE of Lachish (Albright, Wright, Baldi, Bright, Simon).[3] If Debir is a place name, as is almost certain (it appears as such in v. 38), most people think that it should be identified with *tell bēt*

[1] As proposed by W. F. Albright, *ZAW* 47, 1929, p. 3 n. 2.
[2] W. F. Albright, *BASOR* 74, 1939, p. 14 n. 5 (and already in *BASOR* 15, 1924, pp. 7f.); G. E. Wright, *JNES* 5, 1946, p. 110 n. 2, with a bibliography; K. Elliger, *PJB* 30, 1934, pp. 67f.; Schunck, p. 31, n. 84.

mirsim (141–096), rather less than 20 km ESE of Hebron. Noth, Simon and Galling do not accept this identification:[1] the first two propose *khirbet et-tarrāme* (153–098), the third prefers *khirbet rabūd* (153–093). These are 9 km SE of Hebron and some 5 km further to the SE respectively. Beth-horon is a locality which consists of two parts: the upper town 8 km to the NE of Gibeon, and the lower town 11 km to the NE. Between the two there is an ascent which concludes in a gorge a little beyond the upper town. The name has been preserved up to the present day: *bēt ʿur*, consisting of *al-fawqā* and *at-tahtā* (158–144 and 160–143 respectively). Azekah is probably the present-day *tell zakarīye* (144–123), approximately 25 km SSE of Beth-horon and a little to the NNE of Lachish, with which it is connected by Jer. 34.7 and in the ostraka of Lachish IV, line 12 (cf. *ANET*, p.322; *KIA*, no. 194). A little further on, towards the east, Makkedah should be found, though the site of it is still uncertain. During the Byzantine period, it was thought to be a little east of Lachish, on the boundary of the lowland and the hill country, in the neighbourhood of the present-day *idelmā* (*-mīye*) (150–117), perhaps because of the way LXX confuses it with Adullam. This last locality appears to be almost an addition to the text, and is clearly the link which connects it with the following episode (Abel, Baldi); but it must be admitted that geographically it is in place here. Aijalon is the present-day *yālū* (153–138), approximately 3 km east of ʿamwās, between Gibeon and the present-day *abu ghūš*. Hebron and Debir are places which originally belonged to Caleb (cf. 14.6–15; 15.13–20). It is a sign of the work of a late redactor that they are here found assimilated to the pan-Israelite tradition of the conquest.

6. Thus in its present state, our narrative provides the classic description of the holy war: the oracle of salvation (v.8); Yahweh fighting for his people (v. 14b), who as it were receive everything by grace, the whole glory going to their God.[2] The great final massacre which concludes the expedition is equally typical of the holy war. If it is true that this kind of holy war is not well attested in Israel, as Noth has pointed out, it is nevertheless true that similar institutions are known in Moab, and must also have existed in Israel, though certainly not

---

[1] K. Galling, 'Zur Lokalisierung von Dᵉbir', *ZDPV* 70, 1954, p. 135; W. F. Albright, 'Debir', in D. W. Thomas (ed.), *Archaeology and Old Testament Study*, Oxford 1967, pp. 207–320; the latter, without mentioning other proposals, puts forward his identification of Debir with *tell bēt mirsim*.

[2] Cf. above on Josh. 7–8, nn. 2 and 8.

in the total and absolute form described in the prophetic and Deutero-nomic texts.[1]

[1] Adoni-Zedek: although Noth, with LXX, identifies this person with Adoni-bezek who occurs in Judg. 1.5ff., it seems better to follow the majority of commentators in regarding them as two distinct persons. This king bore a theophoric name, formed with the name of the same divinity as in the case of Melchizedek, found in Gen. 14.18ff. It should be noted that in the el-Amarna texts no name formed with *ṣedeq* appears in relation to Jerusalem and its kings. There is only a king whose name is formed with the aid of a Hurrite divinity: *Abdi-ḥepa*. We translate 'integrated with them', following Abel. Literally, the expression is 'in the midst of it' – i.e. of Israel.

[9] A night march of 30 km is long but not impossible and can be carried out in 8–10 hours.

[15] A return to Gilgal here is absurd, historically speaking, and LXX has also suppressed it. But it is an obvious case of the *lectio difficilior*, and as such should be kept. In the present redaction, from ch. 7 on (except for ch. 11), all expeditions set out from Gilgal and return there.

(b) The five kings in the cave at Makkedah (10.16–27)

1. The conclusion of the previous section, which has the invaders returning to Gilgal, should not be omitted, as some commentators would prefer to do, following the example of LXX. It indicates that the present passage was originally an element from a different tradi-tion (Noth; disagreeing with Wright, p. 112 n. 24). Verse 17 provides an implicit confirmation of this. In its present context, the passage describes the destruction of the armies, with the exception of a few who escaped (v. 20), and the execution of the five kings (vv. 4, 26). These are the two necessary conditions for the destruction of the cities mentioned in vv. 28ff., even though, as we have seen, the list of towns does not correspond exactly to that in vv. 1ff. Too much should not be made of this detail (cf. e.g. Kaufmann, ad loc.), since in vv. 38f. Debir is destroyed with its king, while Gezer and its king are not defeated until v. 33: thus it is not to be supposed that the two were in the cave. The aetiological theme in v. 27 is important. There was a cave half closed by great rocks which did not seem to have got there naturally; nearby, there were several trees; and they stood, moreover, in a region where according to tradition Israel had conquered several

[1] Ibid., on Jos. 7.1, 5b ff.

enemy armies and executed their kings. This was sufficient material to provide a localization for the story. This must be emphasized, in disagreement with Kaufmann, who does not think that a cave surrounded by trees, which is a very common phenomenon, is a sufficient factor to give rise to an aetiological legend.[1] But it must be noted that whereas each of these elements individually is quite common, for them all to be found together in one place is exceptional. Besides, the particular configuration of the ground did not create the legend, but suggested that it should be localized there rather than elsewhere (Bright).

Another question arises, which Hertzberg has brought to the fore. Why, in this narrative, did not the kings flee towards their own fortified cities (as those who escaped the massacre did, v. 20), instead of seeking refuge in such a dangerous place? Here an ulterior motive which contradicts the logic of the previous section seems to have intervened, and is a second indication of an independent tradition connected with the cave. We wonder, moreover, if the logic of the present passage does not require *first* the defeat of the troops of the allied cities by means of an encircling operation which cut them off from their cities, and then only *afterwards*, when every other possibility had disappeared, the flight of the kings towards the cave. In this case the order of our passage (with minor syntactical modifications) would have been as follows: vv. 19, 16–18, 21 ff., etc. On the other hand, the present order is well attested in the ancient translations, and there is no apparent reason why the redactor should not have preserved the text in the original order. Thus the present form clearly represents the *lectio difficilior*. In any case, apart from these questions of detail, the various traditional material has been well drawn together into a single narrative context.

2. The problems concerning the site of Makkedah have been examined in the previous section (cf. p. 126). The fact that it can no longer be located with certainty at the present day adds to the existing difficulties that of the impossibility of a topographical and archaeological study of the region. For example, an element such as the 'great stones' might still have existed at the present day, if the circumstances had been particularly favourable; but here, too, there are difficulties, the main one being that of the double mention of these stones, once rolled to close the cave (v. 18), and later heaped up at its opening

---

[1] See the thorough study of the question recently carried out by Kaufmann himself, *Comm.*, p. 140.

with the same purpose (v. 27). And one may well ask, as Hertzberg does, whether one of these two references may not have originally been an allusion to the burial place of the kings whose bodies had been recovered, such as one finds in 7.26, cf. 8.29. In this case there would have been a second mention of the execution, which the redactor would have eliminated.

[24] The action described indicates the total humiliation of the conquered enemy; it is attested as such in I Kings 5.3; Ps. 110.1; cf. Deut. 33.29. It is often to be found in pictures from the ancient Near East (cf. *AOB²*, no. 59; *ANEP*, no. 393). 'Chiefs': in Hebrew *qāṣîn* is usually a term referring to civil officials, from the beginning of the period of the monarchy, and rarely to military leaders.

[27] Cf. the commentary on 8.29.

(c) The campaign in the southern hill country (10.28–42)

Before dealing with this third section, we do best to go over in synoptic form the names of persons and localities mentioned, remembering that they sometimes appear in a different form in LXX (cf. the commentary on v. 3).

v. 1	v. 3	v. 5, 23	v. 28–39
Adoni-zedek of Jerusalem	Adoni-zedek of Jerusalem	The king of Jerusalem	—
—	Hoban of Hebron	The king of Hebron	Hebron
—	Piram of Jarmuth	The king of Jarmuth	—
—	Japhia of Lachish	The king of Lachish	Lachish
—	Debir (?) of Eglon	The king of Eglon	Eglon
—	—	—	Makkedah and its king
—	—	—	Horam, king of Gezer
—	—	—	Debir and its king

One of the differences between v. 3 and vv. 28ff. can be explained by the fact that v. 3 originally mentioned a king of Debir and a king of Eglon, whereas in vv. 28ff. their names were not mentioned. Four kings were mentioned by name and two of them solely by reference

to their cities. To adapt this tradition to that of vv. 16–17, which
referred only to the five kings executed in connection with the cave
at Makkedah, and which did not contain the name of Debir, it was
fairly easy to equate Debir with Eglon, making the first place the
name of the king of the second. In this way the lists of vv. 1ff. and
16ff. came to be the same. On the other hand, in vv. 28ff., the kings
of Jerusalem and Jarmuth who appear in the two previous sections
are lacking, and a list of six kings is given, the kings of Makkedah and
Gezer having replaced the two that are missing; but in this list Debir
is a city.

Thus it appears that vv. 28–39 preserve the memory of an ancient
tradition, revised several times, which presented a list of six kings set
out according to a traditional itinerary (and of these only the site of
Gezer is no longer certain at the present day). We have a proof of the
adaptation of this ancient tradition to the present context in the fact
that the kings executed in vv. 16–27 are no longer mentioned in
vv. 28ff. The other tradition, that of vv. 1–15, which is more recent,
also originally contained a list of six kings, who were later reduced to
five in order to adapt it to vv. 16–27, and it was also followed by an
itinerary. However, although the two lists of kings have three or even
four in common, they were originally different. The persons are the
same, and so are the places: the conquest of the latter is dependent
upon the defeat, and in some cases the elimination, of the kings and
their armies; thus the accounts were originally similar but come from
different traditions. The aetiological section in vv. 16–27 is not so old,
and is either the reason for the reduction of the number of kings in the
first section to five, or the factor allowing the first and third sections
to be united in the same context. The tension remains, however,
between the first and the third section, because of the disagreements
between the two lists. Makkedah, mentioned in vv. 16ff. because of
its cave, and in vv. 28ff. as a city state, may well have been one of the
factors leading to the uniting of the sections in a single text, even if the
join is still quite visible.

2. In section (a) (above p.125) we have already discussed the
topographical and geographical situation of the region. An interesting
detail is that behind vv. 28–39 lies a traditional itinerary which seems
to have been followed by Sennacherib in 701, according to II Kings
18.13, and in 587 by Nebuchadnezzar, according to Jer. 34.7, in
order to lay siege to Jerusalem, after having reduced to submission
the system of fortified cities surrounding it (Baldi, Bright). The logic

of this tactic is absent here, nor is it a question of the permanent conquest of this region, because the narrative tells not of the occupation but of the destruction of these cities (in spite of the Deuteronomic conclusion of vv. 40ff.). Similarly, in vv. 10ff. we possess the vestiges of an ancient itinerary, even though we cannot tell what it contained (for the two itineraries, cf. du Buit).

The Deuteronomic recapitulation in vv. 40ff. introduces a new element. First of all, it describes as having been conquered territories which the previous texts only show as the object of raids. Secondly, it mentions a 'country of Goshen', to which we shall return in discussing 15.48b–51, where it occurs again. The present context in which this country of Goshen appears, in the form of an explanatory gloss for the region situated between Kadesh and Gaza, shows that it refers here to the region which includes the western slope of the southern hill country and the coast adjoining it. This description of the region occupied (which in reality was never occupied, as we have seen) is recognized by most commentators (except Baldi) as being at the very best highly exaggerated.

The archaeological situation in this region is interesting in other respects. All the sites which occur in it (regardless of their precise identification) appear from excavations to have been destroyed towards the end of the thirteenth century by what the disciples of Albright have called a terrible conflagration, and which they have unanimously identified with the operations described in the present chapter.[1] According to the logic of the narrative in Josh. 1–12, the present chapter would form the conclusion of the conquest of the south-central region, while 11.1–15 records that of the northern region; and this gave rise to the idea of a peaceful conquest of the central hill country and especially of the Shechem region.[2] It is not

[1] A good summary of the discoveries and sources is given in Baldi, pp. 89ff; Bright, pp. 608ff; and Lapp, op. cit. Cf. also, for the general problem, our articles: 'Ancient Biblical Tradition and Recent Archaeological Discoveries', BA 23, 1960, pp. 95–100, and 'La conquista israelitica della Palestina nei secoli XIII–XII e le scoperte archeologiche', Protestantismo 17, 1962, pp. 193–208, esp. pp. 97ff and 204ff. respectively. An account of the views of the American school can be found in J. Bright, Ancient Israel in Recent History Writing, SBT 19, London 1956 (on Josh. 10), while for the German school one can turn to M. Noth, 'Der Beitrag der Archäologie zur Geschichte Israels', SVT VII, 1960, pp. 262–82, esp. pp. 277ff.

[2] For the division of Palestine into three or four zones: south, central, north-central, north, in accordance with the findings of archaeology and the nature of the biblical sources, cf. our study already quoted, 'La conquista israelitica . . .', passim.

easy to work out the connection between the archaeological discoveries and ch. 10, given the complexity of the textual traditions. In any case, the texts do not speak of a conquest but only of a victorious raid. The use of the criterion of the 'balance of probability', as J. Bright proposes, makes it possible to admit a connection between the archaeological findings and the present narrative. Nevertheless, one can never be too prudent in this respect: in 14.6–15 and 15.13–19, passages which (as we shall see) are connected with Num. 13, the conquerors of Hebron and Debir are Caleb and Othniel, who have a traditional connection with Judah. One begins to wonder how many operations, and of what nature, were carried out in this region in the space of only a few decades! To take into account only the archaeological findings without comparing them with these factors is too one-sided.

3. For the Deuteronomic history writer the conquest of the south-central region is now an accomplished fact. 'All Israel' marched under the guidance and by the command of Yahweh, 'The God of Israel', and was able to establish itself firmly in the region which, as if by deliberate purpose, corresponded to that occupied by those who had returned from Babylon in the second half of the sixth century.

[33] Gezer is only defeated, but not destroyed nor taken. It was not to be conquered until the time of Solomon (I Kings 9.16; cf. Josh. 16.10).

CHAPTER 11.1–15

The Campaigns in the North

11 ¹When Jabin king of Hazor heard of this, he sent to Jobab king of Madon, and to the king of Shimron, and to the king of Achshaph, ²and to the kings who were in the northern hill country, and in the Arabah south of Chinneroth, and in the foothills, and in the dunes of Dor on the west, ³to the Canaanites in the east and the west, the Amorites, the Hittites, the Perizzites, and the Jebusites in the hill country, and the Hivites under Hermon in the land of Mizpah. ⁴And they came out, with all their troops,

a great host, in numbers like the sand that is upon the seashore, with very many horses and chariots. ⁵And all these kings joined their forces, and came and encamped together at the waters of Merom, to fight with Israel.

6 And the LORD said to Joshua, 'Do not be afraid of them, for tomorrow at this time I will give over all of them, slain, to Israel; you shall hamstring their horses, and burn their chariots with fire.' ⁷So Joshua with all his people of war came suddenly upon them from the mountain, by the waters of Merom, and fell upon them. ⁸And the LORD gave them into the hand of Israel, who smote them and chased them as far as Great Sidon and Misrephothmaim, and eastward as far as the plain of Mizpah; and they smote them, until there was none remaining. ⁹And Joshua did to them as the LORD bade him; he hamstrung their horses, and burned their chariots with fire.

10 And Joshua turned back at that time, and took Hazor, and smote its king with the sword; for Hazor formerly was the head of all those kingdoms. ¹¹And they put to the sword all who were in it, utterly destroying them; there was none left that breathed. And he burned Hazor with fire. ¹²And all the cities of those kings, and all their kings, Joshua took, and smote them with the edge of the sword, utterly destroying them, as Moses the servant of the LORD had commanded. ¹³But none of the cities that stood on mounds did Israel burn, except Hazor only; that Joshua burned. ¹⁴And all the spoil of these cities and the cattle, the people of Israel took for their booty; but every man they smote with the edge of the sword, until they had destroyed them, and they did not leave any that breathed, ¹⁵as the LORD had commanded Moses his servant. So Moses commanded Joshua, and so Joshua did; he left nothing undone of all that the LORD had commanded Moses.

Bibliography: Möhlenbrink, 'Die Landnahmesagen . . .', pp. 265ff.; Rudolph, *Der 'Elohist'* . . ., pp. 209–11; F. M. Abel, 'Les stratagèmes . . .', pp. 335ff.; S. Yeivin, 'The Israelite Settlement in Galilee and the Wars with Jabin of Hazor', *Mélanges Bibliques . . . A. Robert*, Paris 1957, pp. 95–104; F. Maass, 'Hazor und das Problem der Landnahme', *Von Ugarit nach Qumran. Festschrift O. Eissfeldt*, BZAW 77, Berlin 1958, pp. 105–17; Auzou, pp. 123ff.; J. A. Soggin, 'Giosué 11.7', *Bibbia e Oriente* 9, 1967, pp. 87f. *Archaeology*: Y. Yadin et al., *Hazor*, I–II, Jerusalem 1958–60, passim.

[11.1] LXXᴮ renders *mādōn* by Μαρρων, *šimrōn* by Συμοων (LXXᴬ has Σομερων, in Hebrew *šōmᵉrōn* – Samaria (?) cf. V: *Semeron*). The version in LXXᴮ is supported by 12.20, by various Egyptian texts, by El-Amarna no. 225, 1.4, by the Hellenistic Onomasticon (Simoniad) and by that of the modern Arab *sēmūniye*, cf. also 19.15.[1] For *'akšāp* LXX^B has *'Αζειφ* and LXX^A *'Αχιφ*. [2] 'In the northern . . .'; LXX has κατὰ Σιδῶνα τὴν μεγάλην, a phrase which appears in MT only in v. 8, where it is in place; instead of 'In the Arabah' LXX^{BA} read εἰς τὴν *'Ραβα(θ)* (=towards Rabbath [Ammon], the present day Amman[?]). Thus the coalition appears here to have been of much greater geographical extent. 'South of . . .': LXX has ἀπέναντι = *neged*, 'opposite, facing', cf. V *contra. kin^arōt*: LXX^{BA} have different but equivalent transcriptions; T has *gnysr*. 'The dunes': the Hebrew term *nāpāh*, here in the plural with prefixes, has not yet been explained, and until this happens, it is pointless to correct the form found here (as *BH*[3] and Noth do). It appears in the construct in I Kings 4.11, again in a geographical context. The expression we propose is also quite hypothetical, but gives a clear meaning if one considers the configuration of the region. [3] 'The Hittites': LXX^B has 'the Hivites', and the reverse later on in the verse. *mišpā*, which is *mišpē* in v. 8: the two localities are almost certainly the same. [4] LXX has a much shorter text. [5] *mērōm*: LXX has Μαρρων as in v. 1, identifying the two places. [7] 'From the mountain': an addition on the basis of the variant in LXX, ἐν τῷ ὄρει, Hebrew *bāhār* (*b^e* 'from' is well attested in Ugaritic). [8] *miśr^epōt mayim*: LXX has Μασερων, i.e. perhaps 'from Sharon', while it read 'in the east' (*miyyām*) in the mss. 'Until there was none . . .'; for this formula, cf. the note on 10.33. [10] LXX has a shorter text. [14] 'The spoil of these cities': LXX has 'its spoil' (the spoil of Hazor).

1. Josh. 11.1–15 forms the northern counterpart of ch. 10. The sole difference lies in the fact that although there is a geographical link with the facts given previously, which is due to the hand of the 'compiler' or to that of Dtr, this link is very feeble. We do not know when or how, in the opinion of the redactors, the invaders reached the northern hill country, whereas ch. 10 possesses logical continuity with what preceded. This special characteristic of the present passage clearly reveals that its origin is independent of the present context, and that to a certain extent the redactors respected this independence. Naturally, a certain degree of tension results. Whereas in ch. 10 the link with what preceded logically justified the formation of a coalition to stop the invader, there is no justification in the present case for a coalition of this kind, and mere information about events in the south do not form a sufficient reason. The redactor, however, has set out to present ch. 11 in a form similar to that of ch. 10, describing a fresh expedition on the part of Joshua, this time against a northern coalition, followed by another series of destructions.

[1] Cf. Simons, p. 500, and Du Buit, pp. 132f., 224.

The topography of the operations is relatively clear. The sources of the waters of Merom are found near the present Arab village of *marūn* (191–275) and flow there through the *wādī mārūn* to the southeast. The place is mentioned in the list of Thutmose III (*ANET*, p. 243a) and in the campaigns of Thutmose II (ibid., p. 243a and 256b). Hazor, mentioned several times in Egyptian sources and in the El Amarna texts, is the present-day *tell waqqās* or *el-queda* (203–270), and its ancient name has been restored to it by the State of Israel. This site is 7–8 km south of Lake Huleh along the present-day road for heavy lorries which leads towards northern Galilee and Syria. Madon is further south, west of Lake Tiberias, near *qarn ḥaṭṭīn* (194– 245), where the Crusaders were routed by the troops of Saladin in 1187. Its name is still preserved today in *khirbet madīn* and is attested by an Egyptian inscription found on *tell el-ʿurēme*, the ancient Chinnereth on the west coast of Lake Tiberias, here called Chinneroth (v. 2) (201–257). This last city is not regarded as forming part of the coalition and is only mentioned to identify the particular wilderness referred to. In Noth's view the Arabah referred to here is the plain of *ghūwēr*, situated on the western bank of the lake. Dor (*ṭanṭūrah* in Arabic) is on the sea coast, about 20 km south of Carmel (243–225), while Shimron (or better Shimoon) is found in the plain of Esdraelon, about 10 km north of Megiddo (171–234); Achshaph is situated about 10 km south east of Acco, on the present-day *tell kīsan* (164–253). These last three places, two of which have kings whose names are not mentioned, take us far from the area where the operations are carried out, and in Noth's view the last two at least are later additions. Until we know why they were added to the present text, the question remains open. Misrephothmaim in v. 8 (in some manuscripts it is simply *miyyām*: 'in the west') is generally identified with *khirbet el mušrīfe* (161–276), south of *ras en-nāqūrah*, in modern Hebrew *rōʾš hanniqrā*, the traditional frontier between Palestine and Lebanon. This locality is just as far from the area where the operations took place. We know nothing about Mizpah or Mizpeh, vv. 3b and 8b. 'Great Sidon' also appears in 19.28; II Sam. 24.6, and supplies the extreme northern limit.

Once we accept the addition made by LXX in v. 7, the problem of the course taken by the battle of Merom seems relatively simple to solve. The troops of the cities in the coalition were at the bottom of the valley, where they had water and forage. The invaders attacked them 'suddenly from the mountain' and dispersed their forces into a region where they were no longer able to manoeuvre effectively. This favoured the attackers, who, if they were to fail, could have regained the mountains without horses and chariots being able to pursue them. We never find the Canaanites allowing themselves to be drawn into the mountains,[1] on to terrain which was unfavourable to them. The list in v.3 is the usual stereotyped enumeration of the indigenous people of Palestine (cf. the commentary on 3.10b).

3. The fact that two traditions which are originally independent and both substantially reliable lie behind the present narrative was well known even before the excavations at Hazor.[2] The extension to the whole of Israel (vv. 8, 13–14), the figure of Joshua (vv. 6, 10, 12, 15), and perhaps also the theme of the holy war carried to the extreme (as in vv. 6–9, cf. 14–15), are no doubt due to the redactor. The concluding theme of the sacking of the cities is also found in 7.2. The figure of Jabin, king of Hazor, who appears in Judg. 4–5 in a setting in which it is doubtful that he really belongs, seems here to be authentic, as Noth already maintained.[3] But this affirmation has been disputed recently: O. Eissfeldt[4] defended the view that Josh. 11 and Judg. 4–5 originally referred to the same event (it should be noted that the location is the same, the territory of Naphtali, and that the connection between Jabin and Joshua is secondary). On the other hand, it has recently been observed[5] that the battle described in the Song of Deborah took place a good deal further south, and decided the fate of a plain on which Israel had always had difficulties in establishing itself, and therefore belongs to a later phase than that of the establishment of Israel in the northern mountains. Finally, in Judg. 4–5 the real adversary is Sisera and not Jabin.

The excavations carried out on the *tell* of Hazor by J. A. de Rothschild's expedition in 1954 and the subsequent years have shown that the city was destroyed during the final period of the Bronze Age (end of the thirteenth century), together with its sanctuary, the plan of which was similar to that of the temple of Solomon. The site remained

---

[1] Cf. Abel, p. 385, and Baldi, ad loc.

[2] Cf. M. Noth, *Joshua*, p.67; he has always emphasized the lack of aetiological elements.

[3] M. Noth, ibid.; id., *The History of Israel*, London [2]1960, pp. 149f. E. Dhorme remains doubtful, and thinks there are two different places called *Yabīn*, as does A. Alt, 'Erwägungen. . .', *KS* I, pp. 134f., though with different arguments.

[4] O. Eissfeldt, 'Die Eroberung Palästinas durch Altisrael', *WO* II, 5–6, 1955, pp. 158–71, esp. pp. 168ff. (*KS* III, Tübingen 1966, pp. 367–83; 380ff.).

[5] So Maass, p. 111, Hertzberg and Bright, ad loc.

in ruins until Solomon decided to reconstruct it (I Kings 9.15), a fact well attested by the excavations, which exposed, for example, the foundations of a gate of a type well known in Israel and Judah from the time of Solomon on. There is an interesting observation in v. 13, that only Hazor was destroyed, whereas other sites remained intact. This remains to be checked by archaeologists.

Thus the present narrative provides one of the few cases in which the ancient sources, although they have been re-edited, have not been altered to the point where one can no longer recognize what they originally contained. Here we must certainly modify the thesis of an essentially peaceful conquest of Palestine (cf. the introduction §4) for this region at least, even though it can still be allowed that we have here the account of a final phase and not an initial phase of the conquest. Taking into account the character of the text, the argument here in favour of the traditional thesis is stronger than in the case of Josh. 10.

[6] For the 'oracle of salvation' which begins this passage, cf. the commentary on 8.1; for the holy war, cf. the beginning of ch. 7.

[12] 'Servant of the LORD', cf. 1.1.

CHAPTER 11.16–12.24

General Epilogue and List of Conquered Kings

11 ¹⁶So Joshua took all that land, the hill country and all the Negeb and all the land of Goshen and the foothills and the Arabah and the hill country of Israel and its foothills ¹⁷from Mount Halak, that rises toward Seir, as far as Baal-gad in the plain of Lebanon below Mount Hermon. And he took all their kings, and smote them, and put them to death. ¹⁸Joshua made war a long time with all those kings. ¹⁹There was not a city that made peace with the people of Israel, except the Hivites, the inhabitants of Gibeon; they took all in battle. ²⁰For it was the LORD's doing to harden their hearts that they should come against Israel in battle, in order that they should be utterly destroyed, and should receive no mercy but be exterminated, as Yahweh commanded Moses. ²¹And Joshua came at that time, and wiped out the Anakim from the hill country, from Hebron, from

Debir, from Anab, and from all the hill country of Judah, and from all the hill country of Israel; Joshua utterly destroyed them with their cities. ²²There was none of the Anakim left in the land of the people of Israel; only in Gaza, in Gath, and in Ashdod, did some remain. ²³So Joshua took the whole land, according to all that Yahweh had spoken to Moses; and Joshua gave it for an inheritance to Israel according to their tribal allotments. And the land had rest from war.

12 ¹Now these are the kings of the land, whom the people of Israel defeated, and took possession of their land beyond the Jordan toward the sunrising, from the valley of the Arnon to Mount Hermon, with all the Arabah eastward: ²Sihon king of the Amorites who dwelt at Heshbon, and ruled from Aroer, which is on the edge of the valley of the Arnon, and the middle of the valley, the half of Gilead as far as the river Jabbok, that is, the territory of the Ammonites; ³and the Arabah to the Sea of Chinnereth eastward, and in the direction of Beth-jeshimoth, to the sea of the Arabah, the Salt Sea, southward to the foot of the slopes of Pisgah; ⁴and [the territory of] Og king of Bashan, one of the remnant of the Rephaim, who dwelt at Ashtaroth and at Edrei ⁵and ruled over Mount Hermon and Salecah and all Bashan to the boundary of the Geshurites and the Maacathites, and over half of Gilead [up to] the boundary of Sihon king of Heshbon. ⁶Moses, the servant of the LORD, and the people of Israel defeated them; and Moses the servant of the LORD gave their land for a possession to the Reubenites and the Gadites and the half-tribe of Manasseh.

7 And these are the kings of the land whom Joshua and the people of Israel defeated on the west side of the Jordan, from Baal-gad in the plain of Lebanon to Mount Halak, that rises toward Seir (and Joshua gave their land to the tribes of Israel as a possession according to their allotments), ⁸in the hill country, in the foothills, in the Arabah, in the slopes, in the wilderness, and in the Negeb, the land of the Hittites, the Amorites, the Canaanites, the Perizzites, the Hivites, and the Jebusites:

9 The king of Jericho, one; the king of Ai, which is beside Bethel, one; ¹⁰the king of Jerusalem, one; the king of Hebron, one; ¹¹the king of Jarmuth, one; the king of Lachish, one; ¹²the king of Eglon, one; the king of Gezer, one; ¹³the king of Debir, one; the king of Geder, one; ¹⁴the king of Hormah, one; the king of Arad, one; ¹⁵the king of Libnah, one; the king of Adullam, one; ¹⁶the king of Makkedah, one; the king of Bethel, one; ¹⁷the king of Tappuah, one; the king of Hepher, one; ¹⁸the king of Aphek, one; the king of Lasharon, one; ¹⁹the king of Madon, one; the king of Hazor, one; ²⁰the king of Shimron-meron, one; the king of Achshaph, one; ²¹the king of Taanach, one; the king of Megiddo, one; ²²the king of Kedesh, one; the king of Jokneam in Carmel, one; ²³the king of Dor in Naphath-dor, one; the king of Goiim in [Galilee], one; ²⁴the king of Tirzah, one; in all, thirty-one kings.

Bibliography: Auzou, pp. 127ff.; G. Lombardi, 'Ai, la fortezza di Beth-El (Gios 12.9)', *Studii Biblici Franciscani, Liber Annuus* 13, 1962–63, pp. 278–86; and recently V. Fritz, 'Die sogenannte Liste der besiegten Könige in Josua 12', *ZDPV* 85, 1969, pp. 136–61, which we were unable to use.

---

[17] *ḥālāq*: LXX^B has *Aχελ*, while V and T regard it as a common noun: '. . . the part which goes up.' Following one meaning of the root, Dhorme and Abel translate *le mont Pelé*, the Bald Mountain, here and in 12.7. **[21–22]** T interprets Anakim as *gbry'*, literally 'the heroes', as in 12.4 for Rephaim. The term is often used to describe peoples and shows the idea that was held in the period of the Targums of the legendary indigenous pre-Israelite populations. **[12.2]** *gᵉbūl* means here not 'frontier', as usually, but 'territory', as the region contained between frontiers, cf. the description. It should probably be understood in the same sense in v. 5 and ch. 13. T also, with *thwm*, keeps the double meaning. 'Rephaim': LXX has *ἐκ τῶν γιγάντων* as in 13.12; for T cf. 11.21f. **[3]** 'Southward': LXX transcribes *Θαιμαν*, but *tēmān* is a region in southern Arabia which has nothing to do with the present context. **[4]** 'The territory of (Og)' is lacking in LXX and is probably a later addition, erroneous because it is out of line with v. 1, which lists kings and not territories; cf. the general commentary. **[5]** 'Bashan': T read, as in Num. 21.33, *mtnn*. 'Maacathites': T read, as in Deut. 3.14, *'pyqyrws* (*ἐπίκαιρος*), no doubt one of the names current in the region in its own time. In the text one must add *'ad*, 'up to', which has probably been lost by haplography with *gilʿād*. **[7]** 'Baal-gad' and 'Halak'; cf. on 11.17. For the second name LXX^B has *Χελχα* here, and LXX^A has *Ἀλοχ*, in contrast to 11.17. **[9–24]** For the translation 'beside Bethel' see Lombardi's study. We shall mention only the important variants, not simple differences of spelling: for the kings and places which occur in 10.3, see the commentary on that passage. **[16]** 'The king of Bethel' is lacking in LXX. **[18]** 'Aphek': LXX^B adds *τῆς Ἀρωκ* (Sharon?) and omits the king of this region. **[19]** LXX omits 'the king of Madon'. **[20]** 'Shimron' occurs by itself in LXX and V. (LXX reads *Συμοων* as in 11.1). LXX adds a king of Meron, *Μαρρων*. **[23]** LXX^B reads 'Galilee' for 'Gilgal'; all commentators adopt the reading of LXX for the improbable one in MT. **[24]** LXX has three kings less and one more than MT, making twenty-nine in all.

This final section of the first part can be sub-divided as follows: (1) the recapitulation of the conquest (11.16–23); (2) the list of kings conquered east of the Jordan (12.1–6); and finally (3) the list of kings conquered west of the Jordan (12.7–24).

1. The first sub-division, 11.16–23, attempts in vv. 16–20 to summarize the results of the conquest, and this passage is, according to
Noth, the work of the 'compiler' and is based on ancient traditions.
It is interesting to note that, as in 11.1ff., the point of view seems to be
that of Judah. This can be deduced by the great accuracy in references to the south and the adjoining regions. For the 'land of Goshen',
cf. 10.41; the 'mountain' or hill country of Israel is generally identified with the central hill country, which later, in the period after
Solomon's reign, became the centre of the kingdom of Israel. Thus
for Dhorme and Simons the term is equivalent to the more usual
expression 'mountain of Ephraim'; no actual mountain of this name
is known. 'Mount Halak' is the present-day *jebel ḥalāq*, NNE of *'abde*,
the Hebrew and Byzantine *'abdāt* on the watershed of the southern
Negeb. East of this is the mountain of Seir, which corresponds to the
greater part of the territory of Edom. The 'plain of Lebanon' is perhaps only the southern side of the present-day *beqā'*, the plateau
situated between the mountain ranges of Lebanon and Antilebanon,
between Syria and Lebanon; thus there is no objection to the identification of Baal-gad with the present day Baalbek.[1] There are difficulties in any other identifications which have been proposed. These
extreme limits of Israelite territory replace in the present text the
more usual expression, 'from Dan to Beersheba', in other texts. The
frontiers are not as exaggerated as Noth considers, if they reflect the
extent of the empire of David and Solomon, cf. the passages which
place the north-eastern frontier at the Euphrates, and particularly
the commentary on 1.4.

[18] The intention of the 'compiler' seems to be to dispel the impression that the course of the conquest was a rapid one, explaining
that in reality it was only possible to complete the conquest later,
after long and difficult campaigns. This happened mainly because
Yahweh had hardened the hearts of the Canaanites as he hardened
that of Pharaoh in Exod. 1–14.[2] The theme, however, has been played
down, following Deut. 20.10–20, where an earlier stratum lays down
that the cities which surrender should be treated mercifully, while a
later stratum contains the command to wipe out all the Canaanite
cities.

---

[1] O. Eissfeldt, 'Die altesten Bezeugungen von Baalbek als Kultstatte', *FuF* 12,
1936, pp. 51–53.
[2] For this problem, which we cannot discuss in detail here, cf. F. Hesse, *Das
Verstockungsproblem im Alten Testament*, BZAW 74, Berlin 1955, esp. pp. 53ff.

[21–22] Here Dtr has undoubtedly preserved an ancient tradition about the Anakim, who were driven out from Hebron and Debir (cf. above, on ch. 10) and from Anab, a place which it is surprising to find in this context, and which we shall discuss in commenting on 15.50. Similarly it is difficult to explain the mention of three Philistine cities (v. 22) as the place where the survivors took refuge. Noth is certainly right when he indicates that this passage does not give the appearance of being a later artificial construction. We hear of the Anakim and the conquest of their cities in 14.6–15a (Caleb) and 15. 13–19 (Othniel), cf. Num. 13.22,28; Deut. 1.28; 9.2; Judg. 1.20 (Judg. 1.10b mentions the three persons whom Num. 13.22 calls the 'descendants of Anak'). According to Josh. 10.28ff., these places had already been destroyed by the invaders. Nor does our passage altogether agree with chs. 14 and 15, and therefore presents an independent tradition. Noth would insert 14.6–14a between 11.23a and 23b, which seems unlikely. The Anakim are generally considered as a legendary population of giants (cf. Deut. 1.28; 9.2),[1] but it is questionable whether there is any support in the text for this affirmation. All that is said is that they were taller than the Israelites. Only Num. 13.33, which is doubtful from the textual point of view because it is lacking in LXX, says 'we saw the Nephilim (giants), the sons of Anak, amongst the giants'. No text makes any connection between the Anakim and Goliath of Gath, who, according to I Sam. 17 (cf. II Sam. 21.19–22), was more than 3m tall (!), though some commentators relate them to him. What is more important is that the Anakim are probably already mentioned in Egyptian execration texts,[2] which seems to prove their historicity. One may reasonably suppose that they were a people who can no longer be identified at the present day, but who inhabited Palestine at a pre-Israelite period. A possible solution may be found in relating their name to the Greek ἄναξ (Fαναξ*) 'lord', 'chief'. In this case, they would be an Aegaean group, who had settled in the hill country before the arrival of the Philistines during the reign of Rameses II in the first quarter of the twelfth century. They would have been of greater stature than the West Semitic semi-nomads who were invading the country, and their survivors would later have fled to the Philistines, a people who were related to them (for their pentapolis, cf. the commentary on 13.3).

[1] For the Anakim, cf. L. Delekat, 'Enak', *BHH* I, 1962, cols. 404f., and E. C. B. Maclaurin, 'Anak/ἄναξ', *VT* 15, 1965, pp. 468–74.

[2] Cf. *ANET*, pp. 328f.

But this is only a conjecture. The first sub-division concludes with the affirmation that the country is completely conquered. The final formula is typically Deuteronomic (cf. Judg. 3.11,31; 5.31; 8.28, etc.).

2. The kings conquered east of the Jordan (12.1–6).[1] For the mention of the two kings, cf. Num. 21; the passage corresponds to Deut. 3.8–17 (cf. 1.14, and the commentary on Josh. 13.8ff., 15ff.—see the latter text for the general problem and a solution). The localities mentioned here (and in the passages mentioned in Josh. 13) are as follows: Heshbon, the present-day *ḥesbān* (226–134), is about 25 km in a straight line east of the mouth of the Jordan. Aroer is the present-day *'arā'īr* (228–097), while the two rivers are respectively the *wādī el-mūjib* and the *nahr ez-zerqā*, the most important left-bank tributaries of the Jordan. Verse 3 seems to be simply a summary of the regions already mentioned and not a new specification of other territory. Beth-ha-Jeshimoth is near the north-central shore of the Dead Sea, according to indications given by Josephus, Eusebius and Jerome, but there is still controversy about the exact site.[2] The 'slopes of Pisgah', the mountain from the top of which Moses looked at the promised land (Deut. 34.1), probably represents 'a fixed point on the slope of *ras-es-siyaghah* (Baldi). Bashan is the region east of Lake Tiberias; Ashtaroth, which is attested in the execration texts, in other Egyptian sources, and in the el-Amarna letters,[3] has been identified with *tell 'aštarah* (243–244), which has preserved its name, about 40 km south of *qunēṭriye*, a place in Syria which has become celebrated since the Israeli-Arab war of June 1967. The Rephaim are one of the legendary peoples who inhabited Syria and Palestine, sometimes linked by the texts with certain monuments which seem to require great stature (cf. Deut. 2.11; 3.11, as well as Gen. 14.5; II Sam. 21.16–20). The possibility that they are related to the *rp'm* who are referred to at Ugarit remains uncertain. Edrei, which is also found in the list of Thutmose III,[4] is the present day *der'a* (253–224), an important railway station on the Hejaz line, where the junction with the line to Haifa was before 1948. The site of Salecah is still unknown, but some identify it with *salḫad*, on the *jebel ed-drūz* (311–212). 'Geshurites and Maacathites' are two kingdoms which later fell to the Aramaeans (to

---

[1] Cf. The bibliography on 13.14ff., and the articles quoted by Noth and Simons.
[2] See the discussion in Baldi, p. 100.
[3] The list of Thutmose III (*ANET*, p. 242, and the previous pages); *El Amarna*, ed. Knudtzon, nos. 1, 197.
[4] *ANET*, pp. 242f.

what extent were they Aramaean kingdoms at this period?), east of the upper reaches of the Jordan and of Lake Tiberias.

3. The kings conquered west of Jordan (12.7–24). Cf. for the statement in vv. 7–8 the commentary on vv. 1ff.; the commentary on 9.1 for the various regions, and the commentary on 3.10 for the stereotyped list of various pre-Israelite peoples in Palestine.

The list of vv. 9–24 is very important, if only because of the fact that in vv. 13b–24 it is independent not only of chs. 1–11, but also of all the other traditions about the conquest which we possess. The origin of this list is unknown, but it is certainly very ancient; this is the only explanation of its disagreements with the 'official' version. Moreover, the picture of Palestine which it presents gives the best description, though it is not always complete, of the city states of the region as they appear a century and a half earlier in the el-Amarna archives (Noth). We shall only mention the sites which have not already been discussed and those which present some problem.

[13] Geder is an unknown site, which may perhaps be mentioned in I Chron. 27.28. [14] Arad and Hormah are places in the northern Negeb, the first situated on the south-eastern foothills of the hill country near its descent towards the Dead Sea depression, and the second on the south-western foothills (162–076 and 146–069 respectively). Both are mentioned in Num. 21, probably in connection with an attempt to conquer them (cf. Introduction, §39, and Judg. 1.17–19.) [15] For Adullam, cf. 10.1–15 (p.126). [16] Bethel does not appear in chs. 1–11, but only in Judg.1.22ff., though cf. the commentary on chs. 7–8. [17] Hepher has not yet been identified with certainty;[1] for Tappuah cf. 17.8. [18] Aphek, also mentioned several times in the Egyptian list[2] and in the OT, is the present-day rās el-'ain (143–168) in Hebrew rō'š hā-'ayin, a few km east of Tel-Aviv, or possibly the nearby tell el-mukhmar. On the other hand, the variant in LXX places it in Sharon, that is, in the northern half of the coastal plain. LXX seems to be right on this, since in this case MT mentions a region and not a city state. Thus we must seriously consider the possibility that here we have a different Aphek, further north. [20] Alt (quoted by Noth) regards Shimron-meron as the equivalent of the Assyrian samsimuruna,[3] which is identical with the present-day marūn,

---

[1] For the discussion, cf. Baldi, p. 102; Noth, p. 72, ad loc.

[2] List of Thutmose III, no. 21 (ANET, p.243); list of Amenhotep II (ANET, p.246).

[3] On the 'prisms' of Sennacherib and Esarhaddon and the Rassam 'cylinder' of

on the road leading from Tyre to the sources of the Jordan. In this
case, Achshaph would be the present day *khirbet iksāf*, about 14 km
east of *marūn*. But Baldi thinks that it is more likely to have been
khirbet sārūnā near the Israeli *sārōnā*, a few km north east of Tabor; this
locality, too, is mentioned in the Egyptian lists.[1] [21] For Taanach
and Megiddo, see the commentary on 17.11; they were occupied
during the period of David and Solomon, the first half of the tenth
century. [22] Some writers identify Kedesh here with that in Naphtali in the north (Baldi, Dhorme), but Noth and Abel believe it was
on a site not yet identified in the plain of Esdraelon. For Jokneam, cf.
19.11. [23] For Dor, cf. the commentary on 11.2 and 17.11. 'Goiim in
Galilee' (cf. the textual note) is usually identified with Harosheth-ha-
Goiim (cf. Judg. 4.2ff.), probably *tell el-'amr*, near *el-hārithiye*. (24)
Tirzah, finally, is *tell el-far'ah*, a few km north east of Nablus, on the
road for heavy lorries. Our text lacks any mention of Shechem, which,
however, is one of the most important localities.

Concluding our examination of this complex section, we may accept the view of Hertzberg, that the redactor did not want to give us
so much an account of historical facts, as to bear witness to the mighty
acts of Yahweh in history, the conquest being one of the most important of these mighty acts.

Assurbanipal (*ANET*, pp. 287, 291, 294).
[1] List of Thutmose III (*ANET*, p. 243).

PART TWO

THE DIVISION OF THE PROMISED LAND

CHAPTER 13

Introduction to the Division: The Situation West of the Jordan

13 ¹Now Joshua was old and advanced in years; and the LORD said to him, 'You are old and advanced in years, and there remains yet very much land to be possessed. ²This is the land that yet remains:

All the regions of the Philistines, and all those of the Geshurites, ³from the Shihor, which is east of Egypt, northward to the territory of Ekron, which is reckoned as Canaanite, there are five "tyrannies" of the Philistines, those of Gaza, Ashdod, Ashkelon, Gath, and Ekron, and those of the Avvim, ⁴in the south. All the land of the Canaanites, from Arah (or 'from the cave') which belongs to the Sidonians, to Aphek, to the territory of the Amorites, ⁵and the land of Byblos and all Lebanon, toward the sunrising, from Baal-gad below Mount Hermon to the entrance of Hamath. ⁶All the inhabitants of the hill country from Lebanon to Misrephoth-maim, even all the Sidonians, I will myself drive them out from before the people of Israel. Meanwhile allot [the land] to Israel for an inheritance, as I have commanded you. ⁷Now therefore divide this land for an inheritance to the nine tribes and half the tribe of Manasseh [from the Jordan to the Great Sea in the east, you will give it to them; the Great Sea will be their frontier].'

8 At the same time as the other half of the tribe of Manesseh, the Reubenites and the Gadites received their inheritance, which Moses gave them, beyond the Jordan eastward, as Moses the servant of the LORD gave them: ⁹from Aroer, which is on the edge of the valley of the Arnon, and the city that is in the middle of the valley, and [from] all the tableland of Medeba as far as Dibon; ¹⁰and all the cities of Sihon king of the Amorites, who reigned in Heshbon, as far as the territory of the Ammonites; ¹¹and Gilead, and the region of the Geshurites and Maacathites, and all Mount Hermon, and all Bashan to Salecah. ¹²All the kingdom of Og in Bashan, who reigned in Ashtaroth and in Edrei; he alone was left of the remnant of the Rephaim; these Moses had defeated, and driven them out. ¹³Yet the people of Israel did not drive out the Geshurites or the Maacathites; but Geshur and Maacath dwell in the midst of Israel to this day. ¹⁴To the tribe

of Levi alone no inheritance was given; the offerings by fire to the LORD God of Israel are their inheritance, as he said to them.

15 And Moses had given to the tribe of the Reubenites according to their clans: [16]their territory was from Aroer, which is on the edge of the valley of the Arnon, and the city that is in the middle of the valley, and all the tableland as far as Medeba; [17]with Heshbon, and all its cities that are in the tableland; Dibon, and Bamoth-baal, and Beth-baalmeon, [18]and Jahaz, and Kedemoth, and Mephaath, [19]and Kiriathaim and Sibmah, and Zereth-hashahar on the 'hill of the valley', [20]and Bethpeor, and the slopes of Pisgah, and Beth-ha-jeshimoth, [21]that is, all the cities of the tableland, and all the kingdom of Sihon king of the Amorites, who reigned in Heshbon, whom Moses defeated with the leaders of Midian, Evi and Rekem and Zur and Hur, four vassals of Sihon, who dwelt in the land. [22]Balaam also, the son of Beor, the soothsayer, the people of Israel had killed with the sword among the rest of their slain. [23]And the territory of the people of Reuben reached the Jordan. This was the inheritance of the Reubenites, according to their clans, with their cities and villages.

24 And Moses gave an inheritance also to the tribe of Gad, the Gadites, according to their clans. [25]Their territory was Jazer, and all the cities of Gilead, and half the land of the Ammonites, to Aroer, which is opposite Rabbah, [26]and from Heshbon to Ramath-ha-mizpeh and Betonim, and from Mahanaim to the territory of Lo-debar, [27]and in the plain Beth-haram, Beth-nimrah, Succoth, and Zaphon, the rest of the kingdom of Sihon of Heshbon, having the Jordan as a boundary, to the lower end of the Sea of Chinnereth, eastward beyond the Jordan. [28]This is the inheritance of the Gadites according to their clans, with their cities and villages.

29 And Moses had given to the half-tribe of Manasseh; it belonged to the half-tribe of the Manassites according to their clans: [30]a territory extending from Mahanaim, through all Bashan (the whole kingdom of Og king of Bashan), and all the encampments of Jair, which are in Bashan, sixty villages, [31]and half Gilead, and Ashtaroth, and Edrei, the cities of the kingdom of Og in Bashan; these were allotted to the people of Machir the son of Manasseh for the half of the Machirites according to their clans. [32]These are the inheritances which Moses distributed in the plains of Moab, beyond the Jordan east of Jericho. [33]But to the tribe of Levi Moses gave no inheritance; the LORD God of Israel is their inheritance, as he said to them.

Bibliography: (a) *On the first introduction*: W. Rudolph, *Der 'Elohist'* . . ., pp. 211–16; M. Noth, 'Studien zu den historisch-geographischen Dokumenten des Josuabuches', *ZDPV* 58, 1935, pp. 230–5; *UGS*, pp. 182–90; Auzou, pp. 140ff.

(c) *Reuben and Gad*: Noth, 'Studien zu den historisch-geographischen

Dokumenten . . .', pp. 185–255, esp. pp. 230–5; N. Glueck, 'Explorations in Eastern Palestine III', *AASOR* 18–19, 1937–39, pp. 151–251, esp. pp. 249–51; R. de Vaux, 'Notes d'histoire et de topographie transjordaniennes', *Vivre et Penser* I (= *RB* 50), 1941, pp. 16–47 (repr. *Bible et Orient*, Paris 1967, pp. 115–49); N. Glueck, 'Three Israelite Towns in the Jordan Valley: Zaretan, Succot, Zaphen', *BASOR* 90, 1943, pp. 2–23; id., 'Some Ancient Towns in the Plains of Moab', *BASOR* 91, 1943, pp. 7–26; 92, 1943, p. 26; Noth, *UGS*, pp. 182–190; id., 'Israelitische Stämme zwischen Ammon und Moab', *ZAW* 60, 1944, pp. 11–57; J. Simons, 'From Arnon unto Yabboq', *PEQ* 79, 1947, pp. 27–44; R. Rendtorff, 'Zur Lage von Jaser', *ZDPV* 76, 1960, pp. 124–35; Auzou, loc. cit.; H. J. Franken, 'Tell Deir 'Alla', *RB* 72, 1965, pp. 262–7; B. Oded, 'A note on Josh. XIII 25', *VT* 21, 1971, pp. 239–41, which appeared too late to be used.

(d) *Half-Manasseh east of the Jordan*: A. Bergmann, 'The Israelite Tribe of Half Manasseh', *JPOS* 16, 1936, pp. 224–54; J. A. Soggin, 'Machir' and 'Manasseh', *BHH* II, 1964, cols. 1120, 1136f.

[13.2] 'The regions': the expression also occurs in Joel 4.4; LXX has ὅρια, T *thwmy*, i.e. Hebrew *gᵉbūlē*; V reads 'Galilee, the Philistines', which means nothing. The Hebrew *gᵉlīlōt*, therefore, is translated traditionally, following LXX and T, as 'regions', but in reality the term is unknown: in 22.10–11, for example, this translation is impossible. [3] 'Shihor': LXX translates ἀπὸ τῆς ἀοικήτου; V, better, *a fluvio turbido*. It is clear that LXX no longer understood the exact meaning of the term and so translated on the basis of the fact that in the south of Palestine there is a desert. In fact it is an eastern branch of the Nile Delta, the 'Pools of Horus'.[1] The frontier between Palestine and Egypt is normally called *nᵉhar miṣrayim*, the present-day *wādī el-arīš*, with which Abel and Bright would identify the Shihor. 'Tyrannies': cf. Judg. 3.3, is translated in accordance with the current interpretation of a title which the OT uses only for the governors of the Philistines: *seren*, which may be τύραννος. Even if this etymology is not correct (there are some good reasons for doubting whether it is apt), the title well reflects the situation of the Philistine city-states, and is also confirmed by the *ṭūrānē* of T. LXX translates σατραπεία and V by *reguli*. [4] 'The south'; cf. above, 12.2,4. It should not be transcribed, as LXX does. 'From Arah' is missing in LXX[BA] and appears as Γάζα in LXX[MSS]. It is probably the proper name of an unknown locality. MT and T would allow the rendering 'cave' (as Dhorme does), and this would be plausible, since the region contains a famous cave dedicated to Astarte; but then a prefix *mim-*, lost by haplography, would have to be read. [5] 'The land of Byblos': LXX reads τὴν γῆν Γαλιαθ (LXX[B]) or Γαβλι (LXX[A]) Φυλιστιμ, while V has 'their frontiers'; both are improbable. For Baal-gad, cf. above on 11.17;

[1] For discussion, cf. the commentaries by Baldi and Noth.

LXX^B Γαλγαα, LXX^A has the unlikely Γαλγαλ. [6] 'Misrephoth-maim';
cf. on 11.8. LXX assumes our text here. [7] 'Half the tribe': the article
before *šēbeṭ* shows that the text is not in order. Steuernagel, followed by
Baldi and Noth, would move the *atnaḥ* forward to this word, giving 'for an
inheritance to the nine tribes and a half', and would add *kaḥªṣī šēbeṭ* . . .
wᵉʿimmō, i.e. 'and the half-tribe of Manasseh ⁸and with it . . .', this
phrase having been lost by homoioteleuton. It seems preferable to us to
read, with Abel, the longer text of LXX, cf. the section in brackets in the
text. 'Manasseh' would then be used adjectivally as an explanation of 'half-
tribe': for this syntactical form, cf. *GKC*, § 125 d, n. 1. [8] LXX has 'To
the two tribes and the other half of the tribe of Manasseh; to Reuben and
to Gad Moses had given . . .', a text with fewer repetitions than MT (cf.
v. 7 above). [9] 'From': inserted with LXX (Abel, Noth, Hertzberg). [10]
'Territory': cf. 12.2,4. [11] 'Bashan': for the translation of T, cf. on 12.5.
[12] 'The Rephaim' are the 'giants' of LXX, cf. on 12.2,4, and *gbry* in T,
as well as the 'Anakim' of 11.21–22. [13] After 'the Maacathites', LXX
adds 'and the Canaanites'. For the way in which T translated the word,
cf. 12.5. [14] 'Offerings by fire' is lacking in LXX, which has 'Yahweh the
God of Israel is their heritage . . .' V has *sed sacrificia et victimae*, while T
confirms MT. Noth proposes that the phrase be omitted (no doubt as a
gloss) because of the *hū* that follows (cf. v. 33), which clearly refers only to
Yahweh; cf. Abel and Baldi, as well as Bright (though the latter is not
certain). LXX goes on to add: 'and this was the distribution (καταμερισμός)
which Moses made for the Israelites in the "plains of Moab" beyond the
Jordan, opposite Jericho'. [16] For the translation of *gᵉbūl* cf. on 12.2ff.
For Aroer, cf. on 12.2. 'As far as . . .: MT has 'on (or towards? – in this
case we would have to read *'el* instead of *'al*) Medeba'. LXX omits
Medeba and reads 'as far as Heshbon'. T and some Hebrew MSS have MT
but with *'ad*, while the Hexapla has, with*: 'and Medeba as far as Heshbon';
the preposition is lacking in V. Our correction follows T and MSS with 'as
far as . . .', cf. LXX. [17] 'All the cities': MT has 'all its cities', but it is
not clear to what the suffix refers; it is lacking in LXX, but is found in V
and T in similar circumstances to MT: we follow other commentators in
omitting it. [20] 'The slopes . . .'; cf. above on 10.40 and 12.3,8. [21]
'Four vassals': LXX, V and T read the figure as a fifth proper name,
which gives a person called *rebaʿ* or something of the sort. [22] 'With the
sword . . . etc.' is lacking in LXX, which has ἐν τῇ ῥοπῇ, meaning
probably 'at the last moment'; it is difficult to see what could have been
the Hebrew original of this reading. V and T confirm MT. 'Their' in this
context refers to the Midianite chiefs, as is shown by Num. 31.8, from which
the phrase has been quoted here inaptly (Baldi, Noth). [23] 'Reached . . .
etc.': the text is confused, although the meaning is clear. LXX has 'the
Jordan was its frontier . . .', as do V and T, and we take the text in this

sense. 'Their cities . . .' (i.e. Reuben's), with LXX; MT has 'the cities and their villages'. [24] LXX and Syr have 'Gad' only once; the repetition is tautological (it is probably a dittography). [26] 'Lo-debar': MT and T have *lid^ebir*, LXX^B has *Δαιβων* LXX^A *Δαβειρ*, and V and Syr *Dabir*. The usual reading is *lō-d^ebār*, a place mentioned in the region by II Sam. 9.4ff.; 17.27; cf. Amos 6.13 (*BH³*). [27] 'Having the Jordan as a boundary', cf. v.23. LXX has 'the Jordan bounded it as far as . . .', as do V and T. [29] LXX omits the second mention of the Manassites, as do several commentators, regarding it as a tautology. [30] 'The encampments of Jair': this is the only occurrence of *ḥawwōt* in this form in the OT. [33] A repetition of v.14, with the same omission. Lacking in LXX, and may be the addition of a scribe (Baldi).

Chapter 13 is divided into four sections: (*a*) The first introduction to the division of the land (vv. 1–7), with a catalogue of the regions west of the Jordan which remain to be conquered; (*b*) A summary of the conquests east of the Jordan: the second introduction (vv.8–14); (*c*) The tribes of Reuben and Gad and their territory (vv. 15–28); (*d*) The half-tribe of Manasseh and the conclusion of the chapter (vv.29–33).

The first two parts form an introduction to the third, while the fourth part is its conclusion. But in reality these texts are all somewhat different from each other. The geographical references in the first part make no pretence to be other than secondary, as Noth clearly saw. The chapter begins with an order to divide the land, even that part of it not yet conquered, between the tribes who have a right to it (v. 7), in so far as Joshua can still do this personally (because he is old, v. 1). The secondary nature of vv. 2–6 appears clearly from the fact that the summary of the territories remaining to be conquered has little connection with the order to divide the country amongst the Israelites. Moreover, v. 6b is out of place in its anticipation of the division ordered in v. 7. And whereas vv. 1 and 7 refer solely to Palestine west of the Jordan which rightly belongs to Israel, which they assume has been conquered, vv. 2–6 refer to the empire of Israel at its greatest extent, under David and Solomon (cf. above, 1.4).

In this way Dtr introduces chs. 13–21, which, as we saw in the introduction (§3, b), contain bodies of material which are much older, which often differ amongst themselves, and are in any case independent of their present context. This can be seen from 13.1b and 23.1b, which are almost identical, as if the whole section had been interpolated into the Deuteronomic framework.

Verses 2–6 do not present any difficulty, once it is realized that they consist of an interpolation on the part of a redactor, and have the empire of David and Solomon in mind. The 'regions of the Philistines' (v. 2b), which are then listed in detail in v. 3 as the 'tyrannies', traditionally form the Philistine pentapolis, to which Judg. 3.3 also refers. To these are added 'in the south' the 'Avvim', who, in the LXX, and perhaps also in Judg. 3.3, appear as the 'Hivites', and whose southern frontier is formed by an eastern arm of the Nile delta. The sites mentioned in this section are Gaza, the present day *ghazzeh* (099–101); Ashdod (117–129), in Arabic *esdūd*, the modern Hebrew name being the same as the ancient name, situated between the railway and the present-day *sᵉdē ʿuzziyāhū*; Ashkelon, in Arabic *ʿasqalān* (107–118), the modern Hebrew name being the same as the ancient name, is a little to the SE of the present town. The site of Gath is unknown. Excavations on the *tell* of that name, situated near the junction of the Jerusalem road with that from Tel-Aviv to Beersheba (130–114), have shown that it is impossible that that town ever belonged to the Philistines, for there is a complete absence of any Philistine pottery. Perhaps it is to be found on *tell eṣ-ṣāfi* (135–123). Ekron seems to be on the site of *khirbet el-muquannaʿ* (136–131).

The presence of the 'Geshurites' and the 'Avvim' in this context is strange. The former must have been a different people from those bearing the same name who were situated east of Lake Tiberias, in the view of the fact that the present passage places them in the south (here I disagree with Dhorme). They reappear, presenting the same problems and in the same geographical setting, in I Sam. 27.8. The Avvim also appear in Deut. 2.23.[1] The northern zone is the most extensive and that which is described in the least detail: no town called Arah is known on the territory of the city state of Sidon; to obtain the reference to the famous cave of Astarte, the text must be emended (cf. ad loc). Aphek seems to be the most northerly point here, and may perhaps be the Aphek situated in the plain of Acco and mentioned in Judg. 1.31 || Josh. 19.30 (cf. the commentary on 12.17) (160–250). But some commentators think that it is more likely to be located a little to the north of Beirut, as the context suggests. The place of that name situated east of the present-day Tel-Aviv does not seem to be that mentioned here, because it is too far south (against Dhorme), unless our text is saying that the whole coast from Sidon to the northern confines of Philistine territory remained unconquered. In this case, we

[1] The problem is discussed in Noth, *Comm.*

would have here the historically correct statement that the whole Mediterranean coast remained to be conquered (Hertzberg). But of course in the present context, which extends as far as Byblos (*jebēl*), situated between Tripoli and Beirut, the more northerly site is equally possible.

For Baal-gad cf. the commentary on 11.17 and 12.7. The 'entrance of Hamath', a place which also appears in Num. 13.21; 34.8; Judg. 3.3, forms (as we have seen) a variation on the northern frontier of the empire of David and Solomon, which can also be designated by the Euphrates in the NE (cf. the commentary on 1.4). The 'entrance' is on the Orontes, which crosses it in its northward course, and the use of the term therefore assumes that the empire was not as extensive. Noth has rightly pointed out that neither made satisfactory frontiers. But in any case, the writer's intention is clear: it is to describe the extreme limits reached (or rather, to be reached) by the Israelite occupation. Verse 6a, which contains a clear allusion to 11.8, is 'an incomprehensible addition' (Steuernagel and Noth), in which it is no longer possible to tell clearly whether the promise refers to the northern region which has just been described, or if it is once again a question of the whole of Palestine. Seeing that it is followed by the invitation to divide the lands by lot, the second alternative seems more likely.

With regard to the practice of division by lot, this is attested for private land in Isa. 34.17; Micah 2.4–5.

(*b*) *Second introduction* (*13.8–14*)

In the second introductory section to vv. 14ff., which Baldi and Noth rightly consider to be also secondary, three different strata can be distinguished, as Noth has pointed out.[1] First of all there is a description of Israelite territory east of the Jordan in geographical terms: vv. 9, 11a, b. This is dependent upon Deut. 3.8, 10a, and we find it expanded in vv. 14ff., to which, together with our commentary on 12.1–5, we refer. A second stratum is formed by vv. 10, 12, which also finds a parallel in the beginning of ch. 12. They belong to the same context, as can be seen from the plural suffixes in v. 12b (Steuernagel and Noth). They tell us of the territories of the two Amorite kings (the conjunction in v. 10 is probably an illegitimate attempt to unite this statement to that which precedes it). Here the description is historical and no longer geographical. Finally, we have comments on the

[1] *Comm.*, p. 76.

two kingdoms of Geshur and Maacath (cf. 12.5), formulated, as in Judg. 1.27ff. (and parallels in Joshua), in terms of a kind of negative inventory of territories remaining unconquered. The statements here are legitimate when one considers that just as in the case of the great city states of the Palestinian plain and coast, the various Aramaean kingdoms were not conquered until the period of David, and less completely under Solomon. In the case of Geshur, this came about through an alliance: David married the daughter of a king of the country (II Sam. 3.3), so that relations were always friendly (cf. II Sam. 13–15). Maacath, on the other hand, became properly speaking a vassal state (cf. II Sam. 10.6–8; I Chron. 19.7), because it fought against David and was conquered.

For the place names and rivers, cf. the commentary on 12.1–5.

(c) The tribes of Reuben and Gad and their territories (13.15–28)

1. This passage, which sets out to describe the territory received as an 'inheritance' by Reuben and Gad, presents considerable difficulties, which are reflected in the various interpretations of the passage between which present-day commentators are divided: that of N. Glueck, D. Baldi, and J. Bright on the one hand, and that of M. Noth, H. W. Hertzberg and German archaeologists and geographers in general on the other hand.

We must begin by noting that the history of the tribes east of the Jordan, and particularly of Reuben, is extremely complex. If we admit that there is a historical basis in the statements made in Gen. 35.21ff. and in Josh. 15.6 ‖ 18.7, it can be seen at once, for example, that the presence of Reuben is sometimes also attested west of the Jordan, although no incontrovertible historical or geographical conclusion can be drawn from this fact. Here we are only concerned with its position east of the Jordan, but we shall see that this is described within the context of statements referring basically to the period of David and Solomon, and to episodes related to the wars which they conducted in this region. Moreover, Reuben is never endowed in any historical period with well-defined historical and ethnic characteristics. These must have been lost at a relatively early period. If we look closely, the existence of Reuben in a concrete and real form is attested only in the Song of Deborah (Judg. 5.15b–16).

In his articles of 1935 and 1944 (the latter was concluded in 1942), and in the two editions of his commentary, M. Noth maintains that this passage was constructed by Dtr on the basis of ancient material principally contained in Num. 21.21ff.; 32.1ff. (cf. Josh. 12.1–5; 13.7–13). On the other hand, the present text (the other Deuteronomic texts of Josh. 12 and 13) presents a number of important variants on the traditions in Numbers: Num. 32.1 states that Reuben and Gad chose 'the land of Jazer and the land of Gilead' (cf. v. 25 here) to pasture their cattle (cf. the reference in Judg. 5.15b–16). Here there is in fact a confusion between cause and effect: the two groups from the east of the Jordan remained in the nomad state longer than the tribes on the west of the Jordan, who adapted completely to the nature of the country they occupied. Their territory was progressively extended towards the south, first of all as far as the Arnon (and the historical element in the record of the battles against Sihon of Heshbon is usually placed in this framework). This course of events seems to be fully confirmed by other ancient passages in the OT: in Judg. 3.12ff. Benjamin, west of the Jordan, looks across the valley towards Moab and not towards Reuben and Gad, at a time when Ephraim was already firmly settled in the hill country. In the same way, Deut. 34.5ff. describes Moses as dying 'in the land of Moab', which theoretically should have been within the territory of Reuben, cf. Deut. 34.6b and Josh. 13.20a – and this is the reason why the exact site of the tomb of Moses remains unknown!

As Noth showed in his 1944 study,[1] based on data drawn from the *Onomastikon* of Eusebius (104.13–19), the territory of Jazer probably lay between the *wādī eṣ-ṣīr*, i.e. about 30 km in a straight line east of the Jordan (239–151) in the same latitude as Amman, and the place *nā'ūrah*, 7–8 km further south, in the latitude of Jericho (239–141). This location has recently been confirmed and made more accurate by Rendtorff's work: every *tell* in the region studied is Israelite, and Jazer is probably *tell 'arēme*. Gilead, on the other hand, cannot have been the more extensive territory bearing that name, but must be a region in the immediate neighbourhood of that known as Jazer. This can best be seen from I Sam. 13.7, where Gad and Gilead (in the wider sense) are distinct (cf. the commentary on 13.31 below). For this reason, the identification of the two is probably the product of an inaccurate later gloss made in ignorance of the original situation. Furthermore, according to the very ancient song preserved in Num. 21.21ff., 30, the conquest of the region probably took place from north to south, contrary to the impression which the texts intend to give in their present form. This can be seen from the fact that Medeba

1 'Israelitische Stämme', pp. 31ff.

in the south was not conquered until after the defeat of Sihon of Heshbon.

The conquest of the region seems to have been completed only at the period of David and Solomon (cf. II Sam. 24.5 and I Kings 4.19, together with II Sam. 8.2). In the second half of the ninth century Mesha, king of Moab (Mesha stele, lines 4–21), reoccupied the region after a military campaign. In line 10 of the stone, he states that at Ashtaroth 'the men of Gad had always conquered'[1] while Medeba had been occupied by Omri king of Israel (lines 9–10) and that Israel lived there for forty years. The Israelite population of the occupied region was exterminated by means of a kind of ban which is also known in the Old Testament (lines 11–12).

Having established this, Noth states that vv. 15–28 contain three elements which must be clearly distinguished: (a) a list of place names (vv. 17b–20, 27a); (b) a series of fixed points, with the lines that join them, formulated in the same style as that of the tribal boundaries west of the Jordan (vv. 16a, b, 26, 27b); (c) summaries (vv. 16b, 17a, 21a, 25), on the whole making use of geographical names which have already appeared in the text mentioned, ch. 12 and the beginning of ch. 13.

(a) The lists of place-names are also found in Num. 32.34–38, in a context which, as we possess it, seems to depend on Josh. 13, in that its chronology has been brought into line with it. But the list there is recognizably ancient, as can be seen from the fact that it is fuller than that in ch. 13. The style of the list here is the same as in the lists of place names which are found in chs. 15–19.

(b) The lines which join the places that indicate fixed points (linked by the formula: 'from . . . to . . .') trace an almost straight path from south to north across the Arnon and Lake Tiberias. As this cannot represent a road, Noth thinks that it may be a line representing the eastern frontier of the two tribes, set out like that of the tribes west of the Jordan, following a series of fixed points joined together.[2] North of *d^eḇōnīm* this line becomes completely theoretical (v. 26), above all in the section which touches the lake. The line of demarcation between Reuben and Gad seems just as artificial, and it was certainly absent from the original version; there is no trace of any precise definition of this frontier line.

The theses of Noth, repeated and expanded in numerous articles

---

[1] *ANET*, pp. 320f.; *KAI*, no. 181.
[2] Cf. Alt's thesis, mentioned in the Introduction, § 3b.

over more than thirty years, have not been accepted by all scholars, as we saw above. N. Glueck, who has explored the region east of Jordan and the Negeb, and was followed by Baldi and Bright, considers that the lines drawn from one place to another present only the appearance of a boundary, but do not actually form one. According to Baldi, they are at most 'a few reference points formed by the principal centres within the territory, on a basis of which the boundaries can be approximately located'. But we must point out that the division into literary categories which Noth carried out is accepted by all, regardless of the effective historical and geographical validity of the events and situations they describe. In fact it must be recognized, with regard to the fixed points of the eastern boundary east of the Jordan, that as those who disagree with Noth rightly point out, they form far too vague a frontier (especially in the northern part, as Noth himself admits), and often have no contact with any concrete situation. Thus it is clear that on the one hand the intention of the redactor of this passage is to incorporate lists of place names referring to the period of David and Solomon, which were valid until the region was reconquered by Mesha, king of Moab (second half of the ninth century), while on the other hand the same redactor introduced a list of fixed points such as existed in the same literary form only for the tribes west of the Jordan, a list which is of doubtful value here and often improbable in historical and geographical terms. This is true even if this list of fixed points definitely goes back to the pre-Deuteronomic period.

3. We will now discuss the localities in the order in which they occur in the text. We have already examined some of them in commenting upon ch. 12. Most of them are also to be found in Num. 22, 31 and 32.

[15–20] Cf. the commentary on 12.1–6 and 13.8–14 for some place names. Dibon is the present-day *dhībān* (224–101), about 5 km north of the Arnon on the heavy goods road (it is exceptional for the Hebrew *dālet* to change into the Arabic *dal*). Noth believes that Beth-baal-meon is identical with Bamoth-baal (the latter being a gloss for the former), but cf. Baldi, who disagrees. It is the present-day *mā'īn*, about 8 km SE of *mādabā* (219–120), and it appears on the Moabite stele, line 7, next to Kiriathain (v. 9), a place which has not yet been identified, as a part of the 'territory of Medeba'. According to Eusebius, *Onomasticon* (48.3ff.), and Musil (at the beginning of this century), Beth-peor corresponds to *khirbet eš-šaikh jāyil* about 10 km east of

Heshbon (9.10; 12.2). The identification of most of the other place
names is doubtful; cf. the commentaries of Baldi and Noth, as well as
Simons, § 298ff. For the 'slopes of Pisgah' and 'Beth-ha-jeshimoth',
cf. above on 12.3.

[21–23] For the 'vassals of Sihon', cf. a commentary on Num. 31.8.
The relationship between the present passage, this passage and its
parallels in Num. 22; 31; 32 is not always obvious, since, as Noth
points out, the texts in Numbers have been harmonized with the Deuteronomic texts. For the death of Balaam, cf. Num. 31.8. For the western frontier of Reuben (the Jordan), cf. the comment in § 1. above.

[24–28] The territory of Gad includes the 'country of Jezer', cf.
above in § 1; as also for Gilead. The most likely site of Gilead is in the
region south of the Jabbok up to the hill country around Amman, as
can be seen from the various instances where the name *gil'ad*, and
variants of it, occur in the region of *es-salṭ*, on the old road for heavy
goods leading to Amman. Aroer here is not the same as the Aroer of v.
16, with its parallels, but another place near Amman (here called
Rabbah, a shortened form of *rabbat-'ammōn*). *rāmat-hammiṣpeh* is different from the Mizpeh in 11.3, 8 and other places with the same name.
The frequency of this name is explained by the fact that there are numerous heights from which it is possible to 'observe' (*sph*) from a long
way off. In this case the probable site is the present-day *khirbet eṣ-ṣar*
(also known as *qaṣr eṣ-ṣar*) about 16 km north of Heshbon, while Betonim is about 5 km sse of *es-salṭ* on the *khirbet batnē*. Mahanain is nowadays generally identified with *tell ḥejāj* in the valley of the Jabbok
(*nahr ez-zerqa*), on the south of the river (Aharoni: *tell edh-dhahab el-
gharbīye* 214–177), while Lo-Debar is a little further north, although
its site is unknown. Verse 27 also contains a list of place names. Beth-
haram is the present-day *tell iktanū*, near the place where the *wādī
ḥesbān* enters the Jordan depression (214–136); Beth-nimrah is the
present day *tell blēbil*, near where the *wādī sa'eb* enters the depression
(210–146); Succoth is *tell dēr 'allā*, a little to the north of where the
Jabbok turns south (208–178); Zaphon is almost certainly *tell es-
sa'īdiye* (204–186) on the southern bank of the *wādī kafrinjī*; Glueck,
however, proposes a different identification.

(*d*) *Territories belonging to the half of Manasseh east of the Jordan (13.29–33)*

The description given of the territory which was accorded to the
eastern half of the tribe of Manasseh is particularly inadequate, because it includes neither a list of the places which form it, nor the

fixed points which mark its boundaries. The text itself is extremely brief, if we follow Noth in allowing that the only authentic part is v. 30, as far as the first mention of Bashan. The reason for this phenomenon was probably that the readactor had few sources at his disposal. Num. 32.39–42 and Deut. 3.13, passages parallel to these verses, are equally poor in details.

Even the mention of Mahanaim as a fixed point on the east is unconvincing, because of its imprecision. The 'encampments of Jair' are mentioned in Num. 32.41 and Deut. 3.14. Their site is unknown.

A problem which we can do no more than touch on here is that of the connection between Manasseh and Machir. In Gen. 50.23, the latter appears as the 'son' of the former, as part of the following genealogy: Manasseh-Machir-Gilead, which is a further indication that originally there was no connection from the ethnic point of view between Gilead and Gad. It was only when Gad came to settle in Gilead that it was possible to make a link between the two names. Modern criticism is unanimous in holding that Machir left the east of the Jordan to settle west of the Jordan, and did not break away from Manasseh west of the Jordan, in order to settle east of the Jordan.[1]

CHAPTERS 14–17

The Division of Territory carried out at Gilgal

14 [1]And these are the inheritances which the people of Israel received in the land of Canaan, which Eleazar the priest, and Joshua the son of Nun, and the heads of families of the tribes of the people of Israel distributed to them. [2]Their inheritance was by lot, as the LORD had commanded Moses for the nine and one-half tribes.[3]For Moses had given an inheritance to the two and one-half tribes beyond the Jordan; but to the Levites he gave no inheritance among them. [4]For the people of Joseph were two tribes, Manasseh and Ephraim; and no portion was given to the Levites in the land, but only cities to dwell in, with their pasture lands for their cattle

[1] For the links between Manasseh and Machir, cf. M. Noth, *The History of Israel*, London ² 1960, pp. 61f., and below, on 17.1ff.

and their substance. ⁵The people of Israel did as the LORD commanded Moses; they allotted the land.

6 Then the people of Judah came to Joshua at Gilgal; and Caleb the son of Jephunneh the Kenizzite said to him, 'You know what the LORD said to Moses the man of God in Kadesh-barnea concerning you and me. ⁷I was forty years old when Moses the servant of the LORD sent me from Kadesh-barnea to spy out the land; and I brought him word again as best I knew. ⁸But my brethren who went up with me discouraged the people; yet I wholly followed the LORD my God. ⁹And Moses swore on that day, saying, "Surely the land on which your foot has trodden shall be an inheritance for you and your children for ever, because you have wholly followed the LORD your God." ¹⁰And now, behold, the LORD has kept me alive, as he said, these forty-five years since the time that the LORD spoke this word to Moses, while Israel walked in the wilderness; and now, lo, I am this day eighty-five years old. ¹¹I am still as strong to this day as I was in the day that Moses sent me; my strength now is as my strength was then, for anything at all in war. ¹²So now give me this hill country of which the LORD spoke on that day; for you heard on that day how the Anakim were there, with great fortified cities: certainly, if the LORD will be with me, I shall drive them out as the LORD said.' ¹³Then Joshua blessed him; and he gave Hebron to Caleb the son of Jephunneh for an inheritance. ¹⁴So Hebron became the inheritance of Caleb the son of Jephunneh the Kenizzite to this day, because he wholly followed the LORD, the God of Israel. ¹⁵Now the name of Hebron formerly was Kiriath-arba; this Arba was the greatest man among the Anakim. And the land had rest from war.

15 ¹The lot for the tribe of the people of Judah according to their clans: from the territory of Edom, from the wilderness of Zin to Kadesh, towards the south-west. ²And their south boundary was from the end of the Salt Sea, from the bay southward; ³it goes to the region south of the 'Ascent of the Scorpions', passes along Zin, and goes up south of Kadesh-barnea, passes by Hezron, goes up to Addar, turns about to Karka, ⁴passes along to Azmon, goes out by the 'Brook of Egypt', and comes to its end at the sea. This is their south boundary.

5 And the east boundary is the Salt Sea, to the mouth of the Jordan. And the boundary on the north side runs from the bay of the sea at the mouth of the Jordan; ⁶and the boundary goes up from Beth-hoglah, and passes along north of Beth-ha-arabah; and the boundary goes as far as the 'Stone of Bohan the son of Reuben'; ⁷and the boundary goes up to Debir from the plain of Achor, and to the north it turns toward the 'Gilgal', which is opposite the 'Ascent of Adummim', which is on the south side of the 'Torrent'; and the boundary passes along by the waters of En-shemesh, and ends at En-rogel; ⁸then the boundary goes up by the 'Valley of the son of Hinnom' at the southern shoulder of the Jebusites (that is, Jerusalem);

and the boundary goes up to the top of the mountain that lies over against the valley of Hinnom, on the west side and at the northern end of the 'Plain of Rephaim'; ⁹from the top of the mountain the boundary turns to the spring of the 'Waters of Nephtoah', and stops at the cities of Mount Ephron; then the boundary bends round towards Baalah (that is, Kiriath-jearim); ¹⁰and the boundary circles from Baalah westwards to Mount Seir, passes along to the northern shoulder of Mount Jearim (that is, Chesalon), and goes down to Beth-shemesh, and passes along by Timnah; ¹¹and the boundary stops at the shoulder of the hill north of Ekron. Then the boundary bends round to Shikkeron, and passes along to Mount Ballah, and stops at Jabneel; then the boundary comes to an end at the sea.

12 And the west boundary is the Great Sea with its coast-line. This is the boundary round about the people of Judah, including everything given to their clans.

13 According to the commandment of the LORD to Joshua, to Caleb the son of Jephunneh was given a portion among the people of Judah, Kiriath-arba, that is, Hebron (Arba was the father of Anak). ¹⁴And Caleb drove out from there the three sons of Anak, Sheshai and Ahiman and Talmai, the descendants of Anak. ¹⁵And he went up from there against the inhabitants of Debir; now the name of Debir formerly was Kiriath-sepher. ¹⁶And Caleb said, 'Whoever smites Kiriath-sepher, and takes it, to him will I give Achsah my daughter as wife'. ¹⁷And Othniel the son of Kenaz, the brother of Caleb, took it; and he gave him Achsah his daughter as wife. ¹⁸When she came to him, she decided to ask her father for a field; and she alighted from her ass, and Caleb said to her, 'What do you wish?' ¹⁹She said to him, 'Give me a present; since the land you have given me is dry, give me also springs of water.' And Caleb gave her the 'Upper Springs' and the 'Lower Springs'. ²⁰This is the inheritance of the tribe of the people of Judah according to their clans.

21 The cities belonging to the tribe of the people of Judah, toward the boundary of Edom *in the Negeb*, were Kabzeel, Eder, Jagur, ²²Kinah, Dimonah, Adadah, ²³Kedesh, Hazor, Ithnan, ²⁴Ziph, Telem, Bealoth, ²⁵Hazor-hadattah, Kerioth-hezron (that is, Hazor), ²⁶Amam, Shema, Moladah, ²⁷Hazar-gaddah, Heshmon, Beth-pelet, ²⁸Hazar-shual, Beer-sheba and its villages, ²⁹Baalah, Iim, Ezem, ³⁰Eltolad, Chesil, Hormah, ³¹Ziklag, Madmannah, Sansannah, ³²Lebaoth, Shilhim, Ain-rimmon: in all, twenty-nine cities, with their villages.

33 *In the foothills*, Eshtaol, Zorah, Ashnah, ³⁴Zanoah, En-gannim, Tappuah, Enam, ³⁵Jarmuth, Adullam, Socoh, Azekah, ³⁶Shaaraim, Adithaim, Gederah, Gederothaim: fourteen cities with their villages.

37 Zenan, Hadashah, Migdal-gad, ³⁸Dilean, Mizpeh, Joktheel, ³⁹Lachish, Bozkath, Eglon, ⁴⁰Cabbon, Lahmas, Chitlish, ⁴¹Gederoth, Beth-dagon, Naamah and Makkedah: sixteen cities with their villages.

42 Libnah, Ether, Ashan, ⁴³Iphtah, Ashnah, Nezib, ⁴⁴Keilah, Achzib, and Mareshah: nine cities with their villages.

45 Ekron, with its towns and its villages; ⁴⁶from Ekron to the sea, all that were by the side of Ashdod, with their villages,⁴⁷Ashdod, its towns and its villages: Gaza, its towns and its villages; to the 'Brook of Egypt', and the great sea forming its frontier.

48 And *in the hill country*, Shamir, Jattir, Socoh, ⁴⁹Dannah, Kiriath-sepher (that is, Debir), ⁵⁰Anab, Eshtemoah, Anim, ⁵¹Goshen, Holon, and Giloh: eleven cities with their villages.

52 Arab, Dumah, Eshan, ⁵³Janum, Beth-tappuah, Aphekah, ⁵⁴Humtah, Kiriath-arba (that is, Hebron), and Zior: nine cities with their villages.

55 Maon, Carmel, Ziph, Juttah, ⁵⁶Jezreel, Jokdeam, Zanoah, ⁵⁷of the Kenites, Gibeah, and Timnah: ten cities with their villages.

58 Halhul, Beth-zur, Gedor, ⁵⁹Maarath, Beth-anoth, and Eltekon: six cities with their villages.

[Tekoa, Ephratah (that is, Bethlehem), Peor, Etam, Kulon, Tatam, Sores, Kerem, Gallim, Beter, Manochoh: eleven cities and their villages.]

60 Kiriath-baal (that is, Kiriath-jearim), and Rabbah: two cities with their villages.

61 *In 'the wilderness'*, Beth-arabah, Middin, Secacah, ⁶²Nibshan, the 'City of Salt', and En-gedi: six cities with their villages.

63 But the Jebusites, the inhabitants of Jerusalem, the people of Judah could not drive out; so the Jebusites dwell with the people of Judah at Jerusalem to this day.

16 ¹The territory assigned to the descendants of Joseph went from the Jordan by Jericho, the 'Waters of Jericho', to the east, the wilderness going up from Jericho into the hill country to Bethel; ²then going from Bethel to Luz, it passes along to Ataroth, the frontier of the Archites; ³then it goes down westward to the frontier of the Japhletites, as far as the territory of lower Beth-horon, then to Gezer, and it ends at the sea. ⁴This was the inheritance of the people of Joseph, Manasseh and Ephraim.

5 The territory of the Ephraimites by their clans was as follows: the boundary of their inheritance on the east was Ataroth-Arak as far as upper Beth-horon, ⁶and the boundary goes thence to the sea . . .; on the north Michmethath; then on the east the boundary turns round toward Taanath-shiloh, and passes along beyond it on the east to Janoah, ⁷then it goes down from Janoah to Ataroth and to Naarah, and touches Jericho, ending at the Jordan. ⁸From Tappuah the boundary goes westward to the brook Kanah, and ends at the sea. Such is the inheritance of the tribe of the Ephraimites by their clans, ⁹together with the towns which were set apart for the Ephraimites within the inheritance of the Manassites, all those towns with their villages. ¹⁰However they did not drive out the Canaanites that dwelt in Gezer: so the Canaanites have dwelt in the midst

of Ephraim to this day, but have become slaves to do forced labour.

17 ¹Territory assigned to the tribe of Manasseh, for he was the first-born of Joseph. To Machir the first-born of Manasseh, the father of Gilead, were allotted Gilead and Bashan, because he was a man of war. ²And allotments were made to the rest of the tribe of Manasseh, by their clans, the Abiezerites, the Helekites, the Asrielites, the Shechemites, the Hepherites and the Shemidaites; these were the male descendants of Manasseh the son of Joseph, by their clans.

3 Now Zelophehad the son of Hepher, son of Gilead, son of Machir, son of Manasseh, had no sons, but only daughters; and these are the names of his daughters: Mahlah, Noah, Hoglah, Milcah, and Tirzah. ⁴They came before Eleazar the priest and Joshua the son of Nun and the leaders, and said, 'the LORD commanded Moses to give us an inheritance along with our brethren.' So according to the commandment of the LORD he gave them an inheritance among the brethren of their father. ⁵Thus there fell to Manasseh ten portions, besides the land of Gilead and Bashan, which is on the other side of the Jordan. ⁶As for the daughters of Manasseh, they received an inheritance along with his sons. But the land of Gilead was allotted to the rest of the Manassites.

7 The boundary of Manasseh on the Asher side takes in Michmethath, which is opposite Shechem; then the boundary goes along southward to Yashib, the 'Spring Tappuah.' ⁸The land of Tappuah belongs to Manasseh, but the town of Tappuah on the boundary of Manasseh belonged to the sons of Ephraim. ⁹Then the boundary goes down to the brook Kanah (there are Ephraimite cities to the south of the brook among the cities of Manasseh, while the boundary of Manasseh goes on the north side of the brook) and ends at the sea. ¹⁰To the south for Ephraim and to the north for Manasseh the sea was the western boundary; on the north Asher is reached, and on the east Issachar.¹¹Also in (or 'with') Issachar and Asher Manasseh had Beth-shean and its villages, and Ibleam and its villages, and the inhabitants of Dor and its villages, and the inhabitants of Endor and its villages, and the inhabitants of Taanach and its villages, and the inhabitants of Megiddo and its villages and the three of Napheth. ¹²Yet the sons of Manasseh could not take possession of those cities; but the Canaanites persisted in dwelling in that land. ¹³When the people of Israel grew strong, they put the Canaanites to forced labour, but as for conquering them, they did not conquer them.

14 And the tribe of Joseph spoke to Joshua, saying, 'Why have you given me but one territory and one portion as an inheritance, although I am such a numerous people, since the LORD has blessed me?' ¹⁵And Joshua said to them, 'If you are a numerous people, go up to the forest, and there clear ground for yourselves in the land of the Perizzites and the Rephaim, since the hill country of Ephraim is too narrow for you.' ¹⁶The

tribe of Joseph said, 'The hill country is not enough for us; yet all the
Canaanites who dwell in the plain have chariots of iron, both those in Beth-
shean and its villages, and those in the plain of Jezreel.' [17]But Joshua said
to the house of Joseph, to Ephraim and Manasseh, 'You are a numerous
people, and have great power; you shall not have one lot only, [18]but the
hill country shall be yours, for though it is a forest, you shall clear it and
possess it to its farthest borders; and moreover you shall drive out the
Canaanites, though they have chariots of iron, and though they are
strong.'

Bibliography: (a) *Introduction to the division:* Auzou, pp. 142ff.; (c) *The
Territory of Judah: the frontiers:* A. Alt, 'Das System der Stämmesgrenzen
im Buche Josua', 1927, *KS* I, pp. 193–202; M. Noth, 'Studien zu den
historisch-geographischen Dokumenten des Josuabuches', *ZDPV* 58, 1935,
pp. 185–255; R. North, 'Israel's Tribes and Today's Frontier', *CBQ* 16,
1954, pp. 146–53, esp. p. 152; F. M. Cross and G. E. Wright, 'The Boundary and Province Lists of the Kingdom of Judah', *JBL* 75, 1956, pp. 209–
26; R. North, 'Three Judaean Hills in Jos. 15.9f.', *Bibl* 37, 1956, pp. 209–16;
Y. Aharoni, 'The Northern Border of Judah', *PEQ* 90, 1958, pp. 27–31;
Z. Kallai (-Kleinmann), *The Northern Boundaries of Judah from the Settlement
of the Tribes until the Beginning of the Hasmonaean Period*, Jerusalem 1960,
pp. 46ff. (in Hebrew, summary in English); Auzou, pp. 142ff. (d) *Judah:
cities and districts:* A. Alt, 'Judas Gaue unter Josia', 1925, *KS* II, pp. 276–88;
Noth, 'Studien zu den historisch-geographischen Dokumenten . . .', pp.
185–255; A. Alt, 'Bemerkungen zu einigen judäischen Ortslisten des Alten
Testaments', *BBLAK* (= *ZDPV*) 68, 1949–51, pp. 93–210; R. North,
'Israel's Tribes and Today's Frontier' (see above); F. M. Cross and G.
Wright, 'The Boundary and Province List . . .' (see above: with a good
summary of the studies quoted above by Alt and Noth); Z. Kallai
(-Kleinmann), 'Note on the Town Lists of Judah, Simeon, Benjamin and
Dan', *VT* 11, 1961, pp. 223–27; A. D. Crown, 'The Date and Authenticity
of the Samaritan Hebrew Book of Joshua as seen in its Territorial Allotments', *PEQ* 95, 1963, pp. 79–100; K. D. Schunck, *Benjamin*, Berlin 1963,
pp. 139ff.; id., 'Bemerkungen zur Ortsliste von Benjamin (Jos. 18.21–28)',
ZDPV 78, 1962, pp. 143–58; Auzou, loc. cit.; S. Talmon, 'The Town-Lists
of Simeon', *IEJ* 15, 1965, pp. 235–41; id., 'The Lists of the Cities of
Simeon', *'Ereṣ Iśrā'el* 8, 1967, pp. 265–8 (in Hebrew, summary in English);
also A. Charbel, 'Beit Jimāl tra le città bibliche della Shefela (Gios.
15.33–36)', *Salesianum* 31, 1969, pp. 485–96; A. Kuschke, 'Kleine Beiträge
zur Siedlungsgeschichte der Stämme Aser und Juda', *HTR* 64, 1971, pp.
291–313; of which we were not able to make use. (f) *Ephraim and Manasseh:*
W. F. Albright, 'The Northern Boundary of Benjamin', *AASOR* IV, 1922–
23, pp. 150–5; id., 'The Site of Tirzah and the Topography of Western

Manasseh', *JPOS* 11, 1931, pp. 241-51; K. Elliger, 'Die Grenze zwischen Ephraim und Manasse', *ZDPV* 52, 1930, pp. 265-309; G. Dahl, 'The "Three Heights" of Josh. 17.11', *JBL* 53, 1934, pp. 381-3; M. Noth, 'Studien zu den historisch-geographischen Dokumenten . . .', pp. 201-15; J. Simons, 'The Structure and Interpretation of Joshua XVI-XVII', *Orientalia Neerlandica*, Leiden 1948, pp. 190-215; E. Danielus, 'The Boundary of Ephraim and Manasseh in the Western Plain', *PEQ* 90, 1958, pp. 122-44; E. Jenni, 'Historisch-topographische Untersuchungen zur Grenze zwischen Ephraim und Manasse', *ZDPV* 74, 1958, pp. 35-40; A. Kuschke, 'Das Deutsche Evangelische Institut . . .', Lehrkurs 1959, *ZDPV* 76, 1960, pp. 38f. (for Taanath-shiloh, 16.6); Auzou, pp. 147ff.

[14.1] 'Heads of families': *rā'šē 'aḇōt* for *rā'šē ḇēt 'aḇōt*, an expression current throughout the ancient Near East, and meaning the heads of great families bearing a famous name (Baldi). [2] 'By lot': the expression in Hebrew is complicated but clear in itself; the ancient versions and *BH*³ propose paraphrases and corrections which should not be ignored. Perhaps we may follow T in reading *baggōrāl*, as does *BH*³. [7] 'As best I knew', literally, 'as it was with my heart'; LXX refers the expression to Moses '. . . his heart', but this is an error. V, correctly, has 'as seemed true to me'. Noth, on the basis of I Kings 8.17-18 and 10.2, has 'as I had proposed to myself'. [8] 'Discouraged': MT has the form *himsīw*, a real Aramaism (cf. *GKC* § 75 ii) in place of which it is usually proposed to read *hēmassū*, following Deut. 1.28. The expression means literally 'make the heart melt'. [11] '. . . anything at all in war', literally, 'to fight, to go and come'. The juxtaposition of contrary terms in Hebrew usually indicates totality;[1] thus 'to fight' is probably a gloss giving a correct explanation of 'go and come', which was regarded as too vague. LXX transposes the terms, putting 'for war' at the end of the sentence. [12] 'With me': read *'ittī* instead of MT *'ōtī*, 'me', following the ancient versions. [15] 'This Arba . . . Anakim' is clearly a gloss; cf. the commentary. LXX read: 'This was the principal city (μητρόπολις) of the Anakim', suggesting that MT might be (Bright) the product of a confusion between *'ēm*, 'mother', and *'āḏām*, 'man'. [15.1] The lot is not mentioned in LXX, which also presents certain variants in the formulation of the names: we mention them only when they are more than simply a question of spelling. 'To Cadesh, towards the south-west', following LXX (πρὸς λίβα); MT and V have only 'towards the south, on the western side' (or 'towards the Negeb'), which is a tautology. We should also follow LXX in reading 'from the wilderness of Zin' (ἀπὸ τῆς ἐρήμου, i.e. *mimmidbar*, the preposition being possibly lost by

[1] A. M. Honeyman, 'Merismus in the Bible', *JBL* 71, 1952, pp. 11-18, esp. pp. 15f; P. Boccaccio, 'I termini contrari come espressione della totalità in ebraico', *Bibl* 33, 1952, pp. 173-190, esp. p. 182, n. 2.

haplography). This gives us the same frontier line, with a few variations, as is found in Num. 34.3–5. **[2]** 'From the bay', literally, 'from the tongue'; LXX has 'from the height' and T 'from the shore' (*kēpā*'). **[3a]** Lacking in LXX and V. **[4]** 'Their', following LXX and V; MT has 'your'. 'Comes to its end' (Heb.: 'and the ending(s) of the boundary is'); cf. K and Q: the former follows the sense, the latter has the plural agreeing with the subject. **[6]** 'As far as', with LXX, V and T (which has *l^e*), inserting '*ad*. **[7]** 'The "Gilgal"': perhaps the plural was read with 18.17: *g^elīlōt*. 'To the north' is omitted in LXX, which once again has καταβαίνει, 'goes down', for 'turns'; Noth and Baldi prefer the reading of LXX. **[9]** 'The cities of Mount Ephron': LXX has only 'towards the mountain'; this is the *lectio brevior*, especially if one concedes that '*ārē* may be a phonetic dittography for *hār* (Baldi). 'And stops at': instead of *w^eyāšā*, Noth (pp.211f.) proposes *ūmōṣā*, that is, 'and Mosa, towards the cities . . .', cf. *hammōṣā*, which results from the change of *hē* into *aleph* as the final consonant. This gives us the name of a known locality in the region. **[10]** 'Seir': LXX^B has Ασσαρ (ες),which is supported by the modern name *sarīs*. **[12]** 'The Great Sea' is obtained by means of a very slight change in the text, to some extent supported by LXX and T. MT reads 'toward the sea' (or 'toward the west'), but the final letter is no doubt the result of a dittography with the initial which follows. This form is already assumed by V. **[13]** 'Was given': in Hebrew literally 'gave' (the subject being understood: *the lot* gave . . ., v.1). 'The father of . . .' LXX has here, as in 14.15, μητρόπολις. **[15]** 'Kiriath-sepher' is often corrected to *qiryat sōper*, according to the reading of LXX, which has πόλις γραμμάτων, cf. LXX^A which, in Judg. 1.11, has καριαθσωφαρ, and T, which reads *qryt 'rky*. A *bita tupir* is recorded in the Egyptian 'satirical letter', pap. Anastasi I (XXII, 5, *ANET*, p.477b), from the end of the thirteenth century; but there is no indication that it is the present locality (Noth). **[18]** 'She decided': the form *watt^esītēhū* means literally 'she convinced him', and sometimes even 'seduced', but in what follows the only persons present are herself and Caleb; LXX confirms MT (against Baldi), while V has *suasa est a viro suo*; but T, even with its textual variants which give the *qal* and the *hapel* respectively, confirms MT. On the basis of V, some MSS of LXX and the reading of LXX^B in Judges 1.14, it has been suggested that *way^esītehā*, 'he persuaded her', should be read. But the difficulty of this reading lies in the fact that the verb *swt* always has a pejorative sense, 'seduce', 'tempt', etc., towards something bad, and the sense of the text excludes this implication. Thus our translation is itself quite hypothetical (cf. Noth and the discussion in J. Bright). 'She alighted': the meaning of the root *ṣnḥ* is unknown; Baldi, Hertzberg and Bright propose the translation which we adopt, and which fits the context. Noth follows T and Syr. **[19]** 'A present': literally, 'a blessing', a term which is very apt in referring to water in this region. 'Land . . . dry' can also be translated: 'the region . . . the Negeb' or '. . . southern', but the emphasis here is on the nature of the terrain, which only water can cure, and not on its geographical position, which would be defined rather vaguely. In vv. 21-63 the versions present a number of variations in the names; we indicate them only where they are of some importance. [21] 'Eder': LXX^B: Apa, LXX^A Εδραι, LXX^L Αραδ. The last reading is adopted by Baldi, and by Abel, who compares it with 12.14. [22] 'Adadah': LXX^B has Αρουελ/-ες i.e., Aroer; the reading was probably 'Ararah' (confusion between *rēš* and *dālet*); V and T confirm MT. [23] LXX^B makes the two last places into one, probably rightly. [24] LXX^B lacks Telem, though it is found in I Sam. 15.4. [28] 'Villages': following LXX; the term *bizyōt*^e*yā*, confirmed by V, must no doubt be read as *b*^e*nōtēhā* (confusion between *nun* and *zain*), cf. Neh. 11.27 and the introduction, § 5. [32] 'Ain-rimmon' appears as a single locality in LXX (cf. Neh. 11.29), and not as two, as in MT and V. For Shilhim, cf. 13.6. [34] 'Tappuah' is lacking in LXX, which also (LXX^A) has other readings different from MT. [36] 'Gedero-thaim': LXX read 'its hamlets', refering to *g*^e*dērā*, and this accords better with the number 14. The differences between LXX^B and MT can be explained by the wish of the first to give the exact number indicated, 14; in MT and V we have in fact 15 places. [47] For the last phrase, cf. on 13.3. [49] 'Kiriathsepher', with LXX and Syr; MT, V and T have 'K.-Sanna', no doubt as a result of assonance with the previous word. Noth prefers MT, perhaps because it is the *lectio difficilior*.[50] 'Eshtemoh' ought probably to read *'ešt*^e*mōah*; the consonants are, of course, identical. [52] Abel's note on 'Dumah' seems wrong. [53] 'Janum', following Q, LXX^A, V and T; MT has *yānīm*, and LXX^B 'Ιεμαιν. [56] I Chron. 2.44 has 'Jorkeam' (con-fusion between *rēš* and *dālet* and metathesis): the reading occurs in LXX^B: 'Ιαρεικαμ. [57] 'Of the Kenites' is originally an explanation of the previous word (Noth). [59] Here LXX inserts into the text a lengthy passage which seems indispensable in order to restore the list. We have put it in square brackets in the translation. It was no doubt lost by homoioteleuton. The orthography is certain only in the case of the first five places, which occur elsewhere in the OT. This section is also lacking in V and T. [63] 'Could not': Q has the perfect, K the imperfect, with an unusual *scriptio plena* in the first syllable, cf. BH³. [16.1] 'Territory assigned': following MT, V and T; LXX has 'the frontier'. The confusion is probably due not only to the similarity between the two terms *gōrāl* and *g*^e*būl* (of which the latter has an ambivalent meaning, cf. on 13.16 and 12.2), but also to the mixture here of the description of boundaries on the one hand and lists of cities on the other; in the former case the term in LXX is the appropriate one, and in the latter case that of MT. 'The wilderness': some commentators, followed by BH³, would place the *atnaḥ* here. 'Bethel' is juxtaposed with 'Luz' in LXX, whose text reads much more smoothly here, but is thereby suspect.

[3] Here, as in vv. 6 and 8, MT can be understood in two ways: 'to the sea' (LXX and V) or 'towards the west'; in the light of 17.10 the first meaning is preferable. [5] 'Arak', with LXX^B, cf. v. 2; LXX^A, V and T confirm MT as in 18.13. [6] 'Passes along beyond it', cf. 13.14; the pronoun is lacking in LXX and V, and should probably be omitted. The verse is incomplete after 'sea'. [10] After 'this day' LXX adds 'until Pharaoh king of Egypt came up and took it and burnt it with fire; he killed the Canaanites, the Perizzites and all the inhabitants of Gezer. And Pharaoh gave it as a dowry to his daughter.' But it omits the forced labour, as does MT in Judg. 1.29.[1] [17.1] 'Territory assigned'; cf. on 16.1. [2-3] In LXX there are some differences in the names, and the text is in parts shorter. 'The Shemidaites': on the Samaria ostraka this name appears, in fact, as šem⁽e⁾yādāʿ.[2] [4] 'Moses': LXX has 'through Moses'. 'Them': in the masc. in MT, even though it refers to a feminine noun; the change from feminine suffixes into masculine suffixes is frequent in Hebrew. [5] Once again, the list of names in LXX differs somewhat. [7] 'Southward': literally, 'to the right', from the point of view of one facing east, as directions were worked out. 'Yashib', following LXX^B; cf. the commentaries; MT has 'towards the inhabitants of the Spring . . .' At the beginning LXX^B has: 'The boundary of the Manassites includes Delanath, which is opposite the Anathites; and the boundary continues towards Yamush and Yashib . . .' T reads: lwt ytby ʿyn, i.e., 'it leads to the inhabitants of the Spring . . .' [8] LXX differs slightly. [9] 'Ephraimite cities': following Noth. MT has the impossible form 'cities', without the article, followed by 'these', with the article. [10] 'Western' must be added to make the translation comprehensible. [11] Noth suppresses all mention of the 'inhabitants' as redundant. 'Endor' is lacking in LXX and seems to be a dittography which should be omitted from MT, although it occurs in V and T; however, it forms part of the topography of the region being described. 'The three of Naphet' (?) is probably a confusion for nāpēt dor, cf. on 11.2; we would then have to read 'all three, the Dunes of Dor'; for the details, cf. Dahl, op. cit. [13] 'Forced labour'; cf. on 16.10. [15] 'In the land of the Perizzites and the Rephaim' is lacking in LXX. [14] 'Since the Lord' is not clear in the text. Perhaps ʿd is an abbreviation for ʿ/dw = ʿal dᵉbar, which was later understood but not expressed, cf. BH³ and the similar wording in T. We assume this form in our translation. [18] 'Moreover . . .' Some scholars, since R. Smend,

---

[1] For the term 'forced labour', as a rendering of mas ʿōbēd, cf. I. Mendelssohn, 'State Slavery in Ancient Palestine', BASOR 85, 1942, pp. 14–17; id., 'On Corvée Labor in Ancient Canaan and Israel', BASOR 167, 1962, pp. 31–35; also our Das Königtum in Israel, Ursprünge, Spannungen, Entwicklung, BZAW 104, Berlin 1967, p. 86 n. 18.

[2] Cf. D. Diringer, Le inscrizioni antico-ebraico palestinesi, Florence 1934, nos. 3ff. For other places which appear in this list and in the Samaria ostraka, cf. S. Moscati, L'epigrafia ebraica antica, Rome 1951, pp. 28ff.

believe it necessary to insert *lō'* and to read: 'But you shall *not* drive out the Canaanites, because they have . . . because they are . . .' This would be in accordance with the logic of the text, but there is no critical basis for it. Moreover, LXX echoes MT and even adds: You in fact will succeed in conquering him'.

(a) Introduction to the division of territory (14.1–5)

This passage forms a kind of heading (Noth) which is difficult to date (in Abel's view, it is early). **[1–2]** These are among the few verses which are often attributed to P, so that sometimes the whole section has been ascribed to the priestly redactor (e.g. S. Mowinckel).[1] The reason for this is the mention of Eleazar, who no doubt is identical with the son of Aaron mentioned in Exod. 6.25, even though this is not completely certain, as Baldi and Hertzberg imply. With him, as well as with Joshua, the 'heads' act; in Num. 34.17–19 they appear as 'princes' (*neśî'îm*) and are listed in detail. It is interesting to note that in vv. 2–3 the tribes of Israel number twelve plus one: Levi, while in v. 4 they would be nine, if Joseph is to be divided into two and if we are to obtain the figure twelve by adding Levi (for the special grant made to Levi, cf. the commentary on ch. 21; and cf. 13.14, 33). On the other hand, in the general list, chs. 14–21, they number twelve if we count Caleb and if we exclude the tribes beyond the Jordan. Other problems concerning this figure will be discussed in my commentary on Judg. 5.

[2] The lot carries out the task imposed in Num. 33.54; 34.13 (cf. above on 13.6–7). Baldi has pointed out the difficulties to which this procedure gave rise within the biblical tradition itself. Although Num. 26.53–56 speaks of a division by lot, it emphasizes at the same time that the division must be made in proportion to the effective numerical importance of each group (Num. 26.54 explicitly mentions the results of the census). Thus we have here two contradictory conceptions, both present in the tradition but difficult to harmonize. Moreover, apart from difficulties manifested within the tradition itself, the two procedures present other difficulties from the historical point of view. The division of the land by lot would seem to be quite applicable to the rotation of the use of common lands belonging to a tribe or clan (an institution for which there is no evidence in the OT, the only divisions of land being in the passages already quoted: Isa. 34.17 and Micah 2.4–5). But here it seems an excessive simplification

---

[1] Cf. above, Introduction, § 3.

for such complex events, and one has only to glance at the traditions about Caleb which immediately follow this passage, and at Judg. 1 with its parallels in Joshua, to realize this.[1] But a distribution according to the needs of each tribe would seem to be just as improbable in a country which was only partially occupied, and the resources of which could not be known in advance. It also contradicts the oldest tradition which we possess. Consider, for example, the situation of Joseph in Josh. 17.14–18, and the difficulties that tribe underwent because of the inadequacy of the land at its disposal; or again, there is the episode of Judges 19–21, where recent studies have shown that the source of the conflict was probably the territorial difficulties, and the resultant economic problems, faced by Benjamin and Ephraim, two groups which were both expanding. The ethical motivation in the text we are discussing would simply be that of providing a pretext for making war.[2] Thus a historical account either of the distribution by lot or the distribution of land according to the effective needs of each tribe is impossible.

(b) *The territory of Caleb* (*14.6–15*)

The beginning of this chapter, as we saw, implies that Caleb was a member of the tribe of Judah, although there is no connection between his membership of this tribe and the assignation of land of his own to him. The purpose of the narrative seems to be [14] to explain how Caleb came to occupy this region right down to the redactor's time; that is, its origin is local. In Judg. 1.10 the region is conquered by Judah and Simeon, who defeated the three Anakim chiefs. These three chiefs are also mentioned in Josh. 15.14, but there they are defeated by Caleb.

The present narrative refers to the episode where spies were sent into Canaan from the desert, cf. Num. 13–14;[3] Deut. 1.22–28. Here Caleb acts independently of Judah, as in Josh. 14–15. It would be nothing out of the ordinary for the mention in the Pentateuch, deriving from a late stage in the tradition, and as we possess it altered to the point of being unrecognizable, to have referred originally to the conquest of the territory of Hebron by Caleb, an episode which is now incorporated into the context of 'all Israel', the material contained in Numbers and Deuteronomy being reduced there to an exploratory

---

[1] Cf. above, Introduction, § 3c.
[2] Cf. K. D. Schunck, *Benjamin*, BZAW 86, Berlin 1963, pp. 57–71.
[3] M. Noth, *UGP*, Stuttgart 1948 (repr. 1962), pp. 143ff.

episode. In Num. 13.6; 34.19 (where Caleb is already the representative of Judah) and in other passages Caleb is henceforth assimilated to Judah. But here, and in the ancient text of Num. 32.12 (cf. Judg. 1.13), he appears as a Kenizzite, that is, as belonging to a group which Gen. 36.11, 15, 42 associates with Edom. The name borne by the hero (='dog') recalls that of other peoples in the region, as for example that of the Midianite chiefs in Judg. 8.3: Oreb and Zeeb, 'crow' and 'wolf' respectively (Abel). This passage also shows a lexicographical affinity with Deut. 1.22ff.

[22] The secondary character of the situation of the scene at Gilgal clearly appears from the expression 'this hill country', which could not be used in the region of Jericho. Of course it could have been an error on the part of the Deuteronomic redactor, who was writing in exile and no longer had the places clearly in mind.

The original name of Hebron has obviously no connection with that of its inhabitants, but signifies 'four towns', or 'town of the four clans'. It does not seem possible that it could have been based on a pun: Arba, because he was four times bigger than normal (Hertzberg), cf. above on 11.21ff. where the problem of the Anakim is also discussed. For the final phrase cf. 11.23.

The references to Hebron, here and in the following chapter, are, in spite of Baldi's assertions, completely independent of those which appear in Josh. 10, and indeed seem to contradict them.[1]

(c) *The territory of Judah: the frontiers (15.1–12)*

According to Alt's classification,[2] which has generally been accepted, the first part of ch. 15 (vv. 1–12, cf. v. 20) gives us a description of the frontiers of Judah based on a list of fixed points, later completed by the insertion of the appropriate verbs (only Baldi disagrees). This list is clearly independent of the list of districts, vv. 21–63, because it defines a much smaller region, corresponding to the effective territory which traditionally belonged to Judah. In vv. 2–4 we have the southern list of fixed points, which is also given with a few variants in Num. 34.3–5, and which runs from east to west. Then we have the eastern frontier, v. 5a, which is very simple because it is formed by the Dead Sea (the 'Salt Sea'). Then follows the northern frontier, vv. 5b–11, also drawn from east to west, which is parallel to the text des-

---

[1] Cf. R. E. Clements, *Abraham and David*, SBT II, 15, London 1967, pp. 37f., for the most recent discussion on this subject.

[2] Cf. above, Introduction, § 3b.

cribing the southern frontier of Benjamin, 18.15–19, with a few variants: the text in ch. 18 is shorter because it omits Debir, the valley of
Achor (15.7), the gloss on the Jebusites (15.8), the 'cities of mount
Ephron', the gloss on Baalah (15.9) and naturally 15.10–11, the fixed
points in which are not reckoned by ch. 18 as belonging to Benjamin.
Oddly (see below), the list in ch. 18 omits the very areas (with the exception of Achor) about which we know least. Besides, the frontier of
Benjamin in ch. 18 is described from west to east.

Here and in the following passages we shall not go into the technical details (cf. the biblical geographies quoted in the bibliography
and the commentaries of Noth, pp. 85f. and 77, and of Baldi). The
southern frontier is described in a very summary fashion, partly because of the sparse population of this region: we have a few fixed
points situated between the Arabah and the Mediterranean, a region
which is only known in part from the studies carried out on the spot
by A. Musil, C. L. Woolley and T. E. Lawrence, T. Wiegard, F.
Frank and A. Alt. The identifications made by the first of these seem
for the most part to be doubtful or erroneous. The 'bay' of the Dead
Sea, in Hebrew 'the tongue', is not, as the name would suggest, the
peninsula of al-lisān on the east coast of the Dead Sea, which it divides in two (as Dhorme proposes), but the southern extremity of the
Dead Sea. The same expression is found in v. 5b, where it refers, however, to the northern extremity. This clearly follows from the fact that
the whole eastern frontier is defined by the Dead Sea. The 'Ascent of
the Scorpions' is one of the uneven slopes rising out of the valley of the
Arabah towards the southern hill country and its first foothills. It is
certainly the present-day naqb eṣ-ṣafa, to which the Israelites have restored the ancient name, on the north side of the ancient road leading
from the Dead Sea to the Gulf of Aqaba (172–035). Zin seems to have
been the ancient caravan route towards the west, though it is not
clear whether it was also a place name and the name of a region. The
question is complicated by the existence of a desert of the same name,
and of the name of Sinai, the latter having etymological connections
with the other two. Kadesh-barnea is probably the ancient desert sanctuary (cf. the commentary on 10.41), near the present ʿain qedēs, or a
place in the immediate vicinity. In the latter case, one would think
of the present ʿain el-qedērāt a little further north. Both are on the
Egyptian side of the frontier between Israel and Egypt. (1967) The
southern end of the frontier of Judah is the wādī el-ʿariš.

Whereas the eastern and western frontiers do not present any difficulties, the northern frontier presents a complex situation.[1] The number of fixed points which are given, with the degree of accuracy that this assumes, shows how important it was, It reflects the effective maximum northward extension of the tribe of Judah and the groups incorporated within it (though less so, perhaps, in the western zone). It starts from the mouth of the Jordan, it runs in a NNW direction from Beth-hoglah, which is situated on the outskirts of the present-day *'ain hajlā*, in which its name has been preserved, and takes in Beth-ha-Arabah, near the present-day *'ain el-gharabe* on the right bank of the Jordan, near the new motor road from Jerusalem to Amman. For the valley of Achor, cf. the commentary on ch. 7, and Simons §314. The 'Ascent of Adummim' is the next identifiable place name: it is the present-day *ṭal'at ed-damm*, 'the ascent of the red (rock)' (184–135) on the old Jerusalem–Jericho road for heavy goods, which is now largely unused. Those parts of the frontier which are known to us in fact follow this road as far as Jerusalem. En-shemesh is probably the present-day *'ain el-ḥūḍ*, a little east of Jerusalem (175–131), while En Rogel is *bīr 'ayyūb*, in the valley of the Kidron, which is continued by the valley (of the son of) Hinnom. The 'mountain' opposite this valley is the ridge which is now the *abū-ṭūr* quarter by the railway station and the British Consulate, which continues as far as the YMCA and the Terra Sancta convent, taking in the northern part of the 'Plain of the Rephaim', through which the railway now leaves the new town. The frontier then runs north to the waters of Nephtoah, a place which has kept its name down to the present day (168–133). This name is no doubt derived from the corruption of the name of the 'well' or 'waters of Mernephtah' (a pharaoh who reigned about 1235–1227, and whose name is found on the famous 'Israel stele').[2] The name seems to occur as early as the 'message of an Egyptian frontier official'[3] about 1230. The large number of fixed points around Jerusalem is immediately evident; their purpose is to show that the territory of the city state of Jerusalem remains outside the territory of Judah (in 18.16 it is included theoretically within the frontiers of Benjamin). The places which follow present difficulties,[4] except for Ki-

---

[1] For the various changes in the course of the centuries, cf. K. D. Schunck, *Benjamin*, p. 169.

[2] As shown by F. von Calice, 'König Menephtes im Buche Josua?', *OLZ* 6, 1903, col. 224, quoted by almost all commentators.

[3] But cf. the doubts expressed by A. Alt, 'Neues aus der Pharaonenzeit Palastinas', *PJB* 32, 1936, pp. 8–33, esp. pp. 29ff. The text is found in *ANET*, p. 258b.

[4] Cf. Noth, ad loc., and North, op. cit., p. 212.

riath-jearim (159–135) (according to Noth it is wrongly identified
with Baalah; North, p. 215, and Schunck, p. 145 n. 45, confirm this),
Seir, which, if the reading of LXX is followed, is the present-day
sārīs, a few km sw of Kiriath-jearim,[1] and Beth-shemesh (147–148),
where the present-day railway (*har-ṭūb* station) leaves the mountain
zone. From this point it runs directly to the sea, which it meets north
of Ekron (cf. 13.3).[2]

As can be seen, the frontier includes territory which does not strictly
belong to Judah, and therefore takes in what Noth refers to as 'greater
Judah', that is, it includes the groups which were associated with
Judah from time immemorial. This means that its date is unlikely to
be later than the time of David, while Noth[3] sees in it the traces of a
southern amphicytony which was earlier than the earliest monarchy.
Thus there is no question that this text is an ancient one, whether its
latest date is placed at the beginning of the tenth century, or whether
it is dated at an even earlier period. In order to choose between these
two alternatives, one might appeal to the description of the frontier in
the Jerusalem region, vv. 7–9; here the distance between the town
and the fixed points can sometimes be measured in tens of metres.
There are two possibilities here. Either the frontier refers to a period
where Jerusalem was not yet conquered, which would necessarily
mean a period earlier than that of David, or else it refers to the period
which followed the conquest of the city, and simply signifies that it remained an autonomous administrative community, a situation which
is well attested in later centuries, where the mention of Jerusalem is
always distinguished from that of Judah. If one accepts the first alternative, other difficulties arise: the territory of the city state, later
occupied under David, seems to be unduly restricted on the eastern,
southern and western sides, unless the frontier line drawn here is completely unreal, and there is nothing to suggest this, On the other hand,
this is not an insurmountable obstacle, since the el-Amarna archives
show that the territory situated between Jerusalem and the plain of
Esdraelon was almost entirely under the rule of Shechem.[4] This
would confirm the existence of a city state of Jerusalem with an ex-

---

[1] Cf. North, op. cit., p. 213, for a detailed discussion.

[2] Kallai (-Kleinmann), 1958 (for all the frontiers).

[3] M. Noth, *Das System der zwolf Stämme Israels*, BWANT IV, 1, Stuttgart 1930
(repr. Darmstadt 1966), p. 107.

[4] A. Alt, 'The Settlement . . .', *Essays on Old Testament History and Religion*,
pp. 135–69, esp. pp. 152ff.

tremely diminished territory, which would have grown even smaller in later centuries under the pressure of Judah and the groups confederated with it. Thus in the case of Jerusalem, the frontier line with Judah seems to presuppose the existence of a city which was still free, because of its impregnable strategic position, but which in Alt's words, was 'long ripe for the coup de grâce'.[1] On the other hand the implicit inclusion of Philistine territory from v. 11 on also provides a *terminus a quo*. If this inclusion is purely theoretical, the list cannot be earlier than the first decades of the twelfth century, when their pentapolis was founded, while if the list assumes an effective occupation, it brings us down to the period of David, who made these cities his vassals at the beginning of the tenth century (cf. II Sam. 5.17–25 ‖ I Chron. 14.8–16 and II Sam. 8.1 ‖ I Chron. 18.1). In the latter case, we would have to assume the existence of an ancient list, including the territories of the southern amphictyony, extended in David's time by the inclusion of the Philistine territory, only recently brought under the control of his empire. On the other hand, Schunck[2] disagrees with Noth, and argues that the first part of the list is not ancient in the sense that we have defined; he points out that Beth-shemesh and Kiriath-jearim[3] were only occupied under David, so that the whole construction cannot be earlier than his period.

The problem has therefore not found any solution in the present state of scholarship.

(d) Judah: the federated territories of Caleb and Othniel (15.13–20)

This text continues that given in 14.6–15, and includes, in addition to Caleb, Othniel, which belonged to the same ethnic group. Judg. 1.11–15 is almost identical, and there are similarities with Num. 13. The point of the narrative lies in the way in which Othniel was able to take Debir (cf. commentary on 10.38ff., a version of the story which as we have seen was excluded from the present text) and the two springs, which must have belonged to the territory of Hebron (cf. the commentary on 14.6ff.). Caleb and Othniel both belong to the Kenizzite group (cf. the commentary on 14.6, 14), which was related to

---

[1] A. Alt, 'Jerusalems Aufstieg', 1925, *KS* III, pp. 243–57, esp. p. 253.
[2] K. D. Schunck, op. cit., pp. 144ff.; A. Alt, ibid. Alt, however, does not say anything about the state of Jerusalem in our present context, as Schunck, p. 145 n. 44, seems at first sight to affirm.
[3] Which he identifies with Baalah, in disagreement with Noth, on the basis of II Sam. 6.2; I Chron. 13.6.

the Edomites of Gen. 36.9–11, 15, 42. Verse 17 in fact indicates that
Othniel, as a Kenizzite himself ('son of Kenaz'), belonged to the same
ethnic group ('brother'). The two clans were incorporated into 'greater Judah', and for this reason appear as members of this tribe.

The 'springs' have been identified by Baldi and Noth with the
place where at the present day the road for heavy goods from Hebron
to the south crosses the *sēl ed-dilbe*, about 9 km from Hebron. For the
position of Debir, which is still disputed, cf. 10.38ff. The ruins of this
place cannot be very far from the 'springs', even if they belong geographically to the territory of Hebron.

For the Anakim, cf. the commentary on ch. 14. In Noth's view,
their name originally meant 'those who wear the collar' and later became the name of a tribe. For the names quoted, cf. Num. 13.23. Some
scholars think that these are names of Hurrite origin, which would be
of some importance if we consider Gen. 23, where P has preserved
a tradition which records the presence of Hittites at Hebron: the
two peoples, both of Indo-European origin, might well have been
confused at a later period. In this case, of course, the explanation
proposed in 14.13ff. is impossible. Another explanation would regard
them as Aramaean groups, in accordance with post-exilic traditions: I Chron. 9.17; Ezra 10.40 (Bright). This explanation does not
exclude the others, because the groups may have become assimilated
in the meantime.

(e) Judah: cities and districts (15.21–63)

[21b–32a] *District I: the Negeb.* Chief town: in Noth's view perhaps
Hormah, the present *tell el-mšaš* (146–069), a few km east of Beer-
sheba; in the view of Alt and Cross and Wright, Beer-sheba (134–072).
The reference to the latter and its 'villages' (v. 28) suggests that the
list as we have it includes a secondary list of the territories which depended on this place, as well as the original list of cities forming the
district as a whole. A valuable criterion for distinguishing them would
be the list of Simeonite cities in 19.2–6 (cf. I Chron. 4.28–32), a list
which Noth, however, considers as purely artificial, and the work of a
compiler, and therefore secondary in our present context (cf. also Talmon, 1965, p. 236). For a criticism of this opinion, cf. Cross and
Wright, pp. 212ff. The debate whether the Simeonite list was added
at the pre-Davidic and Davidic period, or much later, at the period
of Josiah, has not yet been satisfactorily concluded.[1] It is certain

---

[1] Schunck, op. cit., pp. 162f.

that the Simeonite list presents some variations from the present one in vv. 28–31: Madmannah and Sansannah (v. 31) seems to be replaced in 19.5 by Beth-Marcaboth and Hazar-Susah respectively (in Josh. 19 and I Chron. 4.31 LXX reads Susim for the latter), cf. *BH*³. But it is not easy to tell whether these are the same places, or different ones. In any case, the figure twenty-nine does not correspond with anything: MT has thirty-six names, and LXX has thirty. This disconcerting fact was given a rational explanation by Talmon in 1967: the lists varied in the course of the years according to political and administrative changes, and were published from time to time, while the figures remained the same. An almost perfect example of such a case is found in the incorporation of the Simeonite list into the list of cities of Judah, with the resulting confusion of the two lists; he holds, however, that the figure twenty-nine was the earliest figure in the Judah list. For the identification of each of the cities named, cf. Baldi and Noth ad loc.; the best known place is Beer-sheba.

[**33b–36a**] *District II: The foothills.* Chief city: Azekah, the present-day *tell zakarīye*, cf. 10.10 (according to Alt, Adullam). A good proportion of the places mentioned here are identifiable, so that we are able to trace the dimensions of the district almost exactly. For Jarmuth, cf. 10.3ff., and for the other places, cf. Baldi and Noth ad loc. Noth makes the pertinent comment that this is a territory which Judah possessed from the very earliest period of the monarchy, cf. I Chron. 2.54; 4.18, as well as II Chron. 11.5–10, where several of these cities are included in Rehoboam's system of fortifications (922–901). The figure fourteen is correct if we read the last name (v. 36) following LXX. For some discussions with Noth about the archaeological problem, cf. Cross and Wright, pp. 215ff.

[**37–41a**] *District III:* Chief city, Lachish (cf. 10.3ff.). For Eglon, cf. ibid., and for the identification of the other localities, which is not always certain, cf. Baldi and Noth ad loc. Logically, all the cities mentioned are near the two cities named above. Some of them have a name ending in *-iš* or *-as*, which are non-Semitic endings. Thus it was no doubt a district inhabited by non-Israelite populations, which were later incorporated, but at a very early period, into Judah: II Chron. 11.9 in fact presents Lachish as one of Rehoboam's fortresses.

[**42–44a**] *District IV.* Chief city: perhaps Mareshah (140–111) (according to Alt, Keilah, 150–113). II Kings 8.22 records of Libnah that it rebelled against Judah during the reign of Joram (c. 849–842), but the account is unfortunately incomplete. However, it is a sign that at that period the city already formed part of the Judaean complex of frontier fortresses. For the other places see Baldi and Noth ad loc.

[45] *District V* (Noth, Bright); *XII* (Alt); '*It is not a district*' (Cross and Wright, Aharoni and Simons). Chief city: Ekron, cf. 13.3. Noth regards this as a district in the proper sense, because of the mention of 'towns' and 'villages'. But Cross and Wright deny, no doubt rightly, that this region was a real district, and regard it as an artificial construction (pp. 218f.). In 19.41–46, the places mentioned are included in Dan, and according to Noth the place was never occupied before the time of Josiah, even if some of the regions in it were temporarily invaded.

[48b–51a] *District VI* (Noth, Bright); *V* (Alt, Cross and Wright, Aharoni and Simons): *The hill country.* Chief city: perhaps Goshen, cf. 10.41 (Noth), or better, Debir (cf. Josh. 10.3) (Alt, Cross and Wright), if we accept the identification proposed in the text. It consists of the southern part of the southern hill country, to the north of District *I*.

[52–54a] *District VII* (Noth, Bright); *VI* (Alt, Cross and Wright, and Simons). Chief city: Hebron, cf. 10.3ff., which is also mentioned as one of Rehoboam's fortresses in II Chron. 11.10. It includes the south-central part of the southern hill country. The region seems to be identical with that inhabited by the Kenizzites (cf. above 14.6–15 and 15.13–20).

[55–57a] *District VIII* (Noth, Bright); *VII* (Alt, Cross and Wright, Aharoni, Simons). Chief city: perhaps Maon, the present-day *tell mā'în* (162–090), approximately 15–20 km sse of Hebron. Carmel, now *el-kirmil* (162–092), is a little further north; it is known from the episode in I Sam. 15.12, and above all from I Sam. 25.2ff. This district continues the previous district east of the watershed. It is probably the territory which belonged to the Kenites (v. 57).

[58–59a] *District IX* (Noth, Bright); *VIII* (Alt, Cross and Wright, Aharoni, Simons). Chief city: Beth-Zur. It is north of the two previous districts and east of district *IV*, that is, it comes into the northern part of the southern hill country. Beth-Zur, at the present-day *khirbet et-ṭubēqah* (159–110), was excavated by O. R. Sellers in 1932, and is a few kilometres north of Hebron.

[59 LXX] *District X* (Noth, Bright); *IX* (Alt, Cross and Wright, Aharoni, Simons). Chief city: Bethlehem. This is the most northerly district in the southern hill country. Tekoa, Bethlehem and Etam are the fortresses of Rehoboam in II Chron. 11.6. These last two districts form the country of Judah in the strict sense, with influences from Caleb.

[60a] *District XI* (Noth, Bright); *X* (Cross and Wright, Aharoni, Simons; in Alt's view, this district includes all the places listed in 15.60; 18.25–28). Chief city: Jerusalem. It takes in the southern part of the central hill country, territory which strictly speaking belongs to Benjamin (cf. vv. 7b–9 and its parallel in ch. 18), with the detailed list of places which is given in 18.25–28a. We know that after the breakdown of the personal union on which the empire of David and Solomon was based (I Kings 12.21 ∥ II Chron. 11.1), Benjamin formed part of the kingdom of Judah, and therefore became a district. This explains why ch. 18 includes Jerusalem in Benjaminite territory.[1] The cities in 18.28, of course, may be a later addition.

[61b–62a] *District XII* (Noth, Bright): '*The wilderness*'; *XI* (Alt would also include 18.21–24, while Cross and Wright, Aharoni and Simons regard 18.21–24 as belonging to their District *XII*, with the cities in 15.61–62 alone forming their District *XI*). Chief city: Jericho. According to Cross and Wright it also includes the Ophrah district south of Ephraim and the eastern part of the territory of Benjamin and Judah, which is why the redactor has placed some of the localities in it here and others in 18.21b–24a. The mention of Jericho in 18.21 suggests that it belongs to a period later than I Kings 16.34 (from the end of the tenth century to the beginning of the ninth century), but during the period of David there was some population in the area (cf. II Sam. 10.5). The mention of places which mainly belonged to Ephraim: Bethel (cf. chs. 7–8), 18.22, Ophrah, now *eṭ-ṭayibe*, (178–151), a few kilometres north of *bēṭīn* and of Ophni, 18.24, seems improbable in the context of the conquests of Josiah, as Noth and Alt propose; for these conquests extended much further north and consequently had no need to cut off parts of Ephraim to make a district of Judah out of them. On the other hand it seems quite logical within the framework of the conquest carried out by Abijah the son of Rehoboam (c. 910–908), II Chron. 13.19, cf. 15.8, where Asa, his son (c. 908–868) is in control of the Ephraimite cities in the hill country, and 17.2, where Jehoshaphat (c. 868–847) is still in control of them. Thus the list referring to this district must be dated in this period at the latest (Cross and Wright). Perhaps the region was reconquered by Joash, who, towards 788, defied Amaziah of Israel (II Kings 14.11–

---

[1] In Schunck, pp. 141ff., we have a logical explanation of the reasons which obliged Benjamin, which belonged ethnically to the North, to join Judah.

14 || II Chron. 25.17–24). On the other hand, Kallai and Aharoni point out, for different reasons, that the period in question is one in which the frontiers between the two states in Palestine were continually in movement, although it has not been proved that the cities in question were anything other than Israelite. Consequently, Aharoni suggests (p. 239) that only 18.25–28 belong to the list, and with Kallai (p. 156) he maintains that District *XII* according to Cross and Wright's numbering (the wilderness) contained only the zone in the east, bordering on the Dead Sea, which no other district touched.[1] According to Abel, this latter district was set up by Uzziah (c. 787–736), II Chron. 26.10. Thus for Cross and Wright (pp. 223ff.), vv. 61–62 form a separate district independent of Judah proper, and belonging to Benjamin and Ephraim, an opinion which is supported by Aharoni; the description which Noth gives of his District *XII* seems to Cross and Wright to be a 'geographical nonsense'.

Thus apart from these concluding verses of ch. 15, in their relationship with ch. 18, the districts seem to be relatively clearly defined, even though as we possess it the list cannot be later than the first half of the eighth century; the possibility always remains open that Josiah used this list in order to reorganize his own territory.[2]

The comment in v. 63 recalls that of Judg. 1.21, but contradicts Josh. 15.8; 18.16, 28, where for the reasons given above, Jerusalem belongs at least in theory to the territory of Benjamin.

(f) Ephraim (16.1–10)

This passage, like that which follows in ch. 17, is notorious for its difficulties. The frontiers must have been clearly described originally, but they appear here in a fragmentary form. Similarly, cities appear here and there, artificially inserted into the frontier system (cf. vv. 1, 2, 5–6), while it is not possible to tell whether the other place names given are meant as fixed points in the description of the frontiers, and whether they also form part of the lists of cities. It should also be noted that here and in the following chapter, the order is independent of the traditional genealogy.

There is a parallel to vv. 1–3 in 18.12–13: the northern frontier of Benjamin. This parallel passage presents the following variations on

---

[1] Cf., however, the valid criticisms in Schunck, pp. 157ff.; in pp. 162ff., he treats vv. 21–24 as an addition made at the period of Josiah, cf. II Kings 23.8.

[2] Even Noth recognizes that this list is ancient, cf. *Der Beitrag der Archäologie*, loc. cit.

the present text: Beth-Aven for Bethel (18.12), the identification of
Luz with Bethel (18.13, like LXX in the present passage). Thus the
list in ch. 16 seems the most authentic. For some of the place names
mentioned, cf. chs. 6; 7–8; 10.1–15. For a discussion of the others, cf.
the works quoted in the bibliography and the commentaries of Baldi
and Noth. The 'Waters of Jericho' in v. 1 are the present-day *'ain es-
sultān*, and flow out a short distance from the *tell*, the city on which already belonged to Benjamin. For the 'Archites' in v. 2, cf. II Sam.
15.32. These and the 'Japhletites' (v. 3) are no doubt old Canaanite
enclaves which had remained unconquered. Gezer, mentioned at the
end, became Israelite in I Kings 9.21.

(g) Manasseh (17.1–18)

1. The mention of Machir in vv. 1ff. is out of context (v. 1 in fact
continues in v. 7) and is of particular interest, as we have seen in part
in discussing 13.29–31; cf. the commentary on those verses for a further bibliography. According to Num. 26.28–34 (cf. I Chron. 7.14–
19), the six clans of Manasseh descend from Gilead, the son of Machir.
This differs from the present text (vv. 2ff.). Moreover, if all the statements in Num. 26 and the present text are reliable from the ethnic
and historical point of view, it is clear that the original home of Machir was Gilead on the east of Jordan. Consequently, the groups which
are said to belong to Manasseh and which later conquered the territory of 'Manasseh' west of Jordan also originate there. In other words,
the traditional order of the genealogy should be reversed: Manasseh
and its clans 'descend' from the group of Machir in Gilead. A third
factor is provided by the fact that a large number of the Manasseh
clans appear as place names or regions on the Samaria ostraka.[1] Thus
it is not surprising that Judg. 5.14b mentions Machir instead of Manasseh (a name which perhaps did not yet exist), even if, as the order in
which the tribes are listed clearly shows (Judg. 5.14–15), Machir was
already west of the Jordan. Gilead, on the other hand, is east of the
Jordan (Judg. 5.17a). For the two territories east of the Jordan listed
here, cf. the commentary on 12.2 and 9.10 respectively. Thus it is probable that in the present text Machir occurs in the original form,
while Manasseh is a later addition, made when the former name had

[1] Cf. p. 161 n. 2, and B. Maisler (Mazar), 'The Historical Background of the
Samaria Ostraka', *JPOS* 21, 1948, pp. 117–33; G. E. Wright, *Biblical Archaeology*,
Philadelphia and London 1957, p. 158; [2]1963, p. 162; and recently Y. Aharoni,
The Land of the Bible, London 1966, pp. 315–27.

become synonymous with the groups who lived east of the Jordan (Baldi holds a different view).

The name Zelophehad in v. 3, transformed by LXX into Σαλπααδ and by V into *Salphaad*, is of interest. It may be a theophoric name formed with *paḥad* (cf. Gen. 31.42, 53), which is usually understood nowadays to mean 'parent' and no longer 'terror'.[1]

2. The mention of Asher, situated well to the north of the following place, which is in the south, is surprising (cf. the discussion of the problem in Baldi). Simons (p. 160) would explain it simply as the equivalent of a generality: 'south of Asher'. In 10b the mention of it has more point.

The southern frontier reproduces in a fragmentary way the northern frontier of Ephraim in 16.6b–8. Tappuah is almost certainly the present-day *tell šaikh abū zarad*, about 15 km SE of Nablus, according to the studies carried out by F. M. Abel and W. F. Albright. Nearby is the spring *yāsūf* (cf. the reading Ιασσιβ in LXX, in v. 7): its name seems to have been *ʿain et-tuffāh* in the past (for details, cf. Noth and Baldi).

The territorial claims in vv. 11–13 reflect the situation shown in Judg. 1.27–28. The conquest of these territories probably took place during the reign of David (in II Sam. 24 the census extends from 'Dan to Beer-sheba', which implies that the city states had been conquered). Under Solomon (I Kings 4.12ff.), the division of the ancient tribal frontiers into independent districts presupposed that they had been occupied. The statement that the city states were not incorporated into the empire, but only associated as vassals who were obliged to take a personal oath, is no doubt accurate. In the present context, the mention of the 'inhabitants' may refer to the Israelites who lived there (Abel).

The statement in v. 11 that Manasseh shared cities with other tribes, and even in the middle of their territories, may be an attempt to harmonize lists of reference points on the frontier with catalogues of towns and districts, which were not necessarily identical, as we have seen in 15.1–12, 21–63.

3. Verses 14–18, in which Joshua once again appears 'at home'[2], consists of two parallel narratives: vv. 14–15 and 16–18. The second text seems to be the older, in so far as the intention of the former seems

---

[1] W. F. Albright, *From the Stone Age to Christianity*, Baltimore [2]1957, p. 248; Alt, *KS* I, 1953, p. 26 n. 2, and M. Noth, *Comm.*, ad loc., agree.

[2] A. Alt. *Josua*, 1936, *KS* I, pp. 189ff.

to be to complete it, in the sense that Manasseh is said to have conquered 'Rephaim' territories east of the Jordan (cf. the commentary
on 12.2ff., etc.). Baldi and Hertzberg disagree with this explanation.
The latter believes that the Rephaim also appeared west of the Jordan, north of Shechem (cf. Gen. 15.20; I Chron. 20.4). But the first of
these texts occurs in a stereotyped catalogue of pre-Israelite inhabitants of Palestine, and therefore has no historical value. It is equally
difficult to take seriously the statement in I Chron. 20; cf. the commentaries.

CHAPTERS 18–19

A New Distribution of Territory

18 ¹Then the whole congregation of the people of Israel assembled at
Shiloh, and set up the tent of meeting there; the land lay subdued before
them. ²There remained among the people of Israel seven tribes whose
inheritance had not yet been apportioned. ³So Joshua said to the people of
Israel, 'How long will you be slack to go in and take possession of the land,
which the LORD, the God of your fathers, has given you? ⁴Provide three
men from each tribe, and I will send them out that they may set out and
go up and down the land writing a description of it with a view to their
inheritances, and then come to me. ⁵They shall divide it into seven portions,
Judah continuing in his territory on the south, and the house of Joseph in
their territory on the north. ⁶But you shall describe the land in seven
divisions and bring the description here to me; and I will cast lots for you
here before the LORD our God. ⁷The Levites shall have no portion among
you, for the priesthood of the LORD is their heritage; and Gad and Reuben
and half the tribe of Manasseh have received their inheritance beyond the
Jordan eastward, which Moses the servant of the LORD gave them.'
8 So the men started on their way; and Joshua charged those who went
to write the description of the land, saying, 'Go up and down and write a
description of the land, and come again to me; and I will cast lots for you
here before the LORD in Shiloh.' ⁹So the men went and passed up and down
in the land and set down in a book a description of it by towns in seven
divisions; then they came to Joshua in the camp at Shiloh, ¹⁰and Joshua
cast lots for them in Shiloh before the LORD; and there Joshua apportioned
the land to the people of Israel, to each his portion.

11 The lot of the tribe of Benjamin according to clans came up. The territory allotted to it fell between the tribe of Judah and the tribe of Joseph. ¹²On the north side their boundary began at the Jordan; then the boundary goes up to the shoulder north of Jericho, then up through the hill country westward; and it ends at the wilderness of Bethaven. ¹³From there the boundary passes along in the direction of Luz, to the southern shoulder of Luz (the same is Bethel), then the boundary goes down to Ataroth-addar, upon the mountain that lies south of Lower Beth-horon. ¹⁴Then the boundary goes in another direction, turning westward and southward from the mountain that lies to the south, opposite Beth-horon, and it ends at Kiriath-baal (that is, Kiriath-jearim), a city belonging to the tribe of Judah. This forms the western side. ¹⁵And the southern side begins at the outskirts of Kiriath-jearim; and the boundary goes from there to Gasin to the 'Spring of the Waters of Nephtoah'. ¹⁶Then the boundary goes down to the border of the mountain that overlooks the valley of the son of Hinnom, which is at the north end of the plain of the Rephaim; and it then goes down the valley of Hinnom, south of the shoulder of the Jebusites, and downward to En-rogel; ¹⁷then it bends in a northerly direction going on to En-shemesh, and thence goes to Geliloth, which is opposite the ascent of Adummim; then it goes down to the 'Stone of Bohan' the son of Reuben; ¹⁸and passing on to the northern shoulder of Beth-ha-arabah it goes down to the Arabah; ¹⁹then the boundary passes on to the shoulder of Beth-hoglah northward, and the boundary ends at the north of the bay of the Salt Sea, at the south end of the Jordan; this is the southern border. ²⁰The Jordan forms its boundary on the eastern side. This is the inheritance of the tribe of Benjamin, according to its clans, by the boundaries which mark it off.

21 Now the cities of the tribe of Benjamin according to their families were Jericho, Beth-hoglah, Emek-keziz, ²²Beth-ha-arabah, Zemaraim, Bethel, ²³Avvim, Parah, Ophrah, ²⁴Chephar-ha-ammoni, Ophni, Geba – twelve cities with their villages.

25 Gibeon, Ramah, Beeroth, ²⁶Mizpeth, Chephirah, Mozah, ²⁷Rekem, Irpeel, Taralah, ²⁸Zela-ha-eleph, Jebus (that is Jerusalem), Gibeah and Kiriath – fourteen cities with their villages. This is the inheritance of the tribe of Benjamin according to its clans.

19 ¹The second lot came out for Simeon, for the tribe of Simeon, according to its clans; but its inheritance was in the midst of the inheritance of the tribe of Judah. ²And it had for its inheritance Beer-sheba, Sheba, Moladah, ³Hazarshual, Balah, Ezem, ⁴Eltolad, Bethul, Hormah, ⁵Ziklag, Beth-ham-marcaboth, Hazar-susah, ⁶Beth-lebaoth, and Sharuhen – thirteen cities with their villages; ⁷En-rimmon, Talkah, Ether, and Ashan – four cities with their villages; ⁸together with all the villages round about these cities as far as Baalath-beer, and Ramath-Negeb. This was the

inheritance of the tribe of Simeon according to its clans.

9 The inheritance of the tribe of Simeon formed part of the territory of Judah; because the portion of the tribe of Judah was too large for them; so the tribe of Simeon obtained an inheritance in the midst of their inheritance.

10 The third lot came up for the tribe of Zebulun, according to its clans. And the boundary of its inheritance reaches as far as Sarid (Shadud). 11Then its boundary goes up westward, and on to Mareal, and touches Dabbesheth, then the deep valley which is east of Jokneam; 12from Sarid it turns eastward toward the sunrise to the boundary of Chisloth-tabor; 13thence it goes to Daberath, then up to Japhia; from there it passes along to the east toward the sunrise to Gath-hepher and Eth-kazin, and going as far as Rimmon it bends toward Neah; 14then on the north the boundary turns about to Hannathon, and it ends at the valley of Iphtahel; 15and Kattath, Nahalal, Shimron, Idalah, and Bethlehem – twelve cities with their villages. 16This is the inheritance of the tribe of Zebulun, according to its clans – these cities with their villages.

17 The fourth lot came out for Issachar, for the tribe of Issachar, according to its clans. 18Their territory went to Jezreel, with Chesulloth, Shunem, 19Hapharaim, Shion, Reeroth, Anaharath, 20Rabbith, Kishion, Ebez, 21Remeth, En-gannim, En-haddah, Beth-pazzez. 22The boundary also touches Tabor, Shahazumah, and Beth-shemesh, and its boundary ends at the Jordan – sixteen cities with their villages. 23This is the inheritance of the tribe of Issachar, according to its clans – the cities and their villages.

24 The fifth lot came out for the tribe of Asher according to their clans. 25Their territory was from Helkath, with Hali, Beten, Achshaph, 26Allam-melech, Amad, and Mishal; on the west it touches Carmel and Shihor-libnath. 27On the east it turns to Beth-dagon, and touches Zebulun and the valley of Iphtah-el to the north, then to Beth-emek and Neiel; then it ends at Kabul. 28Then Mishmol, Ebron (Abdon), Rehob, Hammon, Kanah, as far as Sidon the Great; 29then the boundary turns to Ramah, reaching to the fortified city of Tyre; then the boundary turns to Hosah, and it ends at the sea; Mahaleb, Achzib, 30Acco, Aphek and Rehob – twenty-two cities with their villages. 31This is the inheritance of the tribe of Asher according to its clans – these cities with their villages.

32 The sixth lot came out for the tribe of Naphtali, for the tribe of Naphtali according to its clans. 33Their territory was from Heleph, from Elon Bezaanannim, and Adami-hannekeb, and Jabneel, as far as Lakkum; and it ended at the Jordan. 34On the other side the boundary goes westward to Aznoth-tabor, and from there ends at Hukkok, touching Zebulun at the south, and Asher on the west, and Judah of the Jordan (?) on the east. 35The fortified cities are Ziddim, Zer, Hammath, Rakkath, Chinnereth,

³⁶Adamah, Ramah, Hazor, ³⁷Kedesh, Edrei, En-hazor, ³⁸Yiron, Migdal-el,
Horem, Beth-anath, and Beth-shemesh – nineteen cities with their villages.
³⁹This is the inheritance of the tribe of Naphtali according to its clans – the
cities with their villages.

40 The seventh lot came out for the tribe of Dan, according to its clans.
⁴¹And the territory of its inheritance included Zorah, Eshta-ol, Ir-shemesh,
⁴²Sha-alabbin, Aijalon, Ithlah, ⁴³Elon, Timnah, Ekron, ⁴⁴Eltekeh, Gibbethon, Baalath, ⁴⁵Jehud, Bene-berak, Gath-rimmon, ⁴⁶and on the west
Jarkon with the territory over against Joppa. ⁴⁷But the territory of the
Danites was lost to them, so that the Danites had to set out on an expedition. They fought against Leshem, and after capturing it and putting it to
the sword they took possession of it and settled in it, calling Leshem, Dan,
after the name of Dan their ancestor. ⁴⁸This is the inheritance of the tribe
of Dan, according to their clans – these cities with their villages.

49 When they had finished distributing the several territories of the
land as inheritances, the people of Israel gave an inheritance among them
to Joshua the son of Nun. ⁵⁰By command of the LORD they gave him the
city which he asked, Timnath-serah in the hill country of Ephraim; and
he rebuilt the city, and settled in it.

51 These are the inheritances which Eleazar the priest and Joshua the
son of Nun and the heads of the fathers' houses of the tribes of the people
of Israel distributed by lot at Shiloh before the LORD at the door of the
tent of meeting. So they finished dividing the land.

Bibliography: (a) *The territory of Benjamin:* see the bibliographies for chs.
15.1–12 and 16.1–3 for the northern boundary of Judah and the southern
frontier of Ephraim, and also for the cities in the districts of the north of
Judah; also W. Rudolph, *Der 'Elohist'* . . ., pp. 228–36; Auzou, pp.
150ff.; J. G. Vink, 'The Date and the Origin of the Priestly Code in the
Old Testament', *OTS* 15, 1969, pp. 1–44, esp. 63ff., could not be used.
(b) *The territory of Simeon:* W. F. Albright, 'Egypt and the Early History
of the Negeb', *JPOS* 4, 1924, pp. 149–61; Z. Kallai (-Kleinmann), 'Note
on the Town-Lists of Judah, Simeon and Benjamin and Dan', *VT* 11,
1961, pp. 223–7; G. Wallis (ed.), 'Die Geschichte der Jakobstradition',
Wiss. Zeitschr. Halle 13, 1964, pp. 427–40, esp. p. 430 (now in *Geschichte und
Überlieferung*, Berlin 1968, pp. 20ff.); Auzou, pp. 150ff.; S. Talmon, 'The
Town-lists of Simeon', *IEJ* 15, 1965, pp. 235–41; id., 'The Lists of the
Cities of Simeon', *'Ereṣ Isrā'el* 8, 1967, pp. 265–68 (in Hebrew, summary in
English). (c) *The territory of Zebulon:* M. Noth, 'Studien zu den historisch-
geographischen Texten . . .', pp. 215–29. (d) *The territory of Issachar:*
W. F. Albright, 'The Topography of the Tribe of Issachar', *ZAW* 44,
1926, pp. 225–30; A. Saarisalo, *The Boundary between Issachar and Naftali*,
Helsinki 1927; W. Herrmann, 'Issakar', *FuF* 37, 1963, pp. 21–6; Auzou,

loc. cit.; Y. Aharoni, 'Anaharat', *JNES* 26, 1967, pp. 212-5. (*e*) *The territory of Asher*: A. Kuschke, 'Kleine Beiträge zur Siedlungsgeschichte der Stämme Aser und Juda', *HTR* 64, 1971, pp. 291-313, which appeared too late to be used. (*g*) *The territory of Dan*: B. Mazar, 'The Cities of the Territory of Dan', *IEJ* 10, 1960, pp. 65-77; J. Strange, 'The Inheritance of Dan', *StTh* 20, 1966, pp. 120-39; cf. also the article mentioned by Z. Kallai (-Kleinmann) in the note on vv. 1ff. above. (*h*) *The personal territory of Joshua*: A. Vaccari, 'Parole rovesciate e critiche errate nella Bibbia ebraica', *Studi Orientalistici* . . . *G. Levi Della Vida*, Rome 1956, II, pp. 553-66, esp. p. 554.

LXX has a number of variants in the lists of place names, especially in the list of cities, 18.21ff., with some differences between LXX^B and LXX^A. Most of these problems have been discussed in the notes on 15.5b–11; 16.5–10; 15.60–63. [13] Ataroth-addar: cf. on 16.2.5: *'aṭrōt 'erek* would be better. [15] Gasin: following LXX (transcription conjectural); MT has 'towards the west', which is meaningless. [18] Beth-ha-Arabah: with LXX; MT has 'opposite the Arabah', a general indication, while our reading is more exact. [23] Avvim: following Bethel, is reminiscent of Ai. [26] Mozah: cf. the note on 15.9. [28] Kiriath: LXX^A read K.-Jearim, probably rightly. [19.1] LXX and V do not have the tautological repetition of Simeon, cf. in v. 8; the same style is found in 13.15; 15.1; 18.11; 19.24,40. [2] Sheba: in 15.26 we read *šemaʿ*, and this is the translation of LXX^B in the present passage (Σαμαα), cf. LXX of I Chron. 4.28. In the Hebrew it is no doubt a question of a dittography with the previous word. But V follows MT. [3] Balah: 15.19 has Baalah, I Chron. 4.29 has Bilhah. These are phonetic variations of the same name. [5] Beth-ham-marcaboth and Hazar-susah have different names in 15.31. [6] Sharuhen is preferable to the reading of 15.32; Noth would vocalise it *sirḥōn*, following an Egyptian reference, but the identity of the two places is not certain. LXX has οἱ ἀγροὶ αὐτῶν, i.e. *šedōtēhem* or else *šādēhem*. [7] Instead of beginning the verse with two cities, Noth, on the basis of Neh. 11.29, proposes to regard them as a single place with a double name, cf. also LXX and 13.32 (emended text); LXX^B adds the locality Βαλχά, which we transcribe conjecturally: this enables the figure four to be maintained. [10] Sarid: we should no doubt read *šādūd* with LXX ^MSS and Syr (*BH³*). [11] 'Westward': the Hebrew has *layyommāh*, i.e. a form with a preposition, the article and *he* of direction, cf. *GKC* § 90e and *B-M* I, § 45, 3c. This form is rare, but it is attested in texts which are not disputed; nevertheless, it suggests a proper name which has been corrupted and replaced later by a more general term (cf. Baldi and Noth). LXX has the general term 'the sea', V the interesting variant *de mari*, thus making the boundary run not to the west but from the west. This meaning of *l^e* is well attested in Ugaritic,[1] and we may ask whether this is not a similar case: 'from the west to Mareal . . .' On the other hand, it seems likely that this suggestion must be rejected, because it is contrary to the east-west direction of the line, cf. below. [12] 'Turns' refers to the fact that the frontier now runs in a different direction (Noth and Hertzberg); others (Baldi and Abel) prefer to take the term adverbially: 'once again' or 'in the other direction' respectively. One translation does not exclude the other. The sense requires that *min* here and in the following verse should signify 'towards'. [13] 'As far as Rimmon' is obtained by reading *rimmōnāh*, following *BH*[3], instead of the incomprehensible MT; this was already assumed by LXX and V, who took the verb following as a proper name. [14] After the verb we have the incomprehensible *'ōtō*, which is not represented in the translations and which we omit with all commentators; cf. 16.6 for a similar form. [15] Kattath: Judg. 1.30 has Kitron, which is certainly the same place, although we can give no reason for this variant. For Nahalal, the same passage has Nahalol, following the usual change from *a* into *o* in West Semitic. For Shimron, cf. the note on 11.4. For Idalah, LXX[B] has Jericho; the reason is unknown. [17] The tautological expression which mentions the name of the tribe and that of its members, which is the same as in the previous passage, is that of MT; LXX[A] and LXX[B] give only the name of the tribe. [19] Reeroth is lacking in MT, but should be added with LXX[B], cf. the total number of cities, which requires one more city than is given in MT. Here we follow Albright and all other commentators. [20] Rabbith appears as Debrath in 21.28; I Chron. 6.72; cf. also LXX[B] and v. 12, above. [21] Remeth: in 21.29 we have Yarmuth, and in I Chron. 6.73 Ramoth, all variants of the same name. [25] 'From': reading *mēḥelqat* with LXX[B] (ἐξ: *mem* lost by haplography). [26] Shihor is an Egyptian word, cf. the note on 13.3. [28] MT has *'ebrōn*, but it seems better to read *'abdōn* with I Chron. 6.74. It is a case of the frequent confusion between *rēš* and *dālet*. [29] Mahaleb: MT has 'from Hebel', LXX[B] has ἀπὸ Λεβ, but cf. Judg. 1.31 and the Annals of Sennacherib (Taylor Cylinder II, 39, *ANET*, p. 287): *maḥalliba*. Achzib: with Judg. 1.31; MT has a *hē* of direction as a result of the confusion over the previous word. [30] Acco: with LXX[B] and Judg. 1.31; MT has *'umāh*. [34] Aznoth is probably the name of an unknown tool, and the place known by this name, situated close to Tabor, bore the name of the goods it produced. 'Judah of the Jordan' is a strange and inexplicable name for an unknown locality, cf. the discussion of the problem in Baldi, Noth and Kaufmann. 'Judah' is perhaps a form which has been corrupted by dittography with the Jordan, which is mentioned next. [35] The first four words in MT are considered by Alt and Noth, as well as by Kaufmann, as a corrupted repetition of elements contained in vv. 28 and 29, cf. the text of

---

[1] Cf. J. Aistleitner, no. 1422: 2.

LXX. For Baldi and Abel, or the other hand, they do not present a problem. **[42]** The usual reading is *ša'albīm*. **[44]** Eltekeh occurs in LXXᴬ in the form *Ελθεκω*, cf. the Chronicle of Sennacherib (Taylor Cylinder II, 76ff., *ANET*, p.287) which has *altaqū*. **[45]** Jehud: LXXᴮ has *'Αζωρ*, which is a real variant. **[46]** 'On the west', following LXX (*ἀπὸ θαλάσσης*, a literal translation of *miyyām*); MT and V have 'the waters of the Yarkon' almost as if it were a question of a place or a point on the boundary. **[47]** 'Was lost to them': translated according to the figurative derivative sense which *yṣ'* can have (as, for example, in expressions such as 'their heart failed'). It is often corrected to *wayyēṣer*, following the reading of LXX= 'became narrow for them', but this is unnecessary (Noth). Leshem is the Laish of Judg. 18.7, with a final *mem* and a different vocalization. Judg. 17-18 tells at length the episode which is only referred to here. **[50]** Timnath-serah: LXXᴮ and Judg. 2.9 have Timnath-heres, but Vaccari has established that the first reading is correct and not the second, which is the result of a metathesis.

(a) The territory of Benjamin (*18.1-28*)

1. Chs. 18-19 begin a new section in which (vv. 1-10) the redactor's main purpose was to distinguish between the apportioning of land to the 'great' tribes, made at Gilgal (14.6), and that made to the 'small' tribes, carried out at Shiloh. The latter is in Ephraimite territory, even though it is not mentioned in the preceding passages. But there is a great difference between this passage and 14.1-4, and Abel thinks that in ch. 14 we have the beginning of a historical document, attached to the geographical passages when the redaction took place, while the present passage contains material attached by a redactor to a biography of Joshua. It is not possible to make a definite decision about this matter.

The terminology of vv. 1-10 shows characteristics which are close to those of P, and they are frequently attributed to this Pentateuchal source (cf. also the study by Mowinckel mentioned in the introduction, p. 12 n.3). But M. Noth and H. W. Hertzberg have rightly pointed out that the mention of Shiloh has every appearance of being an interpolation, seeing that the division of frontiers according to the points of the compass assumes that the central point is Gilgal. From Shiloh, in fact, Joseph would not be in the north, and the same is true of the whole northern frontier (vv.5, 11-13). Moreover, the mention of the 'camp' in v.9b is in agreement with the term used throughout

the book solely for the camp at Gilgal. E. Dhorme has proposed another hypothesis: that this is an account of the foundation of the sanctuary of Shiloh. This explanation is attractive, but unfortunately the
excavations carried out by the Danish expedition (led by A. Schmidt
in 1926–29 and by H. Kjaer in 1932, at *khirbet sēlūn*, about 18 km
south of Nablus, 163–177) have not revealed the remains of a temple,
so that the statement remains hypothetical.[1]

With regard to the tent of meeting set up in the locality (cf. also
19.51), we have only a single other text: I Sam. 2.22, where the tent is the
location of the sin of the sons of Eli. Thus the presence of the tent in the
place is confirmed by more than a single tradition, and, according to
verbal communications from O. Eissfeldt in the autumn of 1965,
would explain the statement in II Sam. 7.6, that Yahweh never
'dwelt in a house . . . but . . . in a tent', a statement which nowadays is no longer in contradiction with the mention of the existence
of a temple at Shiloh, if we allow that the tent formed an integral
part of the sanctuary and was meant for the 'dwelling place' of God.
It seems certain, in any case, that before the destruction of the sanctuary by the Philistines (c. 1050, cf. I Sam. 4), the ark was then erec-
ted there. However, in spite of all these considerations, the present
passage is clearly secondary and serves to fill a gap. For v. 7, cf. 14.4
and 13.7–8, 15ff.

2. Verses 11–28 begin by describing the northern frontier of Benjamin, on the lines already laid down in 16.1–3, but with fewer details. The western frontier is obtained simply by linking the two points
furthest west on the northern and southern frontiers by a straight line.
This is clearly an artificial procedure, which in Noth's view is a sign
that the whole western frontier was artificial in nature, and created
to make a place for the tribe of Dan. No other tribe shared a boundary
with Benjamin in this region. On the other hand, there is evidence of
Dan in this region in Judg. 1.34 and 13.2, cf. the localities attributed
to Dan in Josh. 19.41–46. If the artificial nature of this line is to be
maintained, some other solution to this problem must be found.

For the southern frontier, cf. 15.1–12 and for the cities cf. 15.60ff.
For Gibeon (v. 25), Chephirah (v. 26), Beeroth (v. 25) and Kiriath-
Jearim (v. 15), cf. 9.17. They formed the Hivite tetrapolis, which
from now on seems to be completely dismantled. For other details, cf.
the commentaries of Baldi and Noth.

[1] Cf. M. L. Buhl—S. Holm-Nielsen, *Shiloh*, Copenhagen 1969, esp. pp. 56ff.

(b) The territory of Simeon (19.1–9)

For the details of the list preserved here, the reader is referred to pp.176ff.: *Judah, cities and districts*, Districts *I* (15.21b–32a) and *IV* (15.42–44). There the problem of the historicity of the situation described and the authenticity of the list is discussed. It should be noted:

1. The situation described is similar in many ways to that of Benjamin, ibid., Districts *XII* and *XI* (15.61b–62a; 18.21–24), a tribe which was virtually surrounded by Judah at the period of the division of the united kingdom of David and Solomon (c. 922, cf. I Kings 12.21). Something similar may also have happened to Simeon, even though there is no trace of this in the sources.

2. The situation of Simeon, on the other hand, is different not only because we possess no details about the way it was assimilated, as we have said, but also because it formed part of Judah from time immemorial: Gen. 49.5–7 already represents this tribe as scattered throughout Israel. It is therefore logical that the memory of certain localities which originally belonged to Simeon should be preserved, although nothing remained of any frontiers that may have existed.

(c) The territory of Zebulon (19.10–16)

This short passage presents considerable difficulties. In the first place, it is generally admitted that the original has been expanded by the incorporation of new elements no doubt borrowed from Josh. 21 and Judg. 1 (cf. the commentary on these passages). This is clearly seen in the disagreement between the total figures and the place names mentioned (details in Baldi and Noth). Moreover, once the additions are removed, the reader is disagreeably surprised to find that very little remains. Noth is no doubt right when he explains the present text as the product of a restructuring carried out on the basis of a text which was in a bad state and which contained large gaps, with the aid of other material dealing with the same region.

Amongst the primitive elements are, in the east, Sarid/Shadud, on the north side of the plain of Esdraelon, which forms the south-eastern corner of the frontier (probably about 10 km sw of Nazareth, near the kibbutz of this name, 171–230). At the west, on the same latitude, there is Jokneam (probably *tell qēmūn*, 161–230). Chisloth-Tabor and Daberath are both close to Mount Tabor (187–232). The name of the latter is certainly preserved in the name of the Arab village *dabbūriye*, north of which we find ruins bearing the same name (north of Tabor,

187–233). For the former place, the situation is not yet clear, and the reader is referred to the discussion by Baldi and Noth. Gath-hepher is the present-day *khirbet ez-zurraᶜ* (180–238), 5 km NE of Nazareth, while Eth-kazin is probably *kafr kanna* (the Cana of Galilee in the NT), about 1.5 km further east (182–239). Rimmon is no doubt the present-day *er-rummāne* (179–244). On the frontier we have Hannathon, already known from the El-Amarna archives (8.17 and 245.32, cf. *ANET*, p.245a), and also from the annals of Tiglath-Pileser III. It is usually identified with the present-day *tell el-badawiye* (174–243). If this identification is correct, then the 'valley' is the *wādī el-mālik*, in modern Hebrew *naḥal ṣippōrī*, which forms part of the new water supply system. Bethlehem here is Bethlehem in Galilee (168–238).

(d) The territory of Issachar (19.17–23)

The section on Issachar consists almost exclusively of the names of places, which for the Galilee tribes is surprising in the present setting (we noted a similar phenomenon is the case of Simeon). Noth believed that the place names given were in fact a series of fixed points on the frontier line, and in fact Saarisalo succeeded in showing that the northern line at least describes the northern frontier as far as the Jordan; cf. the recent study by Aharoni. But for the most part the fixed points in question have not been identified with certainty, except of course for Mount Tabor and the Jordan. Jezreel, the Arab *zerᶜīn* on the southern slopes of Mount Gilboa, which once again has its ancient name in the state of Israel, can be identified with certainty (180–219). Shunem is now *sōlem*, a few km north of Jezreel (183–224). It appears in the El-Amarna archives, 250,[1] and in the list of Thutmose III (*ANET*, pp.234f). According to Aharoni's recent study, Anaharath can be identified with *tell el-mukharkhaš*, between Mount Tabor and the Jordan (197–230). Engannim is the present-day *jenīn* (178–208), south of the frontier between Israel and Jordan (May 1967). For other details, cf. Baldi and Noth.

The date at which Issachar settled in the region presents a particular problem. According to Herrmann, the list dates from the period of the Syrian invasion (c. 734 BC), but this thesis seems difficult to establish.[2]

---

[1] Letter published in *RA* 19, 1922, pp. 91ff.; *ANET*, pp. 485ff.

[2] We cannot discuss this problem here, and refer to the studies of A. Alt, 'Neues über Palastina aus dem Archiv Amenophis IV', *PJB* 20, 1924, pp. 22–41 (*KS* III, 1956, pp. 158–75), esp. pp. 34 (169)ff.; id, 'Megiddo im Übergang vom Kanaanäi-

(e) The territory of Asher (19.24–31)

The section on the territory of Asher mixes frontier lines with lists of towns, which gives rise to some confusion. The most southerly point is Shihor-libnath, which is usually identified with the marshy region south of Carmel and Dor, which is due to the stagnation of the waters of the *nahr ed-difle* and the *nahr ez-zerqā*; in modern Hebrew the latter is *nahar nattannīnīm*. This region has now been completely transformed by drainage, so that it is no longer easy to identify details on the ground. Acco can still be recognized on the sea coast; it is the Saint-Jean-d'Acre of the Crusaders and the Christian pilgrims, NNE of Haifa. Aphek, the more northerly of the two places of that name (162–249; cf. the commentary on 12.18 and 13.4 for the two places with this name, the second being a few km ENE of Tel-Aviv), can also be recognized, as can Kabul (171–253, cf. I Kings 9.10–14, where they formed the price of an agreement between Solomon and Hiram of Tyre, together with the country round about), Sidon and Tyre. Some of the other places appear in Egyptian lists, although it is not possible to locate them exactly. Cf. the discussion by Baldi and Noth.

A place called *'išryt*, probably situated in Lebanon and occurring in the Ugarit texts,[1] was several times connected before the war with the territory of Asher, but it is now clear that this connection cannot be maintained.[2]

(f) The territory of Naphtali (19.32–39)

Mount Tabor, which according to v. 22 forms part of the territory of Issachar, is used here, too, as for Zebulun, as a reference point. This is not surprising, as it is on a terrain which has few other distinguishing features. Thus the frontiers of Naphtali coincide, in part at least, with those of Zebulun and Issachar, which is why the text does not contain any description of the SW and southern borders (with the difficulty, however, that Zebulun does not extend as far as the Jordan, so that a section is apparently missing here, and it is not possible to tell what is referred to by the mysterious phrase 'Judah of the Jordan';

---

schen zum israelitischen Zeitalter', *ZAW* 60, 1944, pp. 67–85 (*KS* I, 1953, pp. 256–74), esp. pp. 77(265)f.

[1] Cf. the list in Aistleitner, no. 447.

[2] Cf. R. de Langhe, *Les textes de Ras Shamra et leur rapport avec le milieu biblique de l'Ancien Testament*, Paris 1945, II, p. 472, and the excursus on this subject in Baldi's commentary, pp. 145f.

cf. Noth) or on the NW side, which touches the eastern frontier of Asher. There is disagreement about the identification of Hukkok. In Noth's view, it is near Tabor, while others (Baldi, Grollenberg, etc.) place it further north, west of the north-west side of Lake Tiberias, on the site of the present-day *yāqūq* (197–254). The places listed in vv. 35ff. (or at least, those of them which are identifiable) form a series of fixed points, that is, of frontier posts running from south to north: Hammath is the Arab *hammam*, on the edge of the lake, a little to the south of Tiberias (202–241), known for its thermal springs. Rakkath is the present-day *tell eqlātiye* (or *qunētriye*), just to the north of Tiberias (200–246). For Chinnereth, cf. the commentary on 11.2. Noth believes that Adamah is *hajar ed-damm*, a few km north of where the Jordan enters the lake, but cf. Baldi's commentary for a different identification. For Hazor cf. the commentary on 11.1ff.; Kedesh, which has preserved the same name in the Arabic *qedes*, is north of Lake Huleh (201–280), which nowadays is largely dried up. For a discussion of the other localities, cf. the commentaries, biblical geographies and atlases.

(g) The territory of Dan (19.40–48)

Here, too, we have a list of place names, with no information about the frontiers of the tribe. The places which can be identified with certainty are: Zorah, the Arabic *sar'ah* (130–150), Ir (Beth) –Shemesh, now *tell er-rumēle*, a very short distance from the modern Israeli Beth Shemesh (128–147), Aijalon, mentioned in the El-Amarna archives (273.20 and 287.57, the latter text being also reproduced in *ANET*, p. 483), cf. also II Chron. 11.10, where, with Zorah, it forms part of the defensive system of Rehoboam. In Judg. 1.35 it forms with Sha-albim one of the localities which Joseph could not take: it is now *yālū* (139–153). Timnah (Timnatna) is the present-day *khirbet tibne* (cf. 15.10). Ekron is no doubt *'āqir* (cf. 13.3) and formed part of the ancient Philistine pentapolis. This is why Noth and Strange maintain that the passage cannot be dated before the period of Josiah, that is, before his revolt against the Assyrians, because there is evidence that the place was in the hands of the Philistines up to the period of Assurbanipal (c. 668–632, cf. the Annals, Cyl. C, *ANET*, p. 294). This assertion becomes much less likely if we consider that the passage includes other places occupied later by Israel and not by Dan (e.g. Aijalon and Sha-albim, as we have seen). The thesis of Noth (p. 14), according to whom the whole passage is a late and artificial construction, does not seem to us to be adequately proved. The legends of Samson (Judg. 13–15) and the statement in v.47, as well as Judg. 17–18, are against this thesis, even though there are many points which are not clear (Baldi, Abel, Hertzberg). The Jarkon is clearly limited here to the eastern part of its course.

Be this as it may, Dan effectively occupied only a small part of the territory defined by the place names mentioned (for the others cf. the commentaries and geographies). Indeed, the redactor accepts this fact, but tries to explain it by the statement (v.47) that Dan lost part of its territory. It is possible that this statement may be true, if we accept that the necessity which the tribe felt at sometimes emigrating to the north was due to Philistine pressure. On the other hand, the situation is not simple. B. Mazar, in his important study, sees in the region described four districts: I. (v.41), the region effectively occupied at the period of the conquest: II. (v.42 plus Elon), a region of mixed population, in which Israel was constantly in conflict with its neighbours (cf. Judg. 1.35), and which was not occupied until the period of David; III. (v.43 less Elon), corresponding to Solomon's south-western district (I Kings 4.9); IV. (vv. 45–46), also set up at the period of Solomon. In Solomon's time District I was annexed to Judah, while at the moment when the actual breach took place in the united kingdom, Districts III–IV no longer belonged either to Israel or to Judah. The rest of the territory was divided between Judah, Benjamin and Ephraim. Thus the original territory of Dan (to which Judg. 13–15 refers) is only that given in v.41. Unfortunately, Mazar does not discuss the connection between the conclusions of his study and Dan's migration to the north.

(h) *The personal territory of Joshua (19.49–51)*

The mention of the territory assigned to Joshua (vv.49b–50) seems to be an interpolation in the text, for it interrupts the conclusion. It is made in order to justify the statement recorded in 24.30 || Judg. 2.9 that the leader was buried on his own land. The statement is important not only because it stresses the personal importance of Joshua, whose territory seems to have enjoyed a kind of extraterritoriality (Hertzberg), but also because it connects the hero with the hill country of Ephraim (cf. Num. 1.10; I Chron. 7.25ff.).

CHAPTER 20

The Cities of Refuge

20 [1]Then the LORD said to Joshua, [2]"Say to the people of Israel, "Appoint the cities of refuge of which I spoke to you through Moses, [3]that the manslayer who kills any person without intent or unwittingly may flee there; they shall be for you a refuge from the avenger of blood. [4]He shall flee to one of these cities and shall stand at the entrance of the gate of the city, and explain his case to the elders of that city; then they shall take him into the city, and give him a place, and he shall remain with them. [5]And if the avenger of blood pursues him, they shall not give up the slayer into his hand; because he killed his neighbour unwittingly, having had no enmity against him in times past. [6]And he shall remain in that city until he has stood before the assembly of judgment, until the death of him who is high priest at that time; then the slayer may go again to his own town and his own home, to the town from which he fled." '.

[7] So they set apart Kedesh in Galilee in the hill country of Naphtali, and Shechem in the hill country of Ephraim, and Kiriath-arba (that is, Hebron) in the hill country of Judah. [8]And beyond the Jordan they appointed Bezer in the wilderness on the tableland (of the Arnon) from the tribe of Reuben, and Ramoth in Gilead, from the tribe of Gad, and Golan in Bashan, from the tribe of Manasseh. [9]These were the cities designated for all the people of Israel, and for every stranger sojourning among them, that any one who killed a person without intent could flee there, so that he might not die by the hand of the avenger of blood, till he stood before the assembly.

Bibliography: M. Löhr, *Das Asylwesen im Alten Testament*, Schr. der Königsberger Gelehrtengesellschaft VII, 3, Halle 1930; N. H. Nicolsky, 'Das Asylrecht in Israel', *ZAW* 48, 1930, pp. 146–75; W. Rudolph, *Der 'Elohist'* . . ., p. 238; M. David, 'Die Bestimmungen über die Asylstädte in Josua XX', *OTS* 9, 1951, pp. 30–48; B. Dinur, 'The Religious Character of the Cities of Refuge and the Ceremonies of Admission into them', *'Ereṣ Iśrā'el* 3, 1954, pp. 135–46 (in Hebrew, summary in English); F. Horst, 'Recht und Religion im Bereich des Alten Testaments', *EvTh* 16, 1956, pp. 49–75 (*Gottes Recht*, Munich 1961, pp. 260–91), esp. pp. 59/273ff.; R. de Vaux, *Ancient Israel*, London 1961, pp. 160–3; M. Greenberg, 'The

Biblical Concept of Asylum', *JBL* 78, 1959, pp. 125–32. See also the appropriate articles in *RGG*, *IDB* and *BHH*. For the root *rṣḥ*: J. J. Stamm, 'Sprachliche Erwägungen zum Gebot 'Du sollst nicht töten'' ', *TZ* 1, 1945, pp. 81–90; id., 'Dreissig Jahre Dekalogforschung', *TR* 17, 1961, pp. 189–239 and 281–305, esp. pp. 296f.; J. J. Stamm and M. E. Andrew, *The Ten Commandments in Recent Research*, SBT II, 2, London 1967, pp. 98f.; H. Reventlow, *Gebot und Predigt im Dekalog*, Gütersloh 1962, pp. 72f.; E. Nielsen, *The Ten Commandments in New Perspective*, SBT II, 7, London 1968, pp. 108ff.; Auzou, pp. 153ff.; H. Schulz, *Das Todesrecht im Alten Testament*, BZAW 114, Berlin 1969, pp. 9–15; B. van Oeveren, *De Vrijsteden in het Oude Testament*, Kampen 1968, was not available to me.

---

[3] *rōṣēᵃḥ* is derived from the verb *rṣḥ*, on which Stamm's study has been available since 1945; its results are now generally accepted. The root is as it were ambivalent: in the Decalogue it means murder, without legal formalities, but in the context of the cities of refuge it means unintentional homicide. 'Without intent'; in Hebrew *biš*ᵉ*gāgā*; David proposes 'without premeditation', which is perhaps better. [4–6] These verses are lacking in LXX, and have all the appearance of an interpretative interpolation. [7] 'They set apart' is the literal sense of the root *qdš*, and is appropriate in this context; but LXX and Num. 35.11 have the root *qrh*, cf. also V, which seems to presuppose *qr'*. These solutions have been adopted by various commentators, who assume a dittography between the verb and the place name that follows; on the other hand, Abel, David and Kaufmann maintain MT, and it seems to us that this presents no difficulty. [8] After 'Jordan' MT adds 'Jericho to the east', which is meaningless and does not occur in LXXᴮ. The words must therefore be omitted, or else, following V, the word *mūl*, 'opposite', must be introduced. We have read *gōlān* with Q. K and LXXᴮ have *gōlāwn*. [9] 'The cities designated': no doubt a technical term for these cities; its meaning is unknown and it is not found elsewhere (cf. the discussion in Noth).

The present text contains Deuteronomic elements (vv. 3–6), but also seems to have undergone a redaction on the part of P.

The right of sanctuary, of which a very interesting form is described here (and in the passages related to this passage), is known throughout oriental and classical antiquity, in particular in relation to certain sanctuaries, whose privilege in this respect was recognized by international treaties. The same right could also be granted on a political and secular level by one nation to the fugitives of another nation, and the norms for the right of refuge and of extradition in the various treaties of alliance and vassality from the ancient East which have come down to us were laid down in this context.

The institution of cities of refuge (also mentioned in Num. 35.9–34; Deut 4.41–43; 19.1–13) is as far as we know without parallel, and consequently seems to be something typical of the life and faith of Israel. This must be clearly emphasized, since the contrary is often stated. The six places mentioned recur in the Levitical cities listed in the following chapter (where their location is discussed). Moreover, some of them form the site of well-known sanctuaries. It seems plausible to connect the right of asylum in these places with the sanctuaries that existed there, even though there is no explicit statement to this effect. Thus a certain parallel is established: just as it is the legislator's intention that the Levites should derive their means of subsistence from the cities themselves, the guest of a city of refuge might have found that they were not only a place of refuge, but also the means of subsistence which an ordinary sanctuary would have refused him. If this explanation is valid, we would have here one of the numerous examples of an advanced social conscience, typical of the whole world of the Old Testament.

Unfortunately no biblical text provides a concrete example of the functioning of this institution. It is not surprising, therefore, that one of the first questions to be raised has been that of the historicity of the institution as such. It is not possible to give a satisfactory reply to this question. All we can say is that there are two periods in which the institution of cities of refuge can be fitted without difficulty: the first is that of the dawn of the unitary state under David, at the beginning of the first millennium, when the king's justice was clearly tending to take the place of the somewhat chaotic situation which resulted from the private practice of the blood-feud. In vv. 6b and 9b there is particular insistence on the fact that someone guilty of homicide must be allowed to appear before the competent court, instead of being killed by the avenger of blood (cf. Löhr, Dinur, Greenberg, de Vaux). The second period is that of the reform of Josiah, which is preferred above all by German scholars (Nicolsky, Noth and Horst). In their view, sanctuaries other than Jerusalem which practised the custom of giving refuge were suppressed by Josiah, and had therefore to set up a lay substitute in the cities in question, with no further connection with a sanctuary. It is interesting to note that these two theses are not mutually exclusive: the reform of Josiah may very well have sought to bring back into force, under different forms, the ancient institution of cities of refuge, which had fallen into disuse.

If this is true, there is no difficulty in supposing that there is a historical basis for the law in question, even if it occurs in a context of late traditions: Deuteronomy, Dtr and P.

The allusion to the death of the high priest (v. 6a), which certainly belongs to a post-exilic period, is inexplicable. At the very least, it is out of context, because it has nothing to do with the appearance of the accused before the competent court (Greenberg). It seems improbable that on a basis of this verse the whole institution should be dated in the post-exilic period, as David suggests and Mowinckel before him (op. cit. in p. 12 n.3 in the Introduction), because of its relationship with P. How could the tiny remnant of Israel which lived in Jerusalem and its immediate neighbourhood in the post-exilic period have any claims on the country east of the Jordan, in which half the cities mentioned are to be found?

CHAPTER 21

The Levitical Cities

21 ¹Then the heads of the fathers' houses of the Levites came to Eleazar the priest and to Joshua the son of Nun and to the heads of the fathers' houses of the tribes of the people of Israel; ²and they spoke to them at Shiloh in the land of Canaan as follows: 'The LORD commanded through Moses that we be given cities to dwell in, along with their pasture lands for our cattle.' ³So the people of Israel gave to the Levites part of their inheritance, by command of the LORD: the following cities and pasture lands.

4 The lot came out for the clans of the Kohathites. So those Levites who were descendants of Aaron the priest received by lot from the tribes of Judah, Simeon, and Benjamin, thirteen cities. ⁵And the rest of the Kohathites, according to their clans, received by lot from the clans of the tribe of Ephraim, from the tribe of Dan and the half-tribe of Manasseh, ten cities. ⁶The Gershonites received by lot from the families of the tribe of Issachar, from the tribe of Asher, from the tribe of Naphtali, and from the half-tribe of Manasseh in Bashan, according to their clans, thirteen cities. ⁷The Merarites according to their clans received from the tribe of Reuben, the tribe of Gad, and the tribe of Zebulun, twelve cities.

8 These cities and their pasture lands the people of Israel gave by lots to

the Levites, as the LORD had commanded through Moses. ⁹Out of the tribe of Judah and the tribe of Simeon they gave the following cities, whose names we list, ¹⁰which went to the descendants of Aaron, of the clan of the Kohathites who belonged to the Levites; since the lot fell to them first. ¹¹They gave them Kiriath-arba, Arba being the father of Anak (that is, Hebron), in the hill country of Judah, along with the pasture lands round about it. ¹²But the fields of the city and its villages had been given to Caleb the son of Jephunneh as his possession.

13 Thus to the descendants of Aaron the priest they gave Hebron the city of refuge for the slayer, with its pasture lands, Libnah with its pasture lands, ¹⁴Jattir with its pasture lands, Esh-temoa with its pasture lands, ¹⁵Holon with its pasture lands, Debir with its pasture lands, ¹⁶Ashan with its pasture lands, Juttah with its pasture lands, Beth-shemesh with its pasture lands – nine cities out of these two tribes. ¹⁷Then out of the tribe of Benjamin, Gibeon with its pasture lands, Geba with its pasture lands, ¹⁸Anathoth with its pasture lands, and Alemeth with its pasture lands – four cities. ¹⁹The cities of the descendants of Aaron, the priests, were in all thirteen cities with their pasture lands.

20 As to the rest of the Kohathites belonging to the Kohathite clans of the Levites, the cities allotted to them were out of the tribe of Ephraim. ²¹To them were given Shechem, the city of refuge for the slayer, with its pasture lands in the hill country of Ephraim, Gezer with its pasture lands, ²²Kibzaim with its pasture lands, Beth-horon with its pasture lands – four cities.

23 And out of the tribe of Dan, Elteke with its pasture lands, Gibbethon with its pasture lands, ²⁴Aijalon with its pasture lands, Gathrimmon with its pasture lands – four cities.

25 And out of the half-tribe of Manasseh, Taanach with its pasture lands, and Jibleam with its pasture lands – two cities. ²⁶The cities of the clans of the rest of the Kohathites were ten in all with their pasture lands.

27 And to the Gershonites, one of the clans of the Levites, were given out of the other half-tribe of Manasseh, Golan in Bashan with its pasture lands, the city of refuge for the slayer, and Be-eshterah with its pasture lands – two cities.

28 And out of the tribe of Issachar, Kishion with its pasture lands, Daberath with its pasture lands, ²⁹Jarmuth with its pasture lands, En-gannim with its pasture lands – four cities.

30 And out of the tribe of Asher, Mishal with its pasture lands, Abdon with its pasture lands, ³¹Helkath with its pasture lands, and Rehob with its pasture lands – four cities.

32 And out of the tribe of Naphtali, Kedesh in Galilee with its pasture lands, the city of refuge for the slayer, Hammoth with its pasture lands, and Rakkath with its pasture lands – three cities.

33 The cities of the several families of the Gershonites were in all thirteen cities with their pasture lands.

34 And to the Levites, the Merarite clans, were given out of the tribe of Zebulun, Jokneam with its pasture lands, Kartah with its pasture lands, 35Dimnah with its pasture lands, Nahalal with its pasture lands – four cities.

36 And beyond the Jordan, opposite Jericho, out of the tribe of Reuben, Bezer the city of refuge for the man-slayer, in the wilderness, in the hill country, with its pasture lands, Jahaz with its pasture lands, 37Kedemoth with its pasture lands, and Mephaath with its pasture lands – four cities.

38 And out of the tribe of Gad, Ramoth in Gilead with its pasture lands, the city of refuge for the slayer, Mahanaim with its pasture lands, 39Heshbon with its pasture lands, Jazer with its pasture lands – four cities in all. 40As for the cities of the several Merarite clans, those allotted to them were in all twelve cities. 41The cities of the Levites in the midst of the possession of the people of Israel were in all forty-eight cities with their pasture lands. 42These cities had each its pasture lands round about it; so it was with all these cities.

Addition LXXᴮᴬ. 42ªIn this way Joshua finished distributing the land in its frontiers. 42ᵇThe Israelites apportioned to Joshua a territory according to the commandment of the LORD, they gave him the city he had asked for: Timnath-serah, in the hill country of Ephraim. 42ᶜAnd he built his own city there and lived in it. 42ᵈAnd Joshua also took the knives of stone with which he had circumcised the Israelites coming from the desert and put them at Timnath-serah.

43 Thus the LORD gave to Israel all the land which he swore to give to their fathers; and having taken possession of it, they settled there. 44And the LORD gave them rest on every side just as he had sworn to their fathers; not one of all their enemies had withstood them, for the LORD had given all their enemies into their hands. 45Not one of all the good promises which the LORD had made to the house of Israel had failed; all came to pass.

Bibliography: W. F. Albright, 'The List of Levitical Cities', *Louis Ginzberg Jubilee Volume*, I, New York 1945, pp.49–73; A. Alt, 'Bemerkungen zu einigen judäischen Ortslisten des Alten Testaments', *BBLAK* (= *ZDPV*) 68, 1949–51, pp.93–210, esp. pp.199ff.; id., 'Festungen und Levitenorte im Lande Juda', 1952, *KS* II, 1953, pp.306–15; H. Cazelles, 'David's Monarchy and the Gibeonite Claim', *PEQ* 87, 1955, pp.165–75, esp. pp.171f.; M. Haran, 'The Levitical Cities: Utopia and Historical Reality', *Tarbiz* 27, 1957–58, pp.421–39 (in Hebrew, summary in English); B. Mazar, 'The Cities of the Priests and the Levites', *SVT* VII, 1960, pp. 193–205; R. de Vaux, *Ancient Israel*, London 1961, pp.366f.; M. Haran, 'Studies in the Account of the Levitical Cities', *JBL* 80, 1961, pp.45–54, 156–165; Auzou, pp.157ff.; A. Cody, *A History of Old Testament Priesthood*,

Rome 1969, pp. 159–65. For the clans and names of the Levites, cf. K. Möhlenbrink, 'Die Levitischen Überlieferungen des Alten Testaments', *ZAW* 52, 1934, pp. 184–231. For the whole problem, cf. also W. F. Albright, *Archaeology and the Religion* of Israel, Baltimore, ³1953, pp. 121–4 Y. Kaufmann, *The Biblical Account* . . ., pp. 40–6.

[5–6] 'According to their clans': correction, cf. *BH*³. [9] 'Whose names we list': the Hebrew has, literally, an impersonal form which is usually rendered by the passive 'were called'. It is not necessary to amend the text, as Noth does. [16] 'Ashan': with I Chron. 6.59 and LXX ᴹˢˢ. The Hebrew has the improbable *'ayin*. [18] 'Alemeth': with I Chron. 6.60 and LXXᴹˢˢ. The Hebrew has *'almon*. [22] Kibzaim: I Chron. 6.68 has the variant Jokmeam. It is not possible to reconstruct the original form. Albright shows a preference for the form in Chron., and suggests that perhaps both names should be retained; but in this case one of them is superfluous to the reckoning. [23] Elteke: cf. on 19.44. [25] Taanach: I Chron. 6.70 has *'ānēr*, which is perhaps the result of a haplography at the beginning and a confusion between *rēš* and final *kap* at the end. Jibleam: with I Chron. 6.70, which has *bil'ām*. MT has *gat rimmōn*, a repetition of v. 24. LXXᴮ is completely different. [27] Golan: cf. on 20.8. [32] Hammoth and Rakkath: cf. on 19.35. [34] MT interpolated 'remaining' after 'Levites', which is meaningless. [35] Dimnah: I Chron. 6.77 has *rimmōnō*, cf. on 19.13. The original cannot be recovered. [36] The beginning and the middle of the verse have been restored on the basis of LXX and I Chron. 6.78; cf. Josh. 20.8. [40] After 'clans' there is the same interpolation as in v. 34. [42a–d] The addition in LXX is interesting because of the statement in 42d. The rest repeats 19.49–50 and is of no importance.

1. As we have it in the present text, the list of the cities assigned to the Levites claims to describe an institution which carries out a command given in the desert (Num. 35.1–8), by way of a remedy for the failure to apportion any tribal land to the Levites (Num. 18.20–24). These texts are generally attributed to P. Num. 35.5 gives measured dimensions for the land apportioned to each of these cities, but the artificial nature of this system is obvious. This fact, together with the further fact that Numbers is generally attributed to the latest of the Pentateuchal sources, has been largely responsible for the widespread opinion that Josh. 21 (and its parallel in I Chron. 6) is also an artificial construction. On the other hand, in his commentary on Numbers, M. Noth has given extremely convincing arguments in favour of the contrary thesis: that Num. 35.1ff. is derived from Josh. 21, and forms part of the redactional elements in the combination of the Pentateu-

chal sources with Dtr.[1] If these premises are accepted, the whole edifice set up by Wellhausen, according to which Josh. 21 derives from P, and is therefore nothing more than one of the numerous utopian and theocratic constructions put forward by this source, falls to the ground. In the present case, in Wellhausen's view, this construction could at best have been due to the traditional memory of famous sanctuaries of the past, situated in some of the cities mentioned, and of the fact that at the period of the final redaction of the source, the Levites, deprived of their revenue under Josiah, belonged thereafter to the class of *personae miserabiles* who needed special protection. The success of the concept of 'utopia', forged by Wellhausen,[2] can be seen from its presence in the works of an author who has criticized the documentary hypothesis as violently as Y. Kaufmann; except that the latter dates the 'utopian' construction earlier, at the period of the conquest.

2. Whereas A. Alt and M. Noth would date the institution of the Levitical cities at the period of the reform of Josiah, at exactly the same period as their dating of the frontiers and cities forming the districts, the studies of W. F. Albright, Haran and Mazar have posed the problem in fundamentally different terms. In his classic study published in 1945, Albright has shown that on the basis of Josh. 21.1–40; I Chron. 6.54–81, it is possible to reconstruct an almost complete list, and he also confirms, on the strength of Alt's study, that this is not based on utopian elements, but on concrete facts. A detailed examination of the place names listed led Albright to observe that several of them were not taken by Israel until the period of David and Solomon: e.g. Gezer, Ajalon and Taanach. Another important statement is that in I Kings 12.31, that after the breakdown of the personal union between Israel and Judah, Jeroboam I deprived the Levites of their office, so that it seems difficult to suppose that the places in the north could still have been in their possession much after 926 BC. This would also provide an explanation of the fact pointed out by Alt and expanded by Mazar, that the Levitical cities in the south form an obvious parallel to the lists of cities fortified under Rehoboam which is found

[1] M. Noth, *Numbers*, OTL, London 1968, ad loc. Cf. already 'Überlieferungsgeschichtliches zur zweiten Hälfte des Josuabuches', in *Studien F. Nötscher . . .*, BBB 1, Bonn 1950, pp. 151–67, esp. pp. 164–7.
[2] J. Wellhausen, *Prolegomena to the History of Israel*, repr. Cleveland 1957, pp. 159ff., and, recently, S. Mowinckel, *Zur Frage nach dokumentarischen Quellen in Josua 13–21*, Oslo 1946; id., *Tetrateuch-Pentateuch-Hexateuch*, BZAW 90, Berlin 1964, pp. 51–57.

in II Chron. 11.6–10, already mentioned in connection with the districts of Judah in Josh. 15 and 18.

3. Thus it seems that Albright, Cazelles, Haran, de Vaux and Mazar are right to date this list in the concluding years of Solomon and the early years of the divided monarchy, that is, in the second half of the tenth century. It is also possible to accept the dating in the period of Josiah, put forward by Alt and Noth, if we admit that the reforming king wished to restore an ancient institution, after having suppressed the sanctuaries which provided the Levites with their income and brought them to the Temple of Jerusalem. That is, it is clear that the two views are not mutually exclusive at all. It is probable that at a post-exilic period there were places where Levitical families lived, but we know nothing about them, about their relationship with the cities in the present text, or about the aims which P had in re-elaborating the traditional lists with the aid of quite fantastic material of its own, as in the case of Num. 35.

4. The connection with the cities of refuge in the previous chapter can be seen at once from the fact that often, as the list proceeds from one region to another, the first place mentioned is explicitly declared to be a city of refuge. The way in which the matter is set out suggests that the city of refuge was a kind of chief city of the district (cf. vv. 13, 21, 27, 32 and 36). Shechem and Hebron were the sites of famous and very ancient sanctuaries, but we know nothing about the other cities; although it seems probable, in view of the general practice in the ancient East and in classical antiquity, that the right of refuge was associated with a sanctuary.

5. Another problem to be resolved is that of the purpose of the institution. We have stated that we have no concrete example of the way in which it functioned, nor even a description of the Levitical cities: the narratives in I Sam. 21.2; 22.9–19 not only do not fit into the chronology established above, but also have no connection with the Levitical cities (although some commentators make such a connection). They are related solely to places where priests lived. The fact that v. 18 mentions Anathoth, which was also the dwelling place of the descendants of Abiathar, exiled from Jerusalem by Solomon (I Kings 2.26), cannot be construed to mean that all the places where priests lived can be taken as examples of the functioning of Levitical cities. If the purpose of the Levitical cities was to provide the Levites with an income, one might at once observe that the sanctuaries in which they officiated would have served this purpose just as well; and

we have no knowledge of the existence of a sanctuary in most of these cases.

The explanation which Mazar proposes is interesting. In his view, the critics of the Levites were 'colonies' (in the Roman sense of the term), that is, places where groups who, like the Levites, were particularly faithful to the tradition, were settled. And in fact a glance at the map shows at once that a large number of the Levitical cities were found in regions which presented political difficulties. In vv. 11–15 we have a series of cities situated in the southern hill country, particularly towards the frontier with the Philistines, an area which had been held in submission only with difficulty since the time of David (II Sam. 5.17ff. and perhaps 8.1). In vv. 17–23 we have places situated within the territory of Benjamin and that apportioned to Dan in ch. 19, in a region which belonged to the Canaanites until the period of David and Solomon. Apart from this latter factor, the ill-feeling of Benjamin towards David (II Sam. 20) is well known. In vv. 25 and 28–35 we have the cities in the northern plain, entirely subject to the well-known Canaanite city states until the period of David and Solomon, and therefore politically uncertain. In vv. 27 and 36–39 we have the area east of the Jordan, precariously occupied by David (II Sam. 8) and gradually abandoned after the time of Solomon. Thus apart from Shechem, the ancient sanctuary of the tribal amphictyony, it is easy to establish that the Levites and their cities were in fact situated in certain 'difficult' regions of the empire. The connection between them and the cities of Judah fortified by Rehoboam is due simply to the application of the same criteria in the period immediately following the break between Israel and Judah. In support of his thesis, Mazar refers to the Egyptian practice of establishing a military colony in certain key localities in occupied territory: in Palestine the typical case is that of Beth-shan. This practice, he holds, was brought back into use, together with other Egyptian practices, particularly in the field of imperial administration, by David and Solomon.

This would also provide a logical explanation for the absence of Levitical cities in the territory of Jerusalem and Ephraim, an absence which several others have commented upon, particularly Noth.

6. As Albright and Mazar have pointed out, the system did not long survive the dismembering of the empire of David and Solomon. The regions occupied west of the Jordan quickly fell into the hands of the indigenous inhabitants, and a number of Levitical cities west of the Jordan were destroyed and conquered by Pharaoh Shishak

(Sheshonq), c. 941–921 (I Kings 14.25–28 ‖ II Chron. 12.2, 9–11, c. 918 BC),[1] particularly those in the north (which in the meantime, as we have seen, had probably been deprived of Levites as a result of the measures taken by Jeroboam I). It is possible that they survived in the south, but without any theological significance or special administrative form. In this case the attempt to restore them under Josiah may have been an attempt to give them a theological significance within the framework of the theology of his reformation.

7. The addition by LXX in v. 42 is important because of the reference to the knives of stone used in 5.2–3. This is an aetiological passage referring to these objects, which were no doubt on show in a sanctuary which existed in the region; but we know nothing about this.

8. The Deuteronomic conclusion of the chapter, vv. 43–45, forms a link with the beginning of ch. 22 and the whole of ch. 23. They no doubt originally formed a unity into which 22.9ff. was later interpolated; cf. the mention of the 'good promises' in v. 45, an idea which is not developed until 23.14–15.

[1] For the campaign of Shishak (Sheshonq), cf. recently B. Mazar, 'The Campaign of Pharao Shishak to Palestine', in SVT VI, 1957, pp. 57–66 (with a bibliography).

PART THREE

APPENDIX

CHAPTER 22

The Return of the Tribes East of the Jordan

22 Then Joshua summoned the Reubenites, and the Gadites, and the half-tribe of Manasseh, ²and said to them: 'You have kept all that Moses the servant of the LORD commanded you, and have obeyed my voice in all that I have commanded you; ³you have not forsaken your brethren down to this day, and it has been a long time, but have been careful to keep the charge of the LORD your God. ⁴And now the LORD your God has given rest to your brethren, as he promised them; therefore turn and go to your tents in the land where your possession lies, which Moses the servant of the LORD gave you on the other side of the Jordan. ⁵Take good care to observe the commandment and the law which Moses the servant of the LORD commanded you, to love the LORD your God, and to walk in all his ways, and to keep his commandments, and to cleave to him, and to serve him with all your heart and with all your soul.' ⁶So Joshua blessed them, and sent them away; and they went to their tents.

7 Now to the one half of the tribe of Manasseh Moses had given a possession in Bashan; but to the other half Joshua had given a possession beside their brethren on the other side of the Jordan on the west. And when Joshua sent them away to their homes and blessed them, ⁸he said to them, 'Go back to your tents with much wealth, and with very many cattle, with silver, gold, bronze, and iron, and with much clothing; divide the spoil of your enemies with your brethren.'

9 So the Reubenites and the Gadites and the half-tribe of Manasseh returned home, parting from the people of Israel at Shiloh, which is in the land of Canaan, to go to the land of Gilead, their own land which they were assigned by command of the LORD through Moses.

10 And when they came to Geliloth of the Jordan, which is still in the land of Canaan, the Reubenites and the Gadites and the half-tribe of Manasseh built there an altar beside the Jordan, an altar of great size. ¹¹And the people of Israel heard say, 'Behold, the Reubenites and the Gadites and the half-tribe of Manasseh have built an altar on the bank of the land of Canaan, in Geliloth of the Jordan, on the side of the people of Israel.' ¹²And when the people of Israel heard of it, the whole assembly of the people of Israel gathered at Shiloh, to set out on a military campaign against them.

13 But the people of Israel sent to the Reubenites and the Gadites and the half-tribe of Manasseh, in the land of Gilead, Phinehas the son of Eleazar the priest, ¹⁴and with him ten spokesmen, one from each tribe of Israel, every one of them the chief of a family among the 'thousands' of Israel.

15 And they came to the Reubenites, the Gadites, and the half-tribe of Manasseh, in the land of Gilead, and they said to them, ¹⁶'Thus says the whole congregation of the LORD, "What is this treachery which you have committed against the God of Israel in turning away this day from following the LORD, by building yourselves an altar this day in rebellion against the LORD? ¹⁷Have we not had enough of the sin at Peor from which even yet we have not cleansed ourselves, and for which there came a plague upon the assembly of the LORD? ¹⁸And now today you must turn away from following the LORD! And if you rebel against the LORD today, he will be angry with the whole assembly of Israel tomorrow. ¹⁹But now, if the land assigned to you is unclean, pass over into the LORD's land where the LORD's tabernacle stands, and have a possession assigned to you among us; only do not rebel against the LORD, or make us as rebels by building yourselves an altar other than the altar of the LORD our God. ²⁰Did not Achan the son of Zerah break faith in the matter of the devoted things, and wrath fell upon all the congregation of Israel? And if only he had perished alone for his iniquity!" '

21 Then the Reubenites, the Gadites, and the half-tribe of Manasseh said in answer to the chiefs of the 'thousands' of Israel, ²²'El, God, the LORD! El, God, the LORD! He knows, and let Israel itself know! If it was in rebellion or in breach of faith toward the LORD, may he not help us today! ²³That is if we have built an altar to turn away from following the LORD; or if we did so to offer burnt offerings or cereal offerings or peace offerings on it, may the LORD himself take vengeance. ²⁴Nay, but we did it from fear that in time to come your children might say to our children, "What have you to do with the LORD, the God of Israel? ²⁵For the LORD has made the Jordan a boundary between us and you, you Reubenites and Gadites; you have no portion in the LORD." So your children might prevent our children from worshipping the LORD. ²⁶Therefore we said, "Let us now make ourselves (. . .)by building an altar, not for burnt offering, nor for sacrifice, ²⁷but to be a witness between us and you, and the generation after us, so that they perform the service of the LORD in his presence with our burnt offerings and sacrifices and peace offerings; lest your children say to our children in time to come, 'You have no portion in the LORD'." ²⁸And we thought, If this should be said to us or to our descendants in time to come, we should say, "Behold the image of the altar of the LORD, which our fathers made, not for burnt offerings, nor for sacrifice, but to be a witness between us and you." ²⁹Far be it from us that we should

rebel against the LORD, and turn away this day from following the LORD by building an altar for burnt offering, cereal offerings, or sacrifice, other than the altar of the LORD our God that stands before his tabernacle!'

30 When Phinehas the priest and the spokesmen of the congregation, and the chiefs of the 'thousands' of Israel who were with him, heard the words that the Reubenites and the Gadites and the Manassites spoke, it pleased them well. ³¹And Phinehas the son of Eleazar the priest said to the Reubenites and the Gadites and the Manassites, 'Today we know that the LORD is in the midst of you, because you have not committed this treachery against the LORD; now you have saved the people of Israel from the hand of the LORD.'

32 Then Phinehas the son of Eleazar the priest, and the spokesmen, returned from the Reubenites and the Gadites in the land of Gilead to the land of Canaan, to the people of Israel, and brought back word to them. ³³And the report pleased the people of Israel; and the people of Israel blessed God and spoke no more of setting out to make war against them, to destroy the land where the Reubenites and Gadites were settled. ³⁴The Reubenites and the Gadites called the altar (. . .), 'For it is a witness between us that the LORD is our God.'

Bibliography: W. Rudolph, *Der 'Elohist'* . . ., pp. 238–40; K. Möhlenbrink, 'Die Landnahmesage . . .', *ZAW* 56, 1938, pp. 238–68, esp. pp. 246–50; J. de Fraine, 'De altari Reubenitarum,' *VD* 25, 1947, pp. 301–13; J. Dus, 'Die Lösung des Rätsels von Jos 22', *ArOr* 32, 1964, pp. 529–46; Auzou, pp. 165ff.; J. A. Soggin, *'Lô* in *Gios.* 22.20', *Bibbia e Oriente* 10, 1968, p. 188; J. G. Vink, 'The Date and Origin of the Priestly Code in the Old Testament', *OTS* 15, 1969, pp. 1–144, esp. p. 77, which was not available to me.

---

[3] 'And it has been a long time': for the adverbial use of *zeh*, cf. Joüon § 143a. [7] 'On the . . . bank': K has the preposition *min*, Q has *bᵉ*. [10] *Geliloth*: LXX^B has Γαλγαλα, i.e., Gilgal. It cannot be the place mentioned in 18.17, which is not on the Jordan. 'Beside': for this rendering of *'al* cf. Ps. 1.3 and the frequent usage in Ugaritic (Aistleitner, no. 1030, 4). [11] The context requires that *'el mūl* should be translated 'on the bank of': the hostility of Israel arises, it seems, originally from the fact that the altar was built on their own territory, west of the Jordan, and not in the territory of the tribes in question east of the Jordan, cf. the discourse in v. 19.¹ LXX^BA avoids the obstacle by translating 'on the edges of the land of Canaan'. For 'on the side of' cf. Köhler-Baumgartner, *Lexicon*; for the

¹ For these problems, cf. the commentaries of Baldi and Noth; and our own view in 'Gilgal, Passah und Landnahme', SVT XV, 1966, pp. 263–77, esp. 263f.

reasons, cf. what has just been said. The translation of Baldi and Bright, 'district of the Jordan', seems improbable. **[14]** 'Spokesmen': cf. the note on 9.14 for this translation of *nāśî*. After 'each tribe', MT adds 'one for each family', which clearly belongs to the second half of the verse and is meaningless. **[19]** 'Do not . . . make us as rebels': cf. Noth ad loc. For the *qal* in MT (= '. . . and do not abandon us'), read the *hiphil* with all the commentaries. The phrase is lacking in LXX and should perhaps be omitted. **[20]** 'And if only he had perished . . .!' Read *lū* for *lō* with V (*Utinam* . . .!). LXX^A read *hᵃlō*; LXX^B, which did not translate *lō* but gives an emphatic statement, seems to have considered it as a *lāmed* of emphasis: 'And surely he died!'.[1] If we accept the theory of V we clearly have an allusion to 7.4, that is, to the number of persons who had to die for the fault of one. **[22]** 'May he not help us . . .': the usual reading is the third person optative, following LXX, V and Syr, instead of the second person of MT. If we keep the latter reading we have: 'No longer help us' (so Hertzberg), and at the beginning of the sentence: 'O, El, God . . . etc.', which of course does not go with 'he knows'. **[26]** After 'make ourselves' in the text the object is missing. Perhaps it was 'an image', cf. v. 28, which would have offended the sensibility of later orthodoxy. **[34]** MT does not give us the name of the altar (which was perhaps considered scandalous); Syr has '*ēd*, cf. what follows.

1. This chapter begins with a preamble, in which the tribes of Reuben, Gad and the eastern half-tribe of Manasseh are permitted to re-establish themselves in their territory: the task for which they had crossed the Jordan with their brethren who still had no land has now been accomplished. Thus the cycle which began in 1.12–18 with the invitation addressed to them by Joshua himself is brought to a conclusion. Apart from the familiar style, the content also reveals that these verses are of Deuteronomic origin. A link with the previous passages is provided by 21.43–45, which are also Deuteronomic.

2. The starting point of the present narrative must have been the presence in the sacral complex at Gilgal, but on the very banks of the Jordan, of an altar of unusual proportions, traditionally attributed to the Reubenites and the Gadites. From v. 34 one may deduce that the altar bore a name (unfortunately not recorded) which connected it aetiologically with an event which took place in the region and concerned these tribes. By virtue of the setting up of this altar they proclaimed and demonstrated the fact that they belonged to 'Israel', although they were outside the territory of Israel proper (vv. 24–25);

---

1 For details, cf. our note '*Lô* in Gios. 22.20', *Bibbia e Oriente*; listed above.

that is, they were on land that was regarded as impure. This view of the land east of the Jordan is in strange contrast to that which we ordinarily find in other passages in the OT, including the narrative of the conquest: if Moses had apportioned the regions east of the Jordan to two and a half tribes, how could their land have been impure? It is clear that here we have a primitive conception, probably very early, according to which only the land west of the Jordan (and, properly speaking only the region of Shiloh, that is the hill country of Ephraim) was 'Yahweh's land', cf. v. 19. Noth tries to explain the reasons for the possible uncleanness of the region west of the Jordan by assuming that Reuben originally lived west of the Jordan, and in support of this thesis he mentions the 'stone of Bohan the son of Reuben' which appears in 15.6 ‖ 18.17; but this is clearly a proof based on a place name which is not very convincing.[1] In any case, the fact that this chapter speaks always of the 'land of Gilead', which concerns only the tribes of Gad and Reuben, and that Manasseh is absent from vv. 25, 32, 33, 34, suggests that this latter tribe was added later when the passage was placed in its present context.

The emphasis on the dimensions of the altar (v. 10; Baldi translates: 'of grandiose appearance') raises a question of the nature and purpose of this edifice. The idea of an altar of disproportionate size, which at the same time is not an altar (vv. 26–28), is, to say the least, strange! Perhaps it was one of the temple-fortresses called *migdal* and studied in detail by B. Mazar.[2] They were meant both for cultic and defensive purposes. If this thesis can be maintained, we have here a fort, the purpose of which was no doubt to control the ford used by those who wanted to reach Gilgal, and which at the same time was of use in the common worship. The unique difficulty with which we are faced here is well known. In Judg. 3, not only do we hear nothing of the altar in question (which in the situation described there would have been bound to exercise its defensive functions), but, as we shall see when we deal with Judg. 3 in detail, there is not even a mention of the presence of Reuben on the far bank of the Jordan, any more than of the presence of Gad. Another possible explanation is that the term

[1] M. Noth, *The History of Israel*, London ²1960, p. 64; but for a contrary view see A. Jepsen, 'Zur Überlieferung der Vätergestalten', *Wissenschaftliche Zeitschrift*, Leipzig 3, 1953–54, pp. 265–81 (139–55 of the extract), esp. p. 273 (147); J. Dus, p. 530 n. 3.

[2] B. Mazar, 'Migdal', *EncBibl* IV, 1962, cols. 633–5. It is regrettable that a study of this importance should have been published only as a short encyclopaedia article: we read too often references to 'an unpublished paper by B. Mazar'!

'*ēd*, 'witness' (vv. 27, 28 and 34), may conceal an original '*ād*, 'pact, alliance', a term for which there is ample evidence in Aramaean in treaties of the eighth century, and which has recently been reidentified in several passages in the Old Testament.[1] In this case the building would have been a monument commemorating an alliance concluded between 'Israel' and the groups east of the Jordan which adjoin Israel, and would not have been a fortified sanctuary. But in this case, it would no longer have been (as in the text) the object of a dispute, but rather the opportunity of commemorating a fortunate outcome. As can be seen, we are still far from solving the problem, but one fact is certain: here we have a case of a conflict between groups east and west of the Jordan, of the same kind as, for example, in Judg. 12.1–6.

In its original form this narrative is unquestionably ancient; probably, with all the uncertainties which it presents, it may be related to the reference in Judg. 3.19, which is the earliest of all we possess concerning the sanctuary of Gilgal, or at least concerning one of its parts.

3. The remnants of the oldest tradition, which are sometimes difficult to recognize, are now to be found, in an obviously edited form, in various contexts. Verses 9–34 show traces of Deuteronomic redaction, and there are whole passages which belong to this redaction. The lengthy and wordy discussion of the nature of the sanctuary constructed comes from Dtr. Underlying it throughout is the conception of a single legitimate sanctuary, that of the tribal amphictyony (which it seems was Shiloh). The groups from east of the Jordan recognize the validity of this theory and declare solemnly that their edifice is only the copy of an altar, not an altar proper (v. 28), a 'witness' of the fact that they belong to Yahweh, to the generations to come who may cast doubt on this fact (vv. 24–29). Consequently, it is not to be used for offering sacrifices (vv. 26–28), which, on the contrary, will be offered in the place appointed for this purpose (v. 27: 'in his presence' in a general sense; v. 29: on 'the altar of Yahweh . . . that stands before his tabernacle', that is, in the sanctuary of Shiloh). The only way in which this passage differs from the traditional theology of Deuteronomy and of Dtr is that the sanctuary in question is not Jerusalem, which was impossible for chronological reasons; and this also explains the reluctance to mention the name of the sanctuary.

[1] F. O. Garcia-Treto, 'Genesis 31.44 and "Gilead", a possible solution', *ZAW* 79, 1967, pp. 13–17.

But it would not be surprising if the sanctuary of Shiloh belonged to the original form of this narrative. The name of Phinehas appears in I Sam. 1.3; 4.4; etc., and may very well have been one of the common names amongst the priests of this sanctuary, as Möhlenbrink rightly observes. He goes so far as to assume a conflict between Shiloh and Gilgal, which, however, cannot be proved (Noth).

4. There is some material which can be attributed to P, e.g. the person of the priest instead of Joshua (vv. 13, 30, 31, 32) and of the assembly, called *'ēdā* (vv. 12, 16), and the mention of the *nᵉśî'îm*. These two latter terms occur with great frequency in P; and it is no doubt possible to observe how the *nᵉśî'îm* have been substituted for other more primitive figures: whereas in v. 14 they are identified with the chiefs who are the heads of families of 'thousands', elsewhere (vv. 21, 30 and perhaps 32) they are distinct from them. The use of the late root *mᶜl* (vv. 16, 20, and 31), which is found frequently in Ezekiel, P and the Chronicler, is also an indication of a redaction, either contemporary with these strata of the tradition, or carried out later still.[1]

A final indication of late redaction is found in the reminiscences of Num. 25 (v. 17) and Josh. 7.1ff. (vv. 20ff.). The first is due to the P redaction, while the latter is Deuteronomic.

The intentions of Dtr are clear. In his preaching, an ancient tradition about the conflicts which came about between groups and tribes now serves to confirm his theory of a unitary conquest, and even to introduce the theme of the single sanctuary, which so far he has not had the opportunity of developing. The part played by P is relatively slight. It is concerned simply with making sure that the priest plays the role which is his due. In the present state of the sources, we can know nothing of the primitive form of the narrative and of the events which underlie it.

---

[1] For the verb cf. K. Koch, *TLZ* 90, 1965, cols. 663f.

CHAPTER 23

The Last Words of Joshua

23 ¹A long time afterward, when the LORD had given rest to Israel from all their enemies round about, and Joshua was old and well advanced in years, ²Joshua summoned all Israel, their elders and chiefs, their judges and scribes, and said to them, 'I am now old and well advanced in years; ³and you have seen all that the LORD your God has done to all these nations for your sake, for it is the LORD your God who has fought for you. ⁴Behold, I have allotted to you those nations who remain as an inheritance for your tribes and all the nations that I have already exterminated, from the Jordan to the Great Sea where the sun sets. ⁵The LORD your God will push them back before you, and drive them out of your sight; and you shall possess their land as the LORD your God promised you. ⁶Therefore be very steadfast to keep and do all that is written in the book of the law of Moses, turning aside from it neither to the right hand nor to the left, ⁷that you may not be mixed with these nations (those left here among you), or make mention of the names of their gods, or swear by them, or serve them, or bow down yourselves to them, ⁸but cleave to the LORD your God as you have done to this day. ⁹For the LORD has driven out before you great and strong nations; and as for you, no man has been able to withstand you to this day. ¹⁰One man of you puts to flight a thousand, since it is the LORD your God who fights for you, as he promised you. ¹¹Take good heed for your lives' sake, therefore, to love the LORD your God. ¹²For if you turn back, and join the remnant of these nations left here among you, and mix with them, and they with you, ¹³know assuredly that the LORD your God will not continue to drive out these nations before you; but they shall be a snare and a trap for you, a scourge on your sides, and thorns in your eyes, till you are driven off this good land which the LORD your God has given you. ¹⁴And now I am about to go the way of all the earth, and you know in your hearts and souls, all of you, that not one thing has failed of all the good things which the LORD your God promised concerning you; all have come to pass for you, not one of them has failed; ¹⁵and just as all the good things which the LORD your God promised concerning you have been fulfilled for you, so the LORD will bring upon you all the evil things, until he has driven you off this good land which the LORD your God has given you. ¹⁶If you transgress the covenant of the LORD your God, which he

commanded you, and go and serve other gods and bow down to them, the anger of the LORD will be kindled against you, and you shall be driven quickly from off the good land which he has given to you.'

Bibliography: W. Rudolph, *Der 'Elohist . . .'*, pp. 240–4; K. Baltzer, *Das Bundesformular*, WMANT 4, Neukirchen ²1964, pp. 71–3; Auzou, pp. 172ff.; F. Nötscher, 'Bundesformular und "Amtschimmel"', *BZ*, NS 9, 1965, pp. 181–214, esp. pp. 196f.; R. G. Boling, 'Some Conflate Readings in Joshua-Judges', *VT* 16, 1966, pp. 292–8, esp. pp. 296f.; L. Perlitt, *Bundestheologie im Alten Testament*, WMANT 36, Neukirchen 1969, pp. 19ff., which was not available to me.

---

[4] 'From the Jordan' is followed in MT by a parenthesis which abandons the geographical description to return to the peoples. If we follow Baldi and Noth in inverting the order of the sentence (cf. *BH*³), and in reading *weʿad hayyām*, the logical sequence is restored. V places the reference to the people at the end of the sentence. [5] For the form *yihdᵒpem* cf. *GKC* § 60a and *B-L* § 18 r. LXX has a longer text, which contains elements added from Exod. 23.28 and Deut. 7.20. [7] 'Be mixed with': literally, 'go in to'. 'Swear' is lacking in LXX; instead of the *hiphil*, since there is no causative sense here, the *qal* is usually read. 'Bow down yourselves': the root *ḥwh* (and not *šḥḥ* as was thought until recently) is the only one for which a causative form in *š* (with a *taw infixum*) is attested in biblical Hebrew.[1] The persistence of this form, found in West Semitic only in Ugaritic,[2] is explained by its traditional character in the formulae of the cult and the court. [11] 'For your lives' sake' is lacking in LXXᴮᴬ. [12] 'Mix with them': cf. the note on v. 7. [13] 'Trap': literally 'bait' (to make the bird fall into the trap). 'Scourge': the traditional translation of a word the meaning of which is unknown. [15] For the form *'ōtᵉkem* instead of *'etᵉkem* cf. *GKC* § 103b and *B-L* § 81 n'.

1. Chapter 23 gives the conclusion of the Deuteronomic edition of the narrative of the conquest. 23.1 takes up 21.43–45 and 22.1–6, while 23.16 is continued by 24.28 ‖ Judg. 2.6. Thus there is an interruption which is due to two major interpolations: 22.7–34, placed in that position, as we have seen, by a Deuteronomic redactor, its

---

[1] Cf. L. Köhler—W. Baumgartner, *Hebräisches und Aramäisches Lexicon*, fasc. 1, Leiden ³1967, ad loc., and our 'Tracce di antichi causativi in š- realizzati come radici autonome in ebraico biblico', *AION*, NS 15, 1965, pp. 17–30, esp. p. 23. In Ugaritic *ḥwy* also exists only in the '*št*' form, cf. Aistleitner, no. 912 and Gordon, no. 847.

[2] Gordon, § 9.38, pp. 83ff.

final form containing **P** elements added later; and secondly, ch.24 and Judg. 1 (+2.1–5?), which we shall examine shortly. There is no doubt about the Deuteronomic character of the chapter.

Joshua appears in a locality which is not stated. The previous chapters suggest Shiloh, while the following chapter suggests Shechem. Moreover, his personal territory was near Shechem (19.50; cf. 24.29 ‖ Judg. 2.9). In this indeterminate locality he addresses 'all Israel', who have gathered together to hear his last words, his spiritual testament. Thus the situation seems to be similar to that in ch.24, except that in ch.24 there are clear traces of a pre-Deuteronomic account. But it is probable that this chapter follows the pattern of ch.24, which it was perhaps intended to replace, because it was not possible to re-edit it fully without emptying it of its original content.

2. Israel receives the peace of Yahweh, which, as Noth points out, is a typical theme in Deuteronomy and Dtr (cf. Deut. 3.20; Josh. 1.13; 21.44; 22.4). Thus the aim of the divine intervention has been achieved. The fact that this does not correspond with reality, as in fact appears from the same narratives in Deuteronomic style in Judges and I Sam., is a difficulty which is overcome by means of the thesis that in the struggles which followed Israel only had to struggle against the remnants of the other nations, those who had not yet been completely routed, and whose strength and resistance was a result of the divine judgment against the unfaithfulness of Israel. And in fact, Yahweh announces this, with Joshua as his mouthpiece, in this very chapter (vv.13 and 15ff.). This threat is fulfilled in the next two books.

3. According to Baltzer, the structure of ch.23 clearly displays the structure of the covenant formula. If this is true, it is not surprising. We have seen that ch.23 was constructed on the pattern of ch.24, from which it borrows certain elements, and it is therefore not surprising that the redactor has also included elements relating to the making of the covenant. It is, moreover, one of the favourite themes of Deuteronomy and of Dtr in their concern to restore this theological theme in the relationship between Israel and Yahweh. The question of the covenant formula, therefore, is not a primitive element in this chapter, but is at best a theme drawn from the original model and applied here very freely.

4. Much more important, on the other hand, is the presence of allusions, deliberately enigmatic but quite clear to the careful observer, to the Babylonian exile. Verses 13–16 stress at length the possibility that Israel may be 'driven off this good land' which has been given to

it. In the first and final allusion to this possibility the verb *'bd* is used; its primary significance is 'perish', but in the *qal* it can also mean 'wander aimlessly' or 'be driven off'. The use of this verb in the present context forms a kind of negative appendix to the 'confession of faith' recorded in Deut. 26.5b–9, where the same verb describes the situation of Jacob, a wandering nomad always close to catastrophe. Thus one can assume that Dtr was aware of, and takes up again here, the theme of the return to the desert, which is found in Hos. 2.14ff.; 12.9ff. (cf. perhaps also Micah 4.10), and to which the exile is compared. Similar though less explicit threats occur in I Sam. 12, accompanied by a reference to the king.

Thus our text is a *vaticinium ex eventu* composed at a period when the threats of the prophets and the resultant judgments carried out by Yahweh towards the people in Judges, cf. I Sam. 7.2ff., had been fulfilled. This proves that the redaction of at least one stratum of Dtr took place at the exile.

And because a text like this could in no sense have been addressed to those who had remained in the country after the exile, and had had land distributed to them by the Babylonians (cf. Jer. 39.10), and had therefore no interest in the return of the exiles to reclaim what belonged to them, it seems logical to assume that it was addressed to the exiles in Babylon. These, in their own circumstances, were of course suffering from the judgment that was proclaimed, but were also looking forward to a new Exodus and a new conquest (themes developed later by Deutero-Isaiah) and had to face a similar choice: fidelity to Yahweh alone, and the refusal of any kind of assimilation (vv. 7 and 12: first of all in Babylon, and then after the return to Palestine), either ethnic or theological.[1]

Thus here we have a kind of exegesis which is, strictly speaking, 'typological': the choices which faced Israel during the carrying out and at the conclusion of the conquest (as Dtr saw them, of course) are the 'type' of the choices with which the people were faced at the moment of the restoration, before they set out on their return to their homeland. That is why Deuteronomy also incorporated in his work such a large amount of geographical material, some of it anachronistic, and some of it incomplete, but serving to keep the people's expectations alive. It would later be the task of Deutero-Isaiah to proclaim that the time was ready to be fulfilled.

[1] Cf. our 'Deuteronomistische Geschichtsauslegung während des babylonischen Exils', *Oikonomia. Festschrift O. Cullmann*, Hamburg 1966, pp. 11–17, esp. pp. 14ff.

CHAPTER 24.1–27; 8.30–35

The Assembly at Shechem

24 ¹Then Joshua gathered all the tribes of Israel to $\begin{Bmatrix} \text{Shechem} \\ \text{Shiloh} \end{Bmatrix}$, *and summoned the elders, the chiefs, the judges, and the scribes of Israel*; and they presented themselves before God. ²And Joshua said to all the people, 'Thus says the LORD, the God of Israel, "Your fathers lived of old beyond the Euphrates (*Terah, the father of Abraham and of Nahor*); and they served other gods. ³Then I took your father Abraham from beyond the River and led him through all the land of Canaan, and made his offspring many (*and I gave him Isaac*; ⁴*and to Isaac I gave Jacob and Esau. And I gave Esau the hill country of Seir to possess*). And Jacob and his children went down to Egypt [(LXX) and became there a great people, numerous and mighty,] ⁵(*And I sent Moses and Aaron*) and I plagued Egypt

$\left.\begin{matrix} \text{with what I did (MT, T, LXX}^\text{B}) \\ \text{with the signs I carried out (LXX}^\text{A}\text{, Syr)} \\ \text{with many signs and wonders (V)} \end{matrix}\right\}$ in the midst of it.

$\left.\begin{matrix} \text{Afterwards I brought you out.} \\ \text{Afterwards I brought out} \\ \text{I brought you out} \end{matrix}\right\}$ 6 $\left\{\begin{matrix} \text{And I brought out your fathers} \\ \text{— — — — — — — your fathers} \\ \text{— — — — — — — — —} \end{matrix}\right.$

$\left.\begin{matrix} \text{from Egypt (MT)} \\ \text{— — — — (LXX}^\text{B}) \\ \text{— — — — (LXX}^\text{A}) \end{matrix}\right\}$ and you came to the sea; and the Egyptians pursued your fathers with chariots and horsemen to the Red Sea.

7 $\left.\begin{matrix} \text{And they cried (MT, T, Syr)} \\ \text{And we cried (LXX)} \\ \text{And you cried (conjecture)} \end{matrix}\right\}$ to the LORD and he put darkness

between you and the Egyptians, and made the sea come upon them and cover them; and your eyes saw what I did to Egypt; and you lived in the wilderness a long time. ⁸Then I brought you to the land of the Amorites, who lived on the other side of the Jordan; they fought with you, and I gave them into your hand, and you took possession of their land, and I destroyed them before you. ⁹Then Balak the son of Zippor, King of Moab, arose and fought against Israel; and he sent and invited Balaam the son of Beor to curse you, ¹⁰but I would not listen to Balaam; and so he had to bless you; so I delivered you out of his hand. ¹¹And you went over the Jordan and came to Jericho, and the nobles of Jericho fought against you (the Amorites, the Perizzites, the Canaanites, the Hittites, the Girgashites, the Hivites, and the Jebusites), but I gave them into your hand. [12]And I sent $\begin{cases}\text{dismay} \\ \text{the hornet (LXX, V)}\end{cases}$ before you, which drove them out before you, the $\begin{cases}\text{two} \\ \text{twelve (LXX)}\end{cases}$ kings of the Amorites; it was not by your (sing.) sword or by your (sing.) bow. [13]I gave you a land on which you $\begin{cases}\text{sing.} \\ \text{versions, pl.}\end{cases}$ had not laboured, and cities which you (pl.) had not built, and you dwell therein; vineyards and oliveyards which you did not plant, and you eat of them."

14 Now therefore fear the LORD, and serve him in sincerity and in faithfulness; put away (the) gods which your fathers served beyond the River, and in Egypt, and worship the LORD. [15]And if you be unwilling to worship the LORD, choose this day whom you will worship, whether the gods your fathers worshipped in the region beyond the River, or the gods of the Amorites in whose land you dwell; but as for me and my house, we will worship the LORD.'

16 Then the people answered, 'Far be it from us that we should forsake the LORD, to worship other gods; [17]for it is the LORD our God who brought us and our fathers up from the land of Egypt, out of the house of bondage, and who did those great signs in our sight, and preserved us in all the way that we went, and among all the peoples through whom we passed; [18]and the LORD drove out before us all the peoples, the Amorites who lived in the land; therefore we also will worship the LORD, for he is our God.' [19]But Joshua said to the people, 'You cannot worship the LORD, for he is a holy God; he is a jealous God; he will not bear your transgressions or your sins. [20]If you forsake the LORD and serve foreign gods, then he will turn and do you harm, and consume you, after having done you good.' [21]And the people said to Joshua, 'Nay; but we will worship the LORD'. [22]Then Joshua said to the people, 'You are witnesses against yourselves that you have chosen the LORD, to worship him.' And they said, 'We are witnesses.' [23]He said, 'Then put away the foreign gods which are among you, and incline your heart to the LORD, the God of Israel.' [24]And the people said to Joshua, 'The LORD our God we will worship; and his voice we will obey.'

25 Then Joshua made a covenant for the people that day, and made a statute and an ordinance for them at Shechem. [26]And Joshua wrote these words in the document [of the law] of God; and he took a great stone and set it up there under the oak in the sanctuary of the LORD. [27]And Joshua said to all the people, 'Behold, this stone shall be a witness amongst us; for it has heard all the words of the LORD which he spoke to us; therefore it

shall be a witness amongst you, lest you deal falsely with your God.'

8 [30]Then Joshua built an altar on Mount Ebal to the LORD, the God of Israel, [31]*as Moses the servant of the Lord had commanded the people of Israel*, as it is written in the $\left\{ \begin{array}{l} \textit{book of the law of Moses} \\ \text{document (of the covenant)} \end{array} \right\}$, 'an altar of unhewn stones, upon which no man has lifted an iron tool'; and they offered on it burnt offerings to the LORD,and sacrificed peace offerings. [32]And there he wrote upon the stones *a copy of the law of Moses (which he had written)*, in the presence of the people of Israel. [33]And all Israel, *with their elders and officers and their judges*, stood on opposite sides of the ark *before the priests* [and (LXX)] *the Levites, the bearers of the ark of the covenant of the Lord*, half of them in front of Mount Gerizim and half of them in front of Mount Ebal, as Moses the servant of the LORD had commanded, *to bless the people of Israel in the past*. [34]And afterward he read all the words of *the law*, the blessing and the curse, according to all that is written in the $\left\{ \begin{array}{l} \textit{book of the law.} \\ \text{document of the covenant.} \end{array} \right\}$ [35]There was not a word of all that Moses commanded which Joshua did not read before all the assembly of Israel, [*the men* (LXX)] *and the women, and the little ones, and the sojourners who lived among them*.

Bibliography: 1. *On Joshua 24*: M. Noth, *Das System der zwölf Stämme Israels*, Stuttgart 1930, pp.65ff.; A. Alt, *Josua*, 1936, *KS* I, 1953, pp.176–92, esp. pp.191f.; G. von Rad, 'The Problem of the Hexateuch', 1938, in *The Problem of the Hexateuch and Other Essays*, London 1966, pp.1–78; K. Möhlenbrink, 'Die Landnahmesagen des Buches Josua', *ZAW* 56, 1938, pp.238–65, esp. pp.250–4; W. Rudolph, *Der 'Elohist' von Exodus bis Josua*, BZAW 68, Berlin 1938, pp.239ff.; Noth, *UGS*, pp.181ff.; E. Auerbach, 'Die grosse Überarbeitung der biblischen Bücher', SVT I, 1953, pp.1–10, esp. pp.3ff.; G. E. Mendenhall, 'Covenant Forms in Israelite Tradition', *BA* 17, 1954, pp.50–76, esp. pp.67–70; E. Nielsen, 'The Burial of Foreign Gods', *StTh* 8, 1954, pp.103–22; C. A. Keller, 'Über einige alttestamentliche Heiligtumslegenden I', *ZAW* 67, 1955, pp.141–68, esp. pp.143ff.; E. Nielsen, *Shechem*, Copenhagen 1955, pp.86ff.; J. Muilenberg, 'The Form and Structure of the Covenant Formulations', *VT* 9, 1959, pp.347–65, esp. pp.357–60; K. Baltzer, *Das Bundesformular*, Neukirchen 1960, pp.29–37; J. L'Hour, 'L'Alliance de Sichem', *RB* 69, 1962, pp.1–36, 161–84 and 350–68, esp. pp.9ff.; D. J. McCarthy, *Treaty and Covenant*, Rome, 1963, pp.145ff.; G. Schmitt, *Der Landtag von Sichem*, Stuttgart 1964; C. H. Giblin, 'Structural Patterns in Jos. 24.1–25', *CBQ* 26, 1964, pp.50–69; Auzou, pp.182ff.; G. E. Wright, *Shechem. The Biography of a Biblical City*, London 1965, chs.VIII–IX and esp. pp.134ff.; S. Herrman, *Die prophetischen Heilserwartungen im Alten Testament*, BWANT V, 5, Stuttgart 1965, pp.78ff.; R. E. Clements, *Abraham and David*, SBT II, 5,

London 1967, pp. 84ff.; L. Perlitt, *Bundestheologie im Alten Testament*, WMANT 36, Neukirchen 1969, pp. 239ff., which was not available to me. 2. *On Joshua 8.30–35*; Noth, *UGS*, pp. 43ff.; C. A. Keller, op. cit., pp. 143ff.; E. Nielsen, op. cit., pp. 74ff.; O. Eissfeldt, *Das Lied Moses, Deut. 32.1–43 und das Lehrgedicht Asaphs Ps. 78*, Berlin 1958, pp. 45ff.; J. A. Soggin, 'Zwei umstrittene Stellen aus dem Überlieferungskreis um Schechem', *ZAW* 73, 1961, pp. 78–87, esp. pp. 82–7; K. Baltzer, op. cit., pp. 36, 66f.; V. Maag, 'Syrien-Palästina', in H. Schmökel, *Kulturgeschichte des Alten Orients*, Stuttgart 1961, pp. 448–605, esp. pp. 536ff.; Auzou, pp. 106ff.

3. *On the patriarchs and their deities*: A. Alt, 'The God of the Fathers', 1929, in *Essays on Old Testament History and Religion*, Oxford 1966, pp. 3–77; 'Die Wallfahrt von Sichem nach Bethel', 1938, *KS* I, pp. 79–88; E. Nielsen, 'The Burial of Foreign Gods', *StTh* 8, 1954, pp. 103–22; L. Rost, 'Die Gottesverehrung der Patriarchen', SVT VII, 1960, pp. 346–59; F. M. Cross, Jnr, 'Yahwe and the God of the Patriarchs', *HTR* 55, 1962, pp. 225–59, esp. pp. 234ff.; V. Maag, 'Sichembund und Vätergotter', *Hebräische Wortforschung, Festschrift W. Baumgartner*, SVT XVI, Leiden 1967, pp. 205–18.

4. *On the confessions of faith*: W. Richter, 'Beobachtungen zur theologischen Systembildung in der alttestamentlichen Literatur anhand des "kleinen geschichtlichen Credo" ', *Wahrheit und Verkündigung, M. Schmaus zum 70 Geburtstag*, II, Paderborn 1967, pp. 175–212.

---

[1] *š^ekemā*: LXX, here and in v. 25, has the reading *Σηλω* = Shiloh. We do not know what lies behind this variant. In the context it is improbable, but it is certainly original within the framework of LXX (the variant *Συχεμ*, found in a few MSS, is clearly secondary). Perhaps it is due to the fact that at the period of the Greek translation, Shechem was inhabited by the Samaritans. But in that case, it would not be clear why the translator should have emphasized this point here. Or again, perhaps it is a harmonization with 18.1, one of the very rare passages from the P source which is found in Joshua. We do not know.[1] [2] *hannāhār*: T and the Arabic version add that it is the Euphrates, as also in v. 3. The mention of the 'father of Abraham' does not fit the plural, and seems to be a gloss, no doubt in order to make it clear that the patriarch did not practice idolatry (Schmitt). *'^elōhīm '^aḥērīm*: T paraphrases: 'the abomination of the pagans', an ethnical and theological reflection of its own time. 'Canaan' is not found in LXX, which had the hyperbolic 'throughout all the earth'. [3] *wā'ōlēk*: cf. *GKC* § 69 x. *wā'arbe*: K has the short form, Q has the long,

---

[1] For the state of the question, cf. H. H. Rowley, *From Joseph to Joshua*, London 1950, pp. 125ff.; G. E. Wright—H. M. Orlinsky, *BASOR* 169, 1963, p. 28 n. 31.

cf. *GKC* § 75gg. Normally the *waw* consecutive has only the short form of the imperfect, so that K seems preferable. At the end of [4] LXX adds: καὶ ἐγένοντο ἐκεῖ εἰς ἔθνος μέγα καὶ πολὺ καὶ κραταιόν, perhaps recalling Deut. 26.5b (quoted, however, according to MT and not LXX). The mention of Isaac, Jacob and Esau in vv. 3–4 is a further intrusive element, because the large numbers of descendants can refer only to Jacob and not to the others, far less to the period preceding Isaac. It is probably a later gloss, and the same is true of the mention of the greatness of the people and the two leaders of the Exodus in the following verse. [5] *wā'ešlaḥ* . . . *'aḥᵃrōn*: lacking in LXX, it destroys the rhythm of the narrative. L'Hour would keep it as a traditional element, cf. Micah 6.1ff. (p. 24), but for the same reason, as is pointed out by Giblin (cf. Schmitt) it can be regarded as an addition. *ka'ᵃšer* makes little sense at first sight, and LXX read: LXXᴮ ἐν οἷς ἐποίησεν followed by T, while LXXᴬ and Syr have ἐν σημείοις, cf. V: *multis signis atque portentis*. The reading of MT becomes comprehensible, however, if one assumes that the reader, or hearer, knows what is being referred to, and the phrase would mean 'I plagued them like this and like that'; this was recognized by Kaufmann and Dhorme. Thus it would not be necessary to modify the text. In general, however, scholars prefer one of the two LXX readings, and Hertzberg argues for the second, because it establishes a link between the sign and its fulfilment. LXXᴮ has neither the last word of v. 5 nor the first of [6], and goes straight on to the mention of the fathers, while LXXᴬ omits the first three words of v. 6. [7] LXX has ἀνεβοήσαμεν but the other versions confirm MT. The proposal made in *BH*³, note a, to read the second person pl. is therefore not acceptable. *ma'ᵃpēl* is a *hapax legomenon* which should be explained (but not corrected, as most commentators do, regarding the *mem* as a dittography with that which precedes it) by the root *'pl*, from which comes *'ōpel*, darkness; moreover, LXX has νεφέλην = a cloud. [8] *wā'ābī'h*: whereas Q reads the normal form, K has a long form, similar to that noted above (v. 3), and which is formed as though the root were *b'h* instead of *bw'*, *wayyillāhᵃmū* is not found in LXXᴮ, while LXXᴬ has the singular *w'šmydym*. LXX and V have the second person pl.; the verb comes somewhat late in the sentence in any case (Schmitt). [10] *'ābītī*: LXX has the third person. *wayᵉbārek*: V and Syr have the first person. [11] *ba'ᵃlē*: LXX has οἱ κατοικοῦντες = *yōšᵉbē* or *tōšᵉbē*. [12] *haṣṣir'ah* is not the 'wasp' or 'hornet' (LXX τὴν σφηκίαν, V *crambonem*, and so Abel, Dhorme and Kaufmann) but 'dismay', a typical consequence of divine intervention in the course of the holy war.[1] *šᵉnē*: LXX has δώδεκα, a variant which we shall discuss below. [14] *yr'w* is vocalized with the aid of elements borrowed from *lāmed hē* verbs, as is often the case with *lāmed 'ālep* verbs, cf. *GKC* § 75 oo. *bᵉtāmīm*:

---

[1] Cf. L. Köhler, *ZAW* 54, 1936, p. 291; G. von Rad, *Der Heilige Krieg im Alten Testament*, ATANT 20, Zurich 1951, pp. 1off.

note the use of the plural to indicate an abstract concept, singular in itself, *GKC* § 124 d. The two terms are well translated by V: *perfecto corde atque verissimo*. *et-ʾelōhīm*: LXX adds τοὺς ἀλλοτρίους = *ʾelōhē hannēkār*, and so does Syr (cf. *BH³*, note a), while T once again has 'abominations' (cf. v. 2), with no other details. In any case, the sense requires that *ʾelōhīm* should have an article in MT. [15] *ʾelōhīm* presents a problem similar to that in the previous verse: here again, the context requires an article. LXX adds τῶν πατέρων ὑμῶν, suppressing the relative. *bēʿeber* appears in this form in K, and in some western traditions of Q, LXX (ἐν τῷ . . .), in a few MSS of T, in Syr and V; while in Q (eastern) and other recensions of T we have *mēʿeber*. The second reading is more recent and ignores the double sense of *bᵉ*, which sometimes can also mean 'from' (cf. C. H. Gordon).[1] *wᵉānōkī* is a good example of the adversative value of this con junction. At the end. LXX adds: ὅτι ἅγιός ἐστιν, an anticipation of v. 19.- [17] The mention of the fathers is not found in Syr, while LXX, on the other hand, lacks the word *ʾereṣ*, and the words from *mibbēt* to *hāʾēlle*, [18] LXX puts the mention of the 'peoples' after that of the Amorites. [19] *qannō*: the ordinary form is *qannāʾ*. It is an example of the tendency in West Semitic to transform *ā* into *ō*. Note the use of the verb *nsʾ* with the meaning 'bear, tolerate'. [20] *kī* is used here with the special value that it has in legal texts, where it introduces a law formulated in casuistic style,[2] and it means, as in Accadian, 'If the case is that . . .'; the most numerous examples are to be found in Exod. 21–23. [22] LXX does not record the reply of the people: Baldi believes that it is not original because if it was it should be followed by 'and Joshua said'. [25] *lāʿām* must be translated 'for the people' (with T), because Joshua is their authorized representative who receives their assent and draws up the agreement, cf. the following verse. LXX has πρὸς and Syr 'with the people', but neither give the exact sense: the words are lacking in V. [26] The terms of the agreement are inscribed *bᵉsēper tōrat ʾelōhīm*. The phrase gives the impression that it is late because it seems to presuppose the existence of a *tōrāh*, a book, a scripture. In fact, at the end of the second millenium and at the beginning of the first, the word *sēper* should have the meaning 'written document of a treaty', as has now been proved by the Aramaic inscription of Sephireh from the middle of the eighth century, III, 1.4.[3] Cf. several places where this translation solves numerous problems: Exod. 24.7; Deut. 27.2–8; II Kings 23.2, 21; Isa. 30.8; Isa. 34.16; etc. One can in any case assume

---

[1] *Ugaritic Textbook*, Rome 1965, § 10.1.

[2] A. Alt, 'Die Ursprünge des israelitischen Rechts', 1934, *KS* I, 1953, pp. 287ff.

[3] For this text, cf. *KAI* no. 224, and J. Fitzmyer, *The Aramaic Inscriptions of Sefire*, Biblica et Orientalia 19, Rome 1967, s.v. in the index (with bibliography); cf. also D. H. Hillers, *Treaty-curses and the Old Testament Prophets*, Biblica et Orientalia 16, Rome 1964, pp. 45ff.

that the word *tōrāh* was added much later, to adapt the expression to a period where this sense of the word *sēper* was no longer in use. *h'lh* would normally be vocalised *hā'ēlāh* = the oak, the terebinth (cf. Gen. 35.4). [27] The translations have certain additions, but they do not alter the sense of the text. [8.30] *'āz* = 'then', assumes that the text follows something which precedes, which cannot be either the Ai episode (as in MT) or the beginning of ch. 9 (as in LXX). On the other hand, these verses fit much better if they are placed after 24.27; they then recount the writing down of the words of the covenant (24.26a) and the setting up of a stone (24.26b), followed by the construction of an altar. The name of Yahweh is that found in v. 2 (cf. ad loc.), *'ēbal* is the mountain dominating the valley of Shechem/Nablus on the north, cf. Deut. 27.4 (where the Samar. rightly reads Gerizim) and 11.29 (where the curse has to be uttered on Ebal). [31] *sēper tōrat mōše* is once again a late expression which presupposes the conception of scripture as a book, but which can equally be related to the meaning mentioned above (cf. 24.25ff.) of *sēper*, a term which is added to in this way in the present passage because it was no longer understood. The result is a post-exilic anachronism. [32] *mišnēh* is translated δευτερονόμιον in LXX. *'ašer kātab* is lacking in LXX[B], and, as Noth remarks (*BH*[3] and commentary), interrupts the context. It cannot, in fact, refer to Moses, but to the work of Joshua; but of course it cannot be understood as an object: 'which *tōrāh* he (Joshua) had written' (Hertzberg), but this makes the construction of the sentence somewhat clumsy. [33] For this somewhat different list, cf. 24.1. *hā'ām yiśrā'ēl* and *wehaḥeṣeyō* seem 'grammatically impossible' (Noth), cf. *GKC* § 127 c.f. While traditional grammar does not allow a double determination on any occasion, this form does in fact exist in the Phoenician inscription of Karatepe, from the second half of the eighth century,[1] where, in 1.1, we find the expression *hbrk b'l* = 'the blessed of Baal', and analogous forms are also to be found in the OT.[2] Thus the anomaly is not as great as has hitherto been supposed. Rather, it shows how ancient the text is (or, which is also possible, the artificial use of archaic forms). [34] 'The blessing and the curse' are not later additions, as is often supposed (e.g. *BH*[3], note a), but belong to the conclusion of the making of every covenant in the ancient Near East. The blessing was destined for the person who observed its stipulations, and the curse for whoever infringed them. [35] *hannāšim*: LXX has τοῖς ἀνδράσι καὶ ταῖς γυναιξίν, an expression which recalls Deut. 31.12, and which perhaps ought to be preferred (*BH*[3], note a).

There is a basic parallelism, in spite of important differences of content, between the farewell discourse of ch. 23 and the address of

---

[1] For this text, cf. *KAI* no. 26.
[2] Cf. our note in *Bibl* 44, 1963, p. 521 n. 2.

Joshua in the present chapter, because ch. 23 is in fact derived from ch. 24. And just as in ch. 23 the narrative was basically Deuteronomic in origin, here too we find Deuteronomic material introduced, becoming dominant in 8.30–35. But by contrast with ch. 23, the underlying narrative contains elements which are certainly authentic and ancient, cf. vv. 25–27, with other passages also: e.g. in vv. 11–12 there are clear links with the Book of the Covenant, especially with Exod. 23.20–31. These elements form a kind of appendix to the Deuteronomic edition of Joshua, and consist only of fragments of the original narrative. The same statement can for the most part be made about the theological issues in the whole chapter, contrary to what is claimed by Schmitt and Richter. Schmitt himself, in fact, recognizes that it is improbable that a post-exilic redactor would have omitted all reference to Sinai, for such an omission is unknown at that period (whereas it is frequent in the pre-exilic period). Moreover, we may add that if the redaction had been carried out in this period it would have supplied the Samaritans with a most telling argument in favour of the supremacy of their Shechem sanctuary. Thus one is virtually obliged to concede that the essential basis of the present passage was composed at a much earlier period. Hertzberg clearly perceived that the theme of ch. 24 is a very primitive one: *Who* is to be worshipped? In ch. 23, on the other hand, the Yahwist answer seems already to have been given to this question, and the problem that arises is *how*. Thus we are faced in ch. 24 with the question, in all its primitive urgency, of the fundamental and inescapable choice with which the assembly is faced by the proclamation of the word of God and the testimony given by Joshua and his supporters.

The Deuteronomic redaction sought to place ch. 24 in the same framework as in ch. 23: the dying Joshua gathers together the tribes of Israel to dictate to them his last wishes and to leave them his spiritual testament. But this construction on the part of the redactor is improbable, as can be seen from the evident logical difficulties which it involves, e.g. the time which must have passed between the departure of those who were sent to call the people together and the arrival of the delegates (consisting in fact of the leading figures of the tribes, according to the Deuteronomic addition in v. 1), particularly as, according to the same Deuteronomic redaction, he had already given his farewell in ch. 23. But the scene becomes perfectly probable if the assembly was called together at the period of the year fixed for this purpose, and if Joshua there carried out the functions of presi-

dent of the assembly. During this assembly, it seems, a festival of the
covenant was held, no doubt by recalling the occasion when it was
originally made and by renewing the people's commitment, following the example of what had happened at the earlier stage of the
conquest. This is why there are no aetiologies in the present passage,
except in the conclusion of the chapter (following Noth, and disagreeing with Alt), nor any ἱεροὶ λόγοι, since these were all linked
with the patriarchs, in whose time the sanctuary already existed.[1]
And this also explains why Joshua (as we saw in the introduction, § 4)
does not seem to have been introduced here at a later period, but to
be 'at home' here, as Moses was in the narratives of the first occasion
when the covenant was made.[2] A. Alt's study has made it virtually
certain that Joshua occupied this position (cf. 24.6.).

However, the work of the Deuteronomic editor reappears throughout the text (one can observe the interest of Deuteronomy and Dtr
in the ancient confessions of faith, cf. Deut. 26.4ff.; 6.20ff.). The
passage retains its basic unity, in spite of many amplifications, as
Muilenburg has shown. He is supported by L'Hour (who emphasizes
the liturgical character of the chapter) and by Giblin (who demonstrates its symmetry and logical progress). This must be maintained
against all attempts to divide the text, the most notable being that of
Möhlenbrink (who divides it into two sources). From v. 11 on (cf. ad
loc.) there is no longer any connection with the pre-Deuteronomic
elements in Josh. 1–12; and similarly, there are none with the
Pentateuch and its traditions, except in vv. 9–10 (cf. ad loc.); and
these were the facts which enabled von Rad and Noth to state, quite
rightly, that the traditions which are recorded here are both ancient
and authentic. If this were not so, they maintain, the later redactor
would have preferred to embroider familiar themes and traditions,
instead of departing from them. Thus we must reject the negative
view of Josh. 24 put forward by Auerbach, who, in rather gratuitous
fashion, considers it a Deuteronomic construction of no value. The
situation of Josh. 8.30–35 is more complex, because the tradition it
contains has been largely obscured by the redactional process. There,
too, however, we shall see that important primitive elements can be
distinguished.

[1] Cf. the study of Keller, pp. 148–54.
[2] Cf. recently, in disagreement with von Rad and Noth, G. Fohrer, *Überlieferung
und Geschichte des Exodus*, BZAW 91, Berlin 1964, pp. 34ff. for the latter problem and
the question of the connection between the tradition of the desert and that of Sinai.

Joshua 24 and Josh. 8.30ff. shows Israel at Shechem, which can be identified with complete certainty with *tell balāṭa*, at the gates of Nablus. But we know nothing about how Israel got there. In fact the OT tells us nothing about any occupation of the town by force at this period (Gen. 34 is much older, and in any case, it does not seem that Simeon and Levi succeeded in occupying the place, cf. Gen. 49.5ff.), nor anything about a peaceful settlement in this region. There is a great deal to be said for the latter possibility, the most important evidence being that of archaeological excavation. There is no trace whatsoever of any battles or destruction throughout the entire second half of the thirteenth century and whole of the twelfth century. The first destruction established dates from the end of the twelfth century, and is usually identified with the act of vengeance of Abimelech, Judg. 9.45.[1] The Bible states that at a very early period the city was included in the territory of Manasseh (cf. Num. 26.31ff.; Josh. 17.2), but was situated almost at the frontier with Ephraim, which explains why it is sometimes regarded as an Ephraimite city (Josh. 20.17; 21.21; cf. I Kings 12.25), in particular since under Solomon (the middle of the tenth century), Ephraim and the frontier region of Manasseh were rapidly amalgamated into a single province: the 'Mountain of Ephraim' (I Kings 4.7ff.). Thus it is not surprising that the hero of ch. 24 is Joshua the Ephraimite (cf. the introduction § 4). And if the theory of a peaceful occupation of the region is true (and we have seen that from the archaeological point of view this is most likely), the logical conclusion is that this occupation was made with the agreement of the local population. There is also important evidence in favour of this conclusion: in Judg. 8 and 9 there are good relations between the Israelites and the people of Shechem, and only the episode of Abimelech disturbed them, leading to the destruction by the king of the rebel fortress.

Once this is granted, it is possible to see in their true light the statements made in ch. 24, which to some extent have been obscured by the Deuteronomic redaction. It will be seen at once that they are frequently concerned with the making and renewing of the covenant, either as an event taking place for the first time, or as something which seems to be traditional. It is not by chance that an important passage, Deut. 27, mentions Shechem in exactly this context. This is why we have placed 8.30–35 after 24.27, because the theme of these two passages is exactly the same.

[1] For this problem, cf. Wright, op. cit. ch. IX.

This situation leads us to ask what kind of covenant was made and celebrated at Shechem. The reply is obvious: it could only have been the covenant of Sinai which was renewed in this place. But there is more to it than this. In 24.15b two ethnic groups face each other: Joshua and his 'house', who have already chosen for Yahweh, and the others, who are invited to make the same choice. Thus there was a moment when the covenant of Sinai was extended to the population of Shechem and its environments (according to the hypothesis of Rost and Bright); or else, as others believe on the basis of the work of Noth, we have here the making of a covenant between the house of Joseph (probably Benjamin and the Rachel tribes) and other groups (perhaps the Leah tribes) who in part were already in the region (and here one may mention the abortive attempt at a complete conquest in Gen. 34) in order to form 'all Israel'. In this case, the Joseph group, to which Joshua the Ephraimite belonged, and which was the bearer of the Exodus tradition, would have invited the others to follow them in the common cult; and their affirmative reply would in fact have led to the setting up of the amphictyony of the twelve tribes of Israel. Of course these two views are not mutually exclusive, and are perhaps complementary. We shall look in their place at the few elements which remain of such an agreement.

At first sight the present passage seems to be out of context, because it has nothing to do with the book. Bright attempted to restore its original context by inserting ch. 24 after ch. 8, which, as we shall see, is not evidently in place in its present context; but this assumes the historical nature of chs. 1.3–5 and 7–8, and this, from all we have seen, is very doubtful. Now if it is not possible to maintain their historicity, it is clear that the position of ch. 24 and 8.30–35 becomes illogical, because the book no longer has any progressive structure in any real sense. We shall return to this presently. In any case, even if we do not have any definite proof of the original unity of 8.30ff. and ch. 24, it is valuable to consider them together, since they deal with identical or very similar things.

Shechem continued to be an important centre: it was first the provisional capital of the kingdom of Israel (I Kings 12.25), and remained important even when it was no longer a religious centre, because of the existence of the new royal sanctuary at Bethel. According to a study by Alt, in fact, the procession which began a festival at Bethel still left from Shechem (cf. the commentary on vv. 25ff.). In the post-exilic period it became the religious centre of the Samaritans, a role which it continued to play during the New Testament period. Even at the present day one can find there the remnants of the Samaritan group; Christians venerate the well of Jacob there and Moslems the tomb of Joseph, while until 1947–48 the latter monument was also the object of pilgrimages on the part of the Jews. In Deuteronomy itself, as we have seen, there are important elements indicating that the book originated in Shechem, until it was taken to Jerusalem to begin a religious reform which later became the model for the whole of post-exilic Judaism (II Kings 22–23). Thus we can divide the passages as follows:

(a) Preamble, vv. 1–2a;
(b) Confession of faith, vv. 2a–13;
(c) Invitation to make a choice and the people's reply, vv. 14–24;
(d) Making of the covenant, 24.25–27; 8.30–35; 24.28;
(e) Various comments on the surroundings of Shechem, 24.29–33.

(a) Preamble (24.1–2a); (b) Confession of faith (24.2b–13)

[1] The beginning of ch. 24 is very similar to that of ch. 23, and reveals the 'hand of Dtr' (Hertzberg), which is evident even in the names of those who are addressed. For the 'scribes', cf. 1.10 and 3.2.

[2] Here the recitation of the ancient Credo presents elements independent of the tradition of the Pentateuch, even though its framework is the same (Noth). It is an autonomous cultic tradition (von Rad, Noth), the content of which is on the whole identical with the episode recorded in the Pentateuch, but which makes use of its own terminology. We find at the beginning the expression 'Yahweh, the God of Israel', which often occurs in relation to the sanctuary at Shechem (cf. Gen. 33.20; Josh. 8.30; 24.2, 23), though not always, as Noth's statement, p. 139, claims rather too categorically. Rost and Cross consider it to be the formula by which Yahweh came progressively to be identified with the supreme Canaanite god *'el*, a thesis which is also maintained independently of these passages by W. H. Schmidt.[1] In any case, the title seems to be an ancient one. Here we have the recitation of the Credo with the precise purpose of obliging the assembled people to make a choice. On the other hand, we have the traditional gods of the patriarchs when they left Mesopotamia,

---

[1] *Königtum Gottes in Ugarit und Israel*, BZAW 80, Berlin ²1966, s. v. in the analytic index.

gods which are presented as accompanying their believers as they change their dwelling place, and as being now ready to be assimilated with the indigenous gods, with the typical tolerance of all polytheist religion (cf. also Ezek. 20.7; 23.1ff.); on the other hand there is Yahweh, who from now on is also the traditional god of the patriarchs, who too accompanied them as they journeyed, the difference being that he whose mighty acts in the past are solemnly affirmed and made a present reality for the assembled community by the confession of faith (cf. the use of the first person in vv. 5b and 7), now makes a totally exclusive claim. A syncretist solution, such as was attempted by many groups amongst the Israelite population, is therefore impossible, and that is why the alternative presented here is a strict either-or. A few centuries later, Elijah on Carmel (I Kings 18.21) adopted the same attitude (the translation of the key words in the passage is doubtful, but the sense is as follows): either Yahweh or Baal, the local god. The idea that a deity has geographical limitations ('the gods beyond the River': Euphrates) is typical of all the ancient Near East and classical antiquity: the gods were roughly equivalent, but under various forms which we might term hypostases, they exercised sovereignty over some regions rather than others. This raised the question of their relationship to each other, particularly for the worshipper who often moved from one place to another: further on, in v. 14, they are joined by the gods of Egypt. Thus the former nomads, at the moment when they settled, could have lost Yahweh who had accompanied them during their wanderings, and abandoned him for the local gods, or at best could have made a place for him in the local pantheon. This conception was a real and living force even in Israel, as can be seen from I Sam. 26.19. To change one's dwelling place meant placing oneself under the rule of other gods.

The description of the religion of Israel's ancestors in Mesopotamia is much more realistic here than in the Pentateuch. The latter makes only a bare allusion to the episode of the teraphim in Gen. 31.19ff., cf. the mention of Yahweh on a level with a pagan god in 31.53. But here we have more explicit detail. We even have a statement of fact about the gods worshipped in Egypt, while the Pentateuch never mentions them. Naturally, no judgment is made about the past; all we have is a simple statement of fact which well reflects the religious practice of that age. The situation of the exiles to whom the Deuteronomic preaching was addressed was very similar. The region was the same, and the problem of a decision which had to be taken was one they faced almost every day.

[3] The current religious practice with regard to the geographical sphere of influence of different gods is violently interrupted here by the divine intervention which shatters what appears to be the natural order of things in the religious field. God calls Abram to him and leads him to emigrate to an unknown country (cf. Gen. 12.1ff. [J.]; 15.1ff., [E.]). He makes him the bearer of a promise which extends to the whole of humanity, and this is in essence one of the most certain elements in the history of the patriarchs. Here and there the text we are examining is interspersed with glosses, which present no problem by their interpretation of it, but make it somewhat laboured.

Thus the alternative lies in a choice between a personal deity, who accompanies those who believe in him wherever they go, and above all in migrations made in his name (an unheard-of thing at that period, found only amongst nomads), and the various local gods who have to be worshipped as soon as one enters their sphere of influence. It was also unheard-of for such an alternative to be posed in such plain terms: would it not be possible, if the worst came to the worst, to worship both Yahweh and the local gods at the same time? We are told that this is radically impossible as far as Yahweh is concerned. Another possibility would be to see in these verses the fusion of the deity of Sinai, associated with the Exodus, and that of the fathers, linked to the persons of the patriarchs, which were respectively the gods of the two groups involved (Herrman in a recent study). The question is no doubt more complex: the reference to the pagan gods whom the fathers are said to have worshipped and the omission of any clear reference to Sinai and the god of Sinai makes it difficult to accept this solution.

In the same verse the confession of faith emphasizes that the first stage of the promise has been carried out. In Isaac, Jacob and Esau, if we accept all the glosses, but at least in Jacob and his descendants, the prophecy of a numerous posterity has been fulfilled. God has faithfully produced the first instalment, which is a certain guarantee that the others will be forthcoming.

[4–5] The historical summary is continued. Its principal components have been considerably amplified by glosses and various additions, an indirect example, according to Hertzberg, of the liberty with which the text was treated (both by additions and perhaps also by

omissions) before the period of literalist orthodoxy. One recension
assumes that Israel knew how God had struck Egypt with various
plagues, while others try to make this clear.

[6–7] With regard to the preservation of the text, the situation is
the same here as in the preceding verses, notably at the end of v. 5
and the beginning of v. 6. One recension assumes that there was great
interest in the believer's regarding the past events as contemporary
with him, while another is more concerned with the actual course
taken by events. The same is true of the main verb in v. 7: LXX once
again has the first person plural, while in MT and elsewhere the third
person plural is found, in conformity with Exod. 14.10. There follows
a 'presentation of the events of the Red Sea in the style of a free paraphrase' (Hertzberg). The description of the disaster to the Egyptians
omits the entry of the pursuers into the water, and only states that it
was by the water that they were destroyed.

[8–10] These verses emphasize the warlike nature of the passage
through the kingdoms east of the Jordan. It is the only passage to do
this (for the Amorites of this region, cf. Num. 21.23–35; chs. 22–24;
32). The assertion in the present passage is in fact contradicted by
Judg. 11.25 and probably by Deut. 23.3ff. Apart from this historical
problem, which is difficult to solve, the astonishment of Israel looking
back upon its own history and realizing the miracle which had
brought it into existence seems to derive from the same tradition. On
the other hand, the tradition concerning Balaam is wholly in agreement, except for its brevity, with that of Num. 22–24. The very
ancient conception of the pagan wise man who also had dealings with
Yahweh, which is found in the Pentateuch, seems also to be accepted
here.

[11–12] The tradition of battles round Jericho is a vestige of the
very ancient traditions which are preserved in fragmentary form in
ch. 2, in 4.12ff. and in 6.22ff., which spoke of an armed expedition and
the conquest of the town with the aid of a ruse. As we have seen, this
tradition was completely, or almost completely, excluded from the
liturgy at Gilgal (chs. 3–6). Here, too, the author of a later gloss has
tried to turn the campaign against Jericho into a struggle against a
coalition formed by the various peoples of the country, quoted in
accordance with a stereotyped list (cf. the commentary on 3.10). This
reference takes the narrative outside the framework of the Jordan
depression and extends it to the whole of Palestine. The dismay which
went before Israel could not but seize all the kings of the country. The

mention of the 'two kings of the Amorites' (who are usually Og, King of Bashan and Sihon, cf. a concordance) does not refer here to the land east of the Jordan, as is the case elsewhere, but to persons from the west of the Jordan, who must be sought either in the Jericho region, or elsewhere within the framework of Palestine. In any case it is strange (unless it should be placed after v.8, as Bright suggests), because it can be explained neither by adopting the reading of LXX ('12') nor by reference to the list of the 31 kings of Joshua 12. The reading in LXX is no doubt intended to give the impression of a great number, and uses the figure 12 because it indicates a round number, a complete number. Another possibility is that we have here, as in the case of the 'Hittites' in 1.4 (cf. ad loc.), a formula employed by the Assyrian annals, in which in fact we find, in a stereotyped form, 12 kings for the region consisting of Syria and Palestine (*ANET*, p.279b). The end of v.12 and [13] emphasize that the carrying out of the promises is an act of grace, especially v.13, which uses a kind of 'inventory of good deeds' formula, well known from oriental treaties. Thus it was neither the bravery, the cunning nor the wisdom of men which had given Israel what it possessed; it was God, who in this way had desired to carry out his ancient promises. This is obvious from the 'dismay' with which the adversary is seized (the translation 'hornets' suggested to Garstang the idea that Egypt had contributed involuntarily to the conquest by weakening the local city states, the hornet sometimes being the symbol of Egypt; but this seems improbable, cf. pp.258ff.). This theme is also attested in Deut. 6.10ff., which presents it in terms very similar to those found here; on the other hand, the theme of a violent conquest occurs more readily in the oldest passages (Gen. 48.22; Gen. 49; Deut. 33; Judg. 5 etc.), where there is an emphasis on the battle, and where, even though the decisive factor is always the intervention of Yahweh, human bravery is considered to have contributed to the success of the enterprise. This change of emphasis takes on a special significance when it is seen in the context of the exiled nation. The prophets had preached judgment to them because they had trusted in their own powers (cf. for example, Isa. 2.7ff.; 30.16; 31.1, etc.; Jer. 51.21; Deut. 17.16; etc.), and here we have an insistence upon the absence of all merit. Israel will not be saved from the exile by its own bravery, nor by any action of its own, and the second Exodus, like the first, will be purely and simply a sign of divine grace towards Israel, and consequently towards the whole of humanity.

(c) The invitation to make a choice and the people's reply (24.14–24)

[**14–15**] Suddenly, the text passes from the direct word of God (for the confession of faith is taken this way) to human preaching. According to the religious ideas of the period, discussed above, entering a new country meant that the people placed themselves under the jurisdiction of new gods, abandoning their traditional deities for those of the country. And this is one of the terms of the choice set out before the united people, which in all probability, as we have seen, was formed on the one hand by the Joseph group, centred on their leader Joshua, and on the other hand either by Canaanite elements sympathetic to Israel or else – though this does not exclude the first – of groups similar to Joshua's group (e.g. the group of the 'Leah tribes', whose presence in this region is attested by Gen. 34). In any case, the groups whose leader was Joshua have already taken their decision and are waiting only for the others to take theirs, following their example. A decision for Yahweh will, it seems, make of two groups who are already ethnically related a true community, in spite of all the differences which divide them. A decision in favour of the religion of the locality will inevitably bring about a breach between the two groups, which hitherto seemed to have enjoyed good relations, as is seen by the peaceful infiltration of one of them into the Shechem region. Joshua's invitation contains no escape clause and no room for compromise: either you do as we have done, and it is logical that you should do, because you have been witnesses of the same marvellous works of God towards us and towards yourselves; or else you decide differently, in which case our relations are terminated. Here Yahweh clearly appears as a god who is not tied to any territory, but who is on the contrary the sovereign of the whole world, so that it is his right, and lies within his power, to grant Canaan to Israel, the people whom he has chosen to carry out his plans in history. A choice between him on the one hand, and on the other hand the gods of Mesopotamia, Egypt or Canaan, all of whom were tied to their own country, may seem possible in itself, but the form in which the choice is presented here makes it absurd, as all paganism is fundamentally absurd, and a consequence of human sin. Thus, as Hertzberg very clearly shows, the choice is implicitly the same as that contained in the first commandment (Exod. 20.1ff. ‖ Deut. 5.7ff.). But at the period of the preaching of Deuteronomy and of Dtr the choice seemed equally inescapable: for Israel in Canaan the gods of Mesopotamia were no longer of any importance, but for Israel in exile in Babylon it was an existential choice which had to be made every day: fidelity or compromise, the hope of returning to the promised land or integration into Mesopotamian society.

A historical fact of the utmost importance can be derived indirectly from this passage: that of the origin of Israel as an amphictyony of twelve tribes. On the one hand we have a group united round Joshua which has already made a choice for Yahweh, while on the other hand there is a second group which is in the process of making the decision. This dichotomy was to recur throughout the whole pre-exilic history of Israel, cf. the division between Israel (the north) and Judah (the south, the only tribe of the Leah group to acquire any ethnical and political importance, to the point at which it became the bearer of the authentic traditions of Israel, which originally belonged to the north!).

[16–18] The reply of the people on this occasion, and every time the festival of the renewal of the covenant was celebrated, represents, in the awareness of the commitments undertaken, an unequivocal decision for Yahweh on the basis of the mighty acts of God in the past. Those who made the choice first were part-witnesses of these mighty acts, and their successors were made contemporaries of them when they were made a present reality in the cult. The people realize, too, that it is not a question simply of choosing a new deity and eliminating others, but of making a fundamental choice, the result of which is a turning away from the chaotic world of religions, as well as that of irreligion, to be drawn into the divine plan of salvation for the whole of humanity; the abandonment of myths for a part in history, an escape from the limited geographical setting of various local deities to become an integral part of the universe, the Lord of which is Yahweh, the God who has no place of his own because every place is his. This dominion is explicitly affirmed by the group of psalms which are usually known as the *yhwh mālāk* psalms, because this formula, an emphatic proclamation of his dominion, occurs in them several times (Ps. 24.7; 47.2; 68.24; 93; 96–99, etc.). It is also one of the corner stones of the preaching of Deutero-Isaiah in the sixth century, at a period when Babylon still ruled in all its power, and where indeed the dominion of Yahweh seemed to be the very opposite of this rule! Thus this theme was also proclaimed with special force to the scattered community of the exile. They were offered the alternative of faith without even having seen in operation the beginning of the divine plan, leading to their return to the promised land. Thus it is no accident that the only Jews to return after the edict of Cyrus (539) were those most determined in their theology and with little or no inclination to condescend to compromise in this sphere. This is why the Samaritans were rapidly expelled from the community (in circumstances about which we know nothing, except what we learn of indirectly through Josephus, *Antt.* IX, 14, 3; XI, 8, 2, where the Samaritans are called 'apostates of the Jewish nation'; cf. also Ezra 4.1ff.). So, too, were all the foreigners who had become part of the nation (e.g. foreign wives who could decide the religious education of their children, Deut. 7.1–4; 23.20; Ezra 9.1ff.; cf. Neh. 9.2).

[19–22] The dialogue could conclude here, but it continues: Joshua insists on reminding the people of an element which, as we have seen, was far from being a peaceful one at that period: the exclusiveness of faith in Yahweh. He also reminds them of the holiness of the God to whom they were adhering; this forceful element can well be described by Kierkegaard's *totaliter aliter*, because the root *qdš* expresses the setting apart of a sphere peculiar to the deity which man can only enter when he is called, or by carrying out the precautionary measures laid down by the deity. To this extent there is no difference from the practice of the multitude of pagan religions, but in the OT this idea also indicates the essential difference which exists between Yahweh and the creature, two strictly incommensurable entities. Thus whereas in the pagan religions it was sufficient to carry out certain ritual and ethical precepts in order to make contact between the deity and man, understood as two beings who were quantitatively but not qualitively different, here the contact is regulated by what appears from a human point of view to be an irrational factor, because it is unpredictable: the incommensurability of the two entities, and therefore the uncertainty of man in the absence of any explicit promise on the part of God. Similar themes in fact exist in pagan religions, but it is only in the OT, and much later in the NT, that they become fundamental. This distance between God and man, which already exists on the ontological plane, becomes even greater because of 'your transgressions and your sins'. At a certain moment the irrational element tends to become secondary and to give way to a rigorous logic, that of judgment. God's calling of particular men shows that his incommensurability with man does not exclude a personal and intimate communion; but this relationship, which can exist between two entities so essentially different, is disturbed in fact by man's theological and ethical situation; and how could God tolerate this happening? The other element is that of the jealousy of Yahweh (cf. Exod. 20.5ff. ‖ Deut. 5.9ff. and Exod. 34.15); in every age there is a danger that the people, although it has accepted Yahweh, may not take his exclusiveness seriously. Therefore there is a second invitation to make a decision, although it remains implicit.

In both elements the difficulty of making a true decision with regard to Yahweh is clearly set out; and Hertzberg is right to point to the connection between the consequences expressed in v.20, and Amos 3.2.

In response to the people's renewed commitment, Joshua declares that from henceforth anyone who violates this commitment will be condemned himself: he will have been aware of all the implications of a positive decision, and will have accepted them, knowing that there is no escape clause and no possibility of compromise. He would be a witness against himself if he violated his promise (this idea is explained by the practice of following the formula of a treaty, after it has been agreed, by a series of curses which the contracting parties call down on themselves if the treaty is violated, cf. Baltzer, p.35). Important examples of this are known from the Hittite, Mesopotamian and Syrian worlds, so that the statement that we have here a passage which is due to the redactors (Muilenburg and L'Hour) must at the least be reconsidered. The symmetry of the present narrative is probably a sign that we have here material which was ancient, but which was quite compatible with the particular emphasis of Dtr on this point. Preaching to a community which had been judged by the prophetic preaching, it was obvious to him that the latter message had been carried out.

[23–24] The passage concludes with a ceremony: the putting away of the 'foreign gods'; Nielsen, 'The Burial . . .', gives analogies from comparative religion to this rite of renouncing gods, but we know nothing of the content of it; the present text does not give any description of the liturgical action to which it refers. But it is clear that once the decision was taken, the carrying out of this ceremony formed the critical moment in the cult: it was in fact possible that these gods were just as powerful and could have taken their vengeance. The rite seems to have been a very early practice at the Israelite sanctuary at Shechem: an E tradition (Gen. 35.1–4) traces it back to the patriarch Jacob, who is shown there doing away with 'the foreign gods' and certain amulets by burying them 'under the

oak which was near Shechem' (LXX adds: 'and he destroyed them
unto this day'), before undertaking his journey to Bethel. It was on
this basis that Alt worked out his famous theory of the pilgrimage from
Shechem to Bethel, at a period when the early sanctuary had de-
clined for reasons which we have no room to examine in detail here.
In spite of what happened at Shechem, the ceremonies began within
the framework of the former sanctuary by the rite of the burying of
foreign gods, no doubt at the foot of the sacred oak, the presence of
which is well attested.[1]

(d) *The making of the covenant at Shechem* (*24.25–27; 8.30–35*)

[25–27] While it is clear that the present passage has been worked
over and re-edited by the Deuteronomic school (but this statement
must be made with caution! cf. v. 27), it is no longer necessary at the
present day to deny that it contains a tradition which in essence is an
ancient one. The tradition underlying these verses in fact describes
the preparation of the document on which the content of the covenant is to be recorded, and the setting up of a stone as a memorial of
the making of the covenant, elements which are completely at home
in the ancient ritual. Naturally, someone reading this passage long
afterwards would easily interpret the term *sēper*, especially after the
addition of the word *tōrāh*, to refer to a book, and to the scriptures
projecting anachronistically into the past the institutions of his own
time. This interpretation, however, is found only at the conclusion of
the autonomous development of the tradition.

It is not clear whether the document was identical with the stone
that was set up, that is, whether the writing was on the stone. 8.30ff.
(see below) seems to state that it was, but the connection between the
two passages is not sufficiently clear to permit the conclusion that
objects in the two texts are identical. On this point, cf. the statement
by K. Koch: 'If the historicity of this tradition is assessed according
to the conventions of Israelite stories, the frequency with which this
fact is mentioned could only mean that stones of that kind actually
existed at the time of the narrator.'[2] Thus Koch would assert that the
inscription in question existed on the stone; but he is not aware of the
discovery of the new meaning of *sēper*.

It is likewise of interest that in the region of Shechem itself the
excavations carried out by E. Sellin in 1926 and the subsequent years

[1] Cf. on this subject Wright, op. cit., pp. 132ff.
[2] *The Growth of the Biblical Tradition*, London 1969, p. 29.

revealed three partially preserved stelae, which unfortunately were later spoiled in several places by the clumsiness of his companions.[1] Sellin at once understood the function of these stelae, but the argument continued for years until finally, after 1956,[2] it was recognized that he was right. No doubt we lack any evidence for the statement that the object mentioned in the present text was one of these stelae, but the agreement between the text and this discovery is striking. The fact that such a stone is mentioned in this context is noteworthy in itself, because at the period of the Deuteronomic redaction (cf. Deut. 16.21), the setting up of stelae of this kind (*maṣṣēbā*) was explicitly forbidden. This is an argument in favour of the independence of the tradition which our text records: the tradition was so strong that no one, not even Dtr, dared to modify it! Finally, it is not possible to be sure of the connection between Yahweh and the god called in Judg. 9 *'ēl* or *ba'al bᵉrît*, even if we admit, as Bright does, that connections may at some time have existed.

Thus the covenant made by Joshua in the name of the people is a later stage in the logical development of the covenant of Sinai; here the covenant unites two groups, this time in the holy land; and so another element in the promise made to the patriarchs is fulfilled.

It is not at all clear why 8.30–35 have been put in their present context. LXX places them after 9.2, and it must be admitted that in their present context they are not in place. They have no link with what precedes them nor with what follows. Thus LXX bears witness to the fact that the problem is an ancient one. On the other hand, 9.1ff. is clearly connected with 8.28–29, which is yet another proof that the passage is now out of place (cf. Holtzinger, and now Bright, who would place ch. 24 there). The present passage derives wholly from the Deuteronomic redaction, and is clearly dependent on Deut. 11.26–32 and 27.1–26. As we have pointed out in the article quoted, one must not deny *a priori* the possibility that there is in fact an ancient tradition underlying it, even though at the present day it is so obscured that its original identity is sometimes unrecognizable. The reason for this is that the existence of an important cultic act celebrated outside Jerusalem, and the mention here also of the stelae (cf. 24.25ff.), are elements which must be regarded as primitive, unless the contrary is proved.[3] Even Noth, in the second edition of his com-

---

[1] G. E. Wright, op. cit., pp. 84ff. and figs. 36–38.   [2] Wright, ibid.

[3] Here I disagree with E. Nielsen, op. cit., pp. 77ff., and Noth, *UGS*, pp. 43, 99.

mentary, recognizes the existence in this passage 'of fragments . . .
of an ancient pre-Deuteronomic historical tradition'. Thus it is clear
that the passage has undergone a large degree of re-editing, but this
is not to say that it is a historical fiction. The text has undergone
numerous corrections, which is often the case with texts deriving
from the Deuteronomic redaction.

[30–31] The dependence of this passage on Deut. 27 clearly shows
that these verses are late, at least in the form in which we possess
them. However, there are archaic elements in them, both in the
grammar and in the description of facts. This is particularly true of
the kind of altar: except in Deut. 27.6, the only other text where there
is such an altar is Exod. 20.25, cf. also I Kings 18.31, where there is
no explicit statement, but where it is clear that Elijah gathered up
the stones in the state in which he had found them. The reasons for
this procedure must be sought in the belief that any kind of tool
would 'profane' (root *ḥll*) the altar, but we are not certain why (the
various reasons put forward seem inadequate, cf. the commentary on
5.3: the desire to leave things as they had left the hands of the
Creator). The question of Mount Ebal is difficult to resolve,[1] because
it only occurs here and in Deut. 27.4 in a cultic context, while in
11.29 (as in the variant of Deut. 27.4 found in the Samaritan Pentateuch) it is replaced by Gerizim, which is the sacred mountain of this
place. It is possible that a polemical point (of course a late one) is
being made against the Samaritans. The emphasis here, as in ch. 1, on
the work of Moses, is a typical element in the theology of Dtr. The
possibility that the expression 'book of the law of Moses' is a recent
paraphrase of the much more ancient expression 'document (of the
covenant)' must be seriously considered: the latter expression would
be authentic, whereas the former would be the result of an adaptation
(and we not know how far it would be an accidental or intentional
misinterpretation) of the older formula, at a period when it was no
longer understood.

[32] The writing on the stones (Deut. 27.2, 8 prescribes that they
should first be plastered, but there is no mention of this here) presents
a number of difficulties, largely of a technical nature. To write on a
dry stone wall (even if it has been made smooth and uniform by being
plastered) is virtually impossible, as Nielsen has remarked[2] (he adds
ironically that if anyone believes the operation is possible, he should

---

[1] For the geographical problem cf. Baldi's commentary.
[2] E. Nielsen, *Shechem*, p. 80.

try to write a law of Moses on a dry stone wall himself!). One might at once observe that it is not so impossible as it sounds, and at the present day there are all kinds of dry stone walls, finished in various materials, which are often covered, in Latin countries, with the most miscellaneous inscriptions! But it is not as easy as this to solve the problem: Deut. 27 clearly distinguishes on the one hand the stones on which the inscriptions are written, and on the other hand the altar of unhewn stone. Did the redactor here confuse them, and fail to distinguish two elements which were originally distinct?[1] If the distinction can be maintained, the following is the line of study which should be pursued. We know that the Hittites, whose political dominion extended until the twelfth century throughout northern Syria, and whose influence on Palestine was always important, practised the custom of writing on orthostats, i.e. tiles which they then embedded vertically in the lower part of the walls of the sanctuary. A classic example of this practice is provided by the sanctuary of Karatepe (eighth century BC, in southern Turkey, near the western end of the frontier with Syria).[2] No doubt this argument should not be pushed too far: in fact up to now we have no example of this kind of orthostat in Palestine, and the lions discovered at Hazor, which are of the type common in Anatolia and Syria, do not bear any inscriptions.[3] Thus at the present moment some links are missing from the chain. But nothing prevents the use as a working hypothesis of the possibility that sanctuaries existed where portions of the text of the covenant were written on plaster (as was done in Egypt, and cf. Deut. 27; in this case, there would be no hope of recovering anything), or inscribed on orthostats set into the altar or on the wall surrounding the sacred enclave. Moreover, as Hertzberg observes, the Deuteronomic redactor does not seem to be concerned about the technical aspects of the question, which assumes, as we have pointed out in the textual notes, either the widespread existence of sanctuaries of this kind in his own time, or else a deliberate invention on his part; but the latter would seem absurd. In the former and most probable case, he would have been content with repeating in his own terms what was contained in a very ancient tradition which was in part contradictory to his own theology (the centralization of the cult at

---

[1] Nielsen, op. cit., p. 78.

[2] O. R. Gurney, *The Hittites*, London ²1961, pp. 197ff.; M. Riemscheider, *Die Welt der Hethiter*, Stuttgart—Zurich 1954, tab. 81, and V. Maag, art. and loc. cit.

[3] Y. Yadin et al., *Hazor*, I, Jerusalem 1958, pp. 89ff. and pl. XXX.

Jerusalem) and his anti-Samaritan polemic (clearly visible in II Kings 17).

The mention of the ark presents a difficult problem: it is the only passage which shows us the ark at Shechem, and we do not know whether the mention of it comes from the ancient tradition underlying this text, or whether it is due to Dtr. The mention of the personnel connected with the ark must in any case be attributed to Dtr, cf. the commentary on chs. 1 and 3.

[30–35] The people seem to have remained in the valley between the two mountains, and to have turned towards them, according to Deut. 11.26ff. and 26.11ff. (where, however, the law is not mentioned). The curses and the blessings (meant respectively for anyone who violates and anyone who carries out the standards of the covenant) are a constituent part of every kind of treaty throughout the whole of the ancient Near East, and are not, therefore, a rhetorical or literary device. They form the conclusion of the document of the covenant, a document written on a stele or on an orthostat.[1]

CHAPTER 24.28–33

The Tombs of Joshua, Joseph and Eleazar

24 28So Joshua sent the people away, every man to his inheritance.

29 After these things Joshua the son of Nun, the servant of the LORD, died, being a hundred and ten years old. 30And they buried him in his own inheritance at Timnath-serah, which is in the hill country of Ephraim, north of the mountain of Gaash. 31And Israel worshipped the LORD all the days of Joshua, and all the days of the elders who outlived Joshua and had known all the work which the LORD had done for Israel.

32 The bones of Joseph which the people of Israel brought up from Egypt were buried at Shechem, in the portion of ground which Jacob bought from the sons of Hamor the father of Shechem for a hundred pieces of money; it became an inheritance of the descendants of Joseph. 33And Eleazar the son of Aaron died; and they buried him at Gibeah, the town

[1] Cf. G. E. Mendenhall, art. cit., pp.64ff.; K. Baltzer, op. cit., p.66 n.7, and D. R. Hillers, *Treaty Curses . . .*, pp.46 and 84ff.

of Phinehas his son, which had been given him in the hill country of
Ephraim.

Bibliography: Auzou, pp. 191ff.

The text presents no difficulties. **[32]** *watteḥî* (subject *ḥelqat*) should be read
instead of *wayyeḥî*.

[28] The account of the Shechem assembly concludes with the
sending of the people to their own homes, and this is how the ancient
ritual of the renewal of the covenant would have concluded. Judg.
2.6 takes up the first part of the verse, continuing it in a different way,
which proves that the work of the Deuteronomic history writer
includes neither the end of ch. 24 nor Judg. 1.1–2.5. In his theology
(independently of the question whether one believes the conquest
had been concluded or not), this decision on the part of the people
had laid the basis of its existence in the promised land. The violation
of the covenant and of the decision to serve Yahweh had led to the
exile, according to the preaching of the prophets and of Deuteronomy
and Dtr. But now that the people were faced with a second Exodus
and a restoration (that is, the bringing back into force of the ancient
promises), it was important that they should remember that the
covenant was the true basis of their existence. Thus there is good
reason why these themes became fundamental in post-exilic Judaism.
[29] For the death of Joshua, cf. 19.49ff. and Judg. 2.6ff. **[30]** The
place is no doubt the present *khirbet tibne* (160–157), in the south-
eastern region of the 'hill country of Ephraim', and therefore a
considerable distance from Shechem. It is no longer possible to
identify the mountain with certainty. The tomb of Joseph is still
shown to visitors at the present day in the immediate neighbourhood
of *balaṭa*, the *tell* of which is the site of Shechem. **[32]** This verse is
composed of fragments taken from Gen. 50.25; Exod. 13.19; Gen.
33.19, with the addition of a note on the inheritance of Joseph; as far
as the tomb of Eleazar is concerned, this is probably an aetiology of a
place otherwise unknown, called Gibeah of Phinehas.